Escape!

Escape!

The Story of the Confederacy's Infamous Libby Prison and the Civil War's Largest Jail Break

Robert P. Watson

ROWMAN & LITTLEFIELD
Lanham • Boulder • New York • London

Published by Rowman & Littlefield
An imprint of The Rowman & Littlefield Publishing Group, Inc.
4501 Forbes Boulevard, Suite 200, Lanham, Maryland 20706
www.rowman.com

86-90 Paul Street, London EC2A 4NE, United Kingdom

British Library Cataloguing in Publication Information Available

Library of Congress Cataloging-in-Publication Data
Names: Watson, Robert P., 1962– author.
Title: Escape! : the story of the Confederacy's infamous Libby Prison and the Civil War's largest jail break / Robert P. Watson.
Description: Lanham, Maryland : Rowman & Littlefield, [2021] | Includes bibliographical references and index. | Summary: "Robert P. Watson provides the definitive account of the Confederacy's infamous Libby Prison, site of the Civil War's largest prison break. Libby Prison housed Union officers, high-profile foes of the Confederacy, and political prisoners. Watson captures the wretched conditions, cruel guards, and the story of the daring prison break, called 'the most remarkable in American history.'"— Provided by publisher.
Identifiers: LCCN 2021006838 (print) | LCCN 2021006839 (ebook) | ISBN 9781538138229 (cloth) | ISBN 9781538138236 (epub)
Subjects: LCSH: Libby Prison—History. | Prisoner-of-war escapes—Virginia—Richmond—History—19th century. | United States—History—Civil War, 1861–1865—Prisoners and prisons.
Classification: LCC E612.L6 W35 2021 (print) | LCC E612.L6 (ebook) | DDC 973.7/445—dc23
LC record available at https://lccn.loc.gov/2021006838
LC ebook record available at https://lccn.loc.gov/2021006839

To my father, who has long had a passion for the Civil War

The mystic chords of memory, stretching from every battlefield and patriot grave to every living heart and hearthstone all over this broad land, will yet swell the chorus of the Union, when again touched, as surely they will be, by the better angels of our nature.

—Abraham Lincoln, First Inaugural Address, March 4, 1861

Contents

Part IV: Escape

Part V: FREEDOM

Preface

Prison escapes have always captured the public's imagination. This is especially true when it involves prisoners of war. Indeed, several stories of prison breaks—both real and imagined—have enjoyed considerable success in bookstores and on the silver screen. So too is American history full of intriguing and infamous escapes from prison. Among the best known is a 1934 escape in broad daylight from the Lake County Jail in Indiana. The prisoner: the legendary gangster and murderer John Dillinger. His escape was even more provocative because the Indiana facility was said to have been "escape-proof." It was also the third time he managed to break out of jail. The man labeled "Public Enemy Number One" used a hand-carved wooden gun covered in black shoe polish to dupe the guards and then went on a crime spree, killing ten men before being caught in Arizona and shot dead by FBI agents.

Another remarkable escape occurred on June 12, 1962, when Clarence Anglin, John Anglin, and Frank Morris cut holes in their cell walls and managed to break out of the notorious Alcatraz Federal Penitentiary. It was yet another prison thought to be escape-proof because of its location in the center of San Francisco Bay. However, the three prisoners ingeniously devised a raft made out of raincoats to cross the dauntingly cold and treacherous bay. Most experts believe the prisoners drowned, but their bodies have never been found. A long FBI investigation produced no answers, which has only added to the public's ongoing fascination with the case, as was evident with the success of the popular film *Escape from Alcatraz*, released in 1979.

There have also been noteworthy escapes by prisoners of war. One of the best known occurred during the Second World War and was the inspiration for the 1963 blockbuster film *The Great Escape*. It happened in 1944 when Roger Bushell, a British officer, organized teams of inmates to dig three tunnels out of the hellish Nazi prison Stalag Luft III. Seventy-six Allied prisoners made it out of the tunnel; however, all but three of them were recaptured. The Nazis summarily shot most of the escapees.

As intriguing as these other escapes are, arguably the most compelling escape in American history remains largely unknown and happens to be the most important breakout of the Civil War and largest in the United States. It occurred at a wretched Confederate facility in the capital city of Richmond when a large group of Union officers pulled off a simple but bold plan to free themselves from almost-certain death behind bars. The shocking breakout prompted a massive manhunt, perhaps second only in size and importance to the hunt for John Wilkes Booth after he assassinated Abraham Lincoln. That largely forgotten breakout at Libby Prison—a disgraceful facility known as the "Bastille of the Confederacy"—is also noteworthy because many of the prisoners made it to freedom.

The book before you is about a brutal and deadly prison that was used for propaganda purposes and as a form of amusement for twisted Confederate leaders. It is also the remarkable story of a group of courageous and resourceful soldiers and a plan that, against all odds, worked. In the words of Major A. G. Hamilton of the Twelfth Kentucky Cavalry, one of the extraordinary men who survived the ordeal, "There is probably no event in the whole history of the Civil War in which the patriotism, energy, courage, and ingenuity of the Union soldier is better displayed than in the celebrated tunnel escape from Libby Prison."[1] Ultimately, some made it to freedom; others did not. Some lived; some died. In the pages that follow, their lives and ordeals are told from firsthand accounts, letters, and military reports.

It is also a story that is too often a part of the human condition and of warfare in particular—and that is the nature of cruelty and malfeasance shown by governments and soldiers toward one another during times of war. Prisoners in every war and in every culture throughout history have suffered the worst of fates. Such incidents during the Civil War are particularly disturbing and worth examining because they involve brothers fighting brothers, neighbors killing neighbors, and fellow Americans treating one another with what can only be described as unfounded distrust, fear, and naked hatred.

The book would not have been possible without the assistance and support of many people. Numerous archivists and librarians at historic sites, museums, and libraries were helpful. In a larger sense, much of history would have been lost but for their dedication and tireless work. For their ongoing support of my writing projects, I am indebted to my colleagues at Lynn University: Katrina Carter-Tellison, vice president of Academic Affairs; Gary Villa, dean of the College of Arts and Sciences; and Jared Wellman, Digital Resources librarian. A special thanks to Avron Fogelman for his generous support of my research endeavors. I would also like to acknowledge my literary agent Peter Bernstein and the team at Rowman & Littlefield—Jonathan Sisk, vice president and senior executive acquisitions editor; Sally Rinehart, designer; Brianna Westervelt, associate production editor; Debbie Justice, copy editor; and Benjamin Knepp, editorial assistant. Additionally, my friends George Goldstein, Bob Seidemann, and Samuel Stockhamer read early drafts and offered helpful ideas. All mistakes, of course, are solely mine. Please note that, where multiple editions of a publication have been cited in the bibliography, I have drawn page numbers from the most recent version.

Last and most importantly, thanks go to my children—Alexander and Isabella—for their patience and support with all my books. And to the readers, I hope you enjoy this shocking but heroic story.

Robert P. Watson, Boca Raton, Florida

Prologue

The Tunnel

> The night was stormy, dark and cold.
> It cramped the frames of young and old.
> While north winds howl and tempers roar,
> A thousand officers or more
> Thin clad and shivering hug the floor
> Of Libby Prison.
>
> —Robert Cornwell, Libby Prison, 1863[1]

The faint light of the flickering candle gradually dimmed until its final flame wavered and then was no more, casting the long, narrow tunnel into complete darkness. Colonel Thomas E. Rose, lying prone, could no longer even see his hands, though they were directly in front of his face. He instinctively dropped the chisel he had been using to dig and reached out in the direction of the candle he had stolen, until he felt the warm remnants of its wax. Even if Rose had wanted, he could not have turned around to look for the second candle positioned behind him near the entrance to the tunnel. The walls were much too narrow. His broad shoulders were wedged against solid rock and densely packed dirt. With much effort, Rose wriggled onto his side and struggled to reach down into his pants pocket for an old box of matches. As he snaked his arm along the tight walls of the tunnel toward his pocket, bits of dirt poured down onto his body and into his mouth. He closed his eyes and tried to wipe the debris from his face. It did not help; he was covered in dirt.

The colonel was over fifty feet deep into the long shaft running under the prison. For weeks, he and a few of his fellow prisoners had been excavating the tunnel from the east corner of the prison's dank, foul cellar, and doing so in complete darkness.

At the moment, the only sounds were Rose's heavy panting as he struggled for each breath and the occasional squeal and chatter of the rats that menaced the diggers. The furry pests were everywhere. Rose and the other diggers constantly felt them scurrying across their exposed hands and running down their backs. Making matters worse, the prisoners could not defend themselves—the tunnel was too narrow to swat at the rats, and there were simply too many of them—so many, in fact, that the infested cellar was nicknamed "Rat Hell"! Nevertheless, the lack of any light and the overabundance of annoying rodents were not Rose's main problem. He was about to lose consciousness.

The flow of life-saving air that had been fanned into the tunnel by a fellow prisoner had, for some reason, stopped. Feeling himself drifting into blackness, the burly colonel tried to focus his clouded thoughts and suppress the feeling of claustrophobia welling up inside him. Rose lacked the energy to cry out for help; even his breathing now came in gasps of desperation. He reached down and tugged on the rope tied around his ankle, a sign that he needed help. Yet there was no response from his fellow diggers.

Rose's friend and fellow prisoner, Major Andrew G. Hamilton, was always faithfully standing on alert outside the entrance of the tunnel. Weeks before, the two masterminds of the plan to escape from the infamous Confederate bastille had discovered the hard way—Rose had nearly passed out and had to be pulled out of the tunnel—that, as they dug deeper under the prison grounds, there was not enough oxygen to keep the candle lit or the digger alive. Undeterred, the two prisoners had continued the excavation of the tunnel, thanks to a few necessary and creative adaptations by Hamilton.

One was in response to the lack of fresh air deep in the shaft. Hamilton described the dilemma: "As the tunnel progressed the air in it became fetid and oppressive, and the candles used refused to burn in the exhalation from the earth." The situation was resolved when the prisoners confiscated a wide-brimmed hat, which doubled as a somewhat-effective fan. Therefore, as Hamilton explained, "One of the party was compelled to stand constantly at the mouth of the opening and fan fresh air—such as it was in that closed cellar—into the tunnel with his hat."[2] The major later built a more effective fan.

Another solution was a rope tied around the leg of the tunneler so that, should he lose consciousness, become stuck, or if the walls of the tunnel collapsed, the men stationed in the cellar could pull him out. The prisoners had also stolen a "piece of clothes-line" for drying clothing, an "old wooden spittoon," and other items, which Hamilton cleverly rigged with a makeshift pulley to create a system to remove the excavated dirt and rocks from the tunnel. The digger entered the tunnel with a chisel and other crude tools they had stolen and took with him the spittoon and clothes-line. Once the "sled," as it was nicknamed by the prisoners, was full of excavated dirt and rocks, it was pulled out by the man stationed at the entrance of the tunnel. The excavated debris was then emptied and the sled sent back into the tunnel by way of the clothesline and pulley, where it would again be filled.[3]

Nevertheless, this trick presented a problem. If the guards entered the cellar, they would likely discover a mound of rocks and dirt covering the floor. Luckily, the cellar contained a large pile of straw that had been sitting there for years. Its only function, it seemed, was to provide a warm place to sleep for the swarms of rats. The mountain of straw offered an obvious solution—the excavated debris was spread under the pile where the guards could not see it. Thankfully, the guards almost never dared to venture into the dark, eerie, rat-infested cellar.

It was then, when Rose was deep in the tunnel and having trouble breathing, that it happened.

CLOSE CALL

Deep inside the chute, the colonel felt himself slipping into blackness but did not yell out. As his mind was shutting down, he correctly guessed the reason the airflow had stopped: the prison guards must have shown up in the dungeon. Sure enough, muffled voices and footsteps were heard from just outside the cellar. The prisoners had frozen; candles had been snuffed out. One had dived into the entrance of the tunnel; another had quickly taken shelter in the large pile of straw, causing rats to shriek and scurry in every direction. Hamilton, stationed by the entrance to the tunnel, had stopped fanning air into the hole and quickly ran for cover.

The steps approached and, to the horror of the prisoners, a few guards entered the cellar through the seldom-used door by the stairs. The light from their lantern flickered across the empty walls and low ceiling. Fortunately, it was the middle of the night, and the cellar was pitch-black. It was also so malodorous and inhospitable that the guards had, until now, avoided going there and would likely not stay long. However, a few days earlier an unsuccessful escape had been attempted. Rumors had also began swirling through the prison that Union forces were nearby, perhaps planning a raid on the prison. The commandant and guards had been spooked; additional sentries had been posted around the perimeter of the complex. Orders had also been handed down to conduct frequent inspections and roll calls.

The prisoners assumed their tunnel was compromised and suspected they were about to be caught trying to escape. However, the guards did not have their weapons at the ready. Nor did they bark out commands or threats. Rather, the Confederate sentries simply walked to the center of the cellar, casually looked around, and then stood conversing in the blackness, their faces partially hidden and distorted by the flickering light of a lantern. The prisoners held their breath and dared not move.

Time passed slowly, and the Union soldiers wondered if their leader trapped in the deep tunnel had lost consciousness when the fanning had stopped. What if he cried out for help? What if he emerged from the tunnel without knowing the guards were there? Either way, they were helpless to render assistance or warn the colonel.

The guards were no longer looking around; they appeared to just be wasting time and relaxing. Then one of the guards stepped toward the pile of straw. He poked around disinterestedly, kicking at the straw and sticking his musket into the pile. Remarkably, he neither touched nor sensed the prisoner hiding just inches from his boot and bayonet. A moment later, and without saying anything, the guards simply turned and walked out of the cellar, closing the heavy door behind them. After a few silent and tense seconds, the prisoners emerged from their hiding places and hurried to the entrance of the tunnel. Grabbing the end of the rope tied around Rose's ankle, they quickly pulled the colonel out of the deep hole. He was weak but alive.

A big and powerfully built man, Rose was an "imposing figure."[4] He sported a thick, black beard and was never one to boast or offer an extra word when only a few would suffice. Rose wore the tattered blue uniform of the Seventy-Seventh Pennsylvania Infantry, just as Hamilton still wore the fancy but weathered attire of the Twelfth Kentucky Cavalry. The colonel also had a noticeably bad limp, the result of a broken foot suffered while trying to escape from the train that had brought the prisoners to Richmond.

The Pennsylvanian was a veteran of several battles, including Shiloh (which Rose and some Union soldiers called Pittsburg Landing), Stones River, and Liberty Gap, where fully one-third of his regiment had suffered casualties, including the loss of their commander. In the heat of that battle, Rose had assumed command of the regiment. Though wounded, he distinguished himself in combat and proved to be an effective leader of the Seventy-Seventh. Yet the colonel's stoic, commanding demeanor was at odds with his occupation before the war: Rose had been a schoolteacher.

The Union officer was now the leader of the plan to escape from one of the most important, high-profile, and deplorable prisons of the Confederacy. It had been his idea to escape: Rose had designed the plan, done the lion's share of the digging, and selected the men, then organized them into tunneling crews. Through his determination and example, Rose had also inspired the prisoners during the many trials and tribulations of the darkest days at Libby.

Despite nearly dying in the tunnel, Rose wasted no time sharing the good news with his friends when he was pulled free of his would-be tomb: The tunnel had finally reached the necessary length to pass outside of the prison complex. It was a chilly February evening, and the terrible war was in its fourth year, but the moment of escape was finally at hand. They had done it: night after grueling night of digging with nothing but a broken shovel, two confiscated knives, and a chisel in the putrid dungeon-like cellar had worked. It had been roughly eight weeks since Rose and Hamilton had began working on the plan. Since then, they had endured multiple setbacks, narrow escapes from the guards, numerous illnesses and injuries, and a few brushes with death.

THE DUNGEON

Beneath the prison, Rose was still catching his breath while his comrades busied themselves with their assigned tasks. Some of the men had been with Rose and Hamilton for weeks, others for days. They had become a well-oiled machine, with three five-man crews digging in shifts all night, every night, and, of late, even during the day. They'd had no choice—the situation inside Libby Prison had devolved alarmingly. Disease was tearing through the ranks, rations had been cut to dangerous levels, and the unpredictable commandant had become increasingly volatile and violent. With the death rate spiking, the prison had fallen into the grip of despair and desperation. Time was not on the prisoners' side.

Each night, a crew of diggers had to sneak undetected from the crowded holding areas on the second and third floors of the prison down into the kitchen on the lower floor and then descend through a curving secret passageway into the vacant cellar. There the prisoners toiled in the "sickening air, the deathly chill, the horrible, interminable darkness" of the prison's dungeon.[5] After a long night of digging, the exhausted men had to run the same dangerous gauntlet back to their barracks in the predawn hour. Rose followed them, but not until he had carefully hidden the tools and covered any evidence that someone had been in the cellar. The entire operation had to take place in complete silence, under cover of darkness, and without alerting either the guards or other curious prisoners.

Back in the tunnel on that fateful night, an exhausted and weak Rose handed Captain W. S. B. Randall of the Second Ohio the chisel they had stolen from the carpenter's room and instructed him to go to the end of the shaft and finish the job. The other men whispered good luck and, filled with excitement, went back to their assigned posts—fanning air into the tunnel, pulling out the excavated debris and hiding it under the straw pile, and standing watch for any sound or movement. It was now time to dig the short distance directly upward to daylight. Randall eagerly crawled the length of the tunnel and began hacking through the remaining few feet of soil overhead.

At the end of the tunnel, the captain thrust the chisel upward one last time and broke ground. A storm of dirt and rubble poured down on his face. He suppressed the urge to cough while violently spitting the earthen debris from his mouth and frantically wiping his eyes. When Randall did clear his eyes, he glanced upward and saw the night sky and stars and felt the cold rush of the February evening against his face. However, just as the captain peered through the small opening to take stock of their position, he was met by a horrifying site—a Confederate sentry was "standing nearby!" A streetlight illuminated the scene, revealing that the guard's path of patrol passed nearly on top of the exact spot of the opening. They had unknowingly dug to a point along the path "where a sentinel walked" on his nightly patrol. Randall estimated the guard was just "ten to twelve" paces from the opening. Worse yet, the captain saw that the hole came up on the wrong side of the fencing around the prison. They were still inside the prison yard.[6]

The sentry stopped next to the hole, walked over to the fence nearby, and leaned on it. He stood there for thirty long seconds. Randall froze and held his breath. His heart pounding, he later remembered, "The events of my life seemed to flit before me." Panic set in. The digger raced the length of the narrow tunnel back to the opening to tell Rose the bad news. "We are caught! All is lost!"[7] Randall babbled, sure that they were about to be captured. Through the dull light of the candle, the prisoners in the cellar saw the look of alarm on the captain's face. In hushed tones, the men discussed their options. Should they run back to their rooms? Hide in the cellar? Make a break for it through the tunnel? Huddled together in the cold, dark dungeon, the prisoners ultimately looked to Rose. Though weak from nearly losing consciousness and the hours of digging, Rose told them to stay put. He mustered the strength to take the chisel and head back into the tunnel to assess the situation for himself. The big man pulled his body through the passageway as he had every night for weeks, hurrying toward the opening. He had one thought: they were too close to freedom for the plan to unravel at the last moment.

At the end of the tunnel, the colonel turned and climbed upward to the opening. Another "small portion" of the ground "caved in" as he poked through the ceiling of the passage. Rose brushed the dirt from his eyes and saw a guard "running to the spot" where the tunnel opened. Had he been seen? Rose froze. Another guard hollered, "What is it?" There were now two sentries. The closest guard replied that he had heard a noise and was investigating. Fortunately for Rose, the slated night sky worked to his advantage. The closest guard looked at the hole but could not see into the burrow. However, the sentry raised his musket and pierced the opening with the point of the bayonet, then began poking and prodding the crevice. The tip of the bayonet came directly toward Rose, who dared not move. Even if he had wanted to, there was little room in the cramped pit to evade the blade. The steel point "grazed" Rose's cheek, but he remained "motionless and breathless." To his relief, the guard eventually yelled to his comrade, "A thundering big rat!" Remarkably, the sentry turned, grumbled, "Nothing but rats," and continued his nightly patrol around the prison grounds, satisfied that one of the prison's many rats had been the culprit.[8]

Rose and his party had caught a very lucky break. He quietly used his shirt to "patch up" the hole, covering it as best and as quickly as he could.[9] He hoped the guards would not detect it during the next day. Bleeding from the cut on his face, the colonel crawled back to the entrance of the tunnel to inform the digging party that the sentry had not seen them. They had made a mistake but were lucky. It was too close to sunrise, Rose whispered, and they all needed their rest. The next day they would simply extend the tunnel beyond the fencing. It would then be time to escape.

Part I

WAR

1

"The Great Unpleasantness"

Shall we expect some transatlantic military giant to step over the ocean and crush us at a blow? Never! All the armies of Europe, Asia, and Africa combined . . . could not by force take a drink from the Ohio or make a track on the Blue Ridge. . . . At what point then is the approach of danger to be expected? I answer, if it ever reach us it must spring up amongst us.

—Abraham Lincoln, Lyceum Address, 1838[1]

The writing was on the wall long before the war had started. Consider the following event involving a preacher named Elijah Lovejoy. Reverend Lovejoy, a well-intentioned abolitionist originally from Maine but living in the Midwest, served as the editor of the *St. Louis Observer*, a newspaper read by opponents of slavery in Missouri and around the country, including Edward Beecher, brother of soon-to-be famous author Harriet Beecher Stowe.[2] Thanks to Lovejoy's hard-hitting editorials, the *Observer* had emerged as a critical and often-lonely voice for abolition in the heartland of the country.

To be expected, the newspaper attracted the attention of angry Southerners who repeatedly attacked the newspaper's office and press. They also threatened Lovejoy and his family. Worried about the newspaper's future and his family's safety, Lovejoy moved a short distance north across the Missouri border to Alton, Illinois. Feeling safer in a Free State, the reverend kept on writing. He also ordered a new press. However, word of Lovejoy's plans spread. On November 7, 1837, as the equipment was being unloaded from a steamboat on the nearby Mississippi River, a rowdy, drunken mob appeared. They marched directly to the warehouse where the newspaper was printed and threatened to burn down the building and destroy the new press. Lovejoy bravely confronted the mob but was gunned down during the attack that ensued. The violent throng then burned his barn and smashed the printing press.

Reverend Lovejoy died in a Free State, defending both his property and the right to a free press. None of that mattered to supporters of slavery. We will likely never know the full story, but it is possible that most, if not all, of the crowd that day did not own a slave. Tragically, support for slavery and regional loyalties trumped foundational constitutional principles and clouded the notion of individual rights.[3]

One year later, a state legislator in Illinois warned of a coming conflict. His name was Abraham Lincoln. In his celebrated Lyceum address, a young Lincoln prophetically suggested the nation's undoing would come not from abroad but from within. He asked his audience that day, "At what point, then, is the approach of danger to be expected? I answer, if it ever reach us, it must spring up amongst us."[4] And so it was that a decade later the congressional session of 1850 opened with a fiery debate over the future of slavery and the growing gulf between North and South. It was an omen of things to come.

Indeed, the decade of the 1850s was marred by a series of violent and divisive issues, including what to do about fugitive slaves, whether new states and territories should be admitted to the Union as free or slave, and the failure to end the institution of slavery. Conflict was inevitable and seems to have been part of the plan by some Southern leaders and plantation owners.[5] Sure enough, by the middle of the decade beliefs erupted into a series of clashes that became known as "Bleeding Kansas," when proslavery mobs attacked abolitionists and destroyed both antislavery newspapers and businesses owned or frequented by abolitionists in the territory, including the popular Free State Hotel in the budding frontier town of Lawrence.[6]

While the situation in Kansas remained combustible, tensions flared back in the nation's capital. A day after the sacking of Lawrence, the floor of Congress descended into bloodshed when Charles Sumner, an abolitionist senator from Massachusetts, delivered his celebrated "Crimes against Kansas" speech. In the oration, Sumner called out Southern plantation owners for the immoral practice of slavery, the systematic rape of enslaved women and girls, and the slavers' moral hypocrisy. Indignant over Sumner's strong language and abolitionist arguments, Preston Brooks, a proslavery congressman from South Carolina, stormed into the Senate chambers and unleashed a bloody assault on his Northern colleague with a metal-tipped cane. The beating was severe. Sumner was left for dead, unconscious and lying in a pool of his own blood. Shocked members of Congress looked on in disbelief but were rendered powerless by Brooks's colleague, Congressman Laurence Keitt, also of South Carolina, who held other legislators at bay with pistols.[7]

One person following the alarming developments in Kansas and Washington was Lincoln. Of the brewing crisis, the future president wrote to his close friend Joshua Speed in 1855, "Our progress in degeneracy appears to me to be pretty rapid. As a nation, we began by declaring that 'all men are created equal.' We now practically read it 'all men are created equal, *except negroes*.'" The future president warned, "When the Know-Nothings get control, it will read 'all men are created equal, except negroes, and *foreigners, and Catholics*.' When it comes to this I should prefer emigrating to some country where they make no pretense of loving liberty."[8] The nation was stumbling violently and hopelessly toward disunion.

DISUNION

Historians have been writing about the causes of the war for over 150 years. As is widely known, it was fought over states' rights and the issue of slavery. Both causes were inextricably linked, as Southerners maintained that it was the right of a state to legalize slavery. This argument stemmed from the view that the rights of states superseded both the powers of the federal government and any rights an enslaved individual may or may not have. Northerners and Southerners differed in their radically opposed interpretations of the Constitution and the corresponding concept of federal supremacy versus states' rights. Southerners were apparently reading the founding document in ways that were quite distinct from how their Northern counterparts read it or how we understand such concepts as individual rights and the role of government today.

There was an obvious self-interest at play among Southern slave owners and political leaders in maintaining that slavery was both legal and proper; some even went so far as to suggest that the "peculiar institution" was natural and derived its legitimacy in Scripture.[9] Such readings of the founding document provided quasiconstitutional cover for both slavery and the notion that the federal government was somehow oppressing White Southerners. It also offered the South a justification for "the great unpleasantness" that was to come.[10] Aside from the obvious—that slavery was a moral issue and a shameful blight on the nation—these two controversies were, at their core, constitutional and economic matters.[11]

The Southern economy was rooted in and utterly dependent on agricultural production. Not only had much of the South failed to diversify its economic output, but they were reliant on only a very few of crops—and therefore were reliant on the slave labor that had made it so profitable for plantation owners to grow those few crops. It would prove to be a vicious cycle. On the other hand, those living above the Mason-Dixon Line had a far more diverse and healthy economic system, one that included not just agriculture, but factories, food processing, machine tooling, railroad suppliers, shipping, finance, and trade. The North also benefitted from having numerous cities, extensive infrastructure, more colleges, schools, and cultural institutions, and a much larger population.

Yet it is next to impossible to make the case that in the years leading to the Civil War White Southern men and slave owners were being disenfranchised or that Southern cities and states were being denied basic rights by a relatively weak and small federal government. It is far easier to link the existence of slavery to the political and economic suppression of non-slave-owning Southern Whites. Most Southerners did not own slaves, just as most White Southerners did not benefit economically, politically, or socially from its presence and the feudal-like society it created, as well as from the bifurcated system of justice promoted by Southern leaders. To be sure, slavery suppressed wages across the South, reduced economic opportunity, stymied social mobility, and limited political power for non–slave owners.[12]

An estimated 3.5 to 4 million enslaved Blacks lived in the American South when the Civil War broke out in 1861. It was an all-encompassing and ever-present dilemma, one that permeated the very fabric of Southern politics and society. Moreover, it is hard for us today to fully comprehend the shared zeal for and devotion to the disgraceful practice of slaving throughout much of Dixie. Put another way, for example, in 1860 and 1861, the Southern half of the country was willing to abandon the Constitution, secede from the Union, and start a war in which they would send their sons to die—all in order to perpetuate human bondage. The inescapable conclusion is that the lynchpin for the South's insistence on states' rights was the perpetuation of slavery. Indeed, years before the fighting started, radical voices in South Carolina and Mississippi had been calling for secession. As it pertains to this book, such an argument demands further assessment, not just in terms of the rush to secession but also to better understand the cruel treatment to which Northern prisoners were subjected during the war.

Whatever the conclusions reached about how to interpret the Constitution and the primacy of states' rights, the root cause of the conflict was a collective inability to compromise, owing to a deep attachment in the South to slavery, a growing cultural identity below the Mason-Dixon Line that was distinct from other parts of the nation, a festering social and political animosity between both regions, and a blatant disregard in the Southern half of the nation for foundational constitutional principles and basic rights. Rather than find common ground, in the years leading up to the war, thousands—and perhaps millions—of hearts were hardened, and both sides drew the sword. There were two Americas, as sectional animus and antipathy overshadowed any sense of nationhood.

As events were spinning out of control in the 1850s, disunion seemed increasingly inevitable. By the time of the 1860 presidential election, many Southerners believed—or at least claimed—that their very way of life was under attack. Southern political leaders continued repeating their threat to secede from the Union if things did not go their way in the 1860 race. Several Southern states even refused to place Abraham Lincoln's name on the ballot. When Lincoln won his party's nomination that year, fear and anger were such that, south of the Mason-Dixon Line, it was construed as nothing less than an "act of war."[13]

President-elect Lincoln did what he could, announcing repeatedly that his aim was not to end slavery or invade the South; rather, it was only to limit the spread of slavery from any new states in the West. He sought practical compromises that would avoid war and disunion, but the time for rational concessions and civility had long passed. As the president-elect tried to preserve the nation, on December 20, 1860—just over one month after his election but still almost three months prior to his inauguration—South Carolina announced it was leaving the United States.[14]

Then, in rapid succession, beginning with Mississippi on January 9, several states from the Deep South followed suit—Florida on January 10, Alabama a day later, Georgia the following week, and Louisiana at the end of the month. As president-elect, Lincoln was powerless to act; he offered words and gestures. With Lincoln's inauguration still weeks away,[15] the rebellious states convened on February 4 in Montgomery, Alabama, for the purposes of forming a new government and drafting their own constitution—which was adopted on February 22. They were no longer bound by the US Constitution nor pledged allegiance to the Stars and Stripes.

Given Montgomery's rather remote location by the standards of 1861 and its inaccessibility by water or road, the new Confederate States of America decided to relocate its capital to Richmond in Virginia. It seemed a wise move: Richmond was a politically influential, economically important, and relatively large city in the South's foremost state. By the summer of that first year of the war, the entire Confederate government was operating in the Virginia capital. This only made Richmond all the more central to the war effort; it was in Richmond that the war was planned and conducted, the weapons built, and the wartime food and supplies stored and shipped. It would also soon be the site of some of the Confederacy's main and most brutal prisons.

Jefferson Davis, former US secretary of war and a sitting senator from Mississippi, was elected president of the new Confederacy. Across the South, people took to the streets to rejoice, while mobs marched on government buildings, confiscated federal property, and tore down the American flag. Paradoxically, in a region opposed to active governance and with a new regime established allegedly to oppose a national government, among President Davis's first acts that same month were to overrule his governors, suspend *habeas corpus*, and declare martial law across the South. Absurdly, he would assume near-dictatorial powers over a government formed on the hypocritical claim that the US government had oppressed them. The situation was now far beyond repairable.[16]

Lincoln was inaugurated on March 4, 1861, amid the secession crisis and growing clouds of war. As late as the day of his inaugural, however, he still pleaded from the podium for peace and unity: "We are not enemies but friends. We must not be enemies." The man born in Kentucky offered hope: "Though passion may have strained it must not break our bonds of affection. The mystic chords of memory . . . will yet swell . . . when again touched, as surely they will be, by the better angels of our nature." Tragically, his vision would take a few years and a lot of blood and would cost Lincoln his life.[17]

The new president was burned in effigy throughout the South. Just days later, on March 9, the new Confederate president issued a call for 7,700 volunteers from five of his brethren states. South Carolina had already organized state militias in preparation for war and announced that it was more than ready to fight. Men and boys from across the rural South rushed to join the cause. Just one month later, President Davis had sixty-two thousand soldiers.

DRUMS OF WAR

South Carolina was not only the first state to secede but also the first to fire on American targets. The state's militia units let loose an artillery barrage from nineteen coastal batteries in the predawn hours of April 12, 1861. Their target: Fort Sumter, a small fortress sitting in the middle of Charleston Harbor, designed to protect the important Southern city. One of the officers in the federal fortress, Captain Abner Doubleday—the man sometimes credited with inventing baseball—described the scene in graphic terms: "The crashing of the shot, the bursting of the shells, the falling of the walls, and the roar of the flames, made a pandemonium of the fort." It is estimated that over three thousand shots rained down on Fort Sumter during the thirty-four-hour barrage.[18]

Sumter's flagstaff had been hit and its colors felled. All around the fort, walls began crumbling, and the defenders, woefully outgunned and running low on supplies and ammunition, were forced to take cover deep within the bowels of the fort. Finally, on Sunday, April 14, at two o'clock in the afternoon, the fort's commander ordered a white flag be hoisted on a makeshift pole. A massive cheer let loose throughout Charleston. As word of the victory spread through Dixie, it imbued a false sense of confidence and buoyed enlistment numbers. The South celebrated the first shots and opening victory in what would be a long war.[19]

After months of appeasement and pleas for "friendship," President Lincoln was left with no choice. Seven states had announced secession, and the South had seized federal ports, forts, and facilities and had now launched the first salvos of war. In Lincoln's view, the South was in "open insurrection." In order to "put down this rebellion," he issued the call for seventy-five thousand troops on April 15, the day after Sumter fell.[20] Prior to the war, the US armed forces had numbered a meager sixteen thousand soldiers and sailors. The regiments and companies in service were poorly trained, ill equipped, and, for the most part, scattered across sparsely populated regions in the American West. In addition, a disproportionately large percentage of the standing army came from the South, and, when the war started, many of them abandoned the nation and joined the Confederacy.

Amid almost-certain war, Lincoln held out one final olive branch; the intended goal, he claimed, was simply to retake federal installations, allow the Confederacy to disarm and return to the Union, and thus "cause the laws to be duly executed." Nevertheless, the response was the opposite of what Lincoln had hoped. On April 17, Virginia joined the Confederacy. In May, the Old Dominion was followed by Arkansas, Tennessee, and North Carolina, while Richmond was announced as the new capital on the 29th of that month, replacing Montgomery. The Confederate Congress would later leave symbolic seats open during sessions as an invitation to delegates from fellow slave-owning states like Kentucky and Missouri. These two states, however, remained neutral through the war.[21]

During the presidential campaign of 1860, the Union had been comprised of thirty-three states. Now, only months later, eleven states constituting nearly the entire Southern half of the United States had formed their own government. A vast area of the nation had split off and established its own government, capital, president, congress, constitution, and even their own borderline-blasphemous motto—"With God as Our Vindicator." The Confederacy encompassed an astonishing 770,000 square miles. Whereas the Louisiana Purchase in 1803 had doubled the size of the country, by adding 828,000 square miles, the nation was suddenly reduced by nearly as much in 1861.[22]

The republic, it turned out, was less united and more a collection of states. Its people had shown their loyalties to be regional, not to the nation, their allegiances divided between slavery and freedom, separation and union, war and peace. There was the very real prospect that the United States would never again exist in its previous form or as envisioned by the framers of the Constitution.

A WAR OF INNOCENCE AND INNOCENTS

The Civil War was the bloodiest conflict in American history and perhaps the costliest. Indeed, it is difficult to estimate the war's total impact in terms of property damage, destruction of infrastructure, loss of trade, and the complete collapse of the Southern economy. More troubling still, of course, was the human cost of that war. To be sure, every town and village—in the North and South—felt the horrors of war, one that cruelly and ironically often pitted brother against brother and bitterly divided the nation. People went hungry, civilians were displaced, and business owners had no choice but to close their doors. Starving armies foraged off the land while ransacking farms for food, confiscating homes for headquarters, and turning courthouses and churches into field hospitals. This was the Civil War.

In total, over three million men along with many boys and some women served in uniform. The terrible war was fought in hundreds of locations across the vast country—from skirmishes in remote deserts in Texas and Arizona in the Southwest, to little-known raids at Saint Albans in Vermont and the village of West Point in Ohio, to maritime engagements off the coast of Florida and as far away as France. The large number of soldiers—approximately two million Union and seven hundred thousand Confederate troops on the battlefields—and the length of the conflict meant that the casualty counts were staggering. The numbers were exacerbated by the combat tactics of the mid-nineteenth century—large groups of men standing shoulder-to-shoulder, exchanging volleys at a relatively short distance. As a result, the Union lost roughly 110,000 soldiers in combat; the Confederacy suffered approximately ninety-four thousand killed in action. Even more soldiers were lost to disease, malnutrition, and the horrors of primitive field surgery at the time than were lost to combat. The number of civilians killed is even harder to estimate but was also appallingly high. But what is known is that, in total, somewhere between 620,000 and 640,000 soldiers died during America's Civil War.

The shocking number of casualties meant the Civil War was the bloodiest and most destructive war in the Western world from 1815 to 1914, a time spanning a full century, from the Napoleonic campaigns across Europe to the start of that continent's Great War. It was also the first major conflict of the new industrial age, whereby the manufacture of weapons and killing occurred on an industrial scale. It would serve as a harbinger of the evil to come in the twentieth century.[23]

To put the magnitude of the bloodshed into context, approximately 2,446 men died during the Spanish-American War of 1898, while thirteen thousand were lost during the Mexican-American War of the 1840s, and twenty thousand soldiers were killed during the War of 1812. As troubling as those numbers are, they pale in comparison to the losses from 1861 to 1865. Shockingly, the states of Alabama, North Carolina, and Virginia in the South *each* lost roughly thirty thousand of their sons and fathers during the fighting; in the North, the numbers were even worse—the states of Illinois, New York, and Ohio all sacrificed *over* thirty thousand of their citizens to combat-related deaths during the war.[24]

Furthermore, on a battle-to-battle basis, the losses were unprecedented in American history. In just two bloody days at Shiloh, a small rural community in southwestern Tennessee, more Americans fell than had been lost in any previous war fought by the United States. Similarly, in a foolish Union assault at Cold Harbor, Virginia, just before dawn on June 3, 1864, roughly seven thousand men died in only a half-hour. The vast majority of them wore blue. Likewise, the battlefield casualties at Chancellorsville numbered a staggering twenty-four thousand. Yet the casualty count was thirty thousand at Spotsylvania, nearly thirty-five thousand at Chickamauga, and fully fifty-one thousand at Gettysburg. Even more than 150 years later, those numbers are hard to grasp. In fact, the death toll from the Civil War alone was beyond the combined losses of all other American conflicts from the Revolutionary War through the Vietnam War in the 1960s and 1970s. What's more, the losses during the Civil War, if taken as a percentage of the total population living in the country at the time, would be the equivalent of losing over six million soldiers in a war today, a statistic that is inconceivable to most Americans.[25]

2

Libby & Son

Libby acquired a reputation as one of the Confederacy's most notorious prisons.

—Emeric Szabad, Libby Prison, 1863[1]

One of the worst prisons in American history had a most-unassuming origin as a large warehouse complex. It would, however, become the Confederacy's key site for processing Union prisoners, the primary prison for high-ranking Union officers, and a place where ghastly scenes of death and despair unfolded. Its story is set along Richmond's famed Tobacco Row, so named for the lucrative crop in a city whose nickname—"City of Seven Hills"—was borrowed from its far more famous cousin, Rome. Richmond is nestled along Virginia's James River just over one hundred miles west of the Atlantic Ocean, and it first became a town in 1742. Richmond's history, however, began soon after Captain John Smith helped found America's most important early settlement, Jamestown, in 1607.

Just a few years after its founding, soldiers and settlers from Jamestown began exploring the river that ran inland to the northwest. Settlers were both encouraged by Jamestown's leaders and enticed by the wide, navigable river to move farther inland and establish new villages along its shores. Soon European explorers and traders were plying the river's length and planning new settlements. However, tensions with the native peoples of the region such as the Powhatan[2] boiled over a decade later. White encroachment into native lands precipitated raids from both sides, which were followed by reprisals. Blood was spilled. Outright war in 1622 resulted in the destruction of every English settlement along the James except for Jamestown. The English persisted and eventually killed, subdued, or coopted the Powhatan and other native populations.[3]

Richmond grew during the colonial period and proved to be a key Southern city during the American Revolution. It was in Richmond's St. John's Church where Patrick Henry delivered his famous "Give Me Liberty or Give Me Death" speech that highlighted the colony's Second Convention in 1775.[4] Interestingly, almost ninety years later Union prisoners escaping Libby Prison would hide near that same church that helped give birth to the American experiment. In 1780, during the thick of the War of Independence, Virginia moved its capital from Williamsburg along the southeastern coast to what was believed to be a safer location—inland, toward the center of the state, in Richmond—where it has remained ever since. Nevertheless, one year later the city was sacked by the British and burned. Undeterred, the proud residents rebuilt and incorporated Richmond in 1782.

The area enjoys a relatively moderate climate, and the James River's navigability gave Richmond access to the prosperous Tidewater, Chesapeake Bay, and Atlantic regions. Additionally, although the South had few railways, fully five of them either bisected or passed near the city. Tobacco grew throughout the region, leading one British visitor to the city to quip, "The atmosphere of Richmond is redolent of tobacco; the tints of the pavements are those of tobacco."[5] Thanks to a growing taste for the crop across the colonies and in Europe, Richmond soon boasted a half-dozen tobacco factories and numerous warehouses and plantations. By the start of the Civil War, in 1861, Richmond's population had swelled to thirty-eight thousand, making it the third-largest city in Dixie. It boasted several machine shops, flour mills, and foundries fed by the coal-laden hills that ringed the city. Nearly one hundred thousand tons of merchandise and agricultural products—mostly tobacco and cotton—flowed in and out of Richmond, making it, with its network of waterways, railways, and highways, one of the largest trading hubs and the most important manufacturing center in the American South.

Richmond boasted the massive Tredegar Iron Works. With nine hundred workers, it was the city's largest employer and the largest ironworks in the South. Operated by Jos. R. Anderson & Company, Tredegar sat along the banks of the James River and Kanawha Canal, next to a series of large tobacco warehouses, including the Libby complex. Just as Richmond would become indispensable to the Southern cause, the James River immediately became the lifeline of the Confederacy. The river and area railways brought raw materials to the city and agricultural products back out of the city, all of which supported and funded the war. Tredegar produced half the cannons used by the Rebel army, the armor for the legendary *Merrimack* warship, and most of the South's rifles, bayonets, swords, shells, naval torpedoes, cannonballs, and other armaments and ammunition, as well as quality iron for trains and railway tracks. Tredegar was the most productive foundry in the South, and its remarkable output was a major factor in allowing the Confederacy to remain in the fight for as long as they did. In short, the South could not have fought war without Richmond, the James River, or Tredegar.[6]

The city was also a hub for that vastly more-troubling commodity. Ships carrying slaves regularly traversed the James to Richmond's lucrative slave auction blocks and houses. These ships unloaded their human cargo along Tobacco Row, within view of the Libby warehouse complex. From there, slaves were placed in livestock pens in the nearby Shockoe Bottom neighborhood, where they were sometimes washed and covered in grease in order to make them look healthier after the long, cramped voyage spent chained belowdecks. Some were branded with hot irons in order to identify or mark them as property. One by one, or in small groups, depending on the interests of the sellers and buyers, they were then dragged and shoved to the public auctions, where the bidding began.

The Shockoe Bottom slave auction in Richmond emerged as one of the main cogs in the North American slave trade. It is estimated that as many as 350,000 enslaved individuals were taken to, processed in, and auctioned at Shockoe Bottom by the James. From there, they were sent to plantations around the area and throughout the South. Because of the miserable conditions on the slave ships and in the holding pens, many perished before the auction. Therefore Shockoe Bottom was also the primary burial site in the region for thousands of Africans.

WAREHOUSES

The lucrative slave and tobacco trades along the James attracted many investors and merchants to Richmond. One of them was John Enders, a prosperous tobacco dealer. Enders also developed properties around the city, including riverfront lots owned by his in-laws—the Ege family. It was an ideal location for business. And so it was there, on the southeast corner of Twentieth and Cary Streets, in the heart of Tobacco Row, nestled beside the James River and Kanawha Canal, adjacent to the docks and auction blocks, and within view of the Tredegar Iron Works. that Enders built three large buildings. Construction on the warehouse complex began in 1845.

Each of the three tenement buildings, measuring roughly 110 feet by 45 feet, was made of brick and sat one beside the other. Accordingly, they came to be known as the East, Middle (or Center), and West Buildings. The three-story warehouses fronted Cary Street on a slight crest and sloped downhill to the edge of the water-front. The buildings included numerous four-foot-high rectangular windows and were framed by large chimneys sitting atop each corner of the warehouses. They were imposing structures but with an uninspired, functional design; in short, they looked like the industrial warehouses they were. A road provided access to the front of the buildings, which faced the city proper, while on the other side the canal and small docks where ships tied up directly next to the warehouses. A nearby railway served not only the ironworks, tobacco factories, and slave auctions that dotted the waterfront but the Libby warehouses as well.[7]

Enders intended for the buildings to be a tobacco factory and warehouse. There the lucrative crop would be dried, rolled, stored, and distributed. Consequently, the interior of each of the three buildings contained eight large rooms—two on the first floor (known as the lower floor) and three each on the second and third floors (known as the upper floors). The cavernous rooms measured over one hundred feet in length and forty feet in width on each floor. The big rooms were open and breezy, ideal for storing boxes of supplies or tobacco, and were connected by wooden staircases. The stairs lacked landings, which meant that, rather than walk halfway to the next floor, reach the landing, and then turn and walk the remaining four feet to the next landing, anyone in the warehouse would have to climb a narrow, steep, eight-foot-high staircase. While the design was optimal for storage, its low eight-foot ceilings, banister-less stairs, and lack of toilets and other amenities would make it less than ideal for warehousing prisoners.[8]

By October 20, 1851, the buildings were nearly complete. That was the day Enders climbed a ladder to oversee the final construction. The ladder broke, sending him careening through a hatch in the ceiling of the Middle Building to his death below. He was killed instantly. Enders was buried in St. John's Churchyard in Richmond, near what would soon become an important safe house and secret hideaway for escaped Union prisoners. The property was passed to Enders' wife, Sarah, who turned the day-to-day management of it over to Poitiaux Robinson, husband of the Enders' daughter Mary Enders Robinson. However, Poitiaux died on September 15, 1852, less than one year after his father-in-law. The widow Sarah Enders assumed responsibility for the warehouses, but as the remaining family members were contemplating the future of the investment, she died on February 27, 1853, just over two months after the construction concluded. Sarah was buried at her husband's side. One can imagine the family wanting nothing to do with the warehouses that were developing a reputation for being cursed. The complex's history was already stained with tragedy and darkness; it was about to get worse. A deed transferring ownership of the property to the two surviving daughters—Sarah Palmer and Mary Robinson—was signed in Richmond on June 1, 1854. It was left to Mary to decide what to do with the investment.[9]

In 1854, Mary leased the complex to Captain Luther Libby, a sailor and transplant from Maine who had come to Virginia in search of business opportunities and eventually settled in Richmond. The Enders family needed money, and the arrangement was for a three-year lease. As for Mary, she would later remarry, to a man named Lea. The curse continued; she passed away in Richmond on the eve of the Civil War.

Luther Libby had worked as a chandler, which was a grocer and supplier for ships, and that was his plan for the warehouses strategically located along the important river. After leasing the three large buildings, he converted two of the three spacious structures into storehouses, while the West Building became the chandlery office from which he sold supplies to the ships docked just feet away. Libby and his son George W. Libby named the business Libby and Son Ship Chandlers and Grocers but abbreviated the title on the sign they hung on the side of the building to L. LIBBY & SON, SHIP CHANDLERS. It was from that block-lettered sign that the infamous prison would later get its nickname.

Libby and Son prospered. In the 1850s, slavery and tobacco were booming industries in Richmond, and Libby's chandlery became a leading food- and supply-distribution center for the many ships docked along Tobacco Row. The former resident of Maine specialized in supplying ships from the Northern states rather than Southern slavers, so when the war started in 1861 and Northern shipping came to an abrupt halt, Libby's chandlery suffered.[10]

With Richmond as the main city in the new Confederacy and the Virginia state capital (and soon the capital of the Confederate States of America), all available space would be needed to accommodate its burgeoning government and the war effort. Accordingly, Confederate authorities began confiscating warehouses for use as prisons. Their former owners were rarely compensated for the loss. Such would be the case in Richmond, where several warehouses along the city's famed Tobacco Row and James River would function as prisons. The government of the new Confederate States of America gave Luther Libby just forty-eight hours to vacate the building in 1861, most likely in or around October. Libby's chandlery and warehouses were about to become one of the most notorious prisons in American history. In the words of Colonel Frederick Bartleson, one of the best-known prisoners held at the wretched facility, the complex would also become the site of "the most remarkable escape that ever took place in this country."[11]

RICHMOND AT WAR

On May 29, 1861, President Jefferson Davis and roughly one thousand employees of the new government officially moved to Richmond. The population of the Confederate capital grew rapidly, from around thirty-eight thousand residents at the time of the attack on Fort Sumter to a whopping 120,000 just two years later, prompting T. C. DeLeon, aide to President Davis, to complain that "The city was thoroughly jammed." Loyal secessionists, would-be war contractors, military commanders, politicians, displaced Southerners, and thousands of "rowdy Confederate soldiers itching for battle" poured into the city in May and June of 1861. Richmond was no longer simply the capital of Virginia or the Confederacy; it had become the symbol of Southern resistance.[12]

In the coming years, the entirety of the South would be overrun by advancing Union troops. Economies throughout Dixie collapsed, and the jewel of the Confederacy became a city of refugees as people fled for the protection and supposed opportunities Richmond offered. Sally Putnam, a secessionist who had moved to Richmond from Alexandria by the border of the federal capital of Washington, offered an interesting look at the city when she complained about the Confederate capital, "I do not believe there is a vacant spot in the city." She and others soon dubbed Richmond the "city of refuge," observing, "the homeless and destitute crowded into our city for safety and support." She did not mean it as a compliment. Putnam was also taken back by the different kinds of people that now lived in the city, from Irish and German immigrants to Jewish merchants. "A strange city," she noted, "from the signs over the doors of the shops," which included business names such as Moses, Jacobs, Levy, and Rosenheimer. Even though Putnam was shocked by what she encountered, the diehard Confederate was happy to be in the capital of the Confederacy, even if the flood of refugees into the city would not let up until war's end.[13]

As was the case for most facets of governance in the Confederacy, the capital's move was poorly planned, and the apparatus of government was makeshift. It was, for instance, uncertain as to whether Richmond would even be the permanent capital should the Confederacy succeed in seceding. Likewise, the city would soon become the South's central receiving site for nearly all prisoners taken during the war, but this too was a *pis aller*—another stopgap arrangement. Countless thousands of prisoners arrived in Richmond and were then incarcerated, paroled or exchanged, or sent to prisons in neighboring states. The city was now absorbing Union soldiers from across the North. Richmond became a city of war and of prisoners.[14]

Both political tensions and armed conflicts were escalating around the country, and so the Confederate Congress scheduled a meeting in Richmond for July 20, 1861, to prepare for total war. In the North, there were calls to strike the Confederate capital before or during the meeting. In Washington, President Lincoln ordered General Irvin McDowell to prepare the army to invade Virginia and strike at Richmond. McDowell was hesitant; he knew the Union troops were very green and supplies were still being organized, and he had little intelligence about Confederate defenses and actions. However, the drums of war were being beaten by the press and Congress.

Union forces set out from the capital city on July 16, still largely untrained and ill-prepared for combat. General McDowell made a costly mistake: the army's pace was entirely too slow. Word spread throughout the South that a federal force of nearly 28,500 men was moving into Virginia. With plenty of advanced warning, Confederate generals were able to scramble forces to intercept McDowell before he moved too far into Virginia. The Union learned another lesson the hard way: all around the United States, North and South, including inside Washington, D.C., were individuals with Southern loyalties. There would be eyes and ears everywhere during the war, reporting on any troop movements.

In Virginia, General P. G. T. Beauregard, fresh off his victory at Fort Sumter, was ordered to organize defenses between Washington and Richmond. He had only a few thousand men, equally untrained. Nevertheless, they raced to block the Union advance, arriving at the strategic railway junction at Manassas, about twenty-five miles outside of Washington. Beauregard had his men dig in behind Bull Run, a small creek near Centreville. On July 17, McDowell dispatched a small unit of forward scouts to test the Rebel defenses and attempt to cross Bull Run at Blackburn's Ford. A brief skirmish ensued before both sides pulled back. So confident were many Northerners of a glorious victory that day—and so slowly had McDowell moved—that many reporters, politicians, and even civilians with blankets and lunches gathered on a nearby hill to watch the battle and be entertained. Cheering was heard not far from the creek.

On July 21, McDowell attacked. Approximately ten thousand Union forces simultaneously struck Beauregard's main line while also attempting to outflank the enemy. The fighting raged all morning, with McDowell's forces initially driving the Confederate line back across Bull Run. The Union Army continued pushing their foe back beyond the Warrington Turnpike to Henry House Hill behind the battlefield. Victory seemed to be at hand. However, in the afternoon and with Southern forces close to defeat, General Joseph Johnston arrived by rail from the Shenandoah, bringing eleven thousand reinforcements and, importantly, artillery. Additional units arrived. The total Confederate forces now engaged far exceeded thirty-two thousand.

One of Johnston's commanders, General Thomas J. Jackson, a professor from the Virginia Military Institute, rushed forward to establish Confederate defenses at Henry House Hill[15] and engaged the advancing blue line. It worked. In response, McDowell sent additional Union units to strike at Jackson's new line while also attempting to outflank him. However, Jackson's hastily organized artillery batteries were able to halt the Union advance on the hill. Jackson bravely held his position against the Yankee onslaught. From his position nearby, Confederate general Barnard Bee watched the momentum swing in their favor and rallied his own men, noting that Jackson was standing strong and proud "like a stone wall."[16] Bee was killed, but the immortal nickname "Stonewall" Jackson lived on.

After a full day of fighting, Northern commanders had failed to coordinate their gains. With momentum switching sides, General Beauregard ordered a counterattack around four o'clock that afternoon. Exhausted, poorly organized, without reinforcements, and now outnumbered, the Union Army was driven back across Bull

Run. The retreating armies did not have lines of communication; nor were they well trained. Order quickly broke down, and confusion reigned. Making matters worse, some Yankee units from Massachusetts and Wisconsin were wearing gray uniforms, while some Virginia units were clad in blue! Soldiers began collapsing from exhaustion, lack of water, and the combination of heat and humidity made unbearable in their heavy wool uniforms. When the advancing Southern line rushed forward, screaming—in what became known as the Rebel yell—it broke the Union's will. Soon the retreat turned into chaos—then to a total rout. Some of the panicked Union soldiers even overran the crested hill where civilians had gathered to observe the fighting.

In addition to suffering nearly three thousand Union casualties that day, across the North the bitter realization set in that they were unprepared for war and that it would not be over after one battle or even a three-month campaign. Approximately one thousand Union soldiers were taken prisoner at Bull Run. Over the next year, thousands more would be captured. Uncertain as to what to do with so many prisoners of war, Confederate troops marched those captured to Richmond to be processed.

3

"What Is to Be Done with the Prisoners?"

Those who deny freedom to others deserve it not for themselves.

—Abraham Lincoln, 1859[1]

It did not take long after war broke out between the North and the South before soldiers began to be taken prisoner. Some of the very first prisoners of war were federal troops at Castle Pinckney in South Carolina, a small outpost located next to Fort Sumter on the picturesque and sleepy shores of Charleston Harbor. Rebel militias had arrested the soldiers as soon as the state seceded from the Union. More arrests and detentions soon followed, as South Carolina militiamen seized other federal facilities. One by one, other Southern states followed suit, and federal installations and small, isolated forts fell throughout Dixie in the spring of 1861, leading to the detention of hundreds of US soldiers and federal employees.

Lacking any plans for dealing with the inevitability of prisoners, in the early months of the war both sides typically released prisoners right away. Neither side had much choice; they both lacked a sufficient number of prisons, adequate food and supplies, trained guards, or a protocol for handling captured soldiers. They thus followed the tradition in Europe of paroling prisoners of war. Initially, the Union tried to exchange prisoners within ten days of their capture, whereas the South had no formal arrangements. However, both Union and Confederate governments prioritized the exchange of officers, and, when such pacts were made, it was typically an even *quid pro quo*—one general for one general, one colonel for one colonel, one major for one major, and so on. It was hit-or-miss for enlisted men. If a prisoner languished more than ten days, given the lack of facilities or guidelines they were usually simply released. Often the terms for release were little more than the soldier's pledge to never again pick up arms after being freed.[2]

One of first to raise concerns about the issue was US quartermaster General Montgomery C. Meigs, who, on July 12, 1861, wrote to Secretary of War Simon Cameron warning, "The United States will have to take care of large numbers of prisoners of war. I respectfully call your attention to the propriety of making some arrangements in time."[3] This letter was written just days before the First Battle of Bull Run. The Union acted on the warning and developed a system for handling prisoners, which included the historic custom of separating officers and enlisted men in different facilities. In October of 1861, they appointed Colonel William H. Hoffman as commissary general in charge of all prisons and prisoners. Hoffman attempted to organize camps, resources, and guards as well as a system for formally exchanging prisoners and assuring the humane treatment of soldiers captured by the enemy. One of the earliest efforts also came courtesy of Europe—cartels. Cartels were created to help fund prisoners and provide for visits, food, mail, and other services. Hoffman also developed basic rules for the detainment and treatment of prisoners, hired commandants, and ordered that inspections and reports be conducted to assure decent treatment.[4]

Nevertheless, the conditions in prisons were deplorable. Neither side was prepared for the scale and length of the war; nor did they prioritize care of prisoners. This state of affairs was most prevalent in the South, where, by year two of the war, there was scarcely enough food to feed the army or citizens, let alone prisoners. In addition to suffering inadequate provisions, prisoners suffered from the animosities between North and South that often brought out the worst in those assigned to administer and guard prisons. This included both Union and Confederate leaders who often demonstrated little compassion for the enemy. For instance, Colonel Hoffman, heading the Union's prisons, once directed a subordinate, "So long as a prisoner has clothing upon him, however much torn, issue nothing to him."[5] Unfortunately, when prisoners were starving and dying, they found little empathy from their captors, in the North or South.

Throughout the war, prison officials made mistakes. Indeed, the North was plagued by "bad management," the South by "still worse."[6] There was little special training for prison guards and wardens. Moreover, with few men available for such duty, those assigned to be prison guards were often the wounded, older men, or those "mentally or physically unfit for field duty."[7] As such, prisons and detention sites were, at best, "makeshift arrangements, haphazardly organized."[8] Emeric Szabad, a Hungarian freedom fighter who had joined the Union effort, had the misfortune of ending up in Libby Prison and described the horrors of these makeshift prisons as "festering centers of maltreatment, humiliation, hunger and death." The "prisoners," he noted, "were crammed into them with total disregard of capacity limits, nutrition, hygiene or sanitation requirements." It did not take long before inmates were suffering and dying from "poor sanitary facilities, substandard and inadequate food, foul water, superficial medical care, trigger-happy guards, inclement weather and boredom," recalled the Hungarian.[9] Indeed, the flood of prisoners quickly overwhelmed both Union and Confederate facilities and resources.

PRISONER ROW

In July of 1861, just days before the First Battle of Bull Run, a few Union prisoners, mostly from the militia skirmishes in South Carolina, had begun to trickle into Richmond. The *Richmond Dispatch* gives us a number, writing on July 2 that "from 75 to 100 of Old Abe's disciples" had arrived in the city. These Union prisoners were paroled "on their honor" and permitted to simply roam around the city. Of course, such a haphazard arrangement would soon become impossible when waves of prisoners began arriving.[10] The first large group of prisoners to arrive in Richmond—631 of them—came by train. After being unloaded at the city's train depot on July 23, they were taken to an old, three-story tobacco factory on the southeast corner of Twenty-Fifth and Main Streets owned by John L. Ligon. The facility, located near the Libby warehouse complex, even resembled the soon-to-be notorious prison. Like Libby, Ligon's Factory proved to be wholly inadequate for containing so many men.

The next day, Confederate authorities inspected the overcrowded building and were so shocked at the cramped conditions that they even apologized to the prisoners, one of whom was Congressman Alfred Ely of New York, who had been watching the fighting at Bull Run when he was captured. On July 27, the prisoners were moved a short distance to two larger buildings—Howard's Factory and George Harwood's Tobacco Factory. They were also provided with a cook, although not much in the way of rations. Imprisoned officers and enlisted men were placed into separate quarters, so as to lessen the chance of escape. Another practice that would later become associated with Libby Prison was that Richmond residents "flocked" to Ligon and Howard's "prisons" to see the Union soldiers. They would, as one of the prisoners grumbled, "soon have hundreds more to amuse them."[11]

In late July and early August of 1861, Union general John A. Dix and his Confederate counterpart General D. H. Hill arranged an informal cartel with the goal of exchanging prisoners within ten days of capture. This initial system not only specified exchanges of equal numbers and ranks but also established a rough formula between ranks such that one general would be exchanged for sixty privates, a colonel for fifteen privates, a captain for six privates, and a lieutenant for three privates. Parolees were also to remain in provisional camps guarded by their own troops and prohibited from reentering the war based on a pledge or signed affidavit.[12]

Another large group of prisoners was brought to Richmond after the Battle of Ball's Bluff, which had been fought in Virginia on October 21. The *Examiner* put the number of captured at over six hundred, writing that "The capacious tobacco warehouse of Robt. A. Mayo, on 25th between Main and Cary Streets, was thereupon engaged for their reception."[13] This warehouse was located next to the Libby Warehouse, which was also about to become a prison.

Confederate authorities were forced to use every available space. One by one, the lucrative warehouses and factories along Tobacco Row were being converted to prisons, with grave consequences not only to the prisoners but also to the city's economy. Richmond's City Jail was equipped to hold only a few inmates, so the city's provost marshal began using the remaining warehouses and tobacco factories, along with any other available building as prisons, confiscating them in a haphazard manner in order to find room for the burgeoning prison population. This included Crew & Pemberton's Warehouse, Whitlock's Warehouse, Gleanor's Factory, Barnett's Factory, Atkinson's Factory, Ross's Factory, and more. Eventually, the Confederacy was also forced to set aside the Henrico County Jail in Richmond for prisoners of war. The flood of prisoners continued through 1861 and 1862, and conditions deteriorated in the makeshift facilities. Despite the lack of space, the South ordered that prisons be segregated.

A CITY OF PRISONS

Initially, Richmond's residents had seemed fascinated by the arrival of so many prisoners of war. As one of the city's newspapers noted, "Many of our citizens evinced some curiosity to get a peep at the captured Yankees."[14] Within weeks, however, a chorus of indignation and annoyance began to pour forth. The large prison population constituted an imminent threat to Richmond's inhabitants in the case of a mass escape. The prisoners, it was argued by the public and press, were also draining city coffers. It was seen as a question of either feeding the city's residents and the Confederate Army or allocating scarce resources to prisoners. The choice was easy. One newspaper, the *Richmond Whig*, framed the situation this way: "The brave men who have periled life and limb in defense of Southern rights deserve our first care and most attentive consideration." Citizens began to call for harsher treatment for Union prisoners and began demanding that draconian cuts be made to their already meager rations. Feeding this narrative, the *Whig* claimed absurdly that the "Yankee" prisoners were "lounging about" Richmond, enjoying the city and "content" to be prisoners. The paper opined that they were "not treated with that rigor which some have supposed."[15]

By the end of September of that first year of war, the *Richmond Enquirer* put the city's prisoner population at 1,700. The newspaper also began publishing articles expressing concern about the threat of a mass prison escape and growing resentment at seeing so many Union prisoners in the city. One of the main complaints raised concerned the cost of housing and feeding so many prisoners. As food supplies began to dwindle across the city and throughout Dixie, Southerners again called for cuts to prison rations, especially coffee, sugar, and other "luxuries." The *Enquirer* fanned the flames of resentment, claiming incorrectly that prisoners enjoyed stores of food "more plentiful and nutritious than that which constituted their usual fare in the Federal camps." It did not take long for Southern newspapers to devolve into little more than half-truths, pro-Confederate propaganda, and a mouthpiece for the new government.[16]

As early as August of 1861, the *Whig* called for removing all prisoners from the city. It was not clear to where they should be moved or how this would happen. One proposal suggested that brutal treatment would deter other Northerners from joining the war effort. Therefore, the proposal noted, once paroled the prisoners would immediately flee northward with stories of the horrors of Richmond's charnel houses. Another proposal called for using Union prisoners as forced laborers. Massive prison-labor camps could thus produce materials for the Southern war effort. The *Richmond Examiner* echoed these sentiments, advocating a very hard line on the prisoner question. The newspaper's editor, Edward Pollard, encouraged a policy of "neglect" and "roughing up" prisoners of war. Much like the stories running in the *Whig*, Pollard's *Examiner* spewed misinformation, such as claims that prisoners were enjoying a "pampered" life in Richmond. The *Examiner* also whipped the city into a frenzy with inaccurate reports of far greater brutalities visited upon detainees in Northern prisons.[17]

Both the *Examiner* and *Enquirer* also stoked animosities by reporting stories of guards shooting prisoners, endorsing the practice even if the prisoner was not in the act of escaping. For instance, a July 31, 1861, story told of a prisoner who allegedly had been talking to someone outside the prison window, prompting a guard to shoot at the inmate. However, the paper lamented, "The shot missed its mark." The prisoners, wrote the *Examiner*, "need taking down a peg or two." Such was the case two months later when the paper celebrated the news that Corporal N. C. Buck of the Seventy-Ninth New York Volunteers had been shot and killed as he stood by the window in Ligon's Prison. Similar stories soon filled the pages of the city's newspapers. Such opinions and articles spread beyond Richmond, as when the *Charleston Mercury* decried the mounting prisoner crisis, writing, "Some people think we ought to feed them on fodder or mixed horse feed, while others say the cheapest plan would be to destroy them outright."[18]

Sadly, it took only a few short weeks after the war's onset for these alarming ideas to begin percolating throughout Richmond. Either way, opined the *Whig*, "Everybody is asking, 'What is to be done with the prisoners?'"[19]

The Confederacy responded to the mounting problem by adopting a centralized system. The plan was to bring all prisoners to Richmond for processing and detainment. Richmond was a city connected to much of Dixie by water, rail, and roads. As such, wagons, trains, and boats full of prisoners made their way to the Confederate capital throughout the war. There were only a few exceptions, such as Castle Pinckney in Charleston, South Carolina, and the Salisbury Prison in North Carolina. At the beginning of the war, Richmond was able to accommodate most of the prisoners, but soon every other problem in the city was exacerbated by the prison crisis.

The number of prisoners in Richmond ebbed and flowed throughout 1861 and 1862, but in August and September of 1862 alone perhaps six thousand Union prisoners arrived into the city. The prisoner population grew rapidly thereafter. With limited resources, meager funds, little chance to plan, and a steady flood of prisoners, General John Winder, the city's provost marshal, was out of ideas. Richmond's prisoner problem would never be adequately resolved during the war, even with the addition of a prison as large as the Libby warehouse complex. The capital soon became a city of prisons and prisoners.[20]

A POX ON THE COUNTRY

Many Northerners wrongly assumed that secession was being fed by only a few agitators and slave owners in the South, even if the overwhelming evidence and quick exodus of Southern states in 1861 plainly suggested otherwise. There was the rather widespread belief north of the Mason-Dixon Line that "love of nation" as well as rationality and the cause of humanity would prevail among most Southerners; or, at the least, Northerners assumed most of their Southern neighbors were opposed to the evils of slavery or at least were not willing to die for the institution. They were wrong. These same Northern politicians and newspaper editors also underestimated the feeling in the South that they were being oppressed by Northern states, just as they had failed to appreciate the widespread sense that Southern cultural identity was distinct from that of the rest of the nation. Indeed, the causes of the American Civil War were complicated and ran far deeper than most Northerners realized.[21]

On both sides of the conflict, leaders and the public were at best naive and at worst flat out misinformed. This included expectations for war: The common belief was that one major battle would suffice to end the conflict. In the North, confidence prevailed. After all, they had more financial resources and manufacturing. The Confederates, they reasoned, would realize that they were outgunned, outmanned, out-financed, out-populated, and therefore outmatched, which would be enough to end the "uprising." The *New York Times* confidently opined that the conflict would end within one month. Even among more cautious estimates in the North, such as editorials in the *Chicago Tribune*, it was suggested a three-month enlistment would suffice to man the conflict. Shockingly, the new recruits to Lincoln's army were therefore mustered for a period of only ninety days.[22]

The South was also confident of success. Many believed their fighting spirit to be superior to the Yankees' and put great stock in their skilled generals. Other Southerners felt God was on their side and that they could therefore not fail. Moreover, many doubted Lincoln's resolve, leadership abilities, or political acumen. There were few voices of reason. One of them was George Wythe Randolph of Virginia—lawyer, planter, and grandson of Thomas Jefferson—who cautioned against the optimism. The man who would briefly serve as secretary of war for the Confederacy and had studied in Massachusetts as a young man, warned his fellow Southerners, "We are in the beginning of the greatest war that has ever been waged on this continent." Indeed.[23]

There is no doubt that the Civil War was the most dramatic and important event in the early history of the United States. As noted historian Shelby Foote reminded us, it is impossible to understand the United States without understanding the Civil War. It was, after all, a seminal event in testing and ultimately reforging the American character. There are, however, complexities in that character, including the fact that slavery was a horrific pox on the nation, one that would end in a terrible war. Nevertheless, there was another great fault in the national character: an often-forgotten dark legacy of the Civil War was the treatment of prisoners.[24]

Few anticipated the long and bloody struggle that ensued. Therefore, given naive expectations and little preparation for a protracted conflict, it is no surprise that there was even less planning for prisoners.[25] It did not take long, however, for the prisoner situation to reach the point of crisis. The Civil War had many controversies, bloody battles, and devastating impacts, but one less-well-known aspect of the conflict was the brutality of wartime prisons. Despite the horrors of the war, in the words of one of the many unfortunate soldiers to end up in a Civil War prison, "no controversy ever evoked such emotions as the mutual recriminations between Northern and Southern partisans over the treatment of prisoners of war."[26]

Across both the North and South, over 150 prisons were in operation at one point or another during the Civil War. They spread as far south as Fort Pulaski by Savannah and the Dry Tortugas off the southwestern coast of Key West, and as far north as Boston and the ill-famed Elmira Prison in upstate New York. One of the worst prisons in the North, Elmira suffered a 24 percent death rate, prompting G. T. Taylor of the First Alabama Artillery to conclude that it "was nearer Hades than I thought any place could be." Prisons were even needed in the Western territories, including as far west as Fort Craig in New Mexico Territory.[27]

While the North generally did not use old stockades, the South did. Desperate for space and often lacking the resources to build prisons, Confederate authorities resorted to placing prisoners in open areas with high wooden fencing or in pens suited to cattle and hogs. Examples include Camp Cahaba in Alabama, Camp Ford in Texas, Camp Salisbury in North Carolina, and the most notorious prison of the war, Camp Sumter in Georgia, also known as Andersonville. Thousands of Northern prisoners were housed in these stockades, and the results were appalling. At Andersonville, prisoners were packed into the sixteen-acre compound enclosed by a fifteen-foot-high fence. Some thirteen thousand Union soldiers died there in just fourteen months. In total, nearly one-third of all those held at the facility perished! Reminiscent of the *Lord of the Flies*, men inside the compound were reduced from the atrocious conditions, lack of food and shelter, and extreme overcrowding to a struggle for survival and primitive state of nature. Gangs of prisoners formed who terrorized fellow prisoners. The situation was so violent and chaotic that the leaders of one gang of "raiders" was arrested and hanged at the prison on July 10, 1864.[28]

In some cases, Confederate authorities were forced to simply order prisoners to ad hoc prisons comprised of open fields of dirt without a wooden stockade. Union soldiers were simply placed on "barren ground" without tents, shelter, or any necessary amenities, such as at Camp Sorghum in South Carolina, East Point near Atlanta, and a field outside of Charlotte, North Carolina. The most infamous of these wretched sites was Belle Isle, a small islet in the James River in Richmond, located near Libby and the city's famous Tredegar Iron Works.[29]

The Belle Isle confinement was a parcel of land less than six acres in size and surrounded by a ditch and earthen mounds. Some ten- to twelve thousand enlisted men were jammed into the small island without barracks, buildings, or other protection from the elements. It is estimated that, on average, ten prisoners died each day on the hellish enclave, with countless more succumbing to exposure and freezing temperatures during the winter of 1863 and 1864. Emeric Szabad, a Hungarian-born Union officer who watched the suffering at Belle Isle from the windows of Libby, recalled prisoners forced by severe food shortages "to skin rats and eat them raw." Szabad's fellow prisoner, the well-known Union raider Colonel Abel Streight, likened Belle Isle's conditions to a "slaughter-pen" for cattle.[30]

Moreover, partially due to administrative ineptness, during the course of the war the South ran out of food, clothing, blankets, medicine, and most everything else. This was true in Richmond in part due to the massive prisoner population that had been flooding the city since the war's earliest days. As the war waged on, far longer than either North or South had planned, Confederate currency was rendered worthless, and so, cut off from European trade and Northern manufacturing, the Southern economy completely collapsed. The entire region was going hungry. In Richmond, "Except for the wealthy, most residents of the city lived in a condition of near starvation that grew worse with each passing week."[31] This prompted a riot among the city's civilians, who took to the streets on April 2, 1863, to demand food.

Hamstrung by a much smaller population and forced to conscript every able-bodied man into service, Southern farms and businesses were being neglected as the war waged on. Consequently, with Southern armies and civilians starving, it was neither possible nor a priority to feed or care for captured Union soldiers. Compounding the problem was the fact that most of the battles were waged on Southern soil. After starting the war, the South soon found itself invaded. It was total war—both by decree from the Confederate government and by necessity. As war dragged on and shortages and suffering reached crisis levels across Dixie, views hardened toward the causes of the war, secession, and Union prisoners, who came to be seen as oppressors and were derided as "Lincoln hirelings."[32] Richmond residents began referring to the city's prisoners not as United States or Union soldiers but as "abolitionist soldiers" and the "abolitionist army."[33] Total war always involves the demonization of the enemy. And so it was among Confederates. The Southern army not only dug in on the battlefield, but Southern hearts were hardened as well.

Because of gaps in records and quick paroles at the beginning and end of the war, it is hard to determine an exact number of prisoners. It is estimated that roughly 410,000 troops were imprisoned during the Civil War, not counting the armies that surrendered on April 9, 1965, at war's end. Of that total, approximately 194,000 were Union soldiers and 214,000 were Confederate soldiers. Shockingly, in excess of fifty-six thousand prisoners of war perished during the conflict. That is a number similar to the total American losses during the Vietnam War, waged a century later. Furthermore, countless thousands died soon after their release, from illnesses suffered during their incarceration. Although there were fewer Union prisoners of war, more of them—just over thirty thousand—died in Confederate prison camps, whereas roughly twenty-six thousand Rebels perished in Union prisons. This amounts to a death toll of over 15.5 percent for soldiers in blue compared to about 12 percent for soldiers in gray. However, the numbers were most assuredly even higher for Union prisoners because of inaccurate and missing Confederate records.[34]

The breadth of losses among both Union and Confederate prisons are deeply troubling. Prisoners died of malnutrition and, in some Southern prisons, starvation. Soldiers perished from exposure to the elements, with some freezing to death in the winter. A bewildering array of diseases plagued the prisons—consumption, malaria, measles, pneumonia, smallpox, typhoid fever, and typhus (known in Libby Prison as "prison fever"[35]). Added to that, sanitary conditions were primitive, prisoners had little opportunity to bathe, and there was inadequate medical attention. In fact, more men died of diseases during the Civil War than were lost on the battlefield. The tales of suffering and abuse are widespread.

4

To War

The time for compromise has now passed, and the South is determined to maintain her position and make all who oppose her smell Southern powder and feel Southern steel.

—Jefferson Davis, 1861[1]

Those detained in the makeshift prison at the Libby warehouses were Union officers, political prisoners, and those accused of disloyalty to the Confederacy. They included schoolteachers, homebuilders, clerks, farmers, physicians, shippers, bankers, writers, merchants, politicians, and professors. Their stories are as varied as their backgrounds. What all of them shared was the terror of being imprisoned in one of the most brutal and important prisons of the American Civil War. The drama that would soon unfold in Richmond included an impressive group of men who would end up either participating in or having a front-row seat to the largest and most remarkable prison break in American history.

LIBBY'S LEADERS

One of them was a mild-mannered yet indefatigable colonel of the Seventy-Seventh Pennsylvania Volunteers named Thomas E. Rose. Surprisingly, very little about Rose's upbringing would explain the extraordinary valor and leadership he would later exhibit on the battlefield and in a wretched Richmond prison. Rose was born and raised in Quaker country in eastern Pennsylvania near the Delaware River, an area known at the time for embracing passivism, racial tolerance, and abolition.

Raised as a strict Presbyterian, Rose was described as quiet, studious, and responsible, though physically he was broad-shouldered and strong, all traits that would end up being on display to his fellow prisoners. As a young man, Rose followed his father's example by becoming a schoolteacher. At age twenty-one, the young man married Lydia Trumbower, and the couple moved to rural western Pennsylvania, where he became the principal of the South Pittsburg School system.[2]

Rose embraced the cause of the Union; so as soon as the war started, the young principal enlisted in the Twelfth Pennsylvania Volunteers, a local Pittsburgh infantry unit. Although he was educated and held a position of leadership in the community, he was willing to join the war as a lowly private. It did not take long for the former principal's superiors to recognize his abilities. Rose excelled in every assignment, was a natural leader of men, and was quickly promoted to the rank of captain. On September 28, 1861, Rose was reassigned to command the B and E companies of the Seventy-Seventh Pennsylvania—two of the ten companies of infantry and one of artillery comprising the regiment, and consisting at various times of anywhere from 80 to 150 soldiers. Rose's companies had been mustered on August 1, 1861, from Chambersburg, Harrisburg, Lancaster, and elsewhere across Pennsylvania.

The Seventy-Seventh's training concluded at the end of September of that year at Camp Wilkins near Pittsburgh. Rose and his two companies were then ordered to Tennessee. Many of the young Pennsylvanians were away from home for the first time and headed off to war in a faraway part of the country, first traveling on the Louisville Railroad, then marching through Kentucky and Tennessee. The Seventy-Seventh finally arrived in Nashville on March 2, 1862. The Tennessee campaign was a difficult one, and Rose's companies were thrown into the thick of the fighting. Functioning as "skirmishers," the B and E companies were charged with the dangerous and stressful mission of moving in advance of the main army to clear hiding enemy soldiers from the forests. In addition to the rough terrain and thick forests, the weather proved to be challenging. The Tennessee campaign endured torrential rains and blistering heat in the summers, bitterly cold winds in winters, and diseases that periodically tore through their ranks.[3]

The men from the Keystone State carried more than their fair share of the burden during the Civil War, and the Seventy-Seventh was no exception. Rose and his companies participated in a number of engagements, including the Battle of Shiloh,[4] one of the largest and costliest conflicts of the Tennessee campaign and overall war. The fight began on the morning of April 6, 1862, when an army of forty thousand Confederates under General Albert Johnston snuck through the woods and surprised the main Union force under General Ulysses S. Grant camped in a clearing. The bloody engagement raged throughout the day and through the night.

Although the Confederates had the element of surprise and had encircled the Union Army, the North's hastily formed defensive positions held. The next day, Grant managed to organize a counterattack, and Union forces backed by artillery drove the Rebels from the field. It was an unnerving and ferocious affair for those involved, including Rose's companies. Nearly twenty-four thousand casualties were suffered in the battle, one of them being General Johnston, who was killed in the fighting.[5]

The Seventy-Seventh Pennsylvania also fought in Tennessee near Corinth and Murfreesboro in the middle of the state as well as at Perryville and La Vergne in the autumn of 1862. They were instrumental in the Battle of Stones River, another massive and bloody engagement that began on New Year's Eve of 1862 and lasted for several days. It pitted the Union's Army of the Cumberland, numbering over forty thousand men under General William Rosecrans, against a Confederate force of nearly the same size, commanded by General Braxton Bragg.

During the fighting, the Rebels struck the right end of the Union line, pushing them back roughly three miles and nearly encircling the men in blue in the process. With the Union forced to fall back and both flanks exposed, the battle threatened to turn into a costly rout. Moreover, at a crucial moment in the chaotic fighting one of the Seventy-Seventh's batteries was captured by the enemy and turned around to fire at the main Union force. Amid the chaos, Colonel Peter Housum, commander of the Seventy-Seventh Pennsylvania, was severely wounded.

Desperately hoping to hold off the Confederate onslaught, General Rosecrans needed a unit to advance against Bragg's attacking Rebel forces. With the battle deteriorating, Rosecrans selected the Seventy-Seventh for the task, and Rose was thrust into command. The burly former principal quickly organized a counterattack at Stones River. Then another. And another. He succeeded in stalling the Confederate advance and helped turn the tide of the fighting. After the battle, a grateful Rosecrans said to Rose, "Colonel, I see that your regiment is all right. Give my compliments to the boys, and tell them that I say, 'It was the banner regiment at Stones River.' They never broke their ranks."[6]

The Union forces ultimately repelled two attacks at Stones River, and, although they suffered nearly thirteen thousand casualties, they managed to force Bragg's large army out of middle Tennessee. Rose was credited with saving lives and helping secure the victory. Colonel Housum later died from his wounds, and on January 24, 1863, a grateful Rosecrans promoted Rose to colonel and gave him command of the Seventy-Seventh. The battlefield nickname "The Banner Regiment at Stones River" stuck, becoming the motto of the Seventy-Seventh. Likewise, Rose quickly emerged as one of the most respected and admired commanders in Rosecrans's army.

The man who would later serve as Colonel Rose's trusted assistant in the plan to break out of the infamous bastille of the Confederacy was from Kentucky. A homebuilder with a passion for horses, Andrew G. Hamilton resisted the inclinations of many of his neighbors who supported the Confederacy. In fact, when Rebel militia units attacked supporters of the Union near his home in Owensboro on September

18, 1862, Hamilton took up arms and fought against the Confederacy. Two months later, on November 17, when the Union Army called for the formation of a mounted unit near his home, Hamilton immediately enlisted.

There was no time for training. Just one week later, on November 25, Hamilton and the Twelfth Kentucky Volunteer Cavalry saw action in Calhoun in his home state. Hamilton proved himself a resourceful and courageous officer and was promoted to the rank of major. The Twelfth went on to see action in numerous battles in late 1862 and through the winter and spring of 1863. That June, the Twelfth Cavalry was attached to the Army of Ohio. Their most famous assignment pitted them against the legendary John Hunt Morgan. He would prove to be a most worthy foe.[7]

Morgan, who was from nearby Lexington in Kentucky and was a veteran of the Mexican-American War, had formed a militia unit as tensions were building in the years prior to the outbreak of the war; he'd then enlisted in the Confederate States Army as soon as the fighting had began. After serving as a scout, he rose quickly to the rank of general. A staunch secessionist and proud Southerner with a charismatic and dashing personality, General Morgan became a household name across Dixie. The Kentuckian led his mounted raiders on a series of successful assaults in 1862 and 1863 against Union facilities and forces. Based out of Tennessee, he and roughly 1,700 raiders ultimately cut a one thousand–mile path of fear and destruction across Kentucky, Indiana, and Ohio. Using lightning strikes and guerilla tactics, they harassed Union forces, disrupted supply lines, and terrorized civilian populations. Morgan even ingeniously traveled with a crude but portable battery and wire in order to tap into telegraph lines to eavesdrop on Union communications.

The Confederate raider was ordered back to Kentucky for missions in June and July of 1863. He ignored the assignment and continued to press into Yankee territory. Time and again, Morgan was able to elude his pursuers while racing through Indiana and Ohio, ultimately capturing an astonishing six thousand prisoners. However, his streak was about to end, courtesy—in part—of Major Hamilton and the Twelfth Cavalry, who, with a force of three thousand, chased Morgan throughout the region. It was light cavalry against light cavalry in a daring cat-and-mouse mission across three states. Ultimately, the Northern cavalrymen caught and defeated the legendary raiders in late July near Lisbon, Ohio. Roughly nine hundred of Morgan's men were captured, killed, or wounded. The remainder of his force escaped into a forest. In one of the most impressive victories of the war, the Union cavalry lost only twenty-five men.

As for Morgan, the dashing raider was captured and imprisoned at the Ohio Penitentiary in Columbus. However, four months later he successfully tunneled out of the prison and escaped, a feat only adding to his fame. Morgan rejoined the military. Interestingly, in between assignments he was summoned to Richmond, where he paid a high-profile visit to Libby Prison. There Morgan once again met

Hamilton and a few of the most senior Union officers who had bested him but were now suffering in the hellish facility. Ironically, Morgan's former nemesis was, at that very moment, planning an elaborate escape, one similar to the breakout pulled off by the famous raider!

LIBBY'S LUMINARIES

Two other prisoners were as interesting and impressive as Rose and Hamilton but far more famous. One of the bastille's best-known inmates was Abel Delos Streight. Born in 1828 in Wheeler, New York, to a family that had emigrated from Holland, Streight grew up in Cincinnati and would later live in Indianapolis. The young man worked for a time as a lumber merchant but then went into the publishing industry and prospered as a publisher of books and maps. Described as a "burly Dutchman," Streight spoke his family's native tongue and spoke English with enough of a Dutch accent that, while imprisoned in Richmond later in the war, the Confederate press even mocked him, suggesting he had "too much Dutch in him to pronounce his own name."[8]

Like Rose, Streight believed in the cause for which the Union fought and had enlisted soon after the war started. Also like the leader of the remarkable escape from Libby, he was quickly promoted and achieved the rank of colonel. Streight served in the Fifty-First Indiana Infantry, but, though he was eager for combat, his regiment saw little action for the first two years of the war. Restless and frustrated by the inaction and lack of progress in ending the struggle, Streight proposed a bold plan to General James A. Garfield, commander with the Army of the Cumberland and future president of the United States.[9] Taking a page out of the playbook of Confederate raider General Morgan, Colonel Streight organized a mounted unit to conduct raids deep in Southern territory. The goal was to disrupt supply lines by hitting railways and armories, much as Morgan's Raiders had done in the North. Streight would attack the Confederates where they least expected it—in remote rural and mountainous areas of Georgia and Tennessee. General Garfield approved the mission.[10]

Perhaps the first harbinger of what was to come was that the Army of the Cumberland lacked a sufficient number of horses. The result was that only mules could be mustered for the operation. Therefore, unlike Morgan's Raiders, Streight's raids would not be lightning strikes using hit-and-run tactics. The mules would slow the assaults; but, on the other hand, they offered a durable way to get to otherwise-inaccessible and mountainous locations. Despite the obvious problems the mules would present, Streight was an imposing, fearless, and convincing leader, and the war was at a critical turning point in 1863. It was worth the risk.

Another celebrity in the bastille of the Confederacy was one of the highest-ranking prisoners of the entire war—Neal Dow. Born March 20, 1804, in Portland, Maine, to a Quaker family whose motto was "Industry, frugality, and temperance," Dow acquired all those traits. The family, whose ancestors boasted Old Testament names and a maternal grandfather with the puritanical epithet "Hate-Evil Hall," stressed Scriptural readings for their son. A lifelong social reformer, Dow was an early abolitionist. His family had even sheltered escaped slaves at their Portland estate, including one woman whose former master was the father of the prison commandant at Libby. Of the remarkable coincidence, Dow noted, "It came to pass that the son of the man who had given this poor Negro girl a home in a free land was for months a prisoner under the guard of a son of her old master."[11]

Well educated and with a passion for literature, Dow attended a prestigious academy and was a classmate of Henry Wadsworth Longfellow and other notable sons of Maine and later joined a literary society called the Portland Athenaeum. Just prior to his twenty-sixth birthday, Dow married Maria Cornelia Durant, on January 20, 1830, and joined his father's tanning business. Entrepreneurial and ambitious, Dow decided to become a banker. Although he made money, it was never his passion. Rather, his restlessness prompted travels around the country and to Canada and all the way to his family's native England. Dow's true passion was public service. Descended from a family of Massachusetts Federalists and reformers, he claimed to have developed his love of politics after attending political meetings regarding Maine's separation from Massachusetts[12] and status as a separate state.[13]

Dow would become the author of *The Maine Law*, an anti-alcohol treatise, which helped make him in the 1850s the nation's foremost advocate for prohibition and a household name. Dow traveled across the country delivering his teetotaling sermons to large audiences of supporters and critics alike. A cerebral, energetic, and physically large man, Dow was a commanding presence on stage. Numerous towns and a few states were inspired by his book and lectures and adopted anti-alcohol laws. He was even nominated for president of the United States by the National Prohibition Party and, when incarcerated in Libby Prison, received a steady stream of visitors who wanted to get a look at a national celebrity, even if most abhorred his message.[14]

When the Civil War first broke out, Dow was already fifty-seven. Moreover, as he admitted, "I had no military experience, not even such as might have been obtained in the state militia." However, despite his pacifist Quaker upbringing and self-professed "birthright to love peace," Dow did not hesitate to enlist "immediately after the attack on Sumter," saying simply, "duty called me to enter the military service of my country." He and his family had supported the Revolutionary War, after all, and they now sided with Lincoln's response to Southern aggression. Dow reasoned that his abolitionist beliefs superseded his pacifist upbringing. In fact, so deep were

Dow's abolitionist convictions that he welcomed the onset of war, hoping it would "break the South's political power" and "result in the destruction of slavery."[15]

Since he was a banker, however, Dow's "first service" to the Union was to secure funding for Maine's war effort. Second, because Dow had traveled throughout England as part of a speaking tour on temperance and was well connected with influential leaders there, he worked diplomatically to make sure Britain did not support the Confederacy by engaging in "sinister commerce" with them. Secession had weakened the United States, but Dow reminded the English of the moral nature of the Union's position; as such, England must be a "counterbalance" by not trading with the slaveholding South. Appealing to abolitionists across the Atlantic, he hoped to keep the European powers "at least avowedly neutral." His efforts were successful and supplemented those of Lincoln and Secretary of State William Seward.[16]

Despite his age and high profile, Dow was nonetheless eager for combat and was given a commission as colonel by the governor of Maine and invited by the War Department to raise a regiment. He did—the Thirteenth Maine Volunteers. During training, the Thirteenth consisted of men who, for the most part, shared his views against slavery and alcohol. Dow also established and financed his own battery to be sent to any unit needing artillery.[17]

Dow's unit was assigned to the Gulf Department. However, several generals such as Benjamin Butler and Nathaniel Banks were anything but enamored of their fellow general and his "radical" views. They worked to minimize Dow's role in the war. Nonetheless, Dow was not without high-placed friends in Washington. These same supporters secured for him a promotion to brigadier general, a rank he would hold while in the dreaded bastille of the Confederacy, making him one of the highest-ranking prisoners of the war.[18]

LIBBY'S LITERARIES

One of the many brave men trapped in Libby Prison who would end up inspiring his brothers in arms through his courage and poetry was Frederick Bartleson. Like the imprisoned soldiers already mentioned, Bartleson was a man possessing a number of impressive traits and was motivated by the most noble of reasons to enlist in the war effort. Born in Cincinnati on November 10, 1833, young Frederick soon moved with his family to Wheeling in what is today West Virginia. There, his father became the publisher of the town's newspaper, the *Times and Gazette*. A few years later, the family again relocated, this time to Brooklyn.

As was the case with the other prisoners of war mentioned, Bartleson was well educated, having graduated with honors from Allegheny College in Meadville, Pennsylvania. Passionate about the law, after graduating, the young man "immediately" secured a clerkship, studying under Judge Vredenburgh in New Jersey. Bartleson impressed the judge and most everyone he met with his legal acumen and "great lucidity and oratorical power." It was widely agreed that he had a bright future in the law. Seeking to launch his legal career on his own terms, Bartleson surprised his friends by moving to the frontier community of Joliet, Illinois, in 1855. Though only twenty-two and a newcomer to the region, the hardworking Bartleson quickly established a successful law practice. In 1856, the young lawyer was elected to a four-year term as district attorney. The following year, he married Kate Murray, described as the "amiable daughter of a worthy citizen" of Joliet.[19]

Bartleson's promising career was put on hold with the outbreak of the Civil War. Like so many of his eventual fellow prisoners at Libby, Bartleson had enlisted as soon as the war had started. In fact, when word had reached Joliet that President Lincoln had issued the initial call for volunteers in spring of 1861, the young attorney became the first man in Will County to sign, enlisting at the very next "public meeting" of the town on April 17. Townsfolk remembered, "After several patriotic speeches had been made" hoping to motivate the young men from the town in attendance, Bartleson stood and approached the table in front of the meeting room "upon which lay the enlistment roll." With the attention of everyone gathered fixed squarely on him, the young attorney "thundered" to the audience, "I will not urge you to do what I am unwilling to do myself; I propose to head that list!" This type of bold leadership would become a defining trait of the young officer known for leading from the front. It would also, however, end up being his undoing.[20]

A company of local men was organized that very spring, and Bartleson was made its captain. The Will County company was assigned to the Twentieth Illinois Volunteers, then later to the One Hundredth Illinois Regiment, where they saw combat in several engagements, such as Fredericktown and Fort Donelson. For his "heroic conduct" under fire, Bartleson was quickly promoted to major and then colonel. He would end up fighting alongside Colonel Rose and also end up in prison with him in Richmond. The stoicism of these two men would end up inspiring their fellow prisoners during the most difficult period in the notorious bastille.

Another future prisoner was born Louis Napoleon Beaudrye, on August 11, 1833, in Highgate, Vermont, near Saxe's Mills, one of seven boys and six girls. At some point after the family had emigrated from France to Quebec, they began spelling their name without the "e" on the end.[21] As a boy, his family moved back to Canada, where young Beaudry grew up speaking French as his first language. Though only marginally literate as a child, he was a voracious reader of the Bible; it formed the basis for much of his education. He would become fluent in English and later learn Spanish and German while incarcerated in Libby.

On March 19, 1854, Beaudry underwent a religious conversion as a born-again Christian and abandoned the family's Catholicism for Protestantism. Soon thereafter, he was ordained as a Methodist minister and began teaching Sunday school and working as an itinerant preacher, devoting his life to his faith. By the time the war had started, Beaudry had a wife and daughter. Although his wife begged him to avoid the war, he traveled to New York City to enlist. In September of 1861, the Fifth New York Cavalry was formed in Staten Island, comprised of just over one thousand men and fifty officers. Beaudry received a commission from the governor as their chaplain. Impressively, all six of his brothers also enlisted to fight in the war.[22]

The Fifth's training concluded on April 1, 1862, and the unit headed into the heart of Dixie, where they took part in several of the most important battles of the war, including Bull Run, Antietam, and the Wilderness Campaign. Arguably, the most important assignment for the Fifth New York was given in June of 1863. As word spread of Robert E. Lee's invasion of the North, the Fifth was placed under the command of the US Third Division led by General Hugh Judson Kilpatrick—who would later attempt to fight his way into Richmond to free Reverend Beaudry and other prisoners suffering in Libby.

However, in July of 1863, Kilpatrick's Third Division was part of the Union's Army of the Potomac, led by General George Meade, which was ordered to central Pennsylvania to stop Lee's advance. On the way to Gettysburg, the Fifth New York Cavalry was hit by a surprise attack from a Confederate cavalry unit. The Fifth prevailed, though there were "heavy casualties on both sides." After regrouping, they pursued their attackers all the way to Gettysburg. The New Yorkers and units from Maine and elsewhere withstood Confederate artillery barrages and multiple attacks near the pivotal engagement at Little Round Top, fighting "until dark" and helping to turn back General Lee's forces. There Beaudry's mounted unit participated in the three days of fighting that would help ensure the Confederacy's defeat.[23]

LIBBY'S LIBERATORS

Two more prisoners in the bastille of the Confederacy had also led intriguing lives, though they were not Americans. These two officers had fought both in order to keep the Union together and to oppose slavery. One of them, Emeric Szabad, was a Hungarian, born in 1822, one of a few hundred Hungarians who served in the Union Army during the Civil War. Szabad's family name was Frereych,[24] but he changed it while fighting in Hungary's War of Independence in 1848. Szabad also at times had listed his first name as "Imre," which is a shortened version of Emeric in Hungarian.

Szabad was a well-regarded professor of English who also worked as a journalist and writer, publishing articles on linguistics, English, politics, and war in popular literary magazines and textbooks, including one book titled *Theoretical and Practical English Grammar with Pronunciation Expressed in Hungarian Sounds.* He had lived in Hungary, England, and Italy and was fluent in all three tongues, plus French. Yet little is known about Emeric Szabad's private life—one biographer labeled him a "somewhat-enigmatic figure"—except that his literary and academic pursuits were interrupted beginning in 1848 with Hungary's revolution against Habsburg rule.[25]

Szabad was but one of many idealistic and revolutionary leaders in Hungary who were seeking independence from the powerful Austrian Empire. He became a military officer and a government official in the resistance during the Hungarian war, which spanned 1848 and 1849 and pitted several nationalities, cities, and subjugated peoples in central Europe against the ruling Habsburgs. Some Germans, Italians, Slovaks, and Slovenians fought alongside the revolutionaries; however, other groups in the region, including the Croats, Romanians, and Serbs, were enticed to join with the Habsburgs. It was but one of several conflicts that engulfed a changing Europe in the nineteenth century.

Szabad had long been frustrated by the world's general disinterest in the plight of Hungarians. His hopes for European intervention in the revolution and a diplomatic solution to the crisis were repeatedly dashed. "The betrayals committed by the House of Habsburgs in Hungary," he wrote in political tracts, "are made possible only by the indifferent diplomacy of Europe." The professor rallied his fellow revolutionaries, writing, "We are left to our own resources, and knowing this, we shall bravely meet the dynasty's cruel bloodhounds."[26]

Szabad and his outmanned revolutionaries had managed to win several battles to the extent that, with the conflict beginning to shift in favor of the Hungarians, the Habsburgs were forced to abandon Vienna. Desperate, the teenaged emperor Franz Joseph I had requested assistance from the Russians. Czar Nicholas I had responded in June of 1849, marching into Hungary with two massive armies numbering some two hundred thousand soldiers with one thousand artillery pieces. Though the Hungarian revolutionaries "fought bravely against hopeless odds," the Russian forces and their brutal scorched-earth policy in Hungary crushed the uprising.[27]

After the Hungarian Revolution, laws allowing for the rights of minority groups and others were overturned by the Habsburgs, and, in a ruthless effort to "restore order," the military began executing leaders of the uprising in 1850 and 1851. Many military commanders who had surrendered to the Russians in August of 1849 were put to death. Lajos Kossuth, famed leader of the Hungarian Revolution, facing certain arrest and death, had been forced to flee to Turkey that same month. He would later travel to America, where he was received with much fanfare and heralded as "the Washington of Hungary." During his nationwide tour, Kossuth was given an audience with President Millard Fillmore on New Year's Eve at the White House, a parade in New York City, and an invitation from Senator Daniel Webster to address a joint session of Congress—only the second foreigner to do so after the Marquis de Lafayette, who had helped the Americans achieve independence from Britain.[28]

Because Szabad both held offices in the revolutionary government and had fought against the emperor, his life was also in danger under Austrian military rule, and he too was forced to flee his native country.[29] Szabad went to Italy, which at the time was comprised of several small city-states as well as the Kingdom of the Two Sicilies, the Grand Duchy of Tuscany, the Papal States, and other political states, some of which had fought with Kossuth's forces. So Szabad and others repaid the favor by supporting Venice in its own struggle against the Habsburgs. Such actions earned Szabad the reputation of a soldier of fortune, yet he always seemed motivated by ideals rather than money or the fight.

Seeing that Venice was not likely to prevail, Szabad fled Italy, following Kossuth to England in the 1850s. There he delivered public lectures and published several books—including one on Hungary's history and politics, another on European history and politics, and one about Napoleon. He also pushed for the election of a shadow government in exile to represent Hungarian émigrés in London; and in this he was unsuccessful and soon began to feel that his revolutionary beliefs were no longer welcome in England. Accordingly, he traveled to Sicily in 1859 to join Giuseppe Garibaldi in his struggle for Italian independence from the monarchy, serving as a captain alongside one of the fathers of Italian unification.[30]

Szabad decided to leave Sicily and join the fight against the Confederacy and the institution of slavery. Szabad and the Hungarian revolutionaries enlisted with the Union and were known as the "forty-eighters" during the war, in honor of the year of their own revolution back home.[31]

Another immigrant who joined the Union was Federico Fernández Cavada. Born in Cienfuegos, Cuba, on July 8, 1830, to an American mother and Cuban father, he spent his childhood in Cuba. However, when his father died in 1838, his mother, Emily Howard Gaiter Cavada, moved her children back to her native Philadelphia. There she remarried—to a man named Samuel Dutton—and the family lived at 222 Spruce Street, just a few blocks from Independence Hall, in historic downtown Philadelphia. Federico was well educated, becoming a civil engineer and topographer, even traveling to Panama to work on an early effort to establish a canal there.

When the Civil War started, Fernández Cavada and his brother joined the Twenty-Third Pennsylvania Infantry, which was organized in Philadelphia in mid-August of 1861. The men and boys of Philadelphia embraced the call to arms, filling the city's enlistment quotas in just three days. The Twenty-Third adopted the fancy red and blue uniforms of the French Zouaves,[32] which were popular at the time, and earned the nickname "Birney's Zouaves," a nod to their commander Colonel

David B. Birney and their uniforms. The regiment was assigned to the Army of the Potomac and sent to Camp Graham on the outskirts of Washington, D.C., in the fall of 1861. Their mission: defend the capital city from a possible Confederate assault. However, the men of the Twenty-Third suffered the fate of many soldiers during the Civil War: while in camp, a cholera outbreak swept through the ranks, killing an officer and fifty enlisted men. They were forced to relocate to a camp near Bladensburg in Maryland.[33]

In the spring of 1862, the Twenty-Third Pennsylvania boarded a steamship and were sent to join the Peninsula Campaign in Virginia where they fought at Warwick River on April 4, the siege of Yorktown in April and May, and the Battle of Williamsburg on May 5. The Twenty-Third suffered high casualty counts at the Battle of Fair Oaks in late May and June. Despite losing their colonel and other officers, the Pennsylvanians continued to fight that fall through Maryland and Virginia, culminating in the disastrous defeat at Fredericksburg in December when Union forces suffered over thirteen thousand casualties. After months of nonstop combat, Fernández Cavada was promoted to the rank of lieutenant-colonel on August 29, 1862. He had a tough assignment: Though battle-hardened, his regiment was suffering from exhaustion, dwindling numbers, and declining morale.

The situation did not improve and the regiment was not given leave. In January of 1863, the Pennsylvanians were dispatched on a mission to pursue General Robert E. Lee's Army of Northern Virginia. The weather deteriorated into days of torrential rain, earning the campaign the moniker "the mud march" for obvious reasons. Making matters worse, an inclement winter and spring were followed by an unusually hot summer. Several members of the Twenty-Third were lost to disease, sunstroke, dehydration, and other maladies when, already exhausted, the regiment was forced to march eighteen miles in a single, scorchingly hot and humid day—June 16. Soon after, they learned the reason: Lee had invaded the North.

The Twenty-Third continued its race to intercept Lee. On July 1, Fernández Cavada received the order that his regiment was to again march on "double-time" and "without halt or rest."[34] Miraculously, the Pennsylvanians covered roughly thirty miles that day. They caught the massive Confederate Army at a sleeping farm community called Gettysburg.

All the Union soldiers discussed above would soon become prisoners and face arguably their most difficult assignment in Libby Prison.

Part II

PRISON

5

"The Castle of Despair"

Libby acquired a reputation as one of the Confederacy's most notorious prisons.

—Emeric Szabad, Libby Prison, 1863[1]

With the war going poorly for the Union in the early days of fighting, trains, wagons, and convoys of Yankee prisoners began arriving in Richmond each week, then every few days, then daily. The city was unprepared for the numbers. At the beginning of the war, the Confederacy had still been using Luther Libby's services for the war effort, purchasing supplies such as rope, resin, tar, and other building materials from him. That ended on October 5, 1861.[2] The large three-building warehouse complex was appropriated to serve another purpose—possibly a prison and hospital, although for a time it continued to be used as a chandlery. As such, it is doubtful the decision was meant to be permanent; rather, on Provost Marshal Winder's orders, during those first few months of the war prisoners were haphazardly put in any available space.

Libby was converted so quickly to accommodate prisoners that they even left the sign hanging over the facility reading, "L. LIBBY & SON, SHIP CHANDLERS." Although the facility came to be known as the bastille of the Confederacy, and Confederate authorities officially referred to it unimaginatively as the Confederate States Military Prison, it was known among prisoners by the name on the sign. Because of the horrific conditions inside the prison, Frederick Bartleson and many of the other prisoners of war also referred to Libby as "The Castle of Despair."[3]

Records are inconclusive, but most likely only a few prisoners were sent to Libby after the First Battle of Bull Run on July 21 and throughout the summer and fall of

1861. The first prisoner recorded as housed in the Libby warehouse was Philander A. Streator of Holyoke, Massachusetts. There is a clue as to when Libby stopped functioning as a warehouse and permanently became a prison: War reports indicate that the first large contingent of prisoners arrived at Libby on March 26, 1862. Payment for "renting" the warehouses was listed as $1,200 per year, and it appears the first installment was made a few months later, on June 6.[4] Libby soon become the primary processing and incarceration center for the Confederacy.[5]

Confederate authorities made another fateful decision: The prison would be designated solely for officers and high-value political prisoners. At first, the Libby warehouses held both officers and enlisted men, along with Southern political prisoners and Union loyalists. Nevertheless, some time in 1862, both sides of the war adopted the age-old practice of separating officers from enlisted men in order to improve security and because of the social conventions of the time. Yankee officers were sent to Libby, while enlisted men would be sent to nearby Belle Isle on the James River and to other factories and warehouses throughout the city.[6]

In many ways, the Libby warehouse complex was a poor choice for a prison. After all, it had been built to be a tobacco warehouse. It was therefore hard to secure. There was no perimeter fencing, each of the three warehouses had its own entrance, and the property was located in the commercial heart of the city on Cary and Twentieth Streets and not far from the population center. There were also inadequate facilities for medical care, sleeping, meals, and other basic human necessities. On the other hand, the same advantages that made the warehouses profitable were attractive to the Confederate authorities, desperate to accommodate the swelling prisoner population. Most obviously, the warehouses had large open rooms that could accommodate hundreds of prisoners at a time. The complex was located near a railway and backed up against a narrow alley known as Dock Street, running along the Kanawha Canal, which connected the facility to the James River and ran parallel to it. It was thus easy to transport prisoners to and from the Confederacy's central receiving point. Because the prison fronted Cary Street, had a large, open lot directly to the east, and bordered a canal and river in the rear to the south, the warehouses were, in some ways, easy to guard. Any would-be escapee could be spotted in the open ground and street. Furthermore, although there were far too few prison guards assigned to the new facilities in Richmond, Libby's rectangular design, with high walls and open spaces surrounding them, put every window and door of the bastille "in full view" of the guards stationed outside. Later, perimeter fencing was erected, the doors dead-bolted and windows barred, and the bottom of the walls on the outside of the warehouses were painted white so that any prisoner attempting to escape would more easily be silhouetted against the buildings.[7]

Through the spring and summer of 1862, prisoners were taken to Libby in large numbers, pushing the population of Yankee inmates to dangerous levels in the low-ceilinged but cavernous rooms on the second and third floors of the warehouses. The decision was also made that same year to designate Libby as the central receiving and processing point for all prisoners of war. The majority of Union soldiers captured during the war were brought to Richmond, where they were identified and assigned to prisons. It is estimated that roughly 125,000 Union soldiers came through Libby to be processed, and as many as forty-five thousand men in total were kept at the so-called Castle of Despair "for a prolonged time."[8]

Determining the exact number of prisoners is difficult, as the population ebbed and flowed, depending on the outcome of large-scale battles, outbreaks of diseases, and the status of the unpredictable prisoner exchanges. Accounts in Richmond's newspapers and spotty records kept by the Confederacy, however, do allow for a snapshot of the situation.[9] For example, July of 1862 was a beehive of activity in Richmond, as prisoners arrived at Libby nearly every day of the month for processing. On the first, 271 prisoners arrived, followed by one thousand on the second, and four thousand the next day. The numbers then shrunk to a few hundred per day for the remainder of the first and second weeks of July, with 250 on the fifth, 200 on the eighth, and 164 on the fourteenth. The unpredictable nature of the fighting and transportation to Richmond were such that records stated only "a few" arrived on the sixteenth and just fourteen two days later.[10] However, fully five thousand were processed at Libby on July 19. And so on . . .

By the end of 1862, records suggest that roughly seven hundred prisoners were being housed at Libby. This amounts to over one hundred men in each of the rooms on the top two floors of the prison. The prison would remain seriously overcrowded until 1865, and the numbers reported are likely significantly lower than the actual number of prisoners in the facility. For example, in January of 1863, evidence exists that between seven hundred and one thousand prisoners were suffering in Libby. Yet on January 10 the *Richmond Dispatch* reported that the population on January 9 had consisted of just 25 Union officers, 69 abolitionists, 210 civilians, 117 "Yankee deserters," and thirty-three "negroes." It must be remembered that Richmond's newspapers also suggested that the conditions inside the prison were acceptable. Such inaccuracy and blatant pro-Confederate propaganda would become hallmarks of the Southern press coverage of the prisons and war.[11]

DESCRIPTIONS

In truth, Libby was less a castle or bastille, as it was often described, than simply a large complex of warehouses. Rather than storing tobacco or shipping goods, Libby was now warehousing humans. One of the prisoners, Colonel Federico Fernández Cavada, offered a colorful and insightful description of the area:

I look out the window on the James River. Immediately below is the canal; beyond it flows the James river, with a rapid, murmuring current, reflecting here and there the purple flush of the morning clouds; there is a cluster of tall factories on the opposite bank . . . and on the other are broad fields, and the rolling hills which fringe a distant curve of the river. Looking up-stream, there is a lovely little island, three long white bridges which span the stream, half concealed by the thick foliage, and beyond these, a full mile off, is Belle Isle, with some white tents . . . a pretty correct idea may be formed of what we are destined to behold every day during our sojourn here.[12]

The three large, rectangular warehouses of the converted prison were referred to as the East, Central—or sometimes Middle—and West buildings, just as had been the case when Luther Libby had operated his chandlery there before the war. However, the prisoners gave each of the rooms inside nicknames based on the battle in which the prisoners in the room had been captured or the general under whom the room's prisoners had served. As such, the "Chickamauga Room"—so named for the major battle fought in September of 1863 along the Tennessee-Georgia border and the many prisoners captured there—was on the southwest side of the second floor. Likewise, the soldiers serving under the General Robert H. Milroy who had been captured in the defense of Winchester in June of 1863 were placed together in a room on the second floor of the West building that became known as "Milroy's Room." Another room became known as "Streight's Room," where the famous raider from Indiana, Colonel Abel Streight, was incarcerated.[13]

Initially, there had been no doors on the upper floors, but when the warehouses were converted into a prison, Confederate authorities ordered that doors be cut into them. Interior doorways now connected the buildings on the second and third floors where the prisoners bunked. Fernández Cavada, the Cuban-born officer, described the living conditions: "The building is of brick, with a front of near one hundred and forty feet, and one hundred feet deep. It is divided into nine rooms; the ceilings are low, and ventilation imperfect; the windows are barred."[14] Six of the large, open rooms on the top two floors of the three warehouses were used to house prisoners. Each of the rooms was, for the most part, unfurnished—containing only a few benches and lacking bunks or beds and other accommodations. A few primitive troughs were built into closets to function as "water closets" where the prisoners relieved themselves. The troughs routinely overflowed, spilling onto the floors. The cramped and crowded conditions were made worse by a low eight-foot ceiling.[15]

The windows in these rooms provided some natural light. However, the open windows welcomed the heat and humidly during summer, along with mosquitoes, flies, and other pests that hovered around the canal. In the winters, cold blasts of air and snow came through the windows and tormented the prisoners. When a few prisoners tried to escape, iron bars were put in the open windows. "Heavy" walls divided the rooms, and guards were stationed at the steep staircases, which lacked stairwells or handrails. Guards were also positioned at the base of the stairs in order to prohibit prisoners from descending to the first floor, except for the kitchen, and then only during mess hour. Importantly, as Colonel Rose would come to discover, the guards were so inept that they were often not at their posts along the stairs. When not reporting for meals or roll calls, the prisoners were, however, permitted to "mingle" with one another upstairs in the rooms. Eventually, however, even that privilege would be denied.[16]

The kitchen was located on the first floor of the middle building, and it contained either two or three—depending on the year of the war—large stoves for cooking. Behind each stove was a fireplace, but they were never used, a convenience later leveraged by Colonel Rose in his escape plan. The kitchen area also contained "long pine tables with permanent seats attached, such as may be commonly seen at picnic grounds." Lest one get the idea of a "normal" kitchen and dining area, the dingy and crowded room sat below an old trough and faucets that regularly leaked, often fouling the cooking area below.[17]

From the kitchen, a large door led out to Cary Street; another sizable door opened to the street from the East building, but they were "always heavily bolted and guarded" from the outside. Other than the kitchen, prisoners were confined to the second- and third-floor barracks of the prison. Later, the inmate population necessitated additional space for cooking, so old cauldrons were placed in the cellar in the East building; but because of the security risks, this temporary cooking room was soon closed. Ironically, the closure allowed Rose, Hamilton, and their friends to later use the area to tunnel out of the prison.[18]

There were other rooms. The first floor of the West building included the offices of the prison staff and sleeping quarters for the guards. By October 1863, the bastille held so many prisoners and the death toll had climbed so alarmingly that the first floor of the East building had to be converted into a hospital. But it was a hospital in name only. Libby lacked an adequate amount of medicines and sufficient number of physicians, especially given the number of sick and dying prisoners. The commandant often simply refused to allow sick and dying prisoners to go to the hospital. Still, the hospital was lined with cots "which were never unoccupied." A small "apartment" sat adjacent to the hospital room and was used as an office by the physicians who periodically worked out of the prison.[19]

There was one other room in Libby. A basement below the warehouses held four small cells, reminiscent of what would be found in a medieval dungeon, where "problem" prisoners and slaves were confined or punished. The dank cellar also contained an old carpenter's shop that was no longer in use, a storage area, and the spare cooking area—which was soon closed. The prisoners referred to this foul area as Rat Hell for obvious reasons. It was an ideal environment for the population of rats that infested the entire complex. Accordingly, the guards avoided the cellar.

Yet it was from this wretched catacomb that the largest prison break of the entire Civil War would commence.[20]

As for the building itself, the large, featureless brick warehouses came to reflect the emptiness and despair of those misfortunate enough to be imprisoned there. Captain Szabad described the prison blandly as "an isolated, three-story building, facing the James River, or rather the canal skirting its left bank." It seemed featureless to the Hungarian officer and lacking in any discerning or unique design. It was, he recorded, "windowed all over, and comprised of nine compartments," of which "the third and second stories were entirely occupied by the inmates; while a part of the ground floor served as the kitchen."[21] Yet it would be much more than an old, three-story building. It was the horrors inside Libby that defined it. Willard Glazier, who had been captured when his horse had been shot out from under him in battle, echoed that point, noting that the wardens and guards who ran the prison were "fiends—I cannot countenance a milder term" and that Libby was no more than "a den of torture for such as may be so unfortunate as to fall into their hands."[22]

6

Captured

The nights like black blots dying out of a dream of horror, seemingly eternal in its duration.

—Andrew G. Hamilton, on Libby Prison, 1893[1]

The remarkable Union officers discussed earlier in the book suffered the humiliating ordeal shared by so many thousands of soldiers during the Civil War; they were taken prisoner.

LIBBY'S LEADERS

One of the officers serving under General Rosecrans in the Western Theater of the American Civil War in Tennessee was Colonel Thomas Rose, the Pennsylvania school principal who had eagerly enlisted at the beginning of the conflict. After stepping up to replace his unit's fallen colonel, Rose had led the Seventy-Seventh Pennsylvania Volunteers during the long and bloody campaign in 1862 and 1863 deep into Confederate territory and across Tennessee. Later, during the bloody Battle of Chickamauga, on September 20, 1864, Rose was captured. The Confederate victory, for a brief moment, ended the Northern offensive into southeastern Tennessee and northwestern Georgia. Because Rose and the Seventy-Seventh were positioned out front, trying to hold their line while the main army withdrew, they suffered many casualties. Every field officer and numerous junior officers, along with scores of their soldiers, were taken prisoner. The proud colonel recalled with disgust that his men were summarily robbed, beaten, and spat upon by their Southern captors.[2]

After the brutal three-day battle, Union prisoners were detained for a few days and then herded into open train cars. The train traveled northward through rolling hills and past farms to Columbia, South Carolina, where they momentarily stopped. Rose was appalled to see locals gathering to mock the prisoners. One elderly woman even goaded the guards to shoot the captured Yankees. Rose and his men had heard stories about South Carolina and so were rightly worried. However, they were surprised and relieved when some Confederate soldiers threw the prisoners old bread. This was the first morsel of food they'd had to eat since their capture a few days earlier. The guards provided little information to the prisoners, except for telling them that they would soon be exchanged. Rose doubted the promise, understanding that saying so was a good way to keep the men from trying to revolt or escape. The Union, after all, was telling its prisoners the same lie.[3]

After departing from South Carolina, they traveled through North Carolina, where a torrential rainstorm soaked the prisoners sitting exposed on the flatbed cars. Rose saw an opportunity to escape. When the train slowed down by the town of Weldon, along the border with southern Virginia, Rose leaped from the train. He'd misjudged the speed, however, and landed heavily, breaking his left foot. Hobbling on one leg, the burly colonel managed to make it into the surrounding pine forests and impassable bogs. He was hoping the storm would offer sufficient cover, but a guard spotted him and sounded the alarm. A Confederate cavalry unit was ordered into the forest. Limited by his injured foot, Rose was unable to get very far. However, the woods provided some cover, and Rose managed to elude his pursuers. That night he hid; he was hungry, thirsty, exhausted, and in pain. The next morning, with his foot swelling, Rose was unable to run and found himself surrounded by the cavalry. He was beaten savagely and placed back aboard the prison train.

On October 3, the train finally arrived at the Richmond depot, and the prisoners were unloaded and paraded through the streets of the capital. The city that greeted the men in blue was crowded and chaotic, and the signs of war were everywhere: Pickets, artillery batteries, and other defenses ringed the important city, while bands of soldiers marched through the streets and wounded veterans still in ragged gray uniforms begged for food on most street corners. So did the locals. The entire population looked like it was suffering from severe shortages of food, medicine, and other necessities. They were not the only ones. The prisoners were hungry and thirsty, and many were wounded, yet they received little in the way of rations and medical attention during the trip.[4]

Throngs of curious onlookers lined both sides of the streets as the prisoners were marched toward the facility that would serve as their new home and, for too many, the site of their final days. Given that Richmond was serving as the Confederacy's central receiving point for most prisoners during the war, its residents had seen more than their fair share of Union soldiers. Still, Rose and his fellow prisoners were a curiosity: though until recently fellow Americans, they were now the enemy that the Southern press, politicians, and propaganda had thoroughly demonized. One of Richmond's newspapers went so far as to proclaim death to be too good for the Yankee prisoners: "First, it gives them no time to repent of their folly and wickedness, and, second, no matter how we treat them, they will invade our territory of fire and brimstone which will make them want to come back here."[5]

While the prisoners were en route to their new holdings, locals hissed, spat on them, and threw rotten food at the straggling blue line. Rascally young boys ran alongside the men, daring each other to touch a "Yankee." Some hurled insults at the armies that had invaded their homeland, while others took pleasure in warning the men of the fate that awaited them at the notorious bastille of the Confederacy. Someone screamed, "Oh, is these the kind of brutes that has come down here to kill our noble sons?" A few residents looked on quietly or with pride at the armies their Rebel forces had bested. Beggars offered to trade for Union jackets and caps or to swap worthless Confederate currency, known as "bluebacks," for Yankee "greenbacks." Occasionally, a generous hand offered a cup of water. It was a spectacle—a parade of the damned.[6]

As the column of prisoners approached the heart of the city and its famed Tobacco Row along the James River, they saw in front of them three large brick warehouses. Each one was three to four stories in height and hugged the edge of a large canal by the river. The imposing rectangular structures had windows with thick bars standing in place of glass. Behind the bars, ghostly, emaciated figures saluted the prisoners with blank, deathly stares that offered the new arrivals a foreboding glimpse of their own futures. A midsized, white sign with black block letters atop the building welcomed them. It read "L. LIBBY & SON, SHIP CHANDLERS." It was Libby Prison, the infamous bastille of the Confederacy. Most of the prisoners that day were surely overcome with anxiety and fear. They had heard horrific stories about Confederate prisons, and in particular Libby.

Colonel Rose's partner in planning the escape from the dreaded bastille would be Major Andrew Hamilton of the Twelfth Kentucky Volunteer Cavalry. After the successful hunt to capture the legendary Confederate raider John Morgan, the Twelfth Kentucky had been assigned to the larger Tennessee campaign. Their mission was to capture key Confederate positions, depots, and towns in the region that happened to be defended by General James Longstreet. From September through December of 1863, Hamilton and the Twelfth Kentucky assaulted Confederate positions, including at Knoxville. Although Longstreet surprised his foes by going on the offensive, winning a few small engagements, the region would soon fall to the Union.

It was during this larger campaign that Hamilton and four other cavalrymen were captured while skirmishing near Jonesborough, Tennessee. They were first taken to Lynchburg, Virginia, and then on to Richmond. His experience in the Confederate capital was similar to Rose's. However, because Libby was so overcrowded, Hamilton and his fellow cavalrymen were placed in Castle Thunder for the night of September 29. The next morning, Hamilton was taken to the bastille to be processed and was assigned to the "Lower Chickamauga Room" on the second floor. One week later, Rose would arrive and be assigned to the same room.

Hamilton and his fellow cavalrymen had arrived at the prison hungry, sick, and very weak, and they described the overbearing feeling of seeing the overcrowded, spartan prison. They were sent to the hospital that, the major recalled, was nothing more than a single room packed with the dying. Those lying about the crude cots were in delusional states, murmuring the names of their mothers or "sweethearts." Some had stopped begging for food and water. Certain death awaited them. "The angel of death," Hamilton noted poetically, "kissed the starved lips of hundreds of men." The conditions in the prison were so hellish that "death was sought" by some of the prisoners.[7]

Hamilton soon realized that escape was "the one thought that was preying upon the minds" of many of the prisoners. The problem was that there appeared to be no possible way to break out of the prison. "The doors and windows were closely guarded," observed Hamilton, such that "to make an exit from either of these sources meant instant death." However, the dim prospects for escape did not deter everyone. "Among us were many strong-minded men—with a courage of steel." Hamilton was about to "form an acquaintance" with one of them—a colonel from Pennsylvania—and their friendship would change the lives of the prisoners in Libby.[8]

LIBBY'S LUMINARIES

Colonel Abel Streight's request to conduct raids deep in enemy territory had been approved, and approximately 1,700 members of the Fifty-First Indiana Infantry were reassigned to serve in his makeshift cavalry unit. Their mission was to disrupt supply routes and neutralize arms depots throughout Tennessee, Alabama, and Mississippi. They would also attempt to cut off the important Western and Atlantic Railroad, which the South needed to resupply their armies in the region. Unfortunately, the raiding unit had been cobbled together without adequate strategic considerations, and the "raiders" were assigned mules. They also lacked accurate maps, reliable information on their targets, and men with experience in the saddle. The mission seemed doomed from the start, but they were led by a charismatic and capable leader.

Among the mounted raiders was Streight's wife, Lovina McCarthy Streight, and the couple's five-year-old son. Feckless though it may have seemed to bring along one's family to war, Colonel Streight and the Fifty-First immediately found Mrs. Streight an invaluable addition. She not only served as the unit's nurse and cook but also inspired the men. It is, after all, hard to overstate the importance that a matronly, caring presence might have had on an army of young men away from home for the first time and missing their families. The soldiers even called her "The Mother of the Fifty-First." Mrs. Streight distinguished herself in other ways: She was captured three times during the war and was the epitome of courage each time, twice being freed in prisoner exchanges and once escaping by using the pistol she'd hidden under her skirt![9]

The shortcomings and lack of horses did not stop Streight. The Fifty-First Indiana deployed to Nashville, then cut a path across Tennessee, making it to Tuscumbia, Alabama, by April of 1863. Streight's raiders continued their assault and drove through Alabama and Mississippi, skirmishing with the notorious Confederate general Nathan Bedford Forrest at Sand Mountain. By the end of the month, Streight managed to best Forrest at the Battle of Day's Gap, inflicting sixty-five casualties upon the opposition, led by the man who would become one of the founders of the Ku Klux Klan after the war. However, the mules proved to be Streight's undoing. His raiders moved too slowly and, on May 3, were caught by Forrest's cavalry near Cedar Bluff, Alabama. The crafty Confederate commander surrounded Abel's exhausted raiders. Streight was a high-value prize for the Confederacy. There was no question as to which prison he would be taken.

Libby's other celebrity resident was General Neal Dow of Maine, known throughout the nation as the "Father of Prohibition." The noted abolitionist had been given orders by General William T. Sherman to take the members of the Thirteenth Maine to Louisiana in January of 1863. The important Southern city of New Orleans at the mouth of the Mississippi River had fallen to the Union, bringing the North a step closer to controlling the entirety of the vital river. That May, Dow assumed control of Baton Rouge and New Orleans. However, the Confederates had yet to fully capitulate. Dow was informed that Rebel forces were outside of Baton Rouge at Port Hudson. He reconnoitered the area and confirmed the worst: a Confederate force of 7,500 had established defensive positions at the port.

The Battle of Port Hudson would be fought from late May to early July, marking the longest siege in American history. Meanwhile, just up the river at Vicksburg, General Grant was concurrently laying siege to the important defensive position overlooking the Mississippi. If the Union could wrest Port Hudson and Vicksburg from the Rebels, the South would be denied the ability to move troops, supplies, or goods on the river. It would not be easy. Both sites sat atop bluffs and were well defended; the Confederates would put up a desperate and stingy but ultimately hopeless defense.

At Port Hudson, Southern commanders had installed artillery batteries and sharpshooters throughout the area, and an open field sat in front of the defensive works. Any attacker would be exposed while crossing five hundred yards of marshy terrain.

Consequently, Dow wisely counseled against a direct frontal assault. However, the command came down from his superiors that "Port Hudson must fall to-morrow." Dow protested the decision but was given his orders. About two hours before sunrise on May 22, Dow and his fellow commander, General Nathaniel Banks, reluctantly gave the order to attack.[10]

The forty-eight-day siege was supported by troops from Connecticut, Michigan, New Hampshire, and New York, constituting a force of roughly thirty-five thousand. It was an enormous undertaking. The commanders had organized teams of mules that pulled wagons of supplies, while cannons were sailed up the Mississippi and gunboats were moved into position along the river. Freed Blacks constituting units from the Louisiana Native Guards were embedded with the army; they carried long poles and ladders needed to cross trenches and scale walls. It did not go well. The terrain was proving to be insurmountable.

After two stalled attacks, a third was organized. Dow's men managed to cross the open fields, though they suffered many casualties from sharpshooters. Dow and a senior officer had ridden forward to examine the progress and inspire the men. They came under fire. Dow remembered that the officer "was soon badly wounded, his leg being shattered below the knee." Moments later, Dow "was struck by a spent ball in the arm, which was rendered useless by the blow and almost immediately swelled to nearly twice its normal size, so that I could no longer control my horse." The famous abolitionist dismounted and led the assault on foot. As he did, he was hit again and knocked to the ground. The musket ball struck Dow in the left thigh above the knee.[11]

Dow was taken to a Union hospital, where the surgeon informed him that he was lucky: The ball had passed clean through the leg and narrowly missed hitting an artery. While recovering, Dow suffered the fate of many soldiers in Louisiana: He contracted malaria. The general was "on death's door." Exhausted, he was given a brief leave of absence. Eager to recuperate and rejoin the army, Dow decided to remain in the South rather than travel back to Maine and was convalescing in the company of medics at the home of a woman named Cage. However, it appears that Mrs. Cage's neighbor, a Mrs. Brown, was loyal to the Confederacy and sent word that a senior Union general was bedridden at the home. Days later, a Confederate officer and four soldiers stormed the home, only to discover that Dow had only moments before departed on horseback for a nearby home. After arresting two Union orderlies, the Confederates raced down the road and caught Dow, who was about to enter the other home.[12]

"Surrender, or I'll kill you!" screamed the Confederate officer. The man held a gun pointed at Dow. The general from Maine, outmatched and in no condition to fight or flee, said calmly, "I'll surrender, sir—I'll go with you." It was June 30, 1863, and the South had captured one of the highest-ranking Union officers of the entire war.[13]

The Southern press had a field day with the news, boasting of the arrest and offering a detailed account of the coup.

The Confederates took Dow to Camp Logan in Louisiana, and then took him by horseback to a safer prison in Jackson, Mississippi. Two armed guards accompanied him at all times. In Jackson, he was detained at Marble-Yard Prison in "a dirty room, without furniture of any kind, with a single window without glass, the light and air being partially obstructed by boards nailed over it." Worse, "this window overlooked a pig-pen." That is how Dow spent July 4, 1863—alone in the small room with the revolting smell of pigs. He was given only a piece of "wretched hard bread," which the guards called "ship-stuff." It was made of "middlings," which Dow later discovered was "mill feed" used for livestock.[14]

Two days later, the general was informed he was being taken to Richmond. For much of the long trip, he rode in the back of an old wagon, all the while accompanied by armed guards. This afforded Dow the opportunity to observe the South and the effects of the war. The countryside was barren, "drained of its materials and able-bodied men." Everywhere they traveled, "the signs of ruin brought by war" were evident, including among the people who were "lean and poor."[15]

Finally, the general was transferred to a train that took him to Montgomery, Alabama. Southerners were curious about the senior Union commander. "All through that journey I continued to be an object of curiosity to the people whom I met," he noted. Everywhere he went, "groups" gathered to see "the abolitionist and temperance Yankee general." The courteous Dow worried about the impression he made; he was, after all, still recovering from his illness and wounds, had not had a chance to bathe, and was wearing only pants and a "travel-stained linen duster." As was common during the war, the guards had stolen his uniform and possessions. He also worried about violence. He knew of the stories of captured Union soldiers being attacked by mobs. Some Southerners seemed "bloodthirsty to the extreme, and determined to hang me at the nearest lamppost," and several newspapers advocated as much. He counted his blessings that he was not attacked on the long trip.[16]

Dow was also interested in Southern mindset about the war and slavery. Throughout the ride to Richmond, Dow was informed by the guards and citizens he met that "there were no Union men anywhere." Everyone in the South, it seemed, supported the Confederacy. At least that is what he was told. Dow doubted the claims. To be sure, he met a man who discreetly whispered in his ear that the war was "all a mistake." He then admitted to being pro-Union: "I am one, and there are many others whom I know." However, they were all afraid to talk or reveal their support for the United States for fear of reprisals from their neighbors or arrest by the Confederate government. Dow found such realities alarming. Though starving, the Southerners, he concluded, were proud, and there was a "determination to fight to the bitter end," even among women.[17]

LIBBY'S LITERARIES

Colonel Frederick Bartleson had set out from Brooklyn to the frontier of Illinois to start his own law practice and would end up inspiring the young men of his adopted town of Joliet to enlist in the war. Like Colonel Rose, Bartleson had risen rapidly to the rank of colonel, distinguishing himself along the way with his acts of bravery and ability to lead men. Also like Rose, he was part of the Union offensive in Tennessee in 1862 and 1863. A precursor of that larger campaign included the Battle of Shiloh in early April of 1862. Bartleson and the One Hundredth Illinois were there, fighting at Pittsburg Landing. It would be another key Union victory in the area, but one of the bloodiest battles of the war.[18]

Leading from the front, as was his trademark, Bartleson would be one of those casualties. He was shot in the left arm, and the wound was so serious that the arm had to be amputated. The colonel was encouraged to resign from the war and return home to recover. Instead, he opted to remain in uniform, saying that his "patriotic ardor burned too brightly." Moreover, the colonel not only longed for a Union victory but also felt that "This Government must be re-established upon the basis of political unity, under the form of a republic." He wanted to be a part of the restoration of the United States.[19]

A short time later, Bartleson was back in the fight, leading the One Hundredth Illinois Volunteer Infantry. Once again, he fought alongside Rose and the Seventy-Seventh Pennsylvania in the Tennessee Campaign, including at the Battle of Stones River on New Year's Eve of 1862 and New Year's Day of 1863. That September, Bartleson was leading the One Hundredth at Chickamauga. However, during a charge against the Confederate line, he was "far in advance" of his men and ended up being surrounded and captured. Ironically, at the earlier Battle of Stones River, Bartleson had captured the very officer who had now captured him![20]

Bartleson and fifty of his men were transported to Augusta, Georgia. Likely on instructions of the Confederate officer who had captured Bartleson, the men of the One Hundredth were treated with "civilities," just as their colonel had earlier treated his captor with respect. With no prison available, the captives spent the night in a Presbyterian churchyard. They were then taken to Atlanta, then Nashville, and then by train to Knoxville. Along the way, local residents complained about seeing Union prisoners, but the lieutenant in charge insisted on decent treatment, with only a few notable exceptions. But, with limited rations of food and water, the prisoners soon began suffering. As was the case with other prisoners headed to Libby, when the train stopped, crowds of curious onlookers gathered. Southern belles in their finest attire would approach the prisoners, only to scream and hurl insults at them. Bartleson even heard a woman in the crowd in Tennessee ask the guards to shoot all the prisoners. The crowds were not shy about heckling their Northern foes. "What do you think of the Yanks?" they would yell to one another. The prisoners gave it back, boasting, "Never mind—Old Rosy will be along here before long," a reference to General Rosecrans, whose army was fighting Confederate forces in Tennessee.[21]

Southern newspapers followed the convoy, reporting with pleasure that more Yankees had been captured and informing their readers that the Northerners were the worst "specimens" imaginable—little more than a "hang-dang-looking set a scoundrels." The Confederate guards joined in, asking their captives whether they "intended to wipe us from the face of the earth." Interestingly, Bartleson felt that the kindred among men in uniform transcended the bitterness between North and South: Both sides would engage in verbal "jousting," with the Rebels yelling "Bull Run!" and the Yankees responding with such Union victories as "Gettysburg! Vicksburg!" Bartleson referred to these exchanges as "wordy warfare" and noted that it was all "in perfect good humor."[22]

Some soldiers and residents came forward with discreet offers to buy the Union soldiers' watches and clothing or to exchange currency. The locals were living in wretched condition but had only worthless Confederate dollars to offer. They were, however, afraid to be seen talking to prisoners or trying to exchange currency. To do so would likely result in a beating or arrest.[23] The lieutenant in charge of the guards informed Bartleson to be careful and bid him farewell—the prisoners were being handed over to a unit from Georgia known for their "mean" streak. Sure enough, the situation devolved. The remainder of the trip, the prisoners suffered "depravities" and "neglect." They were down to twelve loaves of bread for fifty men. When the train again stopped, they were unloaded and forced to march for days.[24]

Bartleson remembered the "sad state" of affairs for his men. The caravan of straggling blue uniforms was forced to cross creeks and climb over logs. There were few decent roads in the region. There were so few guards assigned to the march that it may have been possible to try to run, but the prisoners were "too weary and hungry" to escape. All they could think about was sleep. Utterly exhausted, Bartleson quipped, "Fatigue and exhaustion make a soft pillow."[25]

Fortunately, the exhausted prisoners were again put aboard open cattle cars and taken by train the remaining distance to Richmond. By this time, there were no provisions to be found among the traveling prisoners—no wood for fires, no food, and all their blankets and coats had been commandeered. When the train arrived in Richmond, the prisoners were "welcomed" by General Winder, provost marshal of the Confederacy, with a stern talk, thinly veiled threats, and the ominous news that they were to be taken to the infamous bastille of the Confederacy. Just as had been the case for Rose and others, Bartleson and his men were marched through the streets lined with heckling locals and provided only the "merest trifle of food."[26]

The Reverend Beaudry, just like Colonel Bartleson, would later write poetry while in prison in order to sustain his morale. Like his fellow writer, he also chronicled life in the wretched prison. The chaplain for the Fifth New York Cavalry learned in June of 1863 that General Robert E. Lee was preparing to invade Pennsylvania with his famed Army of Northern Virginia. In response, units from New York and Pennsylvania had been ordered to intercept the Confederate advance. The joint forces were commanded by General Hugh Judson Kilpatrick of New Jersey, who less than one year later would attempt a daring but reckless rescue of the prisoners suffering in Libby. The joint force was part of the massive Army of the Potomac led by General George Meade.

On June 30, the Fifth arrived in Hanover, Pennsylvania, where the locals "received [us] with great joy," recalled Beaudry. However, an advance cavalry unit from the larger Confederate army attacked that same day. The fighting lasted "until dark," with "heavy casualties on both sides." So many men were lying on the field of battle "badly wounded" that the reverend helped the unit's medic "in stopping the blood of one, who would have bled to death." Back in their field hospital, Beaudry also visited and prayed with those who were "very severely wounded" and helped them write letters to loved ones. The physicians and medics were overwhelmed, so Beaudry "took care of" some of the men.[27]

The Fifth New York eventually drove off the Confederate cavalry and began the chase that would take both units to the town of Gettysburg, roughly fifteen miles away. However, the reverend's services were still needed at the small field hospital, so he had stayed behind. The legendary three-day battle, which began on July 1, ended in one of the most important Union victories of the war. Along the way, the Fifth New York fought gallantly, capturing "about three thousand Rebel prisoners." They were brought to the temporary field hospital where Beaudry was working. He remembered, "They looked sorry."[28]

On July 5, as Beaudry was finally leaving the scene of the fighting, he found himself "surrounded unexpectedly by a detachment of Jenkins Cavalry." Although he carried a pistol, he and a few of his comrades were outnumbered and surprised by the cavalrymen who were not supposed to still be in the area. "It was hard to say 'I surrender,'" he later admitted. The Confederate cavalry unit promised the few men of the Fifth that if they surrendered peacefully they would not take their horses or belongings. Beaudry and his orderlies surrendered and were later robbed of their horses, boots, and belongings.[29] Beaudry was shocked by his captors' appearance. He described them as starving, disheveled, and "very much worn out." Little was said. The Confederates muttered "profanity" among themselves. After riding southward all day and part of the night, they finally made camp. Beaudry remembered that both the captors and captured were "weary, about worn out, wet, hungry and sad." There was only bread to eat. And the camp was not much of one; rather, they camped "on the cold earth and slept with a heavy guard around us."[30]

After a few days during which the men of the Fifth were forced to walk and treated "very shamefully," they approached Richmond. Beaudry recalled that everywhere they went, "I saw dead horses by the way." As they reached the capital, bodies of dead prisoners joined the horses. It was a macabre scene. Everywhere "bodies of men stripped of all their clothing, except their undergarments, lay along the road." Some of the soldiers were still alive but had been left to die. Beaudry was allowed to care for a few of them, even though the guards condemned the dying as "those nodal hordes of Lincoln that had invaded [our] territory, stolen [our] servants [slaves] and destroyed our property." Beaudry felt only "disgust" for his captors.[31]

At six o'clock on the morning of July 18, they finally arrived in the city. They were met by soldiers who escorted them to Libby, where they were "closely searched and robbed" of the few items not taken earlier by the cavalrymen who had captured them.[32]

LIBBY'S LIBERATORS

After the failed Hungarian Revolution, Emeric Szabad was one of many resistance fighters who had been forced to flee for his life. When the former professor, author, and military commander learned that the Civil War had broken out in the United States, he had joined the Hungarian expatriates in supporting the Union and cause of abolition. "The Civil War was followed with great interest in Hungary," Szabad later recalled. Like some of his comrades from the Hungarian Revolution, Szabad had traveled to the United States and joined the Union Army. "Hungarians naturally drew a parallel between the struggle of the free North against the slave-holding South and their own recent war against the tyrannical Habsburg rule," explained Szabad. At the time of the war, about four thousand Hungarians lived in the United States. Most were recent arrivals who had fled the failed revolution in their home country.[33]

While it "is impossible to establish" an exact number of Hungarian expatriates who joined the Union cause, estimates are "as high as 800, although a figure of 300 to 400 seems more reasonable," Szabad suggested. Many of them became officers in the Union Army thanks to their extensive military experience and the fact that many who fled had been intellectuals and leaders. The Union also had a shortage of qualified officers, so much so that Secretary of State William H. Seward attempted to recruit officers from Europe, including from Hungary.[34]

Szabad had arrived in the United States in early 1862, writing that he wanted to "fight for the Union, the destruction of which would cause joy to none but tyrants and despots."[35] He volunteered for the war and was assigned to General John C. Frémont's "Mountain" unit. Szabad was given the rank of captain and served as Frémont's aide-de-camp. Soon other Hungarian émigrés joined them. A few months later, Frémont was assigned to the command of General Nathaniel P. Banks[36] and General Irvin McDowell. Refusing to serve under another commander, the headstrong Frémont resigned in late June of 1862. Many of his loyal Hungarian officers joined him, including Szabad.

Back in civilian life, the former professor and author wrote another book, *Modern War: Its Theory and Practice*.[37] After completing the book, Szabad reenlisted in 1863 and was assigned to the controversial and scandal-prone Daniel Sickles, the man who would nearly cost the Union the Battle of Gettysburg when he disobeyed a direct order and left a critical field undefended.[38] During the fighting at Gettysburg in July of 1863 and right after he defied the direct order from General George Meade, Sickles was struck by a cannonball that took off his leg below the knee. He survived the injury, and after the war his leg and the cannonball would be made into a museum exhibit.[39] Szabad survived Gettysburg and was assigned to General William H. French's Third Army Corps. A few months after Gettysburg, French encountered Confederate forces near the Rappahannock River in eastern Virginia. In the late afternoon of October 26, Confederate cavalry were threatening the Union position. Szabad remembered that French "ordered me to reconnoiter our advanced line" the next day. The Hungarian captain requested that cavalrymen join him on the reconnaissance but was informed that additional riders were not available. Rather than wait for the situation to change, Szabad mounted his "unassuming, fleet, good-natured" horse "Dick," ordered one soldier to join him, and "galloped off" to check on the Confederate cavalry.[40]

Scouting the area near Licking Run, a small stream not far from Bull Run in northern Virginia, Szabad saw no sign of the enemy. Nevertheless, reports had indicated that Confederate forces were in the area, so he proceeded with caution. "I trotted on," Szabad recalled, "casting my eyes to the right and left of the railroad, as a reconnoitering officer usually does," while his "orderly" was "lagging a little behind." Then, suddenly, "three cavalry men darted out from the woods on the right side of the railroad, and halting, called out, 'Halt, who are you?'" Szabad was not sure whether they were friend or foe and so did not answer. Though they were some fifty yards away, he saw that they appeared to be wearing "blue coats and McClellan caps."[41] He called out to them to identify themselves and then brought his horse a bit closer. Szabad remembered that he "found out my mistake when it was too late." They were with the Second Virginia Cavalry and were wearing stolen Union jackets and caps. Szabad was now facing three guns, pointed directly at him, and "had a curious feeling" they were about to use them. He "had to obey" their order that he surrender; he handed over his sword. His Union orderly turned and fled.[42]

Szabad's captors confiscated Dick the horse and began taking the captain's personal effects, including his fancy spurs. The spurs and sword had been gifts from "a brave Hungarian general" and were Szabad's prized possessions from the Garibaldi campaign. The Hungarian officer protested, but to no avail. The Confederates both needed and wanted the items "badly." Szabad was taken by the cavalrymen to their captain, whereupon the Hungarian officer "bitterly complained" about his treatment and the theft of his possessions. The captain said only, "it was the laws of war." What befuddled the Confederates was his accent. They could not figure out where he was from and found it "incomprehensible" that a foreigner would fight with the "damned Yankees."[43]

That evening, Szabad was given only "a small piece of bread, and a much smaller piece of dried meat" and told to sleep on the ground. Without a blanket or his jacket, he minded the cold and could not sleep. The next day, he was ordered to walk behind the three cavalrymen. It was a long, grueling walk, after which he was shoved into an open pen, not unlike that used to corral animals, along with "a few dozen privates, who were under arrest for various misdemeanors." It was cold and raining, and Szabad was "tired and hungry," so he asked the guards to contact their superior; he wished to "strongly" protest the "manner in which he, as an officer, was treated." Officers, he pointed out, were to be housed "indoors and separated from enlisted men," much less penned with those under court-martial. The Rebels only mocked him with "half sneering smiles." Of his requests, they joked, "And where is your army?"[44]

The Hungarian captain was eventually taken to Libby Prison, where his experience was similar to that of the other officers imprisoned there. He quickly realized he was not the only foreign-born prisoner in the bastille of the Confederacy. There were several, including Lieutenant Colonel Federico Fernández Cavada, who had joined the Twenty-Third Pennsylvania as soon as the war had started and, like Szabad and Beaudry, had also fought at the Battle of Gettysburg.

The Cuban-born Fernández Cavada had fought at the Second Battle of Bull Run, in the Battle of Fredericksburg, and in numerous other engagements. The former artist and engineer had been assigned to the Union Army Balloon Corps, where he would rise high above the battlefields in the hot-air balloon *Constitution* and sketch enemy positions and report troop movements. Both sides deployed hot-air balloons during the war, but the Union "was far more successful and better organized," Fernández Cavada noted proudly. Designed by Thaddeus Lowe, the hot-air balloons were tough, durable, and flew high enough that enemy guns could not shoot them down. The massive, brightly colored and elaborately decorated balloons carried up to five men in their gondolas.[45]

The Twenty-Third distinguished itself during the fighting at Gettysburg, although they lost several men. One of the casualties of that struggle had been Fernández Cavada. After returning from a balloon flight above the field of battle, the Cuban-born colonel had been caught and taken prisoner by a Confederate unit.[46] Fernández Cavada was taken to Libby, arriving in the summer of 1863. Charismatic, articulate, and intelligent, the balloonist impressed his fellow prisoners and also rendered history a great service by compiling a detailed list of the imprisoned and chronicling their daily ordeals. His fellow inmates encouraged Fernández Cavada to publish his writings after the war in order to tell the world of their struggles—if he lived.

7

"All Hope Abandon,
Ye Who Enter Here"

On our haggard countenances this was written: Give us rest, and food.

—Federico Fernández Cavada, Libby Prison, 1863[1]

Most of the soldiers who ended up in Libby had heard horror stories about the prison. Likewise, those who recorded their ordeals noted their first impressions of Libby and the fear they had felt at the prospects before them. From the moment they arrived, the ghastly faces that looked down at them from the barred windows were an omen of what was in store for them. They were seeing their own future. One of them was Lieutenant James Munroe Wells of the Eighth Michigan Cavalry. The first site Wells remembered seeing in the Confederate capital was the crowded detention center on the small Belle Isle, in the middle of the James River, where thousands of Union prisoners suffered and died. Wells and his fellow prisoners passed overhead on a long railway bridge. After being unloaded at the Richmond depot, they were paraded through town and to Cary Street. In front of them was a large brick warehouse with a sign that read "A. LIBBY & SON, SHIP CHANDLERS AND GROCERS."[2]

Looking up at the barred windows when he arrived at the prison, Lieutenant Wells saw the desperate faces of men "standing a little back" from the windows. They looked like skeletons. Wells said that his first thought was a line from Dante's *Divine Comedy*—"All hope abandon, ye who enter here," the supposed inscription at the entrance to hell.[3] Another prisoner, Charles Carleton Coffin, a New Englander who became one of the most famous newspaper correspondents during the Civil War, said simply that the prison was "the inferno of the slave Confederacy."[4]

After nearly two weeks in transit and while nursing an untreated broken foot suffered while trying to escape, Colonel Rose arrived at Libby and was placed in a very crowded room on the second floor that immediately become known as the "Lower Chickamauga Room" because so many of the prisoners there had been captured in that bloody battle. The former teacher and principal was just thirty-three at the time of his capture, but his beard would soon turn gray from the stress of his ordeal. Like other prisoners, he was robbed and treated poorly during his registration as a prisoner. His clothing was soon torn and quickly became infected with lice—called "graybacks" by the prisoners—and bedbugs—known in the prison as "chinches." Within days, his entire body hurt from sleeping on the hard floor, which was made worse over time by the unhealthy amount of weight he lost. Rose began to note that he had insufficient flesh to cushion his body.

Moreover, for the thirty-three-year-old colonel, every step was an ordeal. He was still limping on an untreated broken foot. However, that had not distracted him: Rose paid close attention to the route the train had taken, memorizing the landscape and towns they had passed. He had also noted the streets in Richmond and the path to the center of the city. He was already planning to escape. Inside the prison, Rose peered out the windows at every opportunity, watching workers enter a large sewer on Canal Street, then exit, guessing correctly that it emptied into the Kanawha Canal. He had already formulated part of his escape plan. Two other prisoners—Major Andrew Hamilton, who would soon become Rose's assistant in the escape plan, and Lieutenant Frank Moran—noticed the colonel's quiet and serious demeanor and how he observed the comings and goings of the guards, warden, and orderlies. Lieutenant Moran wrote, "From the hour of his coming, a means of escape became his constant and eager study." First he had to survive.[5]

"FRESH FISH"

Captain Emeric Szabad had arrived in the Confederate capital by train at eight o'clock in the evening and was greeted by a "shrill whistle . . . announcing our arrival in Richmond." A sergeant oversaw the unloading of prisoners, and the Hungarian officer was both surprised and somewhat relieved that the Confederate guard was "polite." The courtesies, however, would end there. The prisoners were handed over to a detachment of guards who paraded them through the streets. Aside from hecklers, the streets were "dimly lighted and showed little sign of life or movement in the city." At Libby, Szabad was processed by Lieutenant La Touche, who seemed pleased to find someone who spoke his native tongue; the two briefly "conversed in French."[6]

However, the Hungarian revolutionary was robbed of his few remaining possessions. Perhaps because of his language skills, La Touche was willing to "answer sundry questions" from Szabad. But, the deputy warden also took Szabad's money. When the Hungarian officer surrendered his remaining five dollar "greenback" and asked about it, La Touche promised that he would receive an equivalent amount in Confederate currency when—or if—he was released from the bastille. Of course, the Southern currency was worthless and when prisoners were released, the warden would simply claim he could not reimburse them because the records were lost. One of the many ironies of the war was that the Confederate guards, like the residents of Richmond, were desperate for federal greenbacks. Knowing this, the prisoners tried to hide their money during their capture and processing, as it could be used later to bribe the guards.[7]

When new prisoners arrived, Szabad remembered that the inmates would yell, "Fresh fish! Fresh fish!" For a prisoner's first six months in Libby, they were referred to as "fresh fish," but after six months they were known as "a sucker." Once a prisoner was approaching a year in the wretched bastille, he was elevated to "a dry cod" or "a dried herring." A special nickname was reserved for only the longest-serving prisoners, who were called "pickled sardines." The moniker was bestowed on those men, Szabad reasoned, for good reason—after enough time without adequate water, food, hygiene, or bathing, the inmates began to resemble just that![8]

After being processed and robbed, Szabad asked La Touche for a blanket, but the deputy warden simply smirked and told his new charge to submit a written request.[9] Szabad "followed a sergeant to the first floor of the prison," climbed the steep stairs, and was assigned to the upper, central room. There he was met by an awful site and smell. Men resembling skeletons crowded around him, wanting to talk to the "fresh fish." Eager for news, they asked, "Where were you taken?" Others wanted to know "What corps do you belong to?" The more senior prisoners told the "fresh fish" that the Richmond newspapers were "exceedingly unreliable"—little more than thinly veiled Confederate propaganda—and new prisoners were always a welcome source for updates on the fighting. The longtime prisoners gave the newcomers advice and explained the rules for "Hotel de Libby."[10]

After a thirty-minute "debriefing," Szabad informed his new fellow inmates that he was Hungarian. Upon hearing this, the prisoners took Szabad to the top floor to meet a major from Hungary. He initially did not recognize the "tall, emaciated figure" but then realized it was an acquaintance from Hungary, Stephen Kovacs of the Fifty-Fourth New York Volunteers. The two men had fought in Hungary and again at Gettysburg together. They "embraced without uttering a word."[11]

When Szabad asked if there was any food, Kovacs told him that there would be none until the next day; nor did they have blankets. Szabad expressed his frustration not only with the conditions in the prison but also that the day happened to be the anniversary of Garibaldi's victory over Neapolitan forces, and he had been a part of the grand campaign. Oh, how his fortunes had fallen! Kovacs advised his depressed countryman to quickly find a place to sleep. With the prison so crowded, there was not much room remaining. Sure enough, Szabad could not find a single available space on the floor and ended up having to bunk near an open window. With no blanket, the cold air made for an uncomfortable evening. However, the Hungarian captain was so exhausted that he managed to sleep.

Szabad was awakened by "the call of the guards in the street." What's more, he awoke to the realization of where he was. "The first scene" in the dawn light "was of a kind I had never imagined out of the realms of fiction." Szabad realized that his arrival at night had spared him the true horrors of the prison. All around him were "repulsive things" out of a "Victor Hugo" story—shrunken shells of men, unkept and covered in "merde"[12] and "vermin." Szabad remembered wanting to "turn away my eyes from the scene." Just then the guards announced that the men should form for breakfast. His hunger forced him out of the trance.[13]

However, on the way to the prison kitchen, the once-proud Hungarian revolutionary received devastating news. The other prisoners—whom he called "Libbyans"—informed him that the prisoner exchanges had been stopped because "of the difficulty about the exchange of negro soldiers"; tragically, the South had reacted to Lincoln's Emancipation Proclamation by refusing to recognize Blacks as soldiers and threatened to cease exchanges if Blacks were put in uniform. Moreover, Szabad was told that the "cartels" that were organized to initiate the exchanges were done so by towns and units who would see to their own sons. As a Hungarian, he did not have a cartel to represent him. The prisoners summed up the bad news to their new "fish": "You are in for good!"[14]

PROCESSING AND PILFERING

Libby's new arrivals were forced to line up at the entrance to the prison, and then each inmate would be taken into the main office "for a few minutes." The process, much like the overall administration of the prison, was "disorganized" and often descended into violence and abuse. The office was stark except for a few captured Union regimental flags that were displayed on the walls along with the US flag, which was hanging upside down. There, with two armed guards present, prisoners would meet Lieutenant John La Touche, the adjutant, or Captain Dick Turner, the deputy warden, who made sure the prisoners were "relieved of the few valuables we chanced to have left." The men were then processed by Erastus Ross, the diminutive prison clerk, who would record each prisoner's name, rank, and unit. The enlisted men were taken to other prisons such as Castle Thunder or the Belle Isle stockade, while officers would remain in Libby.[15]

Reverend Beaudry of the Fifth New York Cavalry arrived at Libby at dawn in the middle of July. He was taken aback by the treatment of officers during processing, which he felt violated age-old customs of civility. "They treat some officers with gross insults and harshness," he wrote. For example, while stripping prisoners of their possessions, Captain Turner discovered that a lieutenant had kept a piece of a musket ball as a souvenir from the Battle of Gettysburg. After screaming that the prisoner had no right to any possessions, the deputy warden delivered "a terrible blow on the face" to the lieutenant. Those prisoners arriving with illnesses or wounds suffered in battle were "without medical attention," remembered several of the officers, which further contributed to the shockingly high mortality rate within Libby's crowded rooms.[16]

The reverend soon learned that such treatment was a normal part of "the hells of prison." So many prisoners had arrived with him that it had taken all day for Beaudry to be processed. Like everyone, he was "closely searched and robbed" of his coat, blanket, and personal possessions, which made it difficult to sleep at night during the winter months. Finally, well after dark, the chaplain was escorted upstairs to the "middle room, second floor," which, to his dismay, he found to be overcrowded. He noted that the theft of coats and blankets had another consequence in the prison: "I found nearly 200 men so sick, that they were not able to raise their heads from the dirty floor, where they lay without blankets nor even a stick of wood for a pillow."[17]

Beaudry had no blanket, bedding, or boots and had to spend his incarceration sleeping on the bare floor. The prisoners who had shoes or boots used them as pillows at night. The want of possessions was made worse by the fact that the prison lacked silverware, plates, blankets, beds or bedding, furniture, soap, and other essential items. There was no furniture—no bunks or beds in the rooms, just hundreds of emaciated prisoners. Because the barred windows were otherwise open, rain, snow, and bitter winter winds tormented the prisoners; the lucky ones slept in piles in the center of the rooms in order to stay warm and dry, while some unfortunate souls were forced to sleep by the open windows. This was the room where Beaudry would end up spending his time in prison—if he lived.[18]

The next day, Beaudry had the opportunity to meet one of the prison's celebrity inmates—Colonel Abel Streight—which excited him. Beaudry also discovered that he was not the only chaplain detained; there were eight others suffering in the wretched bastille. His sagging spirits were lifted, if only for a moment, the next day when "Brother McCabe, the chaplain of the 116th Ohio," delivered "a good sermon, about 12 noon." Beaudry would later find his own way to inspire those suffering inside Libby.[19]

"STENCH" AND "VERMIN"

The lack of sanitation and awful smell were among the most obvious and initial things the prisoners noticed. There was little accommodation for bathing or hygiene in Libby. Captain Szabad remembered "the want of fresh air, the fumes of the prison being rather too strong," when he entered Libby.[20] What Reverend Beaudry remembered, first and foremost, was "the stench," which he described as "very sickening— at times almost unbearable."[21] It did not help that the prisoners were "packed like sardines" into the warehouse's open rooms and that the sink and toilet "have no door." Without exception, one of the first challenges new prisoners faced was finding room to "bunk." The prison remained in an almost-perpetual state of being overcrowded, and no one wanted to have to sleep near the open toilet.[22] Colonel Fernández Cavada described the situation he encountered when entering Libby: "The room we are in is low, dingy, gloomy, and suffocating. Some two hundred officers are lying packed in rows along the floor, sleeping the heavy, dreamless sleep of exhaustion."[23]

Libby was only occasionally "cleaned" by slaves and Black prisoners. From time to time, the warden would order "a dozen negroes carrying buckets and brooms" into the two upper floors of the prison either at dawn or late in the afternoon. The "cleaning" was done in various ways. One consisted of a "whitewash" painted onto the floors and interior walls of the rooms. While it did cover the dirt and telltale signs of human suffering and death, it left the prisoner's clothing and bodies stained with white lines and smudges.[24] Though thankful that the wretched warehouse was being cleaned, the prisoners complained because they were awakened before dawn by the assistant commandant and ordered to remove any belongings so that the prison floors and water closets could be scrubbed. As much as the prisoners hated being woken up before dawn, it was preferable to having the floors cleaned in the late afternoon. When that happened, the floors and prisoners' possessions were wet and that night they would have to sleep on damp floors.[25]

Sometimes the prison was cleaned by fumigation. Prisoners often resorted to smoking in order to drive away the pests and counter the nauseating smell of human waste and body odor. Consequently, the cavernous holding rooms were often filled with smoke and everything and everyone came to smell like a putrid mix of human waste and tobacco. The warden ordered slaves to "purify the prison with tar smoke," which simply fouled the air and covered the floors, ceilings, and prisoners' clothing with a black grime. The commandant assigned the job to "an old, shrewd negro" who had been a "valet" to Union general Nathaniel P. Banks but had been captured by the Rebels. Whenever the old valet was sent to burn barrels of tar, he would "announce his presence in the morning with the lusty proclamation," such as "Here is a good smoke without money or price!" He would then sing "Home, Sweet Home" or some other Southern folk song in a thick Louisiana drawl while fumigating the prison rooms.[26]

The cleanings had another function. Aside from the foul stench of the place and the overcrowding, the other immediately noticeable aspect of life in Libby were the vermin: lice, fleas, and a bewildering assortment of pests that had invaded every nook and cranny of the prison, the prisoners' personal effects, and their bodies. When General Dow was once asked if he was "lousy," he retorted good-naturedly, "No, I am not, but my shirt is." Reverend Beaudry echoed other prisoners, complaining that the "rooms are filthy and full of vermin." Szabad said quite simply that Libby was "overrun with filth and vermin," while Frederick Bartleson agreed that the "vermin are troublesome," adding, "We have bed bugs, too, and I presume that in the summer, if we are so unfortunate as to be here at that time, we will find them very bad." Indeed, many claimed that the two defining characteristics of Libby were disease and as assortment of bugs, referred to colorfully as "Libby graybacks and chinches."[27]

DAILY DESPONDENCY

Not surprisingly, one of the most common afflictions in Libby was depression, which the men called "melancholia" or the "Libby emotion." Hand in hand with the bouts of melancholia was boredom. Reverend Beaudry said simply of one of the chief struggles in Libby, "Life is very monotonous," which, along with the absolute lack of control over one's life, tore at all the men imprisoned there, including Colonel Bartleson. He and others, he admitted, would "much rather" be "nearer to the front" fighting than be suffering in the prison. Tragically, many prisoners succumbed to the ordeal. Later it was even said among the prisoners that many of their comrades who survived their stay in the bastille "never fully recovered" and would be "permanently broken down in their constitutions."[28]

Bartleson, the one-armed hero and veteran of many battles, had arrived at Libby on September 29, 1863. After four months of captivity, he wrote the first entry in what would become an important diary and collection of poetry, announcing in late January, "I have determined to keep a journal of my prison life." He was inspired to do so largely as a way of dealing with the "monotonous" days and long nights, writing that it was "both for the purpose of occupying my time and to furnish a memorial to which, in later life, I may refer." At the same time, Bartleson noticed that the gravity of the inmates' situation coupled with the barbarity of the prison made many prisoners lose their "pride and self-respect." Bartleson thus wanted to also test a "theory" about "what transpired during the day" that made some men but not others "give up on life." He also worried, "Shall I be the same man that I am now?" Sadly, as we shall soon see, the brave colonel would not get the chance to pursue the next phase of his life.[29]

The long days inside Libby began at daybreak. On Sundays, the morning drill occurred a bit later; though a seemingly small "privilege," it was one for which the exhausted and weak prisoners were thankful. The prisoners were awakened for a daily roll call conducted by Erastus Ross, the diminutive clerk of the prison who was always in the company of armed guards. After that, it was the same routine, day in and day out. Colonel Bartleson summed it up as, "Read, write, walk, talk, and grumble till bedtime."[30] The exception to the routine was when more prisoners arrived or when one of their fellow inmates died, although such losses quickly became a daily part of life in Libby. A second head count of the prisoners was taken at precisely two o'clock each afternoon.[31]

Bartleson wrote frequent letters to his wife, Kate, in which he described the daily ordeal of the prison, including the sleeping arrangements and roll calls. He recorded that the guards would play "Taps" on a bugle each evening at dusk. The age-old military tradition that marks funerals and flag ceremonies concluded with one of the guards yelling, "Lights out!" Some prisoners such as Bartleson had candles and would read or write for a few hours—in his case, until roughly ten o'clock.[32]

Generally, the behavior of Libby's prisoners according to Szabad was one of "decency" and "etiquette." He attributed it to the fact that many were well-educated senior officers. It also helped, he and other officers noted, that the prisoners tried to maintain a military order inside the bastille. A clear pecking order existed, based on military rank and length of time served in the prison. Likewise, in order to maintain some semblance of order and discipline in the face of severe overcrowding and the despair that gripped many prisoners, the officers inside Libby organized "for the general good." With "military precision," the inmates were assigned to "squads," each with a number and each with a "captain."[33]

The exception to good behavior, observed Szabad, when the rules were "willfully disregarded" was due to the "misery" of prison life. The men struggled with boredom, depression, disease, hunger, a lack of hygiene and space, and abuse at the hands of the cruel wardens and guards. They also grew to loath the tedium of standing in line for hours twice each day for the prison roll call, became frustrated by the inability to go outside and put their feet on "terra firma," and quickly lost patience with the lack of any "elbow room." Tempers flared, and frustrations led to a few fights.[34] Colonel Bartleson recalled "one or two of these little affairs" during his time in the bastille; however, the senior officers ordered such dustups to cease and desist right away. There were also occasional wrestling matches among the younger prisoners, but the senior-most prisoners excused these.[35]

Even the act of sleeping was difficult and subject to a routine. With the prison so severely overcrowded, there was precious little floor space. The prisoners were forced to sleep head-to-head in long lines that the prisoners likened to "lines of battle" that were so "tight" that it was difficult to even roll over, much less stand up and make one's way to the makeshift latrine. By necessity, then—especially in winters, when prisoners were forced to pile in "spoon fashion" to stay warm—each squad "captain" would give the order for the sleeping men to turn in unison from their left side to their right. "Attention!" the squad leaders would announce, "Prepare to spoon! One—two—spoon!" This "maneuver" also helped the officers' aching bodies. It was not enough that they had to sleep on a hard, wooden floor, but as the men lost dangerous amounts of weight, they complained that there was not enough meat on their bones to cushion them from the discomforts of the rough surface.[36]

The men awoke sore and starving from their fitful slumber. After the morning roll call, a long line of prisoners had to file to the few latrines, which often overran. Next to the latrine was a tub, which was described by Captain Szabad as "a trough-like affair situated under a faucet of running water in an enclosed closet." Prisoners used this tub to clean their clothing and themselves. It was difficult because of the limited availability of soap and water and the sheer numbers of men in the prison. Consequently, recalled the Hungarian, "It was not unusual for three or four men to bathe at the same time." Prisoners tried to wash their clothing in the mornings so that it had time to dry before lights-out. They also made an agreement to not bathe after nine in the evenings, out of respect to the unfortunate prisoners who had to bunk next to the latrine and bathing trough.[37]

According to General Dow, the chief occupations in the bastille were eating food, planning an escape, and finding a way to pass the long days; each man did what he could to cope. Colonel Bartleson described Libby as a "beehive" of activity. "Except in the dead of night," there were always men up and walking about or engaged in activities to ward off the cold of night and boredom. Other prisoners stayed up late at night either commiserating or arguing. These commotions did not last long; fellow prisoners often threw boots at their noisy comrades or a senior officer shouted out for them to shut up. Several of the men noted that the symptoms of melancholia were more pronounced at night, as indicated by the sobbing heard throughout the prison.[38]

The daily routine also included trying to steal a look out one of the vertically rectangular windows of the prison. Szabad recalled joining others attempting to stick their heads out a window for a quick breath of fresh air. The problem, however, was that the guards had orders to shoot any prisoner who even stood near one of the barred windows or the "deadline," the area around each window that prisoners were forbidden to cross. Most of the sentries took pleasure in carrying out the order, even seeing it as sport. More often than not, there was little for the prisoners to see outside the window, other than the occasional ship on the James River. The windows also periodically brought the "shrill calls" of "frightened negro women" victims of the regular attacks from local men. Still, the prisoners risked their lives for a glimpse outside; Szabad even referred to the blank "gaze" out of Libby's windows as the "despondency."[39]

Libby Prison, observed Bartleson, "has its life and its routine and its characters."[40] Character helped men deal with the despondency. Many accomplished and interesting officers were among the prison population. Szabad, for instance, appreciated the fact that the prison contained men from all across the country, from many different units, and who had fought in as many battles. The mix of compelling characters "served to keep me for weeks in a state of continual surprise," said the Hungarian freedom fighter. This was especially the case for the highest-ranking officers and celebrities inside the prison, who emerged as "objects of special interest" to everyone.[41]

Just over a week after his arrival at Libby, Szabad had undertaken what he called "my reconnaissances" of the prison in order to deal with the boredom, meet his fellow prisoners, and assess the possibility of escape. He especially wanted to visit the main room below his assigned quarter, which he referred to as "the *bon ton* room" because it contained a few of the highest-ranking officers. There he met the "elderly" General Dow, whom he was elated to see "bore his imprisonment with considerable equanimity." Szabad described Dow and a few other senior officers as "distinguished."[42]

The former Hungarian professor was less charitable in his assessment of Americans in general, describing them as "uncouth" compared to Europeans. Szabad was also upset by a few "*mauvais sujects.*"[43] He accused these bad elements of "filching" from their fellow prisoners by trying to sell "for pretty high prices" apples, tobacco, crackers, and other items they received in boxes sent by loved ones. These few prisoners thought only of "profitable prices" and not their starving comrades. On the whole, though, Szabad commented that most of the "gallant gentlemanly officers confined with me" were very "honorable."[44]

The Hungarian officer was particularly impressed with Colonel Streight of the Fifty-First Indiana. Szabad described the famous raider as "gallant" and noted that the colonel returned the compliment. To his delight, Streight invited Szabad to dine with him. Streight, like a few of the highest-ranking officers, had received boxes of provisions and food from home. The invitation, noted Szabad, could not have come at a better time. Rations had been cut, and the situation inside Libby had "considerably deteriorated" to the point where even bread was scarce. Streight's "very welcome offer" likely saved Szabad's life, whose "health was giving way" after his capture.[45]

PIG FEED

The prisoners awoke each morning to "the old sensation of hunger." James Munroe Wells, a young officer from Michigan, complained that mornings were the worst because the pangs of hunger greeted them "with renewed force." Being "constantly hungry," he wrote, caused much "despondency" among the prisoners. There was the word *despondency* again, often used by the prisoners, and for good reason. The morning routine in Libby, however, did include breakfast. After roll call and time for the latrine and washing, the squads of prisoners organized into a "mess" and were marched down the steep stairs to the dining area. Each mess consisted of anywhere from four to twenty men, with eighteen as the average size but with one mess containing thirty members. As a mess, the men often cooked, ate, and even slept as a unit. They shared blankets, knives, forks, and spoons, if they were available at all, and had to pass around a plate or bowl, which were even more "scarce."[46]

The assistant commandant, Captain Dick Turner, supervised the mess and always with armed guards at his side. Colonel Bartleson saw the act of going down the stairs to line up for the morning meal in the open dining room as having the dual "purpose of exercise and fresh air." It was also the only place the incarcerated men were permitted to go. As Bartleson complained, "Out of this prison no one is allowed to go under any pretext." They were otherwise confined to their crowded rooms all day and night, something he found "very irksome."[47]

After the men arrived at the mess area, several guards would come "thronging in." The warden would then order the prisoners to "fall in to ranks." Although the food was of a poor quality and insufficient quantity, the starving prisoners looked forward to what was usually the first of two meals each day. At times, however, and without explanation, breakfast was served very early, Captain Szabad noted, "while it was still dark." The second meal was scheduled in the late afternoon, typically at five o'clock.[48]

At times in Libby, the meals were prepared for the prisoners by slaves and "Northern colored" cooks, who also served the food in a kitchen and dining area on the first floor of the prison. There were either two or three old wood-fired stoves and a fireplace in the kitchen. After rations were reduced at the end of the summer of 1863, some of the prisoners asked the warden if they could prepare their own food; it would give the men something to offset the boredom, and they wanted to try and improve the quality and sanitary conditions of the slop they were being fed. The warden agreed, as it would allow the slaves and Black prisoners to be put to work in other needed areas. But a problem emerged: how could 1,200 starving men share two or three old stoves? Trying to cook breakfast was sheer chaos, remembered Bartleson. Hungry men were crammed into the small kitchen, and soon tempers flared, leaving Bartleson to label the breakfast mess an "army of ferocious cooks." Although Colonel Rose remained calm and on the periphery of the breakfast scrum, he considered every meal an ordeal. Standing in the queue on the broken foot he suffered while trying to escape during the train journey to Richmond was painful; many boots stepped on his foot.[49]

Captain Szabad reported that there were two luxuries available to the prisoners when it came to food. If they happened to have money—and on the rare occasion that the guards did not steal it during processing—the Union officers were allowed to buy butter, coffee, tea, sugar, and vegetables.[50] The warden oversaw this "market," but, as Bartleson observed, he overcharged the prisoners and lined his own pocket with the proceeds.[51] Fernández Cavada explained that on the rare occasion the men "received permission to purchase provisions outside the prison," it was either stolen by the warden or guards or they were charged "fifty percent more than Richmond's residents for the food."[52] The second amenity was that the prisoners at times received boxes from loved ones. These boxes often contained food, clothing, books, paper, and other items. Committees and "cartels" from cities across the North—such as the United States Sanitary Commission, operating across the Union and notably in Philadelphia, and the Western Sanitary Commission, operating out of Saint Louis—routinely sent food, blankets, and provisions to Libby and other prisons during the war. Many of these aid organizations were established at the outset of the war in 1861, inspired by the British organization founded by Florence Nightingale during the Crimean War. Other charities such as the United States Christian Commission sent chaplains to the prisons. The guards, however, often stole the boxes brought by the chaplains.

The Hungarian freedom fighter was fortunate. Another time when he was starving—describing his situation "as if my knees were giving way under me"—Szabad was invited to join the mess of a fellow European who happened to have "a cup, knife, and fork, articles which I at once experienced were not easily to be got in Libby." The European officers, coming from the high echelons of society back home, had managed to get powerful allies to intervene on their behalf to send boxes with "butter and sugar, which were of course a great addition to our spare diet," along with "rye coffee." While grateful for every morsel, Szabad, used to the food of his native Hungary and preferring Italian cuisine, complained of Southern food, calling it "peculiar" and "odd." He described one meal as "smoked tongue, mixed up with crumbs and crackers of different species, struggling to stew themselves into some uniform whole." He tolerated the day that they were served the rare treat of pudding and flapjacks. One can only imagine the delight of the other prisoners with less-discerning tastes![53]

Still, the rations were always insufficient, and throughout the war there were periods during which provisions ran dangerously low and the prisoners did not eat. Bartleson recalled, "One day the Confederate Government is out of meat, another day it is out of rice, and occasionally it may have no food at all."[54] As the entire Southern economy ground to a near standstill during the war, there were severe shortages of food for both soldier and civilian. Providing food for enemy prisoners was never a priority. Colonel Robert Ould, the Confederacy's commissioner in charge of prisoner exchanges, said flatly of the Union prisoners, "I would rather they should starve than our own people suffer."[55] Indeed, Szabad remembered often eating nothing but occasional bits of "a very poor article of corn bread" and sweat potatoes. At other times they were starved for days on end.[56]

Libby's warden and the commissaries in charge of supplies stated that their goal was to provide each prisoner with two ounces of bacon or four ounces of beef, some beans and rice, and a half-pound of bread each day. The prisoners, however, discovered these to be nothing more than empty pronouncements. The South was having trouble feeding their soldiers, much less their prisoners. Making matters worse, the warden frequently "threatened to cut off our supplies."[57] Szabad remembered that it was a rare and special day if the per diem allotment was even close to "a half a loaf of bread, a little more than two ounces of rice, between three and four ounces of meat."[58] The typical rations given to Libby's prisoners, recalled Reverend Beaudry, included some stale bread and rotten meat in the morning and some soup at night. Other days it was "bad" corn bread and Borden's condensed milk in a can. When the inmates prepared their own meals, they used any and all rations to make a hodgepodge soup. It was the best way to consume the inedible food. The rations, estimated the reverend, were "not one-quarter the amount of food we need to maintain health."[59]

Reverend Beaudry noted one troubling ordeal: "This evening our soup was brought to us late—after dark and we have no candles. It is brought up in large dirty pails that remind me of pig feeding in other days." The lack of candles, however, turned out to be a blessing in disguise. "We eat our soup almost without tasting it," he explained. "We are compelled to do so to keep it down." The light of morning brought a gruesome discovery. Beaudry and the prisoners saw the filth in and around the maggot-infested pails from the night prior! Another chaplain named Harvey recorded what he ate as "a small amount of rice, or some black-eyed beans." (It turned out that was only what he *thought* was in the pail.) It was not just the food but the water too that was problematic. Beaudry went on to offer a facetious description of how the prisoners quenched their thirst. "For drink we had the pure extract of James River, always warm and never cold, sometimes thick and sometimes thin." Either way, admitted the chaplain, "We were constantly hungry, and our dreams by night were filled with visions of home and loved ones, and tables spread with every conceivable luxury known to the culinary art."[60] Yet each morning when the sentry ordered the men to awaken, "the old sensation of hunger came back with renewed force."[61]

Not surprisingly, Bartleson and other prisoners described eating as being an obsession inside Libby,[62] an occurrence not uncommon among prisoners of war throughout history. Szabad explained, "A starvation atmosphere existed" to the extent that "malnutrition was the chief contributor to the appalling death rate" inside the prison. Desperate men even "quickly pounced" on the many rats that overran Libby—either that, or go hungry.[63] Reverend Beaudry noted his rapidly declining health due to the lack of food. "I am constantly devoured with hunger and so faint, that I am compelled to lie on the floor most of the time," he wrote. "If I chance to rise up suddenly, my head whirls with dizziness." He shared the sentiments of other prisoners when he despaired, "I do not know but I will starve to death."[64]

"BONEYARD"

Given the prevalence of diseases inside Libby and the lack of hygiene and food, the prisoners were often sick. The commandant was therefore forced to organize a makeshift hospital in the prison, setting up 120 wooden cots, each with a straw paillasse, in a room on the first floor. It was staffed by three surgeons; sometimes they all worked at the same time, and other times there was no physician at all. With severe shortages of food and provisions throughout the South, Libby was also often without adequate medicines or surgical instruments to the extent that it was a hospital in name only.[65]

Reverend Beaudry observed that often there were insufficient cots in the makeshift hospital or not enough medicine for the sick. Likewise, the prisoners who arrived sick or wounded often went untreated entirely. In fact, most of the prisoners who arrived at the prison either wounded or sick died quickly. One night in late 1863, a large group of prisoners arrived. Within days, they were all dead. Similarly, another prisoner recorded that during the summer "about 5 die daily" in the hospital from disease and a lack of food. The sick prisoners were only "fed on half rations of bread and coffee and tea." Weak when he arrived at Libby, Beaudry echoed these concerns, complaining, "I have been so faint and hungry that I could scarcely stand up."[66] Making matters worse, the prisoners' remaining possessions such as "canteens and haversacks" were stolen while they were in the hospital.[67]

Some men, such as Beaudry, recovered. One was Captain Robert Cornwell, who had been taken prisoner on June 13, 1863, at Winchester, Virginia. He had arrived at Libby gravely ill with "fever and ague."[68] Cornwell remained in a precarious state for weeks after his arrival at the prison. However, on October 26 he wrote to his wife, Lydia, "My health is quite restored," although he admitted to her that he was still a wretched sight. "I hardly know myself when I look in that glass you sent me," he mused. He attributed his recovery less to the hospital and physicians than to the fact that his wife had sent him a box with food that the authorities had allowed to be delivered. Although it took some time to recover his "weight and strength," he became the envy of many other prisoners because his wife had also included in the box "a bottle of ink, pen holder and pens, tooth brush, small looking glass, comb, hair brush." Soon he was able to report to her that his "mess mates" have taken to teasing him. "They tell me I am getting fat, and I guess it is true," Cornwell joked.[69]

Death came from many places inside Libby, including the "systematic abuse, neglect and semi-starvation." There were also numerous maladies that haunted the prison, perhaps brought by the abundance of "vermin and fleas," which Szabad claimed "were particularly obnoxious."[70] Among the myriad diseases was smallpox. To combat the periodic outbreaks, prison officials ordered the burning of tar and scraps of leather. The *Richmond Dispatch* wrote after one particularly bad outbreak that this remedy "has been very successful thus far in keeping the disease at a distance."[71] It was an exception. The *Richmond Examiner* even referred to the bastille as simply "a big hospital of sick prisoners."[72]

Some Civil War–era military records from Richmond's hospitals and prisons have survived history, including those from Libby. The records from September of 1862 to November of 1863, for instance, show that one hundred to two hundred prisoners were sick and in Libby's "hospital" room at any one time. Yet it is hard to determine an average number of prisoners who took ill every year, because the numbers spiked in the cold months, when large numbers of prisoners arrived after a battle, and when the prison was in the grips of one of the many diseases that tore through the facility. For instance, reports show that 507 of Libby's prisoners were ill in September of 1862 alone and that an astonishing 1,084 were hospitalized in October of 1863.[73]

The surviving reports also list the death toll at Libby over the course of a full year, when from September of 1862 to October of 1863, 358 prisoners reportedly died. The winter months generally had the highest death tolls, such as when thirty-nine prisoners died in December 1862 and the same number again was lost one month later, followed by seventeen deaths each in February and March. However, sixty-two perished in September of 1862, while 115 died the following October, months when diseases tore through the prison.[74] Of course, the records from Libby's commandant were known for being inaccurate and likely quite understated.

With so many diseases and a high death toll inside Libby, the warden decided that the hospital room would also double as a morgue. Dead bodies were dumped both there and nearby, earning the hospital the nickname the "dead house." The dead were counted, then taken outside the next day for a quick and unceremonious burial in the prison's "boneyard." Colonel Bartleson, who worried about his own declining health, took great joy in discovering that one of the dead prisoners left overnight in the boneyard was not there the next day for the burial. Apparently he hadn't been dead and "had walked off in the night." The fact that the guards could not tell if the prisoner was dead or not when they threw his body in a pile points to the shocking state of starvation and deterioration of the prisoners and the regular and high death toll in Libby. The one-armed colonel summed up the situation saying, "The condition of our men was very deplorable." Other prisoners began to comment, "Hell hath a new name."[75]

8

The Libby Lyceum

'Tis twelve o'clock! Within my prison dreary—
My bed upon my hand-sitting so weary,
Scanning the future, musing upon the past,
Pondering the fate that here my lot has cast;
The hoarse cry of the sentry, pacing his beat,
Wakens the echoes of the silent street:
"All is well"!

—Frederick A. Bartleson, Libby Prison, 1863[1]

Irrespective of how busy the men kept themselves or how strong an officer may have been, life inside the notorious Libby Prison eventually wore down everyone, and often rather quickly. For their part, the commandant and guards worried about a mass uprising, which only resulted in even more brutal crackdowns, and, by the end of the war they were unnerved by the inevitability of what was in store for the South and for each of them. Colonel Bartleson empathized, to a degree. Running a murderous prison and dealing with prisoners of war "is far from being an enviable position," he felt. Still, that thought offered little consolation for the fact that the prisoners were never allowed outside, were not permitted to exercise, and faced the constant peril of disease, starvation, and being beaten or shot by the guards.[2] Colonel Fernández Cavada summed it up, saying, "Fear and hate prevailed on both sides of the prison bars."[3]

Libby certainly provided time and inspiration "for reflection" and "incentives" to plan "a new life" after the war, noted Bartleson.[4] Indeed, despite hellish treatment and conditions inside the bastille, those inmates who did not give up hope tried to find a way of coping. The prisoners fought against the boredom and demoralization by entertaining themselves. As Captain Szabad recalled, his fellow prisoners devised all sorts of activities. "There was," he wrote, "no end of amusements."[5] Chess, checkers, and cards—including a popular game called faro[6]—were enjoyed by most of the prisoners. Other amusements, however, took place at night when the guards called "Lights out!" at nine o'clock.[7]

One form of evening "fun" was to sneak to the windows and look for people passing by the prison. Even though the guards had instructions to shoot anyone near a window or anyone passing the "deadline" perimeter around the window, the prisoners learned the sentries' schedules and used the cover of the dark nights to prank the guards and residents of Richmond. If someone appeared below the window, the prisoners would rush forward and throw crusts of hard, inedible bread, old boots, sticks, and whatever else they came upon out the window, pummeling the unsuspecting passersby with a strange assortment of projectiles. They also sang songs, told jokes, and hollered obscenities at Richmond's residents to the extent that the Hungarian freedom fighter quipped, "A stranger passing by Libby at midnight might have imagined himself to be near a lunatic asylum or menagerie!"[8]

The prisoners also risked being shot or punished in order to catch a glimpse of a woman out the window. Szabad recalled that some of the prisoners were excited by spotting a "half-muffled negro-woman pass by" the bastille on a somewhat-regular basis. The prisoners even developed a rule that whenever a woman was seen outside, the prisoner "on watch" would cry out so that his compatriots could race to the windows for a glimpse. According to Szabad, the code they shouted for such occasions was "gun boat."[9] Fernández Cavada called the men's behavior whenever a woman passed by the prison "vulgar rowdyism." This, he recorded, was nevertheless one of the favored pastimes inside Libby.[10]

The windows also brought the encouraging sounds of artillery in the distance and sight of Confederate troops returning from battle. The prisoners in Libby eagerly tried to get a sense of whether the soldiers in gray appeared to have been victorious or not. If it seemed they had suffered defeat, prisoners caused a great commotion. It also gave the "Libbyans" hope. Likewise, whenever Confederate troops marched by, they were "received by derisive shouts and jeers" from the prison windows. Whenever news of a Union battlefield victory arrived in Richmond, the prisoners celebrated it with "the most jubilant cheering, shouting and singing."[11] General Dow described one celebration that lasted for hours. "Often at night the singing was participated in by large numbers of the men, so that patriotic songs would resound for blocks around." Of course, Dow remembered amusingly that the singing was "more noise than harmony." This would continue until angry guards burst into the rooms with orders to quiet down and threats of beatings and other punishments. Of course, as soon as the sentries went back to their posts, the men "sang louder." The goal, said the famous general, was to be "more noisey, and, if possible, less harmonious than before." The celebrations typically ended only when shots were fired at the windows or a prisoner was dragged to the cages in the dungeon.[12]

The other excitement in Libby was when the men heard the prison bell ring. The large bell, loud enough to be heard for blocks, was rung whenever there was an escape. Prisoners would rush to the windows, and chatter would race through the prison as the men tried to figure out what was happening, who had escaped, and whether or not the attempt was successful. The prison's rumor mill, known affectionately as the "Libby grape,"[13] did not subside until word arrived as to whether the prisoner had escaped, been caught . . . or killed.

All these activities were a form of resistance. There were others, including some that occurred at the expense of the cruel but bumbling guards. An endless array of pranks was devised, Bartleson noted, the purpose of which was to offer a "break in the monotony of prison life and furnish something new for conversation." Prisoners stole items from the hapless guards, fed them false information, and devised ways to interrupt the frequent roll-call tallies. "Tricks are played on them," Bartleson observed with delight; "of course, and much pleasure is felt at their perplexity." It was a risky enterprise, however, because the ploys angered the guards. One prisoner, for instance, liked to stick his head out the window then quickly duck back inside. The guards outside would fire their muskets at the open window but miss, prompting the prisoner to throw a brick or rock at the guards while they were reloading.[14]

One alarming development in the prison was the commandant's order that the doors between the large rooms housing prisoners on each floor be "nailed up." Eliminating the prisoners' ability to move from room to room not only limited their interaction with one another but also had the potential to undermine morale. However, after stealing a few tools, the prisoners "sawed through the lower part of the door" separating two of the main rooms—the Streight and Milroy rooms, so named for the senior commanders incarcerated in them—in order to create a small passageway through which they could "pass and repass with pleasure." The hole, recalled Bartleson, also helped the prisoners pull off one of their favorite pranks: undermining the accuracy of the morning roll call. The prisoners delighted in raising a hand or calling out "present" during the tally, then quickly sneaking to another room and repeating the gesture. The dismay on the prison clerk and guards' faces whenever the roll call did not match prison records always brought cheers and jeers from the prisoners.[15]

LETTERS, POEMS, AND SONGS

Among the many well-educated officers and bibliophiles inside the prison, the men often composed poems or songs about the guards, the commandant, and even the

Confederacy. One outpouring of artistic puns came after Richmond newspapers reported that the Confederacy was so desperate that, in early February of 1864—just
days before the large escape from Libby would occur—it proposed that citizens save
their urine. Southern mines had been running short in their production of salt, po-
tassium, and other necessary substances to make gunpowder. Therefore, they were
experimenting with urine, which, when mixed with other ingredients, made a type
of saltpeter. Speaking of the "First Families of Virginia" (FFV), a few prisoners were
inspired to compose a verse:

> A wise and patriotic Reb, a ways and means provider,
> In breaking up the odious web of the bloody Yankee spider
> A raw material gatherer, with talent rare therefore,
> A powder manufacturer, a parasite of war.
> Tho Richmond's papers ask from all in high and lowly station,
> From male and female great and small, the area of the nation.
> We know full well they eat mule soup, of it not half a ration
> But oh! That F.F.V.s should stoop to such humiliation.
> Now matron fair and lovely miss, here's something you can do,
> More worthy far than bless and kiss,
> To help your country thru
> Your ammunition's nature's gift, and costs not e'en a thankee,
> For every time you live your shift, you shoot a bloody Yankee.[16]

Writing and reading both newspapers and letters from home proved invaluable
to the prisoners' mental health. Both pastimes were, however, contingent on receiving care packages from loved ones back home or from charitable organizations. The
food, clothing, and blankets were desperately needed. However, the officers believed
the letters, books, and paper were just as important to their survival. Colonel Bartleson remembered that he and others were "tickled to death, like a child with a new
toy," whenever they got a box or letter. The arrival of boxes and letters inspired "great
joy" among all the prisoners. "Great crowds gather around" and want to know what
gifts were received and if there was any news from home. The prisoners also enjoyed
receiving letters from members of their units and from former prisoners who had
been exchanged. The sharing of the boxes and reading of letters cemented the fra-
ternal bond among the suffering prisoners. They took an interest in one another's
families to the extent that any good or bad news from the home front for one prisoner became the topic of conversation for all the prisoners. Bartleson chuckled that
the common greeting inside Libby was not "How do you do?" or "How goes it?" but
"Have you got a box?" or letter.[17]

Bartleson always requested letters from his own family members, including from
an aunt and his father. He once mentioned in a letter to his wife back in Illinois, "If

there is anyone in Joliet who wishes to write without expecting answers, I should be extremely well pleased to hear from them." The letters from Bartleson's family and especially his wife, Kate, propped up his will to live. News from home offered an important distraction from the reality of prison life. The prisoners understood this. When one of them was too weak or depressed to write, his fellow prisoners would help in drafting letters. Even the stoic Bartleson admitted to his wife, "The only way to keep a journal is to write it whenever you have an opportunity, whether you feel like it or not." If it was not despair, it was the weather. One February night was so "cold and chilly" that the one-armed colonel remembered his hands being too stiff to write. Around the time of the escape, the frigid winds blowing through the prison even dulled his senses, making it hard to compose his thoughts.[18]

In his letters, the heroic colonel would discuss such mundane issues as whether the family should sell their horse. He also asked his wife to send socks and "one or two shirts" and shared news from the prison. When the prisoners did not receive meat for a two-week period, it was reported in his letters. Bartleson admitted to his wife that he did not miss the rotten meat "except for the purpose of making soup." More news came in the form of an announcement that his "messmate" Captain Ewing was a good cook and shared the food from the boxes he received with the other men in his mess. Bartleson recorded that his mess had expanded when two generals joined it—the well-known Neal Dow and Eliakim Scammon, who Bartleson indicated had been captured in West Virginia and liked to play chess all day. While Scammon, it appears, was a good chess player, perhaps the chess master in the prison was a captain named Wilson. Bartleson also shared the struggles and ordeals of the other prisoners with his wife, including the difficulty they all faced trying to "feel clean" and their battles with outbreaks of smallpox. The colonel was, however, always careful to assure her that, while it was "quite bad elsewhere," Libby was manageable. He signed each of his letters to her, "Faithfully, Fred."[19]

Writing letters and keeping a journal or diary inside Libby was difficult for another reason. The severe shortages of paper and ink in the South made them next to impossible to procure. Prisoners were dependent on loved ones sending paper. To that end, the prisoners resorted to writing as small as possible and reusing paper from books and other sources. Making matters worse, during the difficult winter of 1863 and 1864, the commandant suddenly announced that he was limiting the number of letters a prisoner could send or receive and that all letters sent from the prison would be limited to six lines, could only be sent to family members, and would be read by his staff before being loaded onto the cartel ships. One way around the restrictions, recalled General Dow, was that, because chaplains and surgeons "were generally released soon after being brought to Libby," prisoners slipped them letters or whispered messages to be delivered to loved ones. Dow also passed vital intelligence on to Union commanders in this way.[20]

The strict limit of six lines per letter forced prisoners to be creative. In truth, they doubted the marginally literate guards would either read or enforce the commandant's new decree. But they did not want to take the chance that their lifeline home would be severed. The commandant's volatile and violent disposition was such that, should he discover a violation, it was possible he would simply ban letters and paper altogether. One common response to the new policy was to write in bullet points, as is the case in the following letter:

My Dear Wife.—
Yours received –no hopes of exchange –send corn starch –want socks –no money –rheumatism in left shoulder –pickles very good –send sausages –God bless you –kiss the baby –Hail Columbia!
—Your devoted husband[21]

In his continued intelligence feeds to Union commanders, General Dow now had to resort to writing in code. On the back of his letters, the general passed along intelligence to Union leaders using "lemon juice." This trick, said Dow, made the words "invisible to ordinary inspection, but which upon being exposed to heat became perfectly legible." It allowed him to be in "constant correspondence with the authorities at Washington."[22] Writing letters and feeling he was of service to the war effort even while in prison helped the general cope with the "wretchedness" of being incarcerated. He wrote, "I resigned myself entirely to my situation as a prisoner, keeping myself always cheerful, hopeful and buoyant, not only as a matter of duty to my country, and as important to health, but as an example to my comrades in misfortune." He also noted that, like some of the most-senior officers, his rank afforded him slightly less brutal treatment from the commandants and guards, as did the fact that he was also one of the oldest officers and prisoners of the war. In most of his coded reports, Dow reminded the authorities that the struggle within Libby was such that the "conditions were inseparable from a state of war!"[23]

Although the boxes and letters received were a lifeline to the outside world, the prisoners dared not get their hopes up. The guards frequently demanded bribes from the prisoners before delivering the boxes or letters. As the war dragged on, they simply pilfered them outright. Colonel Bartleson remembered that General Winder put Richard Turner, the deputy commandant, in charge of the boxes and letters in February of 1864, the time of the worst suffering inside the prison and the period of the remarkable escape. Turner saw the boxes and letters as yet another way to punish his charges. For instance, the deputy commandant would, according to Bartleson, "most shamefully" withhold the boxes and letters as retribution. He also enjoyed "breaking them open with his hatchet" in an "utterly reckless" way in order to destroy the contents of the boxes. Another punishment was "tumbling the things out so that they are all mixed together." The only upside to the game played with the boxes was that the guards had no interest in stealing the paper, quills, ink, or anything they could not eat or wear.[24]

Colonel Rose criticized the theft of the prisoners' boxes, causing the cruel warden to explain his motive with a sneer, "Why, gentlemen, they are a d—d [damned] sight better goods than you could buy anywhere in Richmond for the money."[25] It pained the prisoners to see the guards eating the food and wearing the clothing sent from home. By late fall of 1863 and the winter of 1864, the cartel ships were simply lined up along the James River. They were not being unloaded, and prisoners, among them Rose and Bartleson, demanded to know why. No answers were given; when they pressed their captors, they were beaten. It was the withholding of boxes and letters that, along with the declining conditions in the prison, prompted Rose to move forward with his plan to escape.[26]

"LICE-SEE-UM"

There was, according to Bartleson, an "academic side" to Libby Prison. Many of the interred officers were well educated and had lived full and accomplished lives before the war. His fellow prisoners, noted the one-armed colonel, constituted "every variety of character and disposition" and "almost every trade and profession," which made the imprisonment a bit more bearable.[27] Lieutenant Wells of Michigan said simply that Libby contained an impressive collection of "masters of science, art, and literature" as well as talented "preachers, painters, sculptors, orators, and poets." In fact, some of the prisoners were so interesting that Bartleson, Wells, and others delighted in tracking down "every rumor" in the "Libby grape" and trying to both guess and discover everyone's backstory.[28]

The prisoners read the local newspapers and any book that may have been sent to the prison by their family members and soon organized something of a circulating library inside Libby. General Dow claimed reading was his main pastime, noting that the books helped him "overcome hardships" in the prison.[29] Bartleson regularly requested books from his wife and friends on such topics as "Rhetoric." When finished with a book, these men collegially added them to the Libby library.[30]

The "Libbyians" also gambled, played cards, and became accomplished whittlers. Chaplains delivered religious services and lectured on morality, abolition, and religion. Senior officers organized "classes" where languages, philosophy, and other subjects were taught, while the more artistic prisoners even put on theatrical performances for one another. Consequently, the wretched bastille of the Confederacy came to resemble a college, art studio, debate society, publishing office, community theater, and classical academy of learning. In short, the men vowed to survive by establishing a "lyceum" that would help pass the time and provide opportunities for enrichment and self-improvement.[31]

The lyceum included regular sermons from the chaplains among the prisoners, including from Reverend Beaudry. To supplement the work of the Union chaplains inside the prison, local leaders and clergy saw to it that a preacher from Richmond would come and offer sermons. Their faith had prompted them to see that the prisoners received spiritual nourishment but apparently not dietary nourishment.[32] The city's bishop, observed Bartleson, preached "two or three times" to the prisoners. However, many of the men sensed a pro-Confederacy tone in his message of salvation, so they called a meeting to decide whether or not they wanted to hear from any more Southern ministers in the future. The vote was "two to one" in favor of continuing with the local preachers; but, noted Bartleson, "the clergy were a little shy after that" and more restrained in their message. Once a Catholic bishop from Ireland was visiting Charleston, South Carolina, and came to Richmond. He delivered a fire-and-brimstone homily on purgatory with great "zeal." It did not go over well with the prisoners, however, who felt themselves already in purgatory. Or hell. After observing the ardent style of the priest, Bartleson walked out.[33]

The prisoners also organized political and governing "conference meetings" as well as lectures and a debate club known jokingly as "the Libby Lice-See-'Um," a clever nod to the ever-present pests that tormented the prisoners. The lyceum covered an array of topics, both serious and light. On September 8, 1863, for instance, the prisoners debated whether they should shave their faces—the affirmative won the debate. The lectures ranged from such practical topics as "cookery," fencing, and mapmaking to classical subjects like philosophy and Latin. There was even a series of talks by one of the prisoners on Franz Mesmer, noted German physician and scientist, and the benefits of hypnosis.[34] One particularly impressive scholar in Libby, Major John Henry of the Fifth Ohio Cavalry, lectured, in the words of Captain Szabad, "eloquently" on the topic of spiritualism.[35]

In addition to offering sermons every two days, Reverend Beaudry, whose family hailed from Canada by way of France, taught a "large" class on the French language. The popular class grew to thirty-nine pupils, which excited the reverend. Later, when the number of participants passed fifty, Beaudry started offering lessons every day. Besides religion, Beaudry's other passions were photography and phonetics, and he taught classes on the topics. The cavalry chaplain also attended other language classes and taught himself stenography while inside Libby.[36]

Colonel Fernández Cavada, who had been born in Cuba, taught his first Spanish class on August 27, 1863. It was a success, and he too began offering it every day. Fernández Cavada humbly suggested the class numbers had less to do with his teaching ability and more to do with the prisoners being stuck in the large rooms most of the day and looking to find a way to pass the time. Either way, the men enjoyed the course and developed some degree of fluency rather quickly.[37] Bartleson described the many languages spoken in Libby as a source for so many classes. Aside from French and Spanish, lessons were given in German, Hungarian, Irish, and Italian from prisoners with roots in those countries.[38] Szabad, himself a former professor of languages back in Hungary, offered classes, and Captain Cornwell, who was taking German classes and making good progress with the language, echoed Bartleson's observation, writing to his wife, "One finds plenty of natives here to talk with."[39]

The most senior commanders in Libby also partook of the classes, sitting alongside young lieutenants and captains, something that, according to military convention, would otherwise have been discouraged. General Dow, for instance, enjoyed "French and German, debating societies and mock courts." He also "studied tactics," both legal and military, from his colleagues. The general who had written Maine's 1851 law against alcohol and would later, in 1880, be the Prohibitionist Party's candidate for president, gave lectures on temperance, including during the difficult winter of 1864, just days prior to the famous escape.[40] Yet, as Captain Wells noted wryly, even though General Dow "treated us now and then to temperance lectures," the topic, "in a practical view, seemed to be quite unnecessary, as food was very scarce and intoxicating drinks absolutely out of the question." Most men would have given much for a hard drink. Still, lectures from the charismatic Dow were popular.[41]

In fact, the most popular class offering inside Libby was a series of five lectures given by Dow "by invitation of my fellow-prisoners" about the state of the war and conditions in the South. The general had been taken from New Orleans to Mobile and across Dixie and had made a careful study of Southern society. Because these talks were so well attended, and given the sensitive topics covered, the prisoners wisely stationed "two or three officers to be on the watch for the incoming of any of the Confederates in charge." When Dow informed his audience that the Confederacy was in collapse, the prisoners "applauded." This outburst attracted the attention of the guards, who stormed into the room. However, "the signal was given" by the prisoners standing watch, and Dow quickly changed the topic of his lecture to temperance, which bored the guards.[42]

Other officers shared their stories of battles and the war, prompting Szabad to boast, "Added to those I knew before entering Libby, I can say that I have now in memory 127 desperate battles all fought within the last two years!"[43] The bastille had covertly become a military academy. Indeed, the prisoners were so accomplished and diverse, said Bartleson, that among them "you could find out, in all probability, what you wanted." Prisoners such as Bartleson and Szabad, while praising the intellectual and creative nature of many of their fellow prisoners, also made it a point to contrast these traits with the Confederate guards and wardens, who, they noted, seemed "disinterested" in anything and befuddled at the slightest question.[44]

"CONCERT ROOM"

During religious services, it was discovered that several of the prisoners were talented singers. Soon, a vocal troupe known as the Libby Prison Minstrels was organized; it quickly became much more popular than the religious services that had inspired it! Not long after its formation, thanks to so much "musical talent," remembered Szabad, several quartets formed among the prisoners, including both classical and popular troupes and one for "negro spirituals." When the "real artists" among the prison population treated the others to barbershop quartets, Szabad claimed, "the like was assuredly never heard" before in a prison. The music lifted the men's spirits and helped them cope with the wretchedness of prison life. The prisoners especially enjoyed singing at nights, the louder the better, prompting frustrated guards to burst into the rooms, screaming "Lights out!" This is when the entire population in Libby would chime in, which Szabad likened to the "braying of the ass, the cackling of the hen, the hoarse barking of the mastiff . . . the whining of the new-born infant!"[45]

The success of the classes and vocal performances prompted the men to add "theatricals," as they were known in the prison, including concerts, dances, and plays, which were "very popular among the prisoners." They even designated one of the rooms as "The Libby Concert Room."[46] The number of prisoners wanting to sing grew, and men came forward who had experience acting. This inspired the prisoners to undertake a full production of a dramatic play. Unfortunately, as Colonel Bartleson remembered, "it was such a fizzle that a second one was not attempted." However, he and others agreed that the concerts were "respectable."[47]

In 1863, the prisoners also organized an Independence Day celebration. Speakers were selected, and the men tried to save a few precious nonperishables from their meager rations for the event. However, Bartleson pointed out to his fellow prisoners, "Whoever heard of a Fourth of July celebration without a flag? You might as well attempt to have a wedding without a bride." An answer came in the form of prisoners who had red, white, and blue shirts and were willing to tear pieces of the fabric into strips in order to sew a flag. A small committee was appointed for the task, and they produced a passable flag, complete with stars and stripes. It was received by the other prisoners with much joy and appreciation. The ceremony included a remembrance of their "comrades fallen" and the "sufferings, sacrifices, wounds, imprisonments" of so many soldiers. There was a prayer, a reading of the Declaration of Independence by one of the soldiers who had memorized the sacred document, and a keynote address. Of course, the prisoners were careful "not to applaud lest the guard might come in and interrupt" the celebration.[48]

But that was precisely what happened. The prisoners had crammed together in the "Libby Concert Room" but had been *too* quiet. Singers had performed in hushed voices, and speakers held forth in little more than whispers. However, the lack of any noise aroused suspicion among the guards, who burst into the room and announced, "By order of the Colonel Commanding, this fuss must be stopped!" The prisoners were ordered to disperse at once. Angered, Colonel Streight confronted the head guard and questioned him in a commanding tone, "Do I understand you to say that we can't celebrate the Fourth of July here?"[49]

To the men's disappointment, the chief of the guards retorted, "Yes, you can't do it. They ain't been celebratin' the Fourth of July down here for a long time!" The guard even claimed, "In South Carolina it hain't been heard of since 1832." The pronouncement and orders to halt the ceremony outraged the prisoners, and a tense standoff ensued. Many more guards raced into the room along with Commandant Thomas Turner and the deputy commandant, Richard Turner. It was then that the Confederates saw the homemade flag the prisoners had placed on the wall. Bartleson recalled the awkward moment, writing of the warden, "I never saw a man look at a flag so long and intently as he did that."[50]

The commandant gave the order: "That flag must come down!" One of the prisoners who had served under General Ulysses Grant in Mississippi stepped forward and roared, "Let any man touch that flag if he dares." An army of guards lurched forward at the ready, but the proud prisoner stood his ground. Major Turner ordered more guards "within a call" to the room, then repeated the order, "Take down that flag!" No one moved—prisoner or guard. The order was given two more times, but the prisoners refused to obey. Amid the standoff, Turner and a small army of guards fought their way violently through the defiant prisoners and tore down the flag themselves. They wisely and promptly hurried back downstairs.[51]

Undeterred, the prisoners continued the ceremony for another five hours. The next day, they received word that General George Meade and the Army of the Potomac had soundly defeated Robert E. Lee's massive Confederate army at Gettysburg, and there was much "rejoicing." Bartleson said of the exciting news, "You should have heard us cheer!" It was sweet revenge.[52]

The prisoners also organized grand musical performances for Christmas Eve of 1863 and New Year's Day of 1864. The events occurred just as the prison was going through its worst period in terms of overcrowding, disease, hunger, and deaths. Captain Szabad said that the timing of the theatrics was not by coincidence. The prisoners even made a playbill, which announced humorously, "Admission free. Children in arms not admitted." Programs were secretly distributed throughout the prison, detailing the acts and performers, all without the guard's permission or knowledge.[53]

Szabad thoroughly enjoyed the musical and vocal performances. One night, while walking back to his bunk after one particularly delightful evening of song, Szabad passed Colonel Luigi Palma di Cesnola, an Italian aristocrat and diplomat who had received the Medal of Honor for his actions during the Civil War. Cesnola, who would later become the first director of the Metropolitan Museum of Art in New

York, stopped Szabad with the words, "A million for a drink!" The aristocrat was holding a bottle of wine he had received from his contacts outside the prison. Szabad eagerly accepted, and the men drank and talked in "clear moonlight" near the window, unconcerned whether a passing guard would try to shoot at them. "Quaffing the sweet bitters till the last drop was gulped," remembered the Hungarian officer, they found a way to momentarily escape the horrors of the bastille.[54]

THE *LIBBY CHRONICLE*

The men inside Libby were desperate for news of the war and the outside world. Unfortunately, letters and boxes from home were often delayed or stolen. Shipping on the James River during the war was as unpredictable as the temperament of Libby's commandant. That left Richmond's newspapers. The city had a few newspapers, which were made available to the prisoners, most probably because these dailies and weeklies functioned as little more than mouthpieces of the Confederate government; they were filled with pro-Confederate propaganda, overly optimistic assessments of the war, a nonstop barrage of attacks against President Lincoln, the Union, and the city's prisoners. Indeed, a free press was not one of the principles embraced by the Confederate government. Despite all this and the newspapers' unreliability, the officers inside the prison devoured these papers.

Desperate for reading materials, and hoping to prop up morale inside the bastille, one enterprising preacher and amateur poet started his own "newspaper" in the prison. Reverend Beaudry organized a small newsletter called the *Libby Chronicle* that was released under the caption, "Devoted to Facts and Fun." Beaudry was, in many ways, an unlikely writer and editor. As a young man, he had been only marginally literate but had sought to improve his condition through self-study. His passion for writing had also come late—at nineteen, when he had started keeping a diary. At the time of his death, it would amount to a whopping twenty-seven volumes. Beaudry also published the issues of the *Libby Chronicle* as a book in 1889.[55] The year the war ended, he also penned a book about the Fifth New York Cavalry.

Libby's own paper contained an array of writings, musings, jokes, poetry, and "limericks" to "make light of" the brutal conditions in the bastille and help inspire the prisoners. In Beaudry's own words, the *Chronicle* had "some very interesting articles." Unfortunately, because of the shortage of paper, ink, and other materials throughout the South, and especially inside the prison, Reverend Beaudry was forced to often read his paper to the other prisoners.[56] The first "issue" was completed on August 21, 1863; it was a smashing success. So the chaplain started preparing a second issue, for August 27. Each Friday during the summer and fall of 1863, a new issue would be read aloud to the prisoners. That first issue contained a story written as a poem titled "Homer Modernized." It was an ode to lice. Given the infestation inside the prison, it was well received. It read,

> Of Libby's rebel lice,
> To us the direful spring,
> Of woes and pains unnumbered,
> O ye muses sing.[57]

To be sure, one of the main features of the *Chronicle* was the poetry written by Beaudry and the other prisoners. The conditions inside the prison seem to have prompted an academy of poets. One of the more popular poems was a sarcastic account of the nearby prison Castle Thunder, released under the same name, which included the following lines:

> We have eighteen kinds of food, though 'twill stagger your belief,
> Because we have bread, beef and soup, then bread, soup and beef,
> Then we sep'rate around with 'bout twenty in a group,
> And thus we get beef, soup and bread, and beef, bread and soup;
> For dessert we obtain, though it costs us nary red,
> Soup, bread and beef, (count it well) and beef and soup and bread.[58]

"Castle Thunder" occasioned a host of humorous replies and sarcastic contributions to subsequent issues of the newsletter. The following Friday's paper included an editorial by Beaudry saying that, "Yielding to pressing demand from those who heard and from many who did not hear the poem entitled 'Castle Thunder,' we reproduce it this week. We are certain that the uproarious laughter caused by this facetious article . . . has done more good in Libby than cartloads of Confederate medicine."[59] Indeed it did. The prisoners poured forth their wit, frustration, and hopes in verse, the *Chronicle* gave them the perfect outlet.

The *Chronicle* also reflected one of the popular pastimes in Libby: gossip. Referring to the way the men passed their time, Colonel Bartleson recalled, "Such a place for rumors, I think, was never before heard of."[60] The *Chronicle* also contained more serious articles about the war; one common topic was President Lincoln's handling of the war. Understandably, many prisoners felt their government was not doing enough to free them, even though most of the officers understood the complexities of prisoner exchanges and the benefit it provided the Confederacy. The *Chronicle* therefore defended Lincoln. In one opinion piece, it took aim at the president's critics—including the Richmond newspapers—with the words, "These officers evince more the spirit of spoiled children than that of manly courage and intelligence which should characterize the actions of the American soldier."[61]

Part III

TUNNEL

9

"The Underground Road to Liberty"

I bound them by a solemn oath to secrecy and strict obedience.

—Thomas E. Rose, Libby Prison, 1864[1]

By the fall of 1863 and into the early weeks of 1864, Richmond's economy had all but ceased to function, impacting food and medical supplies that had already been meager. At the same time, prisoner exchanges and the delivery of boxes stopped, the prison population ballooned to over 1,200, and the overcrowding precipitated a string of diseases that tore through the bastille of the Confederacy. The deterioration of the conditions in Libby began in late September with the arrival of a large group of prisoners from Maryland, many of whom were malnourished and sick upon arrival. In October, food rations further plummeted, and both Confederate soldiers and Richmond's residents began to starve. Generals, quartermasters, and politicians blamed one another. That month, the paltry rations of meat in Libby ended entirely. Prisoners began to die. The city's newspapers and Libby's commandant began to worry that the situation was so grave that the prisoners might attempt a mass breakout and revolt in the city. A rumor swirled that a Confederate informant inside the prison had heard the prisoners planning an uprising. He notified the commandant, who cracked down on the prisoners.[2]

By November, there were also rumors of a large Union force coming to liberate the city's prisoners. The *Richmond Examiner* warned that prisoners would take to the streets and burn the city to the ground, writing, "Richmond and the prisoners were to blaze at their backs, and the flaming homesteads that dot the Williamsburg road were to form their guide—'a pillar of fire by night, a cloud by day.'"[3] General Winder, Libby's provost marshal, came under pressure to implement further security measures. He complained, "No force under my command can prove adequate to the control of 13,000 hungry prisoners." Commandant Turner doubled the guard detail and curtailed what remained of any liberties inside Libby.[4]

Through November and into December, conditions only further devolved while Richmond fell into the grips of fear. From inside Libby, General Dow managed to get a message to the Union's secretary of war, Edwin Stanton, on November 13, describing the chaos in Richmond and painting a grim picture of the prospects for the unfortunate prisoners suffering in the bastille. Of Richmond, the general noted, "The officers here are very earnest that rebel officers, prisoners, may be placed immediately on precisely the same level that we occupy." The deteriorating conditions throughout Richmond had only hardened Southern hearts and resolve. As for the prisoners starving and now freezing inside Libby, Dow described the situation: "We sleep on the floor without blankets except as we obtain them from our friends. Only one of our rooms has glass; all the others, five in number, have open windows, free to the sweep of the northers." The general advocated action, because both the city of Richmond and its prisoners were on the cusp of perishing. "I am inclined to think," he grimly concluded, "that the starvation rations that we get are due to the extreme poverty of the rebel Government . . . It is very easy to see that the rebellion cannot possibly run on much longer, but must perish from mere inanition."[5]

Most likely, in response to Dow's request, the Union and several sanitary commissions shipped blankets, clothing, and food. The arrival that December of boxes and packages likely saved lives inside Libby. It was only a temporary relief from the suffering, however, because most of the items failed to be delivered. The guards again continued their "wretched jobbing," as Captain Szabad described it, of the boxes.[6] In the words of General Neal Dow, "Every package and can was broken open, and the contents were poured promiscuously into a blanket, so that everything ran in together."[7] Sadly, supplies sent for the Union prisoners were now feeding Richmond's residents and prison guards.

After the surprise delivery of boxes, the Confederacy again cut off all shipments. Captain Szabad later remembered that the imprisoned officers were so desperate and so few provisions had made it past the pilfering guards that, despite their careful rationing, the food was gone "in less than a fortnight."[8] General Dow recorded on December 14 that he had received "information that no more supplies will be allowed to come from our Government or any other quarter."[9] The Confederacy's decision was in response to a complaint from Union authorities that the supplies and food they were sending to Southern prisons was being diverted to feed the Rebel Army. Likewise, that same month the federal government lodged another complaint about the treatment of Union prisoners in Richmond, with particular attention paid to Libby. The Confederacy denied the accusations and then implemented even more extreme measures.[10]

The Christmas of 1863 was marked inside the prison by severe rations of food and hopelessness. It came with the very real prospect that many of the prisoners would not see the New Year. Some prisoners felt that only the holiday concert and performance was helping to keep hope alive inside the bastille. Then a holiday surprise appeared: Captain Szabad described a curious clamor inside the prison when a large ship flying the flag of truce docked alongside Libby on December 26. He estimated that five hundred Confederate soldiers were milling about, suggesting to the prisoners that a very large exchange was about to happen. The men rushed to the windows, hoping their luck had turned. Cheers erupted within the prison, and bets were placed. "Such were the scenes exhibited in the prison on that day," recalled Szabad. No word arrived in the prison, but the ship remained at the dock, with soldiers in gray at her side. Szabad and Fernández Cavada excitedly exchanged their theories as to what was happening. "In this state of happy expectation," the two immigrant officers remembered, "we lived for three days." While they waited for the anticipated exchange, several prisoners perished from starvation.[11]

FROM BAD TO WORSE

Ultimately, their hopes were dashed—as so often had been the case before. There was to be no exchange, and the prisoners never received an explanation as to what had happened to prevent it. They did hear word outside the window and read accounts in the Richmond newspapers that General William W. Averell was raiding Confederate towns and defenses just outside town. Unfortunately, he was stopped just short of Richmond. Szabad, Fernández Cavada, Rose, and others hoped General Averell would at least capture Lynchburg, an important outpost that provided both supplies for and the defense of the Confederate capital. The news worsened, however, when the prisoners discovered that Averell had stopped at Salem, some sixty miles away from Lynchburg. There was no Union victory, no rescue attempt at Libby, and no prisoner exchange—not even boxes!

It was then announced again by the commandant that the Confederacy would no longer be permitting boxes of food and goods sent from benevolent societies and the US government. However, the issuing of yet another stern decree was followed by yet another walk-back. The Confederacy simply needed prisoner exchanges and the food looted from boxes sent by the North in order to stay in the fight. Just days later, on New Year's Day of 1864, another ship arrived at dock. Although it did not fly the hoped-for flag of truce, several crates containing boxes for the prisoners were unloaded. Inside Libby, the men were so desperate for good news that cheers of delight were heard throughout the prison. In anticipation of boxes of food, the prisoners "set tables" and planned a "festive" celebration. Pangs of hunger mixed with the frustration of waiting overtook the excitement when the "authorities delayed delivering these goods," most likely out of contempt and so that they could pillage supplies. Eventually, however, a few boxes were delivered, although the commandant provided no wood for cooking. Once again, much of the contents of the boxes had been stolen. It was, as Szabad remembered, yet another "cruel disappointment." In a great act of generosity and collegiality, the prisoners who had received boxes shared them with those who had not, and, though delayed, New Year's was celebrated.[12]

There would be no more exchanges of prisoners or delivery of boxes that winter. The commandant also announced that rations would be further reduced in January. They now amounted to less than what a man needed per day to just stay alive. As described by Szabad, the hard, stale bread was replaced by "tasteless, flat corn cakes," while "sundry rat-tailed sweet potatoes" were substituted for any meat. That winter, Libby descended into a "starvation panic." As bad as the food rations now were, Szabad noted that "panics of a more serious nature" also began that winter. Beatings and death threats were doled out with increasing frequency by the guards. The "retaliations" from the cruel commandant included forcing the "drawing of lots," whereby one of the prisoners would be "singled out of a few officers, either for sentence of death, or hard labor imprisonment."[13]

At the same time, as General Dow noted, the New Year brought brutally cold weather, which increased exponentially the existing struggles inside the bastille. It had, he maintained, reached "crisis" levels. Colonel Rose had begun planning his escape the moment he had been captured. However, he was prompted to expedite his plans by the desperation within Libby that winter.[14]

SCOUTING

Libby's commandant and Richmond's newspapers boasted that the facility was escape-proof. Nonetheless, there had been some attempts to escape Libby, along with a few successful breakouts. The prisoners, including Rose and Hamilton, were inspired by these few efforts. However, the prisoners risked a lot: If they were not killed in the attempt, those who were captured faced severe punishment and the possibility of being shot. Moreover, the odds were not good for the prisoners. There were few doors in or out of the former warehouse. The guards monitored access to the high windows on the second and third floors and patrolled the perimeter of the compound day and night. If a man managed to get out of the prison itself, he was still in Richmond, the heart of the Confederacy; soldiers in gray were stationed throughout the city, and defensive positions ringed the capital. The vast majority of the residents were loyal to "the cause" and could therefore be counted on to report, turn in, or kill any suspected escapee. On top of everything else, it would be a long and precarious race to the nearest Union camp, especially for a starving, barely clothed, and unprovisioned prisoner.

Some prisoners tried to gain access to the doors on the first floor and then simply walk past the guards. Others went to the hospital on the first floor, where there were few sentries, and then tried to get out through the morgue or "dead room" next to it. A few of the more foolish prisoners attempted to overpower the guards. Other plans were more elaborate, including bribing the guards or getting to a nearby arms depot, where the prisoners hoped to snatch weapons and lead a rebellion to liberate Libby, Belle Isle, and other prisons in the city. Most prisoners viewed such zealous plans as little more than "misadventure," and most attempts failed spectacularly.[15] Moreover, at the first hint of a possible breakout, the commandant responded by doubling the guards. Sentries were also stationed at nearby sites, such as the arms depot, city hospital, and dock; cannons were aimed at the bastille, ready to fire on the prison in the event of a mass uprising or escape.[16]

But one small hope remained: one of the guards was of "Northern birth"; he had been conscripted into the Confederate army. It was suspected that he "was at heart a Unionist" and open to taking bribes to aid the prisoners. Therefore, some prisoners tried to use the Yankee guard to pass notes to other prisoners and to Unionists on the outside. The problem was that the prisoners did not know whether or not he could be bribed or trusted. It was also known that the commandant of the bastille had a few informants among the prison population, prompting the prisoners to worry about which of their comrades could be trusted with "sagacity and fidelity" and which were "snitches." Any mention of escape was therefore consigned to whispers. Sure enough, as Rose was preparing his plan to escape, the prisoners caught "a suspected spy in our midst." This only heightened mistrust and precautions. General Dow was asked to officiate in a mock trial of the traitor. With the other prisoners acting as the jury, the turncoat was found guilty of "treachery." His punishment: "to hang the fellow." There were, the general remembered, "strong suspicions" of other suspected spies among the prison population, prompting Rose and Hamilton to be especially cautious about sharing even their hopes of escape, much less a single detail of their plans with anyone.[17]

It was amid the deteriorating conditions in the bastille and during a "dark, stormy night" in late October of 1863 that Colonel Rose had decided it was time to escape. "At length, after gazing at the fields and forests beyond the James," the burly colonel remembered, "[I] resolved to make the attempt to escape."[18] It was either that or die. Rose's soon-to-be-friend Major Hamilton described Rose as "pale, sallow, resurrected-looking" that winter, "reduced to the narrowest possible limits."[19] But Rose was different from most of the prisoners. While he was, like other officers suffering in the prison, a loyal Unionist and combat veteran who had distinguished himself on the battlefield, Rose was quiet and generally kept to himself. Some of the prisoners whose letters and writings survived the war recalled that he had always seemed preoccupied; after the incredible escape, many were not surprised.

Lieutenant Frank E. Moran of the Seventy-Third New York Infantry remembered Rose: "From the hour of his coming," Moran later wrote, "a means of escape became him constant and eager study; and, with this purpose in view, he made a careful and minute survey of the entire premises." Some prisoners even likened the big colonel to a "monomaniac" because he "mused incessantly upon" escape. One prisoner noted that "eating, walking and sleeping the idea obsessed his brain" and that Rose "can't get it out of his head." He would emerge as the leader of the audacious plan to break out of the notorious bastille.[20]

As soon as Rose had been processed at Libby, the former principal had begun scouting the entire prison for weaknesses in security, observing the trends of the sentry detail, and gazing out the windows at the nearby canal and streets. "Night after night," Rose had watched the guards, documenting the paths of their patrols and timing their movements as well as the location of streetlamps. It was easier to conduct his survey at nights, when there were far fewer prying eyes inside Libby. Furthermore, the guards generally avoided the rooms full of prisoners because of the prevalence of disease and the foul smell—and particularly at night, as it would be unsafe for any guard to be around so many desperate prisoners.[21]

After the prisoners had cut secret passageways into the two upstairs floors when the commandant had ordered the doors sealed, Rose was able to move between rooms at night when the prisoners were unguarded, and he knew from visits to the kitchen that each floor was connected by steep and narrow stairways. The problem was that the guards remained on the first floor at night, locked the few doors out of the prison, watched the windows, and continually patrolled the perimeter of the grounds. Open fields sat on two sides of the former warehouse, with the front and back bordered by a street on one side and the narrow alley and canal on the other. There were options for escaping that were forming in Rose's mind, but none of them seemed good.

Then, one rainy evening, long after the other prisoners had fallen asleep, Rose crept out of his assigned room, climbed the stairway to the top floor, and walked quietly to an isolated window on the west side of the building. Early that morning workers had been outside the window, repairing part of the roof of the prison. As he peered into the night sky, Rose noticed that the high scaffolding used by the work crew was still standing against the western outer wall of the prison. Rose reasoned that, in the downpour, the workers must have run for shelter without removing the scaffolding; with the storm lasting all day and into the night, the guards has still not bothered to remove it. Sentries always patrolled all four sides of Libby. But not that night. It might be a means of escaping!

The colonel was not alone in his desire to escape. Many prisoners obsessed over the idea of breaking out of Libby. Colonel Bartleson admitted, "I think of a release from Libby" always, noting his stay in the facility seemed to be an "eternity."[22] Colonel Fernández Cavada echoed his colleagues. "A prisoner, if he deserves the name, is always more or less occupied with the idea of making his escape," he explained.[23] Another prisoner determined to escape was Major Hamilton, the cavalry officer from Kentucky.

As Rose began climbing out the window to see if he could reach the scaffolding, a lightning strike momentarily illuminated the night sky. In the flash of light, Rose saw that he was not alone. The image of a man standing near him startled the colonel. He was in luck: In the glimmer, both men's faces appeared. It was not a guard. It turned out to be Hamilton. Unbeknownst to one another, Rose and Hamilton had, at the same time, snuck to the same window, seen the scaffolding, and tried to climb onto the high platform. Neither man panicked; rather, in a hushed tone, they exchanged a few cautious words. After a tense moment, both men decided the distance to the scaffolding was too far. They climbed back through the window, wet and cold, and snuck back to their assigned rooms.[24]

THE PLAN

From the large windows on the east side of the prison in what was known as the "Gettysburg Room," Rose could peer across a vacant lot. There were two buildings on the other side of the lot that faced the canal. Rose estimated the space across the open lot to the buildings to be roughly seventy feet. These facts he filed away. The burly colonel also inspected the view from the south windows. He observed the comings-and-goings of the guards, soldiers, merchants, and sailors by the canal and James River, which ran parallel to one another, separated by a narrow strip of land. In the springtime and after heavy rains, the area by the canal flooded, and the high water poured into the cellar of Libby. On such occasions, "enormous swarms of rats come out from the lower doors and windows of the prison and [would] head for dry land in swimming platoons." When the rodents raced out of the prison, it was "amid the cheers of the prisoners in the upper windows." The regular event became something of a spectacle at the bastille. Amid the cheering from his comrades, Rose noticed something else: The rats escaped from a sewer, one large enough that workers had once descended into it. The sewer, running east and west by the prison and to the canal, might be used to escape![25]

It became apparent to Rose that he needed to get into the cellar of the prison to see if it connected to the sewer and thereby might hold the means to escape. The challenge was how to get to the cellar: He would have to sneak out of his room, find a door that was not bolted, and make his way quietly to the first floor. One possibility was the kitchen, as the offices and quarters for the commandant and guards as well as the hospital were, for obvious reasons, impractical. It was time to find out. A few nights after the encounter with Hamilton by the window, Rose took a small candle and headed downstairs. He discovered that the door to the cellar was unlocked. He simply opened the door and descended into the claustrophobic cellar. Once in the dark, dank dungeon, he was greeted by a sea of rats that scurried in every direction. The walls were cold and austere, and the cellar appeared to contain little more than an old, unused carpentry shop and a few tiny cells for isolating problem prisoners. And, of course, there were rats.

Suddenly, the sensation that he was not alone haunted Rose. Someone else was in the cellar. Was he about to be caught? Attacked? A form moved in the dark before being silhouetted by the light of Rose's candle. Amazingly, for a second time, it was Hamilton. The odds that the two men's paths would again cross in the dead of night and while trying to escape was not lost on them. A muffled greeting followed a nervous exhale.

Rose and Hamilton quickly gained one another's confidence and agreed to work together. The cavalry officer described meeting Rose, whom he said was "strong-willed" and "with [the] courage of steel." "Our acquaintance ripened into a mutual friendship and we soon had the full confidence of each other." Throughout the late fall of 1863, the two men "discussed the project" of escaping in detail. Hamilton not only recognized Rose as his senior in rank but also considered the colonel among the "front rank" of all the prisoners. He would support the colonel in every way. It helped that they both bunked in the Lower Chickamauga Room. This made their nightly forays through the prison easier. Additionally, just like Rose, the major was chafing under confinement. He complained that the days and months in Libby were "going by like scarcely moving tears" while the nights were "like black blots dying out of a dream of horror."[26]

Hamilton also brought a valuable skill set to the partnership. He had been a homebuilder before the war and was therefore handy with tools and understood the architecture of buildings. The Kentuckian would soon prove himself to be an innovative problem solver during the difficult attempt to escape. The two men knew there were likely informants among the prisoner population, but they trusted each other and agreed to tell no one else about their plan.

After scouting the prison, they ruled out the feasibility of jumping from a high window. A broken leg or ankle suffered in the effort would impede their ability to run, and Rose was still nursing a broken left foot from his failed attempt to escape during the train ride to the prison. If they could obtain enough heavy rope, they might scale down the side of the window. However, such an effort still failed to account for the guards that kept watch on the windows and patrolled the grounds around the prison. Moreover, the commandant was about to order iron bars be installed in every window. The two men also rejected an effort to simply charge and overpower the armed guards on the first floor or outside the prison. It might attract other armed guards, and they were not sure they could even make it outside of the prison from the first floor. Other ideas were abandoned as well. The best bet remained the unlocked door to the cellar and the sewer, which they had to somehow access.

Rose informed his coconspirator that he had been captured during the Mexican-American War fifteen years earlier and had escaped by tunneling out of the stockade soon after being caught; he would do it again. Hamilton agreed. Rose decided they would escape by digging a tunnel from the cellar beneath the prison, possibly using the connecting sewer. It was a repulsive thought, but it also offered the best chance of getting beyond the prison grounds undetected. Moreover, because the cellar was pitch-black and infested by rats, the guards avoided it; they also avoided the sewer for obvious reasons. There were no easy ways out of the prison, and even this plan was fraught with difficulties. However, Rose and Hamilton were "earnest in purpose, unwearied in persevering." With so many "additional hardships [that] afflicted the prisoners" that fall and winter, the two men agreed that the escape had to occur as soon as possible. The prison was running out of food and they out of options.[27]

Rose and Hamilton worried about the viability of the cellar. With the prison population soaring in the fall of 1863, the commandant was forced to organize a second kitchen. They assumed the spare kitchen in the cellar was the reason why the door to the dungeon had been left unlocked. The problem was that, if Rose and Hamilton excavated from the cellar, the prisoners who went there to cook might see the results of their labor. The two partners then immediately encountered an obstacle: When sneaking back down to the first floor, they discovered that the door to the cellar was now bolted shut. They had to find another way to get inside.

There was a "hospital" on the first floor next to the kitchen and directly above the east cellar. The large, multipurpose room opposite the kitchen had been converted to a hospital in October of 1863 to accommodate the burgeoning population of sick prisoners. Rose and Hamilton decided they could not use the hospital to access the cellar because there were too many sick prisoners occupying cots there and the physicians and orderlies shared a small apartment on the north side of the room. There were simply too many eyes and ears that might detect their movements and digging. Moreover, the large doors from the physicians' office opened to Cary Street, and guards were always posted just outside.

Nor could the two men try to access the cellar from the room on the west side of the first floor, as it contained the offices and barracks for the guards and prison officials. However, from the kitchen area, there was a stairway and an old door. If pried open, it led down stairs to the second, ad hoc kitchen in the cellar. It was not a perfect plan, but it was worth a try. The prisoners snuck down the stairs to the kitchen to inspect the door to the east cellar. It was an option! However, to their dismay, that plan was placed in jeopardy just one week after they had surveilled the cellar and prepared to begin digging. Two prisoners escaped by getting into the cellar and sawing through the wooden bars on the ground-level windows there. In response, the commandant imposed new security measures: both doors to the cellar were bolted shut, and iron bars were installed on the windows. The next night, Rose and Hamilton snuck down to the first floor and discovered that the doors had "been tightly nailed" shut.[28] As Hamilton remembered, "This was a sore misfortune, for this apartment was the only possible base of successful tunnel operations."[29]

In the final days of 1863, as the two men were contemplating other ways to access the cellar, an unexpected prisoner exchange was announced. Rose and Hamilton wondered if one or both of them might be transferred out of Libby. They were not. However, because several prisoners along with the chaplains and surgeons among them were exchanged to alleviate the severe overcrowding, the commandant no longer needed the spare kitchen in the cellar to feed the large population. That was good news. The bad news was that, what with fewer prisoners in the bastille, and with the constant threat of another prisoner escape, he had ordered the spare kitchen "shut off." The cauldrons were carried out of the cellar and placed outside the prison. The entrance was boarded up, and all the cooking was transferred to the main kitchen. At least the cellar would be empty. Rose and Hamilton could excavate their tunnel without worrying about the spare kitchen, but the matter of getting into the cellar remained.[30]

The east cellar stairs were now sealed, and the west cellar both housed Black prisoners and was directly below the guards' barracks. That left the middle cellar. Rose had observed workers going in and out of that cellar. So, the two men snuck downstairs. The doors were bolted shut, so Rose used a piece of wood he had found and whittled into the shape of a lever. From the corner of the kitchen directly above the middle cellar, Rose wedged the wooden lever into a lose plank in the floor. The powerful colonel carefully but forcibly pried the floorboard open just enough for Hamilton to squeeze through and drop down into the middle cellar. What he saw was not good. Disheartened, Hamilton was pulled back up through the hole in the kitchen by Rose's strong hand. Although the middle cellar was empty, there was an enormous "heavy wall between the cellar from the carpenter's shop." It would be next to impossible to dig through such a thick wall with limited tools. Likewise, if anyone went into the middle room, the hole in the wall would easily be discovered.[31]

The two prisoners were in agreement: "There was only one way for us to get out of the prison, and that was to dig out." They just needed to get down into the east cellar undetected. "After considerable deliberation," this time it was Hamilton who "arrived at the conclusion." They would somehow use the main kitchen in the middle warehouse to get into the east cellar. From there they could tunnel southeast, toward the sewer and canal, emerging on the periphery of the prison grounds near Kerr's Warehouse, which could be used for cover. Rose put a positive spin on the plan, telling Hamilton that the sewer would be their "underground road to liberty."[32]

10

"Rat Hell"

They had a rope to make descent
From window sill to street pavement,
And silver watches two in number
To give the guard to hold their thunder.
Then came the point of all the worst,
Who shall run the gauntlet first.
For plain it was for he who did
Of the enterprise its danger hid,
If the guards intent was them to slay
Or otherwise the plot betray
Why he it was, was shot or struck
Or in a dungeon mourned his luck.

—Robert Cornwell, Libby Prison, 1864[1]

From now on, after the prisoners had fallen fast asleep and the bustle of the crowded rooms had quieted down, Colonel Rose and Major Hamilton would sneak down to the kitchen. They would take one of two routes, depending on whether or not a sentry was posted on the steep staircase and on where the guards were patrolling on the first floor. One option was from Milroy's Room—so named for the officers who had served under General Robert Huston Milroy and been captured during the fighting at the Second Battle of Winchester; the other path was from the Chicka-mauga Room—named for that bloody battle. Fortunately, after the fall of 1863, there was a shortage of guards, that both the stairwell and kitchen were usually not secured. The kitchen was full in the mornings and again during the second meal, but it was empty after the lights-out order each evening at nine o'clock. As such, Rose and Hamilton could only work on their tunnel in the middle of the night, which had been Rose's intention anyway.

So, getting to the kitchen was possible; the problem was now getting into the east cellar, nearest the sewer. Unfortunately, as noted earlier, the stairwell to the cellar was now sealed with a bolted door and often patrolled by guards. Directly below the kitchen was the middle cellar, but a thick, sturdy wall separated the middle and east cellars. It would be impossible to breach, and the evidence of any attempt would give the plan away. Rose and Hamilton needed another way into the east cellar. And so, in the dim light cast across the kitchen from a lantern outside, they quietly canvassed the empty room, which they had earlier studied during their daytime meals. Rose estimated the kitchen was roughly one hundred by forty-five feet in size and contained "several long pine tables with permanent seats attached, such as may be commonly seen at picnic grounds."[2] This is where the prisoners ate their meals and lounged while cooking. The planking from one of these tables would soon aid the prisoners in their escape. It also had two old, large stoves, one of which was about ten feet from the door opening to the sidewalk on Cary Street. Behind the larger of the two stoves and against a brick wall was an expansive fireplace with piles of firewood next to it. That, decided the two men, was the key to accessing the cellar.

Hamilton reasoned that they might be able to remove the bricks behind the fireplace and tunnel downward. The fireplace was almost never used, so no one would notice the bricks in the back of it, especially if the two prisoners took care to replace them each morning. It offered the shortest and least-detectable path to the cellar. However, because the fireplace sat above the wall separating the middle and east cellars below, they would have to dig at an angle before dropping down into the east cellar. Also, while the passageway to the cellar would need to be wide enough for a man to squeeze through, it could not breach the wall by the hospital above them or the wall by the carpentry shop below them. Therefore, Hamilton suggested, they should make the passageway from the back of the fireplace "just far enough" to pass the wall below, making sure "to preserve the hospital intact." From there, they would "then cut downward to a point below the level of the hospital floor" and do so in the shape of a "Z." Such an angle would allow them to emerge in the east cellar. Rose agreed with the plan.[3]

They could only work at night, and it would be a meticulous and time-consuming job to dig out the bricks by the fireplace and then cover up all evidence of their nightly escapades each morning before roll call and breakfast. Hundreds of prisoners and the Libby staff congregated around the stoves each day. That meant the bricks had to be replaced and soot and ash spread around the fireplace before pushing the old stoves back into place. There were other challenges: During the excavation, they would have to be quiet so as to not alert the guards outside the door or the prisoners in the hospital next to the kitchen. Rose proposed allowing the prisoners ample time to fall asleep after the call for lights-out before beginning their nightly escapade. Therefore, the colonel proposed they work from ten at night until four in the morning, allowing enough time to be back in their assigned rooms before the "earliest risers would again stir," the morning reveille, and the guards assumed their daily posts. They were close enough to Castle Thunder to hear the "all is well" announcement made each morning at four o'clock. That would be their cue to complete the nightly digging.

At least, that was the plan.

THE PASSAGEWAY

On the evening of December 19, 1863, the two prisoners pushed aside the two large stoves to access the unused fireplace behind them and begin their excavation. After brushing all the soot and ash into a blanket, they began the laborious task of removing the mortar that held the bricks in place, using a small knife given to Hamilton by Colonel Miles. It was painfully slow and tedious work. The two diggers had only the jackknife, and excavation had to be done in near silence. In Hamilton's words, the digging amounted to little more than "scraping."[4]

From the start, Rose made it clear that they had to avoid any mistakes and leave no sign of their work. The cavalry major described the first step: "When nearly all the prisoners were sleeping one night I carefully moved one of the stoves aside, and with the aid of the knife dug the mortar from the bricks. Thus the bricks were loosened, carefully taken out, and our access to the cellar was made." Of course, it was not quite that easy. It meant working in near silence night after night and with only the dim glow from a lantern outside. They also had to make precise estimates without the advantage of having the floor plans for the prison. All the debris from the digging had to be swept into a "rubber blanket" and hidden, lest one of the guards find a pile of dirt and rocks. The two diggers were soon running out of places to hide the debris.[5] Likewise, Hamilton was careful to preserve as much of the mortar "between the bricks" and "to preserve [the bricks] whole" in order to put them back in place each morning. At the busy breakfast, Rose and Hamilton discreetly inspected their work and were pleased. It looked intact. No one would notice that the bricks behind the fireplace had been removed unless they were specifically looking for a breach in the fireplace.[6]

This routine repeated itself for a few nights. Once they had "cut a dozen" of the bricks out, they could squeeze through the narrow hole and start digging downward in Hamilton's zigzagging design. Ultimately, the two men removed roughly fifty to seventy-five bricks to create a tunnel below the fireplace. It was large enough for a wide-shouldered man like Rose to squeeze through but not so big as to risk a cave-in or breach of the walls above or below them. This first phase of the escape went off without a hitch. Rose had been worried about noise and patrols, but the guard stationed outside the kitchen door by Cary Street and his comrades patrolling the perimeter of the building neither entered the kitchen nor detected the digging. So too did the work go unnoticed by the prisoners in the hospital next door. Knowing that a single "thoughtless move would have betrayed us to the Confederate surgeons and doctors that were in the room," Hamilton felt a sense of accomplishment. They were now through the fireplace![7]

After twelve nights of digging in the shape of a "Z," the entrance to the east cellar from behind the fireplace was completed. "I will never forget the satisfaction and relief that our little party experienced when that entrance was completed," Hamilton later recalled. The second phase of the project also went undetected and without problems. "It seemed as though half the battle had been won," Hamilton gushed, adding, "although in reality our labors had been barely commenced." The next dilemma was figuring out how to drop down from the opening into the east cellar without breaking an ankle or making an audible thud. It would be especially painful to Rose, who was still nursing a broken foot. So, "a board was ripped from the top of a bench" and a plank removed from the floor by the powerful colonel. The two wooden beams were thin enough to push through the hole but long enough to reach the cellar floor. Hamilton described what happened next: "With its aid [Rose] went down into the black basement, amid the hurrying, scurrying, squealing rats," sliding the remaining distance to the floor without event, while Hamilton remained on watch in the kitchen. It was December 30, and the two prisoners had managed to make it to the east cellar.[8]

The first thing the colonel noticed upon entering the cellar was the foul smell of rotten food, which he described as a mix of "grease and sewage." It was so overpowering that Rose gagged. The smell of smoke still haunted the cellar, made worse by the low ceiling and limited ventilation. Over the next few weeks, the two men would never get used to the stench, suppressing the urge to vomit every time they crawled down into the cellar. The good news was that no one was there. What Rose did find in the cellar were other inhabitants. It was infested with swarms of rats brought by the nearby river and sewer. It was obvious to the colonel why the cellar had been nicknamed Rat Hell; the rats were an ever-present part of the prison, prowling the upstairs rooms each night and tormenting the prisoners. They were a daily topic of conversation in Libby.[9]

Rose was both pleased and surprised to see an entryway to Canal Street from the east cellar. A lantern outside gave off a dim light that bathed the cellar in an eerie glow, faint enough to help hide the men but sufficient to help them navigate the otherwise-dark dungeon. One night, a "storm raged fiercely," and the periodic lightning strikes momentarily lit up the room. The storm also had the effect of muffling any noise made by the colonel. Rose crept along the wall of the cellar, using the flashes of lightning to look for places to dig the tunnel. A particularly dazzling strike illuminated a small doorframe that led up and out to the street on the south side of the prison. Rose could not believe it had no door! It was another example of the ineptitude of Libby's guards. The colonel made a mental note to later discuss with Hamilton the option of just waiting until the evening sentry was far enough away and then making a dash across the prison grounds. He decided to step up into the doorframe to get a closer look. But just as Rose was peering outside, a guard, musket on shoulder, appeared! The sentry was so close, Rose recalled, that "he could easily have touched this man with his hands."[10]

Crouching just feet from the guard, Rose froze and held his breath. When the sentry moved on, Rose melted back into the blackness of the cellar and watched as the Confederate "repeatedly passed" by on his patrol. Fortunately, the guard seemed distracted by the storm and paced back and forth beside the prison, oblivious to Rose. The colonel continued his surveillance of the cellar, noting details and access points. The idea of just running or sneaking out of the open doorway was dealt a blow when Rose observed the guard taking up his station next to the doorway and spotted other nearby patrols. Over the next few nights, the two prisoners discovered that there were always guards outside the door and that, even if they ran, they had to make it across an open field and scale the fence undetected. If they overpowered or killed the guards, they would only have a few minutes' head start, because the patrols were organized in a way that a missing sentry would very soon be detected.

CACHE

After studying the cellar, Rose identified the approximate location of the nearby sewer. The two men would thus start the tunnel in "rear of the little kitchen apartment at the south-east corner" of the cellar, which marked the closest access point to the sewer. Based on their observations of the workers, Rose and Hamilton guessed that the sewer was nearly six feet high—large enough for a man to pass through. Once they tunneled to the sewer, they would escape by following it to the river.[11]

One challenge of tunneling under the prison was that, with the sewer, canal, and river next to the bastille, its walls were always wet. It made the dirt heavy in places; elsewhere, the sandy soil was not compact and prone to collapsing. The next dilemma was how to dig a long tunnel using only Hamilton's jackknife and their bare hands. An old carpenter's shop solved the problem. As Hamilton wrote, the tools they needed to dig the tunnel were "stolen from the carpenter shop," the most valuable being a chisel, which allowed them to cut through the more-densely packed dirt. The shop sat on the south side of the cellar, and, though it was no longer used, the prison staff never removed all the tools. Rose found a few more items and pieces of tools that could be used for their nightly excavations. These they hid in the cellar each morning before wearily ascending to the rooms above.[12]

On the north side of the cellar was a "series of small cells with padlocked doors" used by the commandant for confining "troublesome prisoners" and "runaway slaves."[13] Fortunately, they were empty at the moment. Rose worried that, should the commandant place prisoners in isolation in those cells, or if the guards needed to come to the carpentry shop, he and Hamilton would have to pause their tunneling until the prisoners being punished were released back into the main holding rooms upstairs. The real problem would be if the commandant and guards showed up unannounced. It was a risk they would have to take. After a careful survey of the cellar, Rose scaled back up the plank and through the snaking passageway to the kitchen to inform Hamilton of what he found.[14]

The next day brought a valuable gift. After it had been announced that additional prisoner exchanges and the delivery of boxes were canceled, a ship had arrived behind the prison. It contained "several bales of clothing and blankets" sent by Union authorities and the cartels. They were destined for Belle Island, where so many Union prisoners were freezing to death in the open stockade next to the bastille. The guards organized a committee of prisoners in Libby to oversee the distribution of the blankets and clothing on nearby Belle Isle. General Dow headed the committee that was comprised of a few of the most-senior officers in the bastille, including Colonel Harry White and Colonel Joseph F. Boyd. All three men happened to be on good terms with Rose, who decided to take a gamble. He asked them to "confiscate" some of the rope used to tie the bales of blankets together. These two colonels would be the first prisoners Rose and Hamilton trusted with their escape plan. Colonel White soon appeared with nearly a hundred feet of rope! It was an inch in diameter, so it would be strong enough for the job at hand. Now the problem was not a lack of rope but concealing the cache until it could be taken down to the cellar.[15]

After the call for lights-out at nine o'clock, Rose and Hamilton snuck back down to the kitchen to begin their "underground road to liberty." In the kitchen, Rose again pried loose the piece of the floorboard while Hamilton tied the rope to one of the thick posts that supported the prison. The rope was knotted every foot or so "to make into a ladder to be used in getting in and out of the cellar from the kitchen fire-place."[16] After disassembling the bricks by the fireplace, both men crawled down the narrow passageway to the cellar, using the rope and board to ease their descent. Once in the cellar, they observed not one but two sentries patrolling along the south side of the building. Fortunately, the guards proceeded on their nightly route without inspecting the cellar. Rose and Hamilton very quietly went "groping about" the old carpentry shop in the dark to pick up the tools Rose had hidden. The cache contained "a board-ax, a saw, two chisels, several files, and a carpenter's square," which supplemented Hamilton's small jackknife. They later obtained an old, broken shovel, "an old hinge,"[17] and two "case-knives."[18] For the desperate prisoners, it was a veritable treasure trove! They could now begin the excavation of the tunnel.

CLOSE CALLS!

The two prisoners made their nightly forays to the cellar, repeating the arduous steps to get into the cellar from the kitchen, and always with sentries outside the cellar door and patrolling the prison grounds. Rose began excavating a narrow tunnel, which proceeded slowly and with great difficulty. The men took turns, with one digging while the other stood guard. One night, while taking a brief break from the digging, they decided to test whether it would be possible to simply step out of the open doorway and race or sneak across the prison grounds.

So, once the sentry had passed on his course, Rose crept out of the dungeon. However, before he was able to go even a few feet, a second guard spotted him. The men had failed to spot the second guard, who "called lustily for the corporal of the guard."[19] Rose raced back into the cellar, where he and Hamilton hid in the dark shadows, along the wall. The first sentry—presumably the corporal—suddenly appeared by the doorway and cocked his musket. His head and the tip of the weapon were silhouetted in the doorframe. "Who goes there?" he yelled.[20] Rose and Hamilton remained motionless and assumed they had been caught. To their surprise—and relief—the two guards did not enter the malodorous cellar. They simply stood at the doorway.

After a few tense moments, and as soon as the guards left, Rose and Hamilton hurried back up the passageway to the kitchen. Much to their relief, it was still empty. They quickly replaced the plank on the floor, but as Rose was about to hide the rope, the beam of a lantern illuminated the kitchen door. The prisoners dashed for cover, but finding places to hide in the open room was not easy. Rose dragged the large coil of rope with him. It seemed futile—they had been spotted. A moment later, the search party burst into the kitchen and "looked into every barrel and under every bench, but no sign of Yankees appeared." A few workers who were repairing the prison's roof were lodging temporarily in the small room on the north end of the first floor. From their hiding places, Rose and Hamilton heard the corporal announce to his comrades that they must have seen one of the workers by the cellar door. The sentries soon abandoned the kitchen and marched into the next room, where they roused the workers from their sleep and angrily interrogated them. The corporal accused them of being out on the prison grounds, but the workers denied the accusation. The corporal insisted it had been one of them and issued a stern warning to stay in their room. Typical of the guards, they were anything but thorough and moved on, presumably to check other rooms.[21]

Luck was again with Rose and Hamilton. They hid the rope and snuck back upstairs, distressed by the narrow escape and "depressed in spirits" by the prospect that the guards might begin inspecting the kitchen and cellar nightly.[22] Accordingly, the men avoided the cellar for the next few nights. After a few days, when there had been no word of an attempted escape and no apparent change in the prison's protocols or patrols, Rose and Hamilton decided to resume their digging.

The two prisoners cautiously crept out of their room and down to the kitchen once again. Everything seemed to be normal; however, just as they prepared to pry loose the plank and collect the rope, a man walked into the kitchen. Rose grabbed a "broad-ax" from the fireplace and lunged at the man "with the intention of braining him if he attempted an alarm."[23] The intruder did not cry out but cowered as the two prisoners grabbed him. The intruder turned out to be one of the workers. Rose warned him, "For God's sake don't come down here ever again!"[24] The worker agreed and, unnerved, slunk back to the room on the first floor where the work crew slept. Rose and Hamilton decided to not press their luck and returned to their barracks. They took another few nights off from digging.

SPITTOON AND KNAPSACK

Nothing came of that close call; it seemed the worker had been sufficiently frightened. So, a few nights after that second incident, Rose and Hamilton returned to the cellar. Every night, it was the same routine—sneaking undetected out of the barracks and down to the kitchen, where the plank of wood and rope were used to descend to the cellar. For the time being, it was working, but the endeavor was proving to be very tiring, very stressful, and very slow. Hamilton also complained of the "unhandy means of getting into the cellar." They spent far too much time loosening the bricks by the fireplace and sliding down the passageway. While they dug, they also constantly worried that any noise or misstep would "arouse" the guards or that someone would enter the kitchen and notice the missing plank and hole behind the stoves and fireplace. They had been lucky thus far but began to feel that they were on borrowed time. The tunnel had to be expedited.[25]

The prison grounds were mostly "brittle, marly sand," which made it easier to excavate but increased the likelihood of a collapse. To overcome the problem of wet, loose soil and sand, Rose found an area in the cellar where the dirt was more compact and angled the tunnel accordingly. However, as they dug deeper, the potential for a cave-in increased. There were other problems: The deeper they tunneled, the darker it became, until the men were in complete blackness. The men stole candles and matches, which had to be used sparingly and were hidden in the cellar each morning before they returned to their barracks. Still, there were too few candles. Much of the work would have to be in pitch-blackness. The air also thinned deeper into the tunnel, to the point where breathing became difficult. Rose had insisted on doing the lion's share of the digging but began to worry he would pass out.[26]

Hamilton came up with two clever inventions. A rope would be tied around Rose's ankle so that he could be pulled out of the hole if he were to lose unconscious, should the tunnel collapse, or if they needed to flee the cellar quickly. The tunnel, after all, was so narrow that it was impossible to turn around, especially for the stout colonel. Rose had to back out of the tunnel after his long nightly shifts. Second, the Kentucky cavalryman stole a wide-brimmed hat, which he would use to "fan" air into the tunnel. Night after night, standing on alert in the cellar while Rose dug, Hamilton fanned air into the tunnel to keep the candles lit and his friend breathing. It worked for a while.[27]

The main "difficulties" in "excavation," according to Hamilton, "resulted from a lack of quality tools and the unpleasant feature of hearing hundreds of rats squealing and running over the diggers almost without fear." Fortunately, "the earth was soft and moved easily." The chisel, he added, was proving to be "a fortunate possession," allowing them to pry loose rocks. Still, "hands and fingers were constantly in use in loosening and removing the dirt." Yet as soon as they overcame this one problem, another obstacle arose.[28]

They now faced the dilemma of how to more efficiently remove the excavated dirt and rock from the tunnel and what to do with all of it. Initially, they had moved the dirt and rocks "with an old sugar scoop stolen from the hospital quarters."[29] However, Rose and Hamilton agreed that they needed a better "receptacle" and more efficient system than simply backing out of the tunnel every few minutes with more dirt. Getting in and out of the tunnel was a chore unto itself. Hamilton devised a solution. "Wooden cuspidors that had been taken from the rooms above" could be rigged with rope to be pulled out of the tunnel by the digger's "companion at the entrance"—usually Hamilton. The old, broken shovel they found in the carpenter's shop was used to push the dirt into the spittoon. It was also used to swat at the rats that tormented them in the tunnel.[30]

Hamilton fashioned an "old-fashioned knapsack" he had stolen onto "a wooden frame." Rose would thus fill it with the excavated debris. But rather than drag the knapsack out of the tunnel every few minutes, "a cord was attached" to it, allowing it to be "drawn out" by Hamilton. Once the full knapsack was dumped outside the tunnel, the empty knapsack "was then shoved back to the digger with a pole." It worked! The digger could remain in the tunnel. Hamilton continued to experiment with the system. For instance, prisoners were allowed to have a small clothesline to hang and dry their clothing. Rose and Hamilton accumulated enough clothesline to attach to the knapsack and use it like a pulley, so that the digger and dumper could soon efficiently pull the spittoon and knapsack in and out of the tunnel. The simple process saved the men time and effort.[31]

However, the large amount of dirt and rock coming out of a long tunnel had to be dealt with. Rose and Hamilton knew they could not simply pile it up or spread it throughout the cellar. Any guard or prisoner who happened upon the room would surely notice the mess. Luck was again with them. A "large quantity of loose packing straw, covering the floor to an average depth of two feet" sat unused in the corner of the cellar.[32] The straw was left over from what was used to fill the mattresses in the hospital and presently was home to the cellar's "large colony" of rats. To the chagrin of the rats, the debris was "carefully hidden under" the straw. Therefore, the dirt and rocks were "safely out of the way" should anyone inspect the cellar.[33]

The tunnel was progressing, but still too slowly. The longer the project took, the greater the chance it would be discovered. The two men worried that it was only a matter of time before the guards or one of the prisoners stumbled upon their nightly escapade. It was difficult, after all, keeping the project a secret from 1,200 prisoners. Each night Rose and Hamilton had to sneak to the kitchen, remove the bricks from the fireplace, and dig in complete silence, then hide the tools, replace the bricks around the fireplace, cover their tracks, and sneak exhausted and undetected back up the steps. There had to be a quicker, more efficient way to dig the tunnel.

Rose and Hamilton were also depriving themselves of sleep. They worked all night, every night, pushing themselves to the brink. They were digging as fast as possible and at every available moment; there was little else they could do to expedite the digging. What if they became sick? They were, after all, spending long hours in a cold, damp cellar in the middle of the winter and getting neither adequate nutrition nor sleep. The lack of sleep might soon cause a fatal error. Sure enough, that was when it happened.[34]

Libby Prison, Richmond, Va., April 1865
Library of Congress

Libby Prison, Union prisoners at Richmond, Va.
Library of Congress

Interior view, Chickamauga Room (2nd Floor)
Courtesy Civil War Richmond

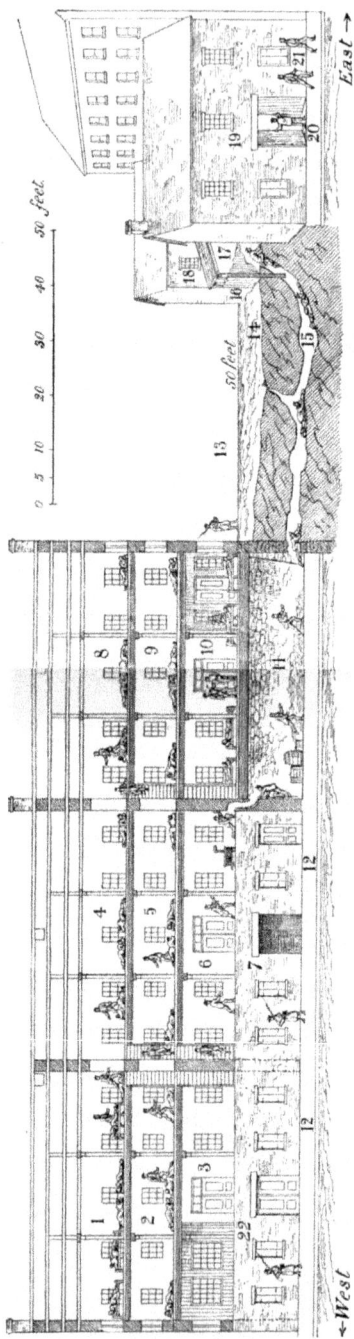

Cross-section diagram of the escape tunnel
Century Magazine, March 1888, p. 786–87

Elizabeth Van Lew
Encyclopedia Virginia

Thomas E. Rose, head-and-shoulders portrait, facing left, Colonel, 77th Pennsylvania
Library of Congress

Major A. G. Hamilton

Neal Dow, General, seated, facing left
Library of Congress

Abel Streight
Project Gutenberg

Frederick Bartleson

Federico Fernández Cavada
Courtesy University of Miami Cuban Heritage Collection

Major Thomas P. Turner, Commandant of Libby Prison, in Havana, 1865
Courtesy of Documenting the American South, University of North Carolina

Richard Turner, "Jailer" of Libby Prison
Courtesy of the *Richmond Dispatch*, 1901

Erastus Ross, Clerk of Libby Prison
Courtesy of Civil War Richmond

President Lincoln riding through Richmond, April 4, amid the enthusiastic cheers of the inhabitants
Library of Congress

Libby Prison (Chicago Museum)
Library of Congress

11

Close Calls

Colder, Colder grows the weather,
Filth, Hunger, Cold confined together . . .
Four whistling winds and driving rain
From North & West across the plain,
Of Libby's Western second floor
To Southeast corner entrance door.

—Robert Cornwell, Libby Prison, 1864[1]

It happened . . .

One brisk evening in late December 1863, Colonel Rose and Major Hamilton once again made their way down to the prison kitchen, removed the fireplace bricks, and began crawling down the Z-shaped passageway to the cellar. The long rope that had been confiscated from the bales of blankets was tied to a support beam and then taken in hand by the burly colonel. Rose, as was usually the case, went first and began the difficult ordeal of squeezing down the narrow hole. To descend, the men would brace themselves with their feet pushed forward against one side of the wall, with their backs flat against the opposite wall. Every bit of progress downward was painful and difficult. There was so little room in the narrow, curving passageway that the tunnelers even had to remove their jackets before beginning the descent. The bitterly cold weather bit at their exposed skin that night, but Rose and Hamilton did their best to block out the chill. That is, until their streak of luck caught up with them.

Partway into the hole, Rose lost his grip on the rope, and his feet slipped. He fell a few feet down the narrow shaft. The colonel found himself trapped, wedged at an uncomfortable angle in the passageway. He tried to move but was unable to budge. One of the prisoners described Rose's predicament as "wholly powerless either to drop lower or return." With his arms pinned against his side, it was impossible to push himself back up or downward. Rose was trapped. Adding to the situation, the men recalled, "the bend of the hole" was "such as to cramp his back and neck terribly and prevent him from breathing." With his chest compressed, the colonel felt himself losing consciousness. Hamilton crawled down into the hole, but there was not enough room to both climb back out of the passageway *and* yank the big man out. He estimated that it would take a few nights to dig down to his friend and widen the passageway. That was not an option. Rose was soon "gasping for breath and rapidly getting fainter." The cavalry major decided to get help.[2]

Hamilton quietly called down the hole to Rose that he would be back with help and then raced upstairs to the rooms crowded with slumbering prisoners, "trampling upon arms, legs, faces, and stomachs, leaving riot and blasphemy in his track."[3] The only men with whom the two collaborators had shared their plan were the two colonels who helped procure the rope from the bales of blankets delivered to the prison a few days earlier. One of them, Colonel White, had later joined the two tunnelers in the cellar to help them find tools in the carpentry room. Hamilton considered finding Colonel White and a friend who was in the Chickamauga Room—Major George H. Fitzsimmons of the Thirtieth Indiana Infantry. But in the dark he could find neither man. The question was now, "Who could be trusted?"[4] Time was limited. He opted to awake another friend, Lieutenant Frank F. Bennett of the Eighteenth Regulars, who also bunked in the Chickamauga Room. Hamilton quickly and quietly shared the details of what had just happened. As the two men began heading down to the kitchen, they encountered Major Fitzsimmons, who hurriedly followed them. In their haste, they risked alerting the sleeping prisoners, but they had little choice. The three rushed down the stairway. There they found Rose still conscious but desperately gasping for each breath.

With the frantic assistance of Bennett and Fitzsimmons, the men were able to widen the passageway. After digging and clawing wildly, they reached the colonel and dragged him out of the shaft. Rose was weak but alive. While he recovered his breath and senses, Hamilton and the two veterans of the Battle of Chickamauga worked furiously to hide all the debris and loose bricks from the hastily dug expansion. Once all evidence of the mishap had been concealed and the bricks and stoves pushed back into place, the men carried Rose upstairs to the barracks before the morning roll call. It seemed to be a costly setback, if not an end to the planned escape, yet would only be a frightening but minor delay.[5]

Rose was eager to return to the digging the next night, and, although he was still sore from the fall and all four men were unnerved by what had happened, time was of the essence. Rose immediately set about widening the passageway. After twelve nights of digging, the two decided it was time to invite additional prisoners to join them in the cellar. Digging all night, every night, was physically exhausting for only two men. Their backs and hands ached, and their knees and elbows were perpetually raw and scratched. Both men were having trouble staying awake at nights from the lack of sleep, which increased the potential for another mishap. They needed more help.[6]

More men meant they could rotate the digging with fresh muscles and thereby make more progress. It was also difficult for Hamilton to fan air into the tunnel with the hat, remove the debris with the knapsack, spittoon, and rope, and hide the dirt under the straw pile, all while remaining on alert for any guards. A small crew could more effectively cover each job. However, adding more men to the effort brought a new concern—how to keep it a secret. Roughly 1,200 men were imprisoned in Libby in December of 1863. Despite digging for two weeks, Rose and Hamilton had only informed four other prisoners of their plan—the two colonels who had helped obtain the rope and then the two who had been brought by Hamilton into the kitchen when Rose was trapped. More diggers exponentially increased the possibility of a leak. Moreover, Rose and Hamilton both knew that there were "toadies" inside the bastille. Commandant Turner recruited such informants. Some willingly offered to spy on their fellow prisoners. Starving, weak, and desperate, they sold their loyalty for an extra ration of food or the promise of being exchanged. So Rose and Hamilton would have to choose carefully. They decided it was worth the risk.[7]

NEW YEAR, NEW CREW

Rose and Hamilton thought carefully about the decision. The men had to be healthy enough to work, and they had to be trustworthy. It was agreed to keep the number to an absolute minimum. Rose believed that three crews would be optimum for sharing the digging, spreading out the workload and yet limiting the number of prisoners who knew about the plan. As Hamilton described it, they recruited "three reliefs—five in each." In January of 1864, they recruited thirteen new compatriots to fill the three crews. The first shift to descend to the tunnel for the new operation included Lieutenant John C. Fislar of the Seventh Indiana Artillery, Captain John F. Gallagher of the Second Ohio, and Major George H. Fitzsimmons of the Fortieth (or Thirtieth) Indiana, who had helped to rescue Rose when he'd become trapped in the passageway. The crewmember who "had the honor of breaking the first dirt" of the new phase of the tunnel was Captain Isaac N. Johnston of the Sixth Kentucky Cavalry. Regrettably, Rose and Hamilton appear to have forgotten the name of the final member of that crew.[8]

Other prisoners would later join the effort, including Captain John Sterling of the Thirtieth Indiana, Lieutenant Frank Moran of the Seventy-Third New York, and Lieutenant Frank F. Bennett of the Eighteenth US Regulars—the other man Hamilton had awoken the night Rose was trapped in the passageway. Colonel Harry White and Colonel Joseph F. Boyd, who had stolen the rope from the delivery of blankets, also joined the project and helped Rose and Hamilton plan the escape. Hamilton admitted that "possibly one or two others that I cannot recall by name" also joined the crews toward the end of the project. Throughout the coming days, they worked together and earned one another's trust. Rose and Hamilton, however, always worked on the same crew. They were, as Hamilton described, "a band of fifteen, sworn to secrecy."[9]

In addition to the thirteen prisoners who joined the two leaders of the escape plan, a few others ended up joining the effort over the next few weeks.[10] There were also a few more prisoners who were either told of the plan or learned of it by noticing that colleagues were missing from their barracks at night or stumbling upon the information in other ways. Hamilton referred to them as "what we had called our 'silent partners.'" Although they were not part of the digging crews on account of poor health or advanced age, these "silent partners" assisted Rose and Hamilton by obtaining materials such as candles that "were very beneficial," reporting on the movements of the guards, and so on.[11] Colonel Bartleson was, much to his disappointment, unable to crawl down into the cellar or dig, having lost an arm in combat, but he would help in other ways. Rose and Hamilton also sought advice from such senior commanders as General H. C. Hobart and General Dow, as well as from such trusted leaders as Colonel Streight, Colonel Cavada, and Captain Szabad.[12]

Another contribution by the "silent partners" was to help cover for prisoners during the morning roll call. As Bartleson later noted, a challenge of the nightly tunneling was "how to dig it and yet have the workman answer to his name at roll-call so as to avoid suspicion." Rose was vigilant in making sure all the members of the crew replaced all signs of the nightly work and were back in their assigned barracks before their fellow prisoners awoke. However, there was always the chance something would go wrong or that a surprise tally would be conducted in the middle of the night. From time to time, Commandant Turner would send the guards bursting into rooms or the kitchen for unscheduled inspections. Fortunately, the cellar was so repulsive that it "was but little visited by the authorities of the prison" and the guards would leave as quickly as they entered.[13]

Rose organized the three crews and met with each new member of what he called the "secret party," giving them firm instructions about the need for confidentiality. As such, he "bound them by a solemn oath to secrecy and strict obedience." He personally led each team down into the cellar every night and trained the new crewmembers on what he wanted them to do. One member would dig, and then pull gently on the rope to indicate to the second man that the knapsack or spittoon was full. The second member would pull the dirt out using the clothesline fastened like a pulley system on either end of the knapsack or spittoon. That second member also emptied the dirt under the straw pile. The third member constantly fanned air into the tunnel with the hat. However, Hamilton later built a more effective "invention" for bringing oxygen into the tunnel, something that became necessary the deeper they dug—a rubber blanket stretched tight across a wooden frame. The fourth member of the crew took turns relieving the other three, while the final member stood watch as the "lookout." If needed, he could also stay in the kitchen by the fireplace to keep an eye on the entrance to the passageway.[14]

Each digger selected their preferred tools for the task from among the broken shovel, chisel, knives, and other items that had been found or confiscated. Each crew worked for a full night and then rested for two. On nights off, the other two crews would still help to monitor the movements of the guards and be ready to alert the diggers. However, their leader soon realized that a full night of digging was exhausting. The crews would be more productive in shorter shifts. Moreover, some of the new recruits struggled with working in such a putrid, claustrophobic, and dark cellar. As Rose recalled, "The indescribably bad odor and impure atmosphere of the cellar made some of them sick." It seemed impossible to get the smell of sewage, rotten food, grease, and rat droppings out of their nostrils, hair, or clothing. The lack of oxygen inside the tunnel also took a toll on some of the men. Crawling on their stomachs in the dark, the men lived like moles. Of course, no one ever got over the rats. Accordingly, Rose began having the men rotate jobs and work shorter shifts, prompted by hearing the prison guards call out, "All's well" every hour, on the hour.[15]

Some of the new members of the expedition voiced their preference for certain tasks. Others preferred to work only part of the night. As such, Rose tweaked the rotation. Men selected their preferred tasks and after a few hours would "quietly pass to their quarters above, awaken the next relief, and go to sleep themselves."[16] Working only two or three hours proved more productive than toiling all night and had the added advantage of keeping morale higher. All the while, the objective remained the same—to dig down under the east wall and then tunnel south, toward the sewer.[17]

If any man was too weak or ill to fulfill his duty, Rose covered his shift. Lest anyone mistake it, Rose was still in charge and remained the most industrious digger. Lieutenant Moran admitted that Rose was, "by long odds, the best digger of the party, while Hamilton had no equal for ingenious mechanical skill in contriving helpful little devices to overcome or lessen the difficulties."[18] Perhaps the main role for Rose, however, was imbuing the men with confidence that the plan would work. The physical and emotional demands were taxing and tedious. Rose realized that "the scheme seemed impractical as soon as the first burst of enthusiasm was over."[19] However, he kept the men motivated and focused.

Fortunately, the cellar remained "entirely unguarded and seldom visited even in the daytime." Ironically, an impediment ended up being a blessing in disguise: Because the door to the cellar had remained "locked and bolted," the commandant imposed no additional security procedures. Working in this three-crew rotation, the tunnel was moving along at a faster rate—until an unexpected and potentially insurmountable series of obstacles arose.[20]

SECRECY

The plan remained to get to the sewer and then use it to access the canal and river. From there, the escapees would use the cover of darkness to make their way out of Richmond. Rose only occasionally tweaked the latter details, based on intelligence he had discreetly gathered from each new prisoner in Libby as to the closest and most feasible locations of Union forces. One night in January, however, the plan changed, in part because of the rapidly declining conditions inside Libby. The idea was Hamilton's. The Kentuckian proposed that he and Rose go to the south side of the cellar and simply overpower the one or two sentries and escape. All the sentries carried their muskets on their shoulders in "parade" style, and, though vicious, most of the guards were inept. Rose was a powerful man, and the two believed they would have no problem subduing the guards. With the additional thirteen members of the digging crews, it would be a mismatch.

There were problems, however. One was that additional guards patrolled every side of the warehouse complex and were posted at the gates. If the prisoners were seen trying to get to the gates, they would be shot. Another hurdle they still had to contend with were the armed guards at the gates. A final concern raised by Rose was that they would not have long before the missing sentries were detected and alarms were sounded throughout the prison and city. As the capital city, Richmond was filled with Confederate troops. Expecting a Union assault, the city was also "strongly guarded by a labyrinth of breastworks that encircled the city."[21] Hamilton's idea did not provide enough time to get out of the city before the escape would be detected.

Still, the opportunity for such an audacious escape attempt presented itself.

Two sentries usually patrolled the area near the cellar door, while others were stationed around the perimeter of the prison grounds and near the gates to the streets. But one night, there were fewer sentries, and, from the vantage point of the prisoners tunneling in the cellar, they did not appear to be on alert. All members of the tunneling crews were summoned to the cellar. Rose announced a change of plan: In the black night, the prisoners could spring forth from the cellar and overpower the two unsuspecting guards. From there, they could race to the unguarded gate and out of the prison. Rose had earlier rejected this plan, but they were becoming desperate.

All members of the three digging crews were in the cellar and ready for the command from Rose to attack the closest sentry. As the colonel prepared to give the order, however, their colleague stationed by the passageway from the kitchen gave a signal with his hand. It was the warning sign Rose taught everyone to use in the event of an emergency. The prisoners abandoned the attack and rushed, single file, back up the passageway and into the kitchen. To their horror, they were informed by their lookout that a group of armed guards was gathering outside the kitchen door, near the exit to Cary Street. The men froze in the kitchen, believing that they had been caught. However, the guards turned and marched away from the kitchen.

The prisoners wasted no time, hurrying back to their rooms on the top floors. As they did, Rose remained behind to quickly replace the floorboard and hide the rope ladder. No sooner had he stowed the long rope than the assistant commandant, Dick Turner, entered the kitchen. A group of guards followed him. Rose was caught; there was no time to flee from the kitchen or hide. The quick-thinking colonel simply sat down "without suspicious haste" at the nearest table. Then, "putting an old pipe in his mouth, coolly awaited the approach of the Confederates." Turner seemed perplexed by what he saw, yet Rose gave the impression that he was simply enjoying an evening smoke. The deputy commandant lifted a lantern and held it at Rose's expressionless face, "stared at him for a second, and without a remark or a halt marched past him." Believing Rose was not trying to escape, Turner "ascended with his escort to the Chickamauga room" and went about his business.[22]

Unfortunately, this near miss resulted in a change in security. The guards must have been tipped off. Rose and Hamilton guessed that one of the "toadies" inside the prison must have reported the suspicious comings and goings of the crews to the commandant. Beginning the next night, the guards began a stepped-up patrol around the entire perimeter of the prison. They began questioning prisoners, searched for suspicious activities, and tightened the daily roll calls. Paranoid, they even began the gruesome task of bayonetting each of the corpses in the "dead house" before taking it outside for burial. The heightened security posed new problems, not the least of which was that the entire prisoner population began gossiping and speculating about a planned escape. The dilemma was now whom to trust and how to continue the excavation without detection. Rose now vetoed the idea of simply overpowering the guards and running.

Upstairs, Lieutenant Moran later remembered, Rose's crews were "soon eagerly plied with guarded inquiries, and besought by their questions to admit them to their confidence." Several prisoners had apparently seen the tunnelers running back into their rooms after the close call. The next day, one of the prisoners even confronted Rose and asked him if he was trying to escape. It forced Rose to organize the crews and their "silent partners" to conduct a discreet but quick audit to determine how many prisoners knew about the plan. They estimated that fully seventy prisoners had some knowledge of or suspicion about the escape. Yet the conspirators all agreed that it was impossible to determine exactly who did and who did not know about the plan and how much anyone really knew. Rose guessed that upward of four hundred prisoners might have seen them racing back into the upper barracks after nearly being caught. The secret was out![23]

Rose and Hamilton concocted a plan to deal with their many curious comrades. They admitted they had been attempting to escape, yes, but had no choice but to abandon the plan. Rose then completed the ruse, asking all those with information on the attempted escape to swear an oath of secrecy. This, he believed, just might work and would buy the tunnelers time to figure out their next step. Hamilton proposed they bring many additional prisoners into the operation. Moran agreed, believing they had no other choice. Colonel Fernández Cavada argued that the plan was "more impossible" than they realized. Rose split the difference, inviting a few additional prisoners into the plan, swearing each to "secrecy" and "obedience." They could not wait, Rose explained. The conditions inside the prison were getting worse, and too many prisoners knew what they were up to. They had to move fast.[24]

CAVE-IN

The months of December and January saw the weather grow even colder. Richmond was in the grips of bone-chilling temperatures. Gusts of frigid winds tore through the open, barred windows of the prison, making it impossible for the prisoners to stay warm. It was too cold to sleep. Christmas day of 1863 passed without celebration. Commandant Turner had prohibited boxes from being delivered, and the severe shortages of food amplified the hunger pangs and depression of the prisoners. Captain Szabad later remembered that no blankets or food were provided that Christmas. The prisoners lacked wood to light fires to stay warm and so were forced to break the remaining wooden benches for fuel. Captain Cornwell recalled that the weather remained "intensely" frigid for the next few weeks. The prisoners, he recorded in his journal, stayed up all night on New Year's Eve. It was not to celebrate; rather, they were too hungry and too "bitterly cold" to sleep. "These walls," he wrote, "contained few sleeping eyes" that holiday.[25]

Not even the lyceum and assortment of classes and games that once had filled the prison with hope could lift their spirits. Cornwell spoke for his peers when he admitted, "it has been so cold that I could not enjoy them much."[26] Once again, morale plummeted among the prisoners. With spirits sagging, however, a few men tried to mark the occasion with song and words of encouragement. When the guards cried out, "Twelve o'clock, and all is well," the mood changed. Those stoic prisoners began to sing. It prompted a response by the entire prison. Once again, "the old building resounded with the good old national song of 'The Union Forever.'"[27]

The cheer was short-lived. By mid-January, there was no more meat and no relief from the cold weather. Commandant Turner had also ordered that Colonel Streight be confined to one of the small cells in the dungeon. Though Streight was a "silent partner" and could be trusted, his detainment there limited the crews' access to the tunnel. Their concern was that guards might enter the cellar to check on their prisoner or to escort him back up to the general population. Streight was finally returned to his barracks on January 8, but after suffering in solitary confinement in Rat Hell, the famous raider's health was severely deteriorated.[28]

In early January, the Lyceum ceased to function. Boxes and letters were not delivered. The prisoners largely stopped their daily routines. Instead, a frozen hush settled over the bastille. Just about the only activity inside the prison was in the "Dead House," where slaves carried the dead from the room near the hospital out to be buried, in increasing numbers. Despite the weather and deteriorating conditions— or, rather, because of them—Rose ordered the crews of diggers to continue to work on the tunnel. Hamilton later remembered Rose telling the men that the plan had not changed, "our objective point [still] being a sewer that we believed to be empty enough to allow an exit." It was either that or die.[29]

The crew's hopes were dashed in January. As Hamilton described it, "to our disappointment we found that the sewer was flooded." As they dug to the walls of the sewer, the soft sand and soil collapsed, sending near-frozen sludge and water pouring into the tunnel. Rose tried to divert the flow back toward the sewer, but it was futile. They lacked the necessary tools, and the water quickly became too deep. The stench was overbearing and threatened to attract the attention of the guards. The excavation was again put on hold while the prisoners hurriedly cleaned the spill and plugged up the tunnel in order that it not be discovered.[30]

Lest his fellow diggers abandon hope, Rose immediately announced that they would find a more suitable location from which to dig a new tunnel. Hamilton remembered that, for his friend, "failure was never thought of." Although the men seemed willing to give up, Rose's "undaunted" strength, "stubborn patience," and optimism kept them going. Yet this new tunnel would be delayed until "a place was found where the earth was firm enough to support a tunnel." Rose believed they could not afford to fail again.[31]

The colonel reconnoitered the grounds around the prison and canal and identified a second, smaller sewer that was not far from the east cellar and appeared to connect to the main one. Despite the earlier flooding, Rose stayed with the idea of tunneling into the sewer; but this time it would be through the adjoining one. He shared his idea with the three crews, and they agreed and immediately began another tunnel from the southeast corner of the cellar. It would run below the prison and street to Dock Street, about twenty feet away and beside the canal. This time, however, Rose instructed the diggers to avoid excavating too deeply and thereby avoiding another flood.

The spirit of the prisoners was also somewhat rejuvenated when one of them stole a hatchet and another found a small iron bar and an auger left behind by a work detail that had recently replaced the wooden bars with the new iron ones. The irony was not lost on Captain David Caldwell, who quipped to Hamilton of their captors, "They were industriously engaged in making . . . the prison proof against escape, yet . . . they were affording us at the same time, the opportunity of procuring the very identical tools with which we did make our escape."[32] Lieutenant Moran remembered that, with the new tools, "It was confidently believed that an entrance to the main sewer would be gained on the night of January 26." The men felt that they were getting close to the date of escape.[33]

On the night of January 25, as the digging crew neared the objective, Rose snuck back upstairs to inform the other members that it appeared they would reach the smaller sewer the following night. All was going well. However, later that night the new tunnel ran into solid rock and thick timbers, described by the diggers as "a series of stone fenders." To their dismay, it was oak—"hard as bone," according to Moran.[34] Hamilton said simply, "Our progress was stopped by a number of logs that had driven into the earth as a foundation." The three massive oak pillars held up the lower side of the prison by the canal. There was no digging through or around this "formidable barrier," said Hamilton, with just chisels, small knives, and their "meager stock" of "simple tools."[35]

Rose proposed that they try burrowing below the foundation in order to still gain access to the sewer that ran from the prison to the canal. He launched into the effort, digging furiously, perhaps to imbue the men with confidence or perhaps to allay his frustrations. Rose and the crews attempted to avoid the main beams but discovered that these extended well below what they had thought was the base. Several precious nights were wasted on this second tunnel—sawing, digging, and chipping away—in order to try to angle below the pillars. Lieutenant Moran remembered some of the "feeble" tools easily breaking.[36]

They finally dug to the bottom and began digging the remaining few feet up to the sewer. Only a few yards from it, however, the ceiling of the tunnel collapsed, and "water began to filter in—feebly at first." The wooden lining of the smaller pipe had been breached. The stench was again overbearing. Men felt the bile rising in their throats as they tried to plug the hole. One of the crew fainted from the smell. Then, the crew watched in panic as the trickle of sewage and water suddenly "broke in with a rush that came near drowning Rose, who barely had time to make his escape." Lieutenant Moran claimed it gushed "so rapidly" that the men could not initially stop it. Rose was engulfed in a putrid cascade of human sewage and was suffocating in the narrow tunnel, which Moran remembered to be only about two feet high by eighteen inches wide. Fortunately, Rose had tied a rope around his good foot when he had crawled into the hole, allowing a quick-thinking Hamilton to drag his friend, "choking," out of the water to safety.[37]

Even though he had nearly drowned, Rose immediately returned to the tunnel, crawling through raw sewage. He had to plug the leak before the smell and flood would give away the secret excavation. The colonel succeeded in packing the hole. In doing so, however, he discovered the secondary sewer line was "too small to let a man through it."[38] Rose considered trying to widen the sewer, but that too was futile. They now had to clean the floors and fill the tunnel with dirt. The crew was not only covered in sewage but also soaking wet. Rose and the others made it out alive, but the filth that now covered their clothing and skin would surely give them away when they returned to the barracks upstairs. After trying to clean themselves, the men risked the obvious and returned to their assigned rooms, climbing the rope ladder to the kitchen.[39]

The next day, Rose and Hamilton peered out the window and surveyed the grounds. They saw one of the large, brick stoves that had been in the spare kitchen in the cellar. Apparently, the guards or workers had removed it and placed the heavy cooker on the grounds beside the sewer. Rose had inadvertently tunneled right under it, and its weight had caused the cave-in. The guards had seen the hole on the prison grounds; however, the prisoners' luck held when the Confederates blamed it on rats tunneling underground.[40]

It had been difficult digging in the winter, as the prisoners did not have adequate warm clothing and January brought snowfall and freezing temperatures; ice now covered the James River. The excavation slowed: The men could not stop shivering, worried they would all catch pneumonia. "All the labor expended had been in vain," noted Captain Isaac N. Johnston, who spoke for everyone when he said, "The feelings of that little band, who can describe! From hopes almost as bright as reality, they were suddenly plunged into the depths of despair." They had "lost heart and hope" and informed Rose that they were done trying. Uncharacteristically, Rose disbanded the crews. Even he had to admit, "The spirits of the party were by this time considerably dashed by their repeated failures and sickening work." It was a second failure within the month of January. The escape attempt appeared to be over.[41]

12

The Evil Turners

And if [Turner] ever falls into our hands, "God have mercy on his soul."

—Emeric Szabad, Libby Prison, 1863[1]

One of the constant torments for the inmates of Libby Prison was the staff—the commandants and guards. Likewise, blame for the terrible conditions also rests with the person responsible for Richmond's prisons. His name was General John Henry Winder. Like the Union, the Confederacy had appointed commissaries who were in charge of obtaining provisions for prisons and administering prisoner exchanges. It was Winder, in his capacity as provost marshal of Richmond's prisons and, later in the war, marshal of all prisons and prisoners in the South, who would bear primary responsibility for the suffering in Libby.

Winder, born on February 21, 1800, in Somerset County, Maryland, would follow his father into a career of military service. His father, General William Henry Winder, had the dubious distinction of leading American troops during the Battle of Bladensburg in August of 1814 during the War of 1812, a conflict that would be remembered as one of the most embarrassing defeats in US history. He also bore some of the responsibility for the British subsequently marching into the undefended capital city and putting it to the torch. After burning the president's house, the Capitol Building, and much of the city, the British marched to Baltimore. In the face of another attack, the elder Winder recommended abandoning the strategically important port city. Thankfully, local leaders and militiamen failed to heed the advice, defending and ultimately saving Baltimore, despite Winder.[2]

It was the attacks on Washington and Baltimore that had prompted the young Winder to enroll in the US Military Academy at West Point. According to John Winder's biographer, the young man had hoped to atone for his father's failures and redeem the family name. He would end up further soiling the Winder legacy. After graduating eleventh in a class of thirty cadets from West Point in 1820, Winder was given a commission as an officer. He served in an artillery unit in both the Second Seminole War from 1835 to 1842 and the Mexican-American War of 1846 to 1848, during which he was recognized for his bravery under fire and promoted to the rank of major. During his long career in uniform, Winder also taught infantry tactics at West Point. With the outbreak of the Civil War, Winder had mixed loyalties. Like many of the Confederacy's officers, he had graduated from West Point and spent years in the US Army. However, he had moved to North Carolina, and, like his fellow leaders of the Confederacy, he ultimately chose the South over his nation and oath as an officer.[3]

Winder had taken a leave of service in May of 1860 and then resigned his commission on April 27, 1861, a few weeks after Southern states had seceded from the Union and just days after South Carolinians had opened fire on Fort Sumter in Charleston Harbor. At sixty-one, Winder was too old for battlefield command but was given an appointment as brigadier general in the Confederate Army. He accepted the position on June 21. Less than one year later, with Richmond facing a prisoner crisis, Winder was named provost marshal of Richmond, whereby he was placed in charge of the city's defenses and security as well as its prisoners. His portfolio would later be expanded in 1863 to include responsibility for the city's hospitals, both civilian and military. One year later, despite his obvious failures in his duties, Winder was given control over all of the Confederacy's prisons and prisoners.

Winder, known as "Old Pig," would prove to be a controversial figure, and criticisms of him abound. The *New York Times* described him as excessively "harsh and strict rule" and "high-handed and antagonistic."[4] The paper echoed complaints by prisoners when it wrote, "He is perfectly capable of stealing the money sent to the relief of our prisoners. . . . His known character for meanness and dishonesty would convict him before any jury of army officers, and if it could be believed that any man would steal the pennies from a dead man's eyes, Winder is the man to do it."[5] Indeed, criticisms abound, including that he was "unfeeling," "short-tempered," and "aloof."[6] Even Richmond's residents came to loathe their provost marshal, especially after he enacted martial law and price controls on the city's food supply in a failed effort to stabilize runaway costs and rampant shortages. Ultimately, part of Winder's failed command included the establishment of three of the most wretched and notorious prisons in American history, all of them in Richmond—Castle Thunder, Belle Isle, and Libby. It was also Winder who later built and oversaw a prison built roughly sixty miles from Macon, Georgia.[7] It was nicknamed Andersonville.[8]

COMMANDANTS

Richmond's prison population had exploded with the onset of war, worrying residents that a mass escape was possible. They were right to be concerned. The first escapes from the city's overcrowded prisons were attempted in September of 1861, as reported by the city's newspapers on the fourth, sixth, fourteenth, and eighteenth of the month, and were blamed on lax security procedures and incompetent guards. One of the Confederate prison commandants, Captain George Gibbs, attributed the mistakes to his guards' drunkenness: "I can account for the escape of prisoners only by supposing that some particular sentry was drunk on post," he wrote General Winder, bemoaning his inability to prevent them from drinking, claiming that drunkenness ran wild among the Confederate guards. The problem, he wrote, would continue "unless the grog-shops in the neighborhood of these prisons are closed."[9] General Winder was even prompted to order the mayor of Richmond to close the pubs. It did not work. Residents complained of the threat arising from housing so many prisoners within the city but were not alarmed enough to abandon their alcohol.[10]

Captain Gibbs's replacement, Major J. T. W. Hairston, also placed blame for the escapes squarely on the guards, whom he described as "incompetent." This, the commandant claimed, was the case throughout the city's prisons. To his discredit, Winder responded by hiring more incompetent and violent wardens and guards.[11] One of them was David H. Todd, half-brother of none other than Mary Todd Lincoln, wife of the president of the United States.

The Todds were a prominent Kentucky family, and two of the first lady's other brothers also fought for the South, while most of the rest of the family swore loyalty to the Confederacy. On July 1, 1861, David Todd was commissioned as a lieutenant and placed under General Winder to help administer Richmond's prisons. Todd would later be assigned to Libby, where he further contributed to the brutality there.[12] An alcoholic with a violent streak, he was described by Captain Szabad as "belligerent, cruel and drunken." Lieutenant Todd quickly became known for his "foul and scurrilous abuse" of the prisoners, such as when he would arbitrarily stab and beat them with his sword.[13]

Lewis Horton, a Union sailor incarcerated in the bastille of the Confederacy, remembered Todd ordering the prisoners to be shackled together and marched through the streets of Richmond to be jeered at by residents. Horton also recalled that Todd one day cut a prisoner "to the bone" because the man had used "a small bit of lighted candle" in an effort "to dress a wound." There were other occasions in which Lieutenant Todd attacked his defenseless charges, such as "when upon the street near our window one day, [he] overheard some conversations that did not suit him." Enraged, Todd "drew his sword and rushing upstairs, stabbed the first man he came across, wounding him so that he had to be removed to the hospital." Todd was also fond of boasting, "I would like to cut Old Abe's heart out!"[14]

Yet another account of the violence Libby's prisoners faced at the hands of Lieutenant Todd and other commandants and guards comes from Dr. Charles Carroll Gray, a captured Union army surgeon who had been sent to Libby Prison in early August of 1861. Dr. Gray noted, "The guards are mad enough to murder all & make themselves as disagreeable as possible." Nevertheless, one of the worst was Lieutenant Todd, who, according to Gray, was a compulsive liar who boasted continuously of his imagined feats of bravery on the battlefield and felt the need to make others pay for whatever angered him. The Union physician summed up Todd in a single word: He was a "humbug."[15] However, the prisoners were soon spared. The lieutenant was so violent that General Winder could not control him. Needing every available able-bodied man, his superiors sent Todd into combat, where he died in July of 1863 from wounds suffered at the Battle of Vicksburg.[16]

Another notorious prison commandant of the Civil War was Heinrich "Henry" Hartmann Wirz, the Swiss-American warden in charge of Camp Sumter in Georgia, also known as Andersonville, the bloodiest of all the Confederate prisons. As a physician in Kentucky and later a private in a unit from Louisiana, Wirz had caught the attention of General Winder, who then brought him to Richmond and promoted him to sergeant. Wirz assisted Winder in Richmond's massive prisoner-of-war operation and, despite a reputation for cruelty and having prisoners beaten, was promoted to the rank of captain and placed by Winder in command of Andersonville. After the conclusion of hostilities, in 1865 Wirz was convicted of war crimes and hanged.

Winder's streak of hiring the wrong people included another cruel prison commandant.

THE WARDEN

Major Thomas P. Turner ran Libby. The commandant had attended West Point for three years but quit the military academy without graduating, apparently due to poor performance and ongoing disagreements with Northerners over the rising sectarian tensions in the years leading up to the Civil War. The testy cadet also refused to swear allegiance "to a Government I despise and abhor!"[17] On March 16, 1861, shortly before leaving West Point, he had written to the newly forming Confederate army, announcing his interest in joining them. Turner shared his secessionist views in the letter, grumbling, "A position in the US Army [is] very tempting. But I can not without a very great sacrifice of principle, agree to take the oath of allegiance to this Black Republican Government."[18]

Turner was not given a commission in the Confederate army. Therefore, the native of Clarke County, Virginia, enrolled at the Virginia Military Institute, which had been founded in 1839 in the town of Lexington. After just one year at VMI, Turner left his second military academy without graduating. The Civil War was starting, and the twenty-one-year-old wanted a commission as an officer in the Confederate States Army. He was again denied, which, given the South's desperate need for men, suggests the extent of Turner's unsuitability and unsavory character. He was forced to accept a commission as a lieutenant in the Virginia state militia.

Turner continued to write letters to Confederate officials asking for a commission. In them, he claims to have been at VMI for two years; in other requests, he boasts of three years of service at VMI. The young man's efforts eventually paid off, but not in the way he had hoped. On April 24, 1862, the ambitious Virginian was named commandant of Libby by General Winder and given the rank of lieutenant commandant. Turner was just twenty-three and completely "inexperienced." It would immediately show.[19]

Running the high-profile prison was not enough for the restless young officer. On September 8, 1862, Turner wrote yet another letter to the Confederate command, this time asking why he had not yet been promoted. "You may be aware that until within the last few weeks, I have for some time past been in charge of the Mil Prisons at Richd," he complains before then appearing to concoct another lie: "Just before Genl. Longstreet's Division left the Peninsula I was offered a position on Genl Kemper's Staff which would have been advantageous for me to have accepted." The compulsive liar blamed his failure to be promoted on Winder, who, he alleged, "would not agree for me to leave the prisons at that time & promised me that I should at any rate be promoted, & did recommend me for promotion."[20]

In another lie, Turned boasted that when General Robert E. Lee had requested a new provost marshal of Richmond, "I had the honor to receive the appointment." He went so far as to suggest, absurdly, that he had declined the honor, because "I was unwilling however to accept it unless my rank was increased." Throughout the war, the problematic commandant repeatedly misrepresented and exaggerated his accomplishments while continually claiming to have been promised promotions in rank, even though there is no such record and it is fantastically implausible that either Lee or Winder would have offered these positions—which included the defense of the Confederate capital—to a young and inexperienced lieutenant, and a scoundrel and compulsive liar at that![21]

Instead of promoting Turner, on October 27, 1862, General Winder selected Captain George Washington Alexander to oversee Richmond's prisons, though Winder would retain his position as provost marshal. Alexander was just one of a cast of unqualified and corrupt characters selected by Winder. Captain Alexander not only looked like a pirate—wearing head-to-toe black, accessorized by a bright red sash, double pistols, and blackjack, and coiffed with long black hair and a long black beard—but he had actually been a pirate and convict who had escaped imprisonment.

He was also put in charge of Castle Thunder, where, accompanied by his massive Russian boarhound, Nero, he brutalized his charges and profited from his position by organizing a scheme of bribes.[22]

Commandant Alexander also wrote a musical play called *The Virginia Cavalier*, in which he performed in the lead role. To a rousing chorus of "Yo! Ho! He is my only joy; he is the darling of my heart; my Southern soldier boy," Alexander made his entrance, riding a black horse across the stage, trailed by Nero. Critics panned the play, saying, "The dialogue is stupid, the incidents are stale, and the plot ridiculous." One paper noted that the more "literary" members of the audience immediately headed for the door. Yet many residents and even the city's newspapers were enamored of their cruel pirate-warden. The *Richmond Enquirer* gushed, "He is not only one of the most gallant but one of the handsomest men in the Confederate service." This despite the fact that Alexander's play had been produced on the Confederacy's dime.[23]

Quite the contrast from the swashbuckling Alexander, Turner was described as an "undersized man" with a chip on his shoulder. He was weak and unimpressive physically and had a loathsome personality. The two commandants did, however, share a few traits. What he lacked in physique, Turner made up for in brutality and vengeance. The prisoners who survived Libby offered countless uncomplimentary descriptions of him as "sadistic," "cruel," "arrogant," and an "infernal brute." Chaplain James Harvey of the 110th Ohio Infantry summed up the warden: "He is a man that is entirely devoid of humanity. There is not a good streak in him, from the end of his toes clear up to the ends of his hair." Another prisoner said of his commandant, "Utter depravity seems to have gained a full and complete expression in every lineament of his countenance." Yet another described an alarming "demon from the pit of perdition," more a monster "than an intelligent human being." Wow![24]

Captain Szabad remembered Turner robbing newly arrived prisoners and accepting bribes, noting the commandant was "as greedy for greenbacks as a pig is for green corn."[25] The "rigid disciplinarian" also took delight in stealing the prisoner's blankets in winter and was quick to order beatings and punishments, including solitary confinement in Libby's dreaded cellar, for offenses as minor as "spitting." Turner's frequent and arbitrary "arrests" and punishments were designed to instill fear.[26]

Despite harboring their own jealousies, Turner and Alexander worked together to hunt down escaped prisoners. One of them was Private Charles Goodwin of the Thirty-Second New York Regiment who had broken out of Libby on November 18, 1862. Turner asked Alexander to help hunt down the "deserter" and requested that the job be carried out by the ruthless "detective officers" who did the commandant's bidding at Castle Thunder.[27] Indeed, both commandants took it personally whenever a prisoner escaped; if caught, the escapees were treated mercilessly. As they prepared their flight from Libby, Rose and Hamilton would have been well aware of what was in store for them should they be caught trying to escape . . . or if they were recaptured.

Turner would eventually get his longed-for promotion, first to captain and later to major. Yet it seems his elevation in rank had less to do with his performance and everything to do with the manpower shortage faced by the South. The prisoners in the bastille of the Confederacy would never forget him. One of them, Reverend James Harvey, although a man of the cloth, said flatly, "If ever Captain Turner falls into the hands of any of the Union officers that have been confined in that prison it will be a sad day for him."[28]

THE PRISON STAFF

The assistant commandant, whose title was "inspector," appears to have been no better than Major Turner. Inspector Richard Randolph Turner, though sharing the same last name as the commandant, was not related to his boss. Inspector Turner, unlike his superior officer, had experience, serving as a jailer before the war, and then enlisting in the Confederate army as a private. Unlike the slight-built major, the inspector was physically imposing, described by Captain Cornwell as a "powerful man."[29]

Known as "Dick" Turner, the inspector seems to have shared several personality traits and a management style with the commandant. For instance, one prisoner described him as "hot-tempered," another as having a "ferocious temper," while other prisoners remembered his "severe" treatment of the prisoners.[30] A German immigrant named Domschcke, who would die soon after the war ended from his treatment in Libby, wrote that the inspector was "a large and foul-tempered individual, quick to resort to violence," adding colorfully that the man was the "son of perdition itself, vicious, sinister, a born turnkey and a beadle by nature."[31] Captain Szabad accused the jailer of instituting "numerous petty regulations" seemingly as an excuse to "frequently" punish the prisoners. The Hungarian officer remembered that, like the commandant, one of his preferred penalties was "solitary confinement in basement cells."[32]

The third in command at the prison was Lieutenant John LaTouche. Described as a "stocky" man who was "outwardly friendly and ready to laugh, but treacherous and spiteful."[33] The Frenchman served as the adjutant of Libby from spring of 1863 to the end of the war. In that capacity, LaTouche, who retained his native accent when speaking English, functioned as the senior assistant to the commandant and oversaw the guards.[34]

Other than the guards, the only other officials at the prison were Doctor Edgar G. Higginbotham, chief surgeon, and his staff of three physicians—A. W. Thomson, C. W. Coleman, and W. S. Nowlin—as well as a quartermaster[35] named Jackson Warner who worked on General Winder's staff as liaison between the Confederate army and the prison. And then there was Erastus Ross, the clerk. Only twenty-one when he had begun working at Libby, the clerk was known to the prisoners as "Little Ross" because of his diminutive stature. Reverend Beaudry remembered him as "the infamous and pompous little clerk," while others described Ross as a "comical little fellow." He held the rank of sergeant and handled all the paperwork, reports, and requisitions for the prison.[36]

Apparently Ross had a penchant for dressing in fancy clothing and had a quirky and feminine demeanor, prompting some prisoners to refer to him as "a peacock." Captain Szabad noted that the prisoners enjoyed giving the clerk a hard time and teased him about his clothing. Although Ross swore a lot and frequently threatened the prisoners, his bark was worse than his bite, as "Little Ross" also liked to joke and could, at times, be affable. Likewise, despite his warnings and complaints, he was supportive of the prisoners, often showing leniency and even covering up their violations of prison rules. When "Little Ross" conducted the daily roll-call tallies, the prisoners often coughed, jeered, called out "Here" in unison when a man's name was called, and interrupted the counting in other creative ways. Ross would curse them and issue threats but rarely acted on them.[37]

Unbeknownst to the prisoners, "Little Ross" kept a secret throughout the war. He was the nephew of a "Unionist" named Franklin Stearns, a wealthy whisky distiller and member of a secret movement of Southerners opposed to the Confederacy. They aided and abetted the Union. More importantly, Ross was also working for a wealthy and eccentric spy in Richmond named Elizabeth Van Lew, who had used her social connections to place the clerk in his job inside the prison. From there, Ross could pass information to Van Lew and do what he could to protect the prisoners from the Turners. For example, in 1863, likely on instructions from his handler, the clerk confronted one of the prisoners named Captain William Lownsbury of the Seventy-Fourth New York Infantry. Punching the captain in the stomach, the clerk gave the order, "You blue-bellied Yankee, come down to my office. I have a matter to settle with you." Nearby prisoners protested, asking what Lownsbury had done and begged for leniency. A bewildered Lownsbury complied with the order. When he arrived in Ross's office downstairs, the little clerk abruptly turned and walked out of the office. Sitting behind the counter was a Confederate uniform in Lownsbury's size. The captain put it on and simply walked out the main gates of Libby.[38]

On the street outside the prison, a slave approached Lownsbury with a request to follow him. Though apprehensive, the New York infantry officer followed the slave through Richmond, up Church Hill, and ultimately to the mansion on East Grace Street owned by the eccentric spy. There she instructed the captain on how to get out of Richmond to the nearest Union lines. He did as she instructed and escaped. After the war, Captain Lownsbury mailed Ross a box of fine cigars as thanks for what he had done.[39]

Colonel Bartleson, the former lawyer who had lost an arm in combat, recorded in his wartime diary that there were often escapes reported by the prison authorities. Each time this happened, the prisoners awaited the news with excitement but concern over the corresponding violent crackdown or word that the escapees had been caught or killed. Yet, more often than not, such reports turned out to be false alarms. The roll call conducted by "Little Ross" would show that all the men were present and accounted for, even though the prisoners suspected that several of their compatriots were missing. The clerk was likely covering for those who may have escaped and would soon try to help when Colonel Rose and Major Hamilton organized the largest prison break of the war.[40]

"FIENDS OF PERDITION"

There were too few guards at any of the Confederate facilities to deal adequately with the swelling prison population. The *Richmond Enquirer* estimated that through 1861 there were only 150 guards in the entire city. Given that it housed officers and high-profile prisoners, Libby received priority staffing. General Winder responded by trying to recruit more trained guards. It was nearly impossible, and the quantity and quality of Confederate guards remained wholly inadequate throughout the war; after all, the Confederate needed every available man in the fight, meaning only the worst conscripts and those deemed unfit for active duty were assigned to be prison guards. One of the prison commandants, Major J. T. W. Hairston, even claimed his guards "were generally so awkward and inefficient that I hazard little in saying there was seldom a day while I was in charge of the rebel prison, when the whole crowd of Federal prisoners . . . might not have marched out and away with impunity."[41]

One of the main complaints among the prisoners in Libby had to do with the guards. They were untrained, uncaring, and prone to drunkenness. But they were also violent and dolled out savage punishments, and often in retribution for Union victories in the course of the war. Moreover, with so few guards and so many prisoners, the sentries were forced to work very long shifts, enforce an impossible array of rules and regulations, and do so in the face of the constant threat of an uprising, attack, or escape. They therefore overreacted when confronted with the most minor of infractions. The guards, one prisoner grumbled, always seemed "to find some pretext, whether real or imaginary, for which to inflict suffering and humiliation upon their unfortunate victims." It was agreed that the guards were not so much sentries as "fiends of perdition."[42]

Another frequent complaint was that the guards were always robbing the prisoners. As was mentioned earlier, the prisoners were robbed when they first entered Libby, and then any letters and boxes sent from loved ones were pilfered. The guards stole food, money, and personal possessions, including letters and "mementos" from loved ones that held "intrinsic value" to the men. Even their uniforms were taken, leaving prisoners half-naked, uncomfortable, and freezing in winter. Colonel Bartleson recalled that one friend of his had all his clothing "pillaged from his box." Despite their loathing of the Union, the guards had no reservation about wearing better-quality blue "Yankee" uniforms.[43]

Bartleson also remembered that the thefts continued during roll calls when the guards searched for weapons and unauthorized "contraband." This included an array of items, but it was also an excuse for the guards to steal whatever they had earlier missed. The search would last "four or five hours," during which time the prisoners were not served breakfast and had to stand in formation. Guards would even confiscate the "many little trinkets" of bone and wood that had been whittled by the prisoners into "ornaments." Later, the guards even forbid the prisoners to whittle, carve, write, or perform any other activity designed to cope with the boredom and oppression inside the bastille. In such cases, Bartleson observed, the guards, like their commandants, seemed to exhibit an "entire absence of all feeling." When the roll call and pilfering would come to a close, the prisoners would find whatever possessions the guards had not wanted cast carelessly about the floor. They then continued whittling and writing.[44]

As foul as they were, the guards happened to be so incompetent and ignorant that they also served as a source of never-ending amusement to the officers inside Libby. The prisoners stumped the guards with basic questions, threw things at them, and amused themselves with stories of their laziness and ineptitude. They often held the same view of the Confederate units in and around Richmond. For instance, Bartleson wrote that the Confederates rarely practiced firing their artillery and when soldiers paraded or drilled near the prison, they did so without rigor, regularity, or discipline. He concluded, "It is no great exaggeration to say that in ordinary battles one regiment in which the men are marksmen is a match for a dozen who have paid no attention to the subject of practice."[45] Others, such as Rose and Hamilton, spent their days studying the guards and observing their routines. Rose quickly concluded that the appalling incompetence of the guards would aid his plan to escape.

Part IV

ESCAPE

13

Desperation

The scheme seemed impractical as soon as the first burst of enthusiasm was over.

—Colonel Thomas Rose, Libby Prison, 1864[1]

The opening weeks of 1864 constituted the darkest times in Libby. As excavation of the second tunnel ended in failure, conditions inside the prison further deteriorated. The frigid and nasty weather extended from January into February, a month described by General Dow, who barely had the energy to write, as simply "cloudy, windy, cold, misty, damp."[2] Commandant Turner continued to impose strict security measures inside the bastille of the Confederacy. Meanwhile, the prison, like much of the city, ran out of food. Meat was no longer served; but now, so too were turnips and most everything else off the menu. Some days, there was nothing to be served at all. Breakfast and dinner mess times were suspended. A state of desperation ensued.

One prisoner complained in his diary in late January, "No rations have been issued for the past eight days except half a loaf of corn bread, very coarse and as hard and heavy as lead. Once in a while a hand full of rice to a man."[3] Captain Szabad shared similar descriptions, noting that he received only two rations of meat the entire winter. Even then, he described one was "half salt meat" and the other as "some mysterious flavor." By late January even the mystery meat was no longer served.[4] When food was available, it was often contaminated to the point of being inedible or, in the words of Szabad, "bloated with the pestilential atmosphere of the prison."[5] Even the bread was not fit to eat. It was so old and hard that the prisoners had to mix it with water to make a nauseating "bread meal" to make it "more palatable" and so they would not lose a tooth while biting into it.[6] General Dow shared the Hungarian officer's concern, commenting that the only ration was one-half of a small loaf of "miserably made" corn bread. It was "heavy as lead," he remembered, rendering it inedible. He managed to eat it only because he was starving.[7] Colonel Fernández Cavada summed it up thus: "We have never been reduced to so wretched a condition, with regard to provisions."[8] Szabad, the Hungarian freedom fighter, went so far as to suspect the Confederacy of adopting a deliberate policy of "gradually starving the prisoners."[9]

It was within that state of despair among the inmates that on January 22 the warden banned the few remaining freedoms the prisoners had enjoyed. One of them was visiting one another in the large rooms upstairs; this allowance had also made possible the Lyceum and numerous classes, games, and activities the prisoners had organized in order to cope with their ordeal. "We have become today the victims of a new grief," observed one prisoner with despair. "Heretofore, we have been permitted to pass through all the six rooms of this building in which prisoners are confined. But today, with no apparent motive than to render us the more uncomfortable, the doors communicating between the three departments have been nailed up."[10] The men were forced to spend their days and nights stuck in a single severely overcrowded room.

This draconian measure was followed on February 1 by restrictions on inmate mail with the deputy commandant's announcement that all "abolitionist officers" from "the 'so-called' United States" would hereby be limited to "only one letter to each officer . . . each week." These "one page" letters could be "no more than six lines . . . and should be handed in on Mondays." From now on, all incoming mail would be inspected by his censors to make sure they "discuss only topics that were strictly personal in nature." Any letter not adhering to the new rule would be discarded.[11] Thereafter, in an effort to transmit intelligence, some of the prisoners such as General Dow and Colonel Streight wrote in code or using lemon and onion juice, which rendered the words invisible upon initial inspection. When heated by fire, however, the message would appear, as if by magic. Lamentably, Commandant Turner later discovered the practice and tightened security even further.[12]

To prisoners who had become dependent on news from home to keep their hopes alive, as well as for those who were "prolific" writers and others who had passed hidden messages along to Union commanders, the new order was devastating. All letters were routed through the "Commissioner for Exchange," and the prisoners assumed that some of the correspondence was screened; however, they correctly guessed that the Confederacy was so understaffed and consumed by the war that most of the threats to read letters were hollow.[13] Colonel Bartleson suspected that the motive for restricting letters had less to do with security than with "mere spite" and "gross ignorance." The indignant and resentful Turner, Bartleson concluded, was driven by "revenge" perhaps more than anything else. Bartleson recalled that the new policy "provoked merited contempt and ridicule" from the prisoners but also completely eroded any will remaining in the bastille.[14]

It was not only the restrictions on letters that devastated inmate morale. The practice of exchanging prisoners also ceased. Captain Szabad blamed this decision on the Confederacy's hatred of Union general Benjamin Butler, the officer in charge of exchanges. The Hungarian rationalized that any exchange involving the man "with whom the rebels refused to treat" with any respect was doomed.[15] There was no longer hope of a prisoner exchange or even the delivery of boxes, only "disappointment" and "despair"—or escape.[16]

ESCAPES

Not surprisingly, prisoners were desperately trying to escape in late January and early February of 1864. One of them was Major Bates of the Eightieth Illinois, who fled at the end of January. Colonel Bartleson recalled that the major had been in "sick-call" and somehow obtained civilian clothing. Acting as a local resident visiting the prison, he asked the guards where the commandant and other guards were. They foolishly answered the question! Armed with the information, Bates simply walked out of the prison at the point he'd learned was no longer guarded. Bartleson believed Bates received the clothing from the clerk, Erastus Ross, remembering the prisoner exited the prison "immediately after the clerk of the prison and his guard have passed out" of view.[17]

Unfortunately, Major Bates was recaptured "about 16 miles" outside of Richmond. According to Captain Cornwell, Bates, already weak, "became exhausted from travel after so long a confinement, and called at a house for something to eat, where he was betrayed." The prisoner who had served as Bates's lookout at the upper window had been Captain John E. Porter of the Fourteenth New York Cavalry. Porter had also gone to see Ross, who had provided him with a Confederate uniform, which Porter had worn under his overcoat. Porter shaved off his moustache and cut his hair in preparation of leaving but was still nervous. Bartleson, the one-armed hero, propped up the man's courage and even agreed to stand by the window and serve as Porter's lookout.[18]

Bartleson decided Porter should act like a messenger and carry two letters, allegedly to be given to the commandant, and then hand them to any sentry he encountered on the way out of the prison. It would make him appear more official. In addition, Bartleson reasoned, what prisoner would walk up to a guard? So, on January 29, after Ross and a guard had departed from the prison gate, Porter followed. Another sentry was nearby, so Porter approached him and handed him one of the letters. Bartleson was pleased with the progress of the plan but then became greatly concerned because Porter "overdid his party, walking almost too slowly." However, the timing worked to his advantage; the guards were preparing to change detail, and the sentry on duty wanted to leave. "A few moments later," recalled Bartleson, "I saw him walking eastward on Main Street, still clinging to that letter as if it were his guide and conduction." Porter made it to a Union safe house, presumably based on information given to him by Ross or a spy in the city such as Miss Van Lew.[19]

The morning after the escapes of Bates and Porter, Commandant Turner stormed into the kitchen, where the men were assembled, and ordered them into formation by rank. He announced that they were to remain there all day: They could not stand near the stoves for warmth, they were not permitted to talk, and they were not given breakfast. After the warden gave the orders, his assistant addressed the prisoners. He claimed in a "condescending" tone that the reason for the protocol was that someone had "insulted" a guard and therefore everyone would be punished. The prisoners knew the excuse to be a lie.[20]

"After two or three hours," the prison's clerk arrived with more guards and ordered the prisoners to "form in four ranks" for another roll call.[21] A rumor spread through the prison—during the punishment, a slave who worked in the kitchen galley had escaped. In the middle of the roll call, another guard appeared and informed Ross that a few more slaves may have escaped. The prisoners quietly absorbed the news with delight. The dim-witted commandants and guards were having trouble conducting the roll call in the small crowded kitchen, so Inspector Turner angrily ordered everyone to assemble in the East Room. There the prisoners were forced to pass between the guards one at a time when their names were called. After the tally, they were sent to their assigned rooms.

The news kept coming. As the roll call was being completed, another prisoner named Carothers picked up a hammer and construction equipment and simply walked out the back door of the prison, passing himself off as one of the workers. One of the guards stationed outside spotted the suspicious incident and "commanded him to halt," but Carothers kept walking. Rather than pursue the prisoner, the guard rushed into the prison to inform the officers of yet another escape. Inspector Turner and two guards ran out to apprehend the escapee. A man in a blue Union coat was seen "some distance" away, heading toward the downtown, so the three Confederates gave chase. After hurrying out the prison gate, they bumped into one of the construction workers, who was nearly knocked over by the collision. The guards caught the person of interest and "rudely and roughly" dragged him back to the prison for questioning. The man turned out, however, to be one of the many Richmond residents wearing Union uniforms. The guards realized the man with whom they had collided when leaving the prison was likely the escapee, pretending to be a worker. Carothers was gone. Bartleson recalled that Inspector Turner was furious and ordered yet another roll call, but it failed to match the earlier tally. The prisoners, despite being forced to stand for hours, enjoyed watching the hapless guards and their cruel commandants argue over the count.[22]

The next day saw the end of January and was spent conducting multiple roll calls. According to Bartleson, each tally produced a different count, leaving the "officials" quite "perplexed." At one tally, Dick Turner and Erastus Ross counted an additional twenty-four men. So they organized another count, which also failed to match prison records. Extra guards were summoned, and prisoners were forced to assemble in the easternmost room of the prison and then proceed one at a time through a gauntlet of guards. The recounts took "all day" and were announced as "unsatisfactory." Ross ordered all the prisoners to line up yet again for a slow and methodical count. It too was "unsatisfactory"; the count exceeded the prison population by forty. After a long and frustrating day, the commandant and guards lost their patience; tempers flared, threats were made, and then General Winder, the provost marshal, was brought in to conduct the count. It too was "unsatisfactory." Confused, the guards and commandants concluded that some citizens, attempting to avoid being drafted into a bloody and failed conflict, had snuck into the prison. Reports surfaced of Southerners bribing prison guards to let them in to the city's prisons. That was how far the Confederate capital had fallen.[23]

Prisoners had been trying to escape from Libby since the facility's opening. However, the vast majority of the attempts had been unsuccessful. Still, the desperation that pervaded during the infernal winter of 1864 had prompted additional attempts. Bartleson remembered, "many of the prisoners are aglow with the desire" to escape.[24] An attempt, even if unsuccessful, inspired other attempts. Without forethought or discretion, the day after the roll-call fiasco, five more prisoners tried to pass themselves off as workers, guards, or residents of the city and walk out of the prison. Four of the five were captured within forty-eight hours.[25]

Of course, none of this was good news for Colonel Rose and Major Hamilton. The rash of attempts resulted in an increase to the guard detail. "The escape of a few officers a day or two before," noted Bartleson, "have made [the guards] unusually vigilant."[26] Around the same time, Captain Cornwell discovered that a handful of prisoners "intend attempting to escape tonight by bribing the guard." Cornwell added that the guard in question even asked to go with the prisoners, mentioning that "seven of his company here already crossed our lines."[27] Such were the hopeless conditions in Richmond and in the Rebel army. Not just the prisoners but the guards too "suffer for something to eat," remembered one of the prisoners.[28] However, the problem with trying to bribe one of the prison staff was that "the guards are so unreliable that it is a dangerous experiment." The planned breakout never happened because the plotters "were frustrated in their designs by an attempt of other parties" that resulted in aggressive enforcement of the rules and frequent inspections and roll calls. Other attempts were thwarted by the weather. Captain Cornwell changed his mind about escaping, explaining, "Last night was very cold. Oh!"[29]

Along with the delivery of boxes from aid organizations and family members, prisoner exchanges in Libby had ended. But then one day in early February a ship arrived behind the prison that appeared to be a flag-of-truce ship. Would there be a large exchange? Surprise and skepticism circulated through the prison population. Sure enough, a group of ninety surgeons and physicians held in Libby were assembled and led out to the dock. One of the surgeons scheduled to be released, however, was so close to death that he could not stand, and the guards refused to allow the prisoners to assist the suffering man. The men were ordered to leave the surgeon on the floor. However, as the physicians were filing out to the ship, one of the prisoners slipped undetected into their ranks. The head count on board was conducted—ninety. It matched the conditions of the exchange, and the ship set sail with the quick-thinking prisoner.

The ship made it to the Union lines at City Point,[30] but "some traitorous tongue frustrated the design." The prisoner pretending to be a physician was discovered and dragged off the ship. When Commandant Turner learned of the near escape, he erupted in anger and ordered all prisoners to assemble for a new round of threats and reprisals; but the prisoners refused to cooperate. The beatings and sentences of isolation in the dungeon no longer held any meaning. His threats frustrated, Turner ordered that Colonel Charles W. Tilden of the Sixteenth Maine be brought to him. The colonel was told to talk: Turner demanded to be told what the prisoners were planning, or everyone would be starved to death. Tilden said nothing. To Turner's amazement, the men stood in solidarity with their comrade, hollering in unison, "Starve us!" The support was a "unanimous exclamation," recalled Captain Szabad.[31]

That January, Colonel Streight attempted to escape. The "burly Dutchman" was a member of a secret society in the prison known as "The Council of Five." They represented five groups of leaders in the prison who, back in November of 1863, had developed a plan known as "The Great Escape Plot." The members of the council, which included Rose, planned to start a riot in Libby that would occur concurrently with uprisings throughout the city's prisons. Based on newspaper accounts, Streight estimated that there were at least thirteen thousand Union prisoners in Richmond. The Dutchman had encoded messages distributed to senior officers in the other prisoners by way of encrypted letters and couriers working for Union spy Elizabeth Van Lew. This most unlikely spy, known by the code name of "Union Lady," had a network of spies throughout the city and had even placed Unionists on the inside of a few prisons, including Libby. Many of her informants and couriers were her Black servants, who passed unsuspectingly in and out of the prisons and fortifications while bravely delivering and receiving orders. Through "Union Lady's" couriers, Streight had been able to assign each prison specific objectives. For instance, one would be sent to capture President Jefferson Davis, while another would attack the Confederate arsenal in the city, and a third would destroy the important Tredegar Iron Works factory. The escaped prisoners would then head toward Union lines in Williamsburg, which would be expecting them, ready to meet at a point between the two cities.[32]

The ambitious plan, however, was betrayed just before it was about to commence. As the prisoners were preparing to launch their riot, they learned that Confederate general George Pickett, who had led the disastrous charge at Gettysburg that July, had been summoned to Richmond with a full division of soldiers to put down any attempted uprising. At the same time, authorities ordered that the guard detail be doubled inside the bastille and surrounded the prison with cannons. The artillery was aimed at the prison and given orders to fire if a riot started. Furthermore, as punishment for the plot, the commandant dealt swift and harsh retributions.[33]

The failure did not deter Streight, who continued to try and escape. One earlier escape attempt had occurred around the time Rose and Hamilton were first starting to dig their tunnel. The infamous raider had received a letter from a guard with shocking news: He had been offered an opportunity to simply walk out the gate of the prison with his colleague, Captain Reed. The author of the letter asked for a hundred-dollar bribe and two "nice" watches; in return, he would assure that guards were not on duty at one of the gates. Streight went along with the offer. He managed to get the money from his contacts outside the prison, while Reed got ahold of two watches. Streight informed Rose of the arrangement, and he then helped with the details, including obtaining rope to be used to slip out of the window nearest the gate.[34]

The men in Streight's confidence met on the second floor, affixed the rope to a foundation, and then dropped it out the window. Captain Reed went first, climbing carefully to the ground. Streight hesitated, worried whether, given his age and size, he would be able to scale the distance to the yard below. Encouraged by Rose, he made it. As agreed, a guard was there to take the cash and watches. Rose watched from the window as the men were taken to the gate, but as they prepared to exit the prison grounds, a group of Confederate soldiers suddenly appeared and seized the two prisoners. Streight and Reed were roughed up and locked in isolation in the cells in the middle cellar.

Through the early weeks of 1864, the commandant announced even more reprisals, but, since no privileges remained inside the bastille, he ended up removing the few remaining medical staff from Libby's hospital. Although the prisoners felt a sense of purpose for the first time that winter, they understood that having no surgeons or medicine inside Libby was a grave predicament. The developments "created a stir and bustle" inside the prison, and men immediately began dying of starvation and a host of ailments. The death toll spiked, and panic threatened to overwhelm the prison. "I shall never forget," remembered Szabad, that no longer was "there was some sort of life left in Libby."[35] There was, however, someone on the outside ready to facilitate an escape.

"CRAZY BETTE"

Elizabeth Van Lew was not only an unlikely spy but atypical of the Southern belles gracing Richmond's social scene. She was the eldest daughter of Unionists! The Van Lews were part of a prominent Philadelphia family whose patriarch, Hilary Baker, served as that city's mayor. After a yellow fever epidemic had struck the city in 1793, claiming the lives of family members, including the mayor, Baker's daughter had been sent to live with relatives in Richmond. That young woman grew up to be Elizabeth's mother.[36]

Elizabeth's father and mother married in 1818 in Richmond's St. John's Episcopal Church—where Patrick Henry had once famously uttered the words, "Give me liberty, or give me death." Their daughter had been born exactly nine months later. Elizabeth's father ran Van Lew and Tailor, a lucrative hardware business, and the family became one of the wealthiest in the city. Despite being Quakers, Elizabeth's father owned slaves and, when he passed, specified in his will that they not be freed. However, his daughter, who believed that "slave power is arrogant—is jealous, and intrusive—is cruel—is despotic," not only freed the family slaves but even helped some escape to Pennsylvania, then hired former slaves who would go on to assist her in helping the Union prisoners in Libby.[37]

Miss Van Lew never married and was seen by residents of the Confederate capital as "brassy" and "high-strung." When the debate over secession had arisen in 1860, she had publicly advocated that Virginia remain loyal to the Union. "Lizzie's" out-spokenness and abolitionism were initially seen as quirky and eccentric, later as trea-sonous, and earned for her the nickname "Crazy Bette."[38] One Richmond newspaper had written that she was "noted for her pluck"; that was putting it mildly. Far from being "crazy," though, Van Lew developed an elaborate spy network throughout the city and worked tirelessly and heroically to save and support the Union prisoners. One of her most effective informants was Robert Ford, a free Black from the North who served as a teamster with the Union Army. After being captured in 1862 in the Shenandoah Valley of Virginia, he had been sent to Richmond and made to work for the deputy commandant. Ford eavesdropped and smuggled information to a Black servant, who in turn had passed it along to Van Lew and other secret Unionists. Later in 1864, after the famous prison break, Ford, suspected of being a collaborator, would be severely whipped and beaten.[39]

Van Lew even used her reputation to her advantage, as she understood that women—especially "crazy, harmless Bette"—would not be suspected of espionage.

She was permitted to visit Libby's prisoners, where she charmed the guards into not searching a "Southern lady" and appealed to Libby's commandant and to General Winder through both buttermilk pastries and gingerbread and an understanding of flattery and their egos. She once quipped, "Oh, I can flatter almost anything out of old Winder; his personal vanity is so great." And so it was that, when she was banned from entering the prison and suspected of treason, she baked and flattered her way past Confederate policies. Of course, when her "charm, flattery, and bribery" were not enough to influence the prison authorities, she simply bribed the guards.[40]

Once in the prison, Van Lew passed notes to prisoners through hidden compartments in the bowls of food she prepared and maps "sewed up" in her servants' clothing and in hollowed-out eggs at the bottom of a basket.[41] In turn, the Unionist collected intelligence from the prisoners and passed it through her contacts to senior Union generals at Fort Monroe in Hampton.[42]

The Van Lew home was a lovely, three-story, fourteen-room mansion on Grace Street in Richmond's Church Hill neighborhood, featuring wide hallways, high ceilings, and, from the top floor, a commanding view of the James River from which Elizabeth could see the old warehouse that now held Union officers. The Van Lew home had become one of the landmarks of Richmond, hosting a stream of celebrity visitors, including famous singer Jenny Lind, known as the "Swedish Nightingale," former Chief Justice John Marshall, and author Edgar Allan Poe, who was said to have read his poem "The Raven" in the parlor. It was from this conspicuous address that Elizabeth Van Lew took her Sunday walks down to the warehouses on the waterfront.[43] Her spacious home and expansive grounds became the main headquarters and hiding place for the city's secret society of "Unionists," network of spies, and both escaped prisoners and runaway slaves.[44]

Van Lew's activities attracted attention. And scorn. She became a marked target for the wrath of the city's residents and leaders. The *Richmond Enquirer* wrote of her, "Two ladies, a mother and daughter, living on Church Hill, have lately attracted public notice by their assiduous attentions to the Yankee prisoners." Not so thinly veiled threats were made. "These two women," the newspaper charged, "have been expanding their opulent means in aiding and giving comfort to the miscreants who have invaded out sacred soil."[45] Van Lew emerged as the prisoners' leading public advocate, causing the *Richmond Dispatch* to warn that her actions must end or be "exposed and dealt with," as she was becoming one of the Confederacy's "alien enemies of the country."[46] Sure enough, mobs soon gathered in front of the Van Lew mansion, issuing threats. The brave abolitionist stood her ground, demanding they leave her property. Van Lew continued to face ridicule, a loss of friends, and the specter of arrest. She struggled with anxiety and concern for the safety of her mother and siblings as well as for her servants. As she recalled, "I have had brave men shake their fingers in my face and say terrible things. We had threats of being driven away, threats of fire, and threats of death." She learned to live with insults and threats, writing with disappointment, "I am held in contempt & scorn by the narrow minded men and women of my city for my loyalty." Van Lew was eventually completely ostracized throughout the city, describing it as "Socially living as utterly alone in the city of my birth, as if I spoke a different language."[47]

Van Lew repeatedly risked her life getting food and intelligence to the prisoners in Libby, including information to Rose and Hamilton on nearby Union positions in Virginia.[48] She had also managed to place Erastus Ross, Libby's clerk, inside the prison, learned how to write with "invisible" ink—made of lime or lemon juice, which, when heated up or doused in milk, reveals the words—and how to use an encrypted codex containing thirty-six letters and numbers on a six-by-six matrix, provided to her from a spy for senior Union generals.[49] She was also preparing a hidden chamber upstairs in her home in which to hide escaped prisoners.[50]

PANIC

That winter of 1864, the James River froze over, and the wind blowing across the ice "whistled" through the open windows of the prison. Men crowded together on the floor each night and huddled next to one another by day, in the hopes of staying warm. Captain Szabad worried that he and his comrades would not make it until spring, fearing that their resolve was at an end. One of the few things sustaining them was "the feeling that the rebellion has no possible chance of much longer resistance." Then amid the suffering that winter came an unexpected delivery of mail. Commandant Turner's limitations on the mail had been frustrating, and so the men were even more eager to receive news from loved ones. All celebrated the joyous moment, as the prisoners shared photos and reports from home with one another and with those who did not receive a letter. Szabad recalled that the prisoners were eager to see pictures of a "cleanly attired mother surrounded by the more lively faces of affectionate sisters," the "half-muffled smile of a charming coquettish lady love," and even "the sorrowing face of a dear wife holding on her lap a blooming infant."[51]

Unfortunately, after the initial excitement had faded, another emotion took control of the men—a "morose and gloomy" longing for home. To be expected, morale plummeted once again. With nothing to eat, nothing to do, and no hope of an exchange, box, or escape, prisoners began to give up hope. "Some sought refuge from hunger in sleep," observed Szabad. "In every room you would find a few prisoners stretched on the floor, vainly endeavoring to forget their misery." All appeared hopeless and, in the words of the Hungarian captain, "the gloom appeared thus to thicken around us."[52]

Indeed, Richmond had run out of everything, including basic goods and essentials. Major shortages of food and most anything else, along with escalating prices, had become commonplace in the capital by 1864. Colonel Fernández Cavada remembered newspaper reports that "empty shelves and empty boxes meet the eye everywhere" in the city. Children roamed the city streets barefoot, barely clothed, and hungry. Soon, the prisoners in Libby, starved and close to death, reported seeing residents gather below Libby's high, barred windows begging for food. Although themselves starving, with virtually no food, and facing the threat of being fired on by the guards should they venture too close to the windows, sympathic prisoners would throw pieces of bread out to the beggars below. "We throw them spare fragments of corn bread, and occasionally a macerated ham bone, which they scramble for greedily, to carry home with them," wrote Fernández Cavada. It was, he noted, an irony that "The poverty-stricken begged from the impoverished."[53]

Inside Libby, General Dow remembered that the prisoners received only "a very small piece of soap" that winter, which he described as "miserable," along with a "very wretched" candle. The conditions that winter prompted the guards, who had always "stolen" boxes, money, and clothing from the prisoners, to simply take whatever remained from their charges, especially coats. Dow remembered, "Every day, we see Rebel soldiers and officers with our overcoats and pants." With Union forces successfully blockading Southern ports, capturing railway depots, and disrupting most any movement within the South, the entire city was starving. Its grotesquely mismanaged economy had ground to a standstill.[54]

A clerk in the Confederate War Department named John B. Jones said of the conditions in Richmond, "We are all good scavengers now, and there is no need of buzzards in the streets. Even the pigeons can scarcely find a grain to eat." With his own ribs becoming more and more pronounced from his emaciated body, Jones worried about rebellion from the city's desperate residents. "A riot would be a dangerous occurrence, now: the city battalion would not fire on the people—and if they did, the army might break up, and avenge their slaughtered kin."[55] Elizabeth Van Lew summed up the situation simply: "There is a starvation panic upon the people."[56]

The war was now well into its third bloody year. Families across Dixie had lost sons, brothers, and husbands, and Southerners were tiring of the shortages on the home front. Sure enough, as John B. Jones had predicted, civil society collapsed, and the people began to riot. The Confederate government seemed unable and perhaps unwilling to assist its residents. Then, on January 19, 1864, a fire nearly burned down the White House of the Confederacy. The cause remains uncertain, but it is likely the blaze was arson. The South was tearing itself apart from within. Yet, rather than rise up against their government, as they had done to the US government during more prosperous and peaceful times, or broker an end to the war, most Southerners remained loyal to the "cause." Instead, their frustration was taken out on slaves and Union prisoners, particularly those at the high-profile bastille, while the Confederate government, though professing a love of liberty and still complaining of imagined abuses under the United States, further cracked down on its own people.

History's frequent scapegoat was also targeted. The few synagogues in the South were ransacked. Even though many of the Jewish merchants and traders living in the South during the war had both supported and supplied the Confederacy, Jews were decried as "Richmond Yankees," and many were forced to flee Richmond and towns throughout the South. The magazine *Southern Punch* had even began referring to Richmond as "Jew-rue-sell-em."[57]

Perhaps to alleviate the overcrowding and specter of disease, or perhaps due to concerns over possible escape, some of Libby's inmates were moved almost 150 miles to the west, to Danville. However, the former warehouse still remained overcrowded, and the transfer simply brought the diseases from the bastille to Danville. The *Richmond Examiner*, for instance, reported that winter that roughly three hundred Union soldiers arriving at the new Danville jail were infected with smallpox. Soon "several wagon loads" of dead prisoners were carted away each day.[58] The same gruesome scenes, of course, were already commonplace in Libby. Perversely, Southern newspapers celebrated the "good news" that so many Union prisoners were dying, the accounts of which were read with alarm by Rose, Hamilton, and the men inside Libby.[59]

Captain Cornwell recorded in his diary that his friends and messmates had become sick or too weak to move. In those days, everyone seemed to be ill with some malady and too weak to move. "Three of our men froze to death last night," he noted one January morning. "It pains me to think of it."[60] The numbers only worsened in February. General Dow described "several" prisoners suffering from "fever and ague," and they began to die in alarming numbers from smallpox, the bitter winter, and hunger.[61] One macabre scene unfolded during the morning roll call that winter. A prisoner did not heed Major Turner's repeated orders to fall in line. The tyrannical commandant personally stormed over and kicked the man covered in an old blanket. There was no response. The cruel warden soon realized the reason, gasping, "My God, I've been kicking a dead man."[62] Many prisoners did not survive the winter of 1864.

ONE LAST TIME

These dismaying developments were monitored by Rose and Hamilton, whose plans to escape had seemingly ended. The two friends decided they had four choices: die in Libby, try to live until the end of the war, pray for prisoner exchanges to resume, or escape. Inspired by the urgency of the situation that winter, they chose escape, and Rose began planning another route. Both men agreed that if they were to be successful—or to survive the winter at all—escape had to happen immediately. Although their previous efforts had failed repeatedly, after thirty-nine tiring nights and three attempts, with nothing to show for the efforts, Rose vowed to find another way out of the prison.[63]

The colonel again surveyed the grounds and decided to try a new tunnel; but this one avoided the sewers. He informed Hamilton that the northeast side of the east cellar appeared to contain more-compact dirt and so it was less likely to cave in. The ground was a bit higher, so the soil would be drier. This tunnel would extend "under the street east of the prison" and be designed "to reach the yard of the warehouse." As such, they would be tunneling across an open yard to a vacant lot on Libby's east side. If the plan worked, they would emerge by a sidewalk and archway, near where sentries patrolled and wagons dropped off supplies. It would be challenging: This would be their longest tunnel yet, and the perimeter of the prison yard "was paced at night by sentinels."[64]

Another problem was that the gate was closed at night and illuminated by a gas lamp. However, a shed near the gate on the other side of the high fence functioned as a small storage space and sat near the archway exiting onto Canal Street, which was sometimes called Dock Street. These small alleys were directly behind the prison and ran parallel to their namesakes and the James River. Rose decided the long tunnel had to extend beyond the fencing and "then pass to the street through an unoccupied building that faced on Dock Street." On the other side of the fence, they hoped to avoid being seen by the sentry. If the tunnel ran into the shed, it could also be used as cover. Once out of the prison grounds, of course, a new set of challenges would arise, including bypassing the ring of soldiers around Richmond and traveling miles in their severely weakened condition to the nearest Union lines.[65]

Rose began estimating the distance from the cellar to the gate. He guessed the new tunnel would need to be at least fifty feet long. The key would be to dig the tunnel to the exact spot, beyond the wooden fencing. Rose assigned Captain John Gallagher of the Second Ohio the task of ascertaining the precise distance from the east cellar to the shed. Cleverly, Gallagher made a request to the guards: Could they go with him to the shed to look for a box he had been expecting? In the past, such requests had always been denied. Presumably, Gallagher had offered the guards a share in whatever was in his fictitious box. Perhaps the pangs of hunger and desperation were the reason the guards agreed. Rose had told Gallagher to be very deliberate in his steps. They even practiced in the barracks until the Ohioan's measured steps were precise. Each step would be three feet in distance. Gallagher set out with the guards, walking methodically. Of course, there was no box in the shed; on his return, he then recounted his steps on the way back. It was fifty-two to fifty-three feet in distance.[66]

It was now time to begin digging. Rose and Hamilton returned to Rat Hell in early February of 1864 to start the new tunnel. Unfortunately, when the colonel informed the crews that he had devised a new plan, they were unenthusiastic. Rose remembered that the men remained "demoralized" from the repeated failures, so he announced that he and Hamilton would dig the tunnel by themselves. In his usual understated way, the colonel said simply, "Hamilton and myself continued our dreary work alone, as before."[67]

Rose attacked the project with renewed vigor. "From this time forward," recalled Lieutenant Moran, who would later join the escape, "he never once turned over the chisel to a relief. All day long he worked with the tireless patience of a beaver."[68] Hamilton concurred, noting that he "did but little of the digging," while Rose dug for long hours alone in the tunnel, using the chisel and what tools had not broken in the previous efforts. He even clawed at the dirt with his bare hands. "I had charge of the kitchen fire-place entrance the greater part of the time" keeping watch, Hamilton later recalled, although he "frequently" went into cellar to fan air into the tunnel. "The completion of this [final] tunnel was carried out," remembered Hamilton, almost exclusively by Rose.[69]

It was a slow process, and the old problems with the previous tunnels reemerged—too little oxygen, too much work for just two men, and too little sleep to recover from the arduous nightly efforts. The deeper they dug, the harder it was to breathe or keep the candles lit. The problem was that whenever Hamilton stopped fanning to stand watch, pull the dirt out of the tunnel, or spread it under the pile of straw, the candlewick fizzled. They had to bring in more diggers; the crew was asked to rejoin the effort. Rose's energy and determination, coupled with the continued deterioration of conditions inside the prison, convinced most of the old crewmembers to answer the call. A few did not but were replaced by new recruits. Captain Johnston of the Sixth Kentucky explained the change of heart: "The hard fare and confinement of our prison, the monotony of which had become unendurable, and the possibility of escape at last roused us up to exertions almost superhuman."[70] Rose again organized three five-man crews, with one man digging, a second member fanning at all times, a third man dragging out the dirt and rock to hide it under the straw, the fourth serving as lookout, and the final member of the crew relieving the others.[71]

Because they were out of time, Rose decided the crews would dig around the clock—day and night. Digging during the daytime was far riskier, and they would have to find a way around the frequent roll calls. However, Rose believed they had no other choice. The men were assembled in the cellar for instructions for the new endeavor. The digging had to be precise both in terms of the direction of the tunnel to the shed and its exact length. Lieutenant Moran remembered, "Soon the knives and toy saws were at work again with vigor."[72] This tunnel would measure roughly two and a half feet high and two feet wide. Rose pushed the crews harder than ever before, but he pushed himself the hardest of all.

14

"Godspeed!"

A prisoner, if he deserves the name, is always more or less occupied with the idea of making his escape.

—Federico Fernández Cavada, Libby Prison, 1864[1]

The depleted food rations, periodic roll calls, increasingly violent tendencies of the guards, chilling temperatures, reduced privileges, and bouts with disease had taken their toll on Libby's prison population. But just when the inmates thought it could not get worse, February brought the most difficult struggles yet. By this point, many of the prisoners were unable to stand or walk, much less dig a tunnel to freedom. Even more security measures had been imposed, and the guards, themselves suffering, harassed the prisoners with heretofore-unseen bouts of rage and frequent shootings. These cruelties, remembered Colonel Fernández Cavada, constituted "a flail which threshes the chaff out of human pride."[2] Lieutenant Cyrus P. Heffley of the 142nd Pennsylvania summed it up: "We are starving by inches."[3] Captain Cornwell recorded simply that "The month of February 1864 was the most difficult."[4]

On February 4, the guards announced that they had reason to believe a mass escape attempt was imminent and anyone suspected of participating would be shot on sight. Sure enough, gunshots were heard throughout that long evening. The prisoners' anxiety and depression were furthered deepened, knowing that stacks of boxes and supplies sent by the sanitary commissions and loved ones still sat in the storage building next to Libby. The men knew the guards had rifled through them, as they saw the guards eating their food and wearing their clothing. Lieutenant Heffley expressed the sentiment of his fellow prisoners when he groaned, "I hope someone will set fire to the building in which the boxes are . . . 15 or 20 ton have been laying there for over a month."[5] The deteriorating conditions in Libby were disconcerting for Rose, who responded by urging his crews to dig with renewed determination.[6]

The weather had been bad all winter, to the point where Rose was concerned about its impact on the escape. Then, in February, a cold front had descended on Richmond—as cold as "Minnesota," according to the prisoners. It was followed by an outbreak of a disease that swept through the prison. Without physicians, medicine, or blankets, no effort was made by prison authorities to mitigate the inmates' suffering. So many prisoners were dying that the "dead house" had no additional room; the extra corpses were taken to the cellar in the west building, where they were stacked in piles. From the east cellar, Rose and his crews counted their blessings—happy to be alive and lucky the guards had not used the east cellar as an overflow to the "dead house." The death toll also diverted the rats that had plagued the prisoners; they simply went to the other cellar to eat the carcasses. Daily, slaves and Black prisoners were sent to load the stiff cadavers into coffins, which were then rolled out in what the prisoners called "the dead cart," pulled by gaunt mules, to nearby Oakwood Cemetery for a quick and unceremonious burial. From the high windows, prisoners watched the spectacle with dismay. Sorrow turned to outrage when the guards started announcing each wagonload by jeering, "A load of dead Yankees!" One of the prisoners, Robert Knox Sneden, recalled that, on a hunch, the prisoners began marking the coffins: Their theory was proven correct—the same coffins were being used repeatedly. The bodies were simply being dumped into shallow pits and the coffins brought back to Libby by night.[7]

Additional rumors swirled that the Union was mounting an assault on Richmond, which reduced the capital city to a state of panic. Newspapers speculated that the city's prisoners were once again planning to rise up and attack the capital. Colonel Fernández Cavada described a "scare on" throughout the prison and city. Accordingly, there were three roll-call tallies on February 6, and then the next day the prisoners awoke to the sounds of church bells ringing throughout the city. Local militias were being called out to reinforce the defensive positions surrounding the city. There was only one roll call that day inside Libby, as the guards were distracted by their own preparations for the invasion.[8]

Outside the prison, Elizabeth Van Lew was receiving reports from her informants that something was about to happen at the bastille. "There was to be an exit." In anticipation, Van Lew had her servants prepare the home to accommodate escaped prisoners. They nailed blankets to cover windows, had a small fire burning around the clock, organized cots, and stockpiled goods. "We were ready for them," the Richmond spy wrote.[9]

SHOOTING SQUIRRELS

In response to the increased likelihood that none of them would walk out of the prison alive, Rose drove the digging crews day and night, "unceasingly." His compatriots described the "severe" but "patient and energetic labor," but there seemed to be a renewed sense that this tunnel would work. Their colonel's "cheery enthusiasm" and stoicism inspired the men to work through the exhaustion and brutal month.[10] Moreover, they were now avoiding the sewers, so there were fewer rats in the tunnel, and the smell was no longer overbearing. But really, there was no other option than to escape.

Rose ordered them to excavate downward to account for the building's foundation, then "slightly ascended" to a point a few feet below the surface. The remainder of the tunnel was dug "nearly level." Much of the tunnel measured roughly twenty-four inches in height by eighteen inches in diameter but diminished to a tight sixteen inches across when they encountered hard clay. As they neared the exit, over fifty feet from the cellar, Rose had the tunnel "gradually enlarged" to roughly two feet wide, so as to accommodate the escape. Their target remained the storage shed by the fence.[11]

With the crews working days and nights and in shorter, rotating shifts, they made better progress. Rose remained concerned about another cave-in. Although the dirt was firmer along the new path, the sheer length of the tunnel was problematic. As expected, the deeper they dug, the more problems they had keeping the candle aflame; the tunnelers were forced to work in complete darkness. As they neared the end of the tunnel, the diggers also felt as though they were suffocating. "It was," Johnston said simply, "impossible to breathe the air of the tunnel for many minutes altogether."[12] When someone felt himself losing consciousness, he tugged on the rope tied around his leg and was pulled out. This became increasingly common, noted W. S. B. Randall; "We often pulled out our comrades, suffocated and exhausted, nearer dead than alive," he later recalled.[13] Rose started alternating the diggers in short shifts.[14]

Rose's other concern was the rash of attempted escapes. The guards were on heightened alert, which meant frequent roll calls and unannounced inspections of the cellar. The escapees were, however, usually caught, which sent a wave of distress across the prison. In one such instance that February, four prisoners broke out. One of them, Lieutenant King, was caught "on the road" just outside of Richmond; he refused to talk or state his name and so was "dragged" to Libby for questioning. He still refused to talk, and the authorities became uncertain whether the man in custody was actually an escapee from Libby. Commandant Turner took the suspect to room after room and ordered the prisoners assembled to identify the man. As usual, the prisoners feigned ignorance when asked if the man, now back in the population, was Lieutenant King. Perhaps wise to the ploy, the commandant ordered that Colonel Streight be brought to one of the rooms. Unaware of what was happening, Streight inadvertently greeted King by name when he saw him. Turner had his man.[15]

The next day, a second of the four escapees, Lieutenant Cupp, was captured quite some distance from Richmond and just sixteen miles from Union lines at Williamsburg. Then on February 3, Lieutenant Carothers, the third prisoner to escape, was rearrested and brought back into Libby. The only member of the party still on the loose was Lieutenant Porter. The captured prisoners were dealt with very harshly, and their plight upset the prisoners. "There perhaps could not be a more unfavorable time to escape, for the whole country is filled with patrols to arrest conscripts fleeing to our lines," reasoned Captain Cornwell. "Every citizen is a policeman."[16] This reality was not lost on Rose and Hamilton.

The digging was interrupted by another alarming development. The guards almost never ventured into Rat Hell; the cellar was simply too foul. However, that February Commandant Turner began ordering surprise visits even to the cellar during the day. Rose had ordered the crews to be extra vigilant, which likely saved all of them. When the guards approached, the lookout posted by the fireplace entrance was able to quickly sound the alarm. The crew would dive into the mouth of the tunnel and crouch in the shadows behind the large, thick beams that comprised the prison's foundation.

It was no longer just a matter of being caught. The guards had standing orders to fire on prisoners standing by any window or caught trying to escape. Over the next few days, inmates standing near windows were nicked, hit, and killed. This included a captain from Ohio who had been sitting by the window in order to use the natural light to read a newspaper; he was shot in the head and died instantly. Throughout the day and into the night, shots struck the walls and ceiling by the windows, unnerving the prisoners. Even though the guards were not skilled marksmen, they seemed to view the new policy as sport, vying to see which of them could hit a prisoner in the head and boasting "pretty much after the fashion of boys after squirrels."[17]

During one breakfast that month, the prisoners tried to lift one another's spirits by singing songs as they marched down to the mess for their meal of rotten turnips. The commandant fumed, ordering them to cease with "your villainous Yankee songs." As punishment, on more than one evening Turner ordered the men to stand at attention for hours at a time. Indeed, Commandant Turner was on edge. Short-tempered, erratic, and violent, the major had begun taking "hostages" and ordering beatings and executions. The adjutant, Lieutenant John LaTouche, announced to the prisoners that he wanted to be "rid of them." It seemed they would be summarily executed in groups.[18]

THE ROLL CALL

Even though the tunnel was progressing quickly, the added guard patrols and frequent roll calls were creating new problems. The commandant ordered that roll be called frequently. Erastus Ross, the clerk, oversaw these daily tallies. Rose worried how his five-man crews would dig during the day without being discovered during a daytime tally.[19] However, one of the tactics used by the prisoners to undermine the count was "repeating." After the head count in one room, members of the crew would sneak quickly through the cuts they had made in the walls in order to again be counted in the next room. It was, Rose said, a "hazardous business," because if they were caught "stooping down and running toward the foot of the ranks," they would likely be put to death, and the men in the cellar would be detected and subjected to a similar fate. Consequently, when the commandant ordered roll calls in February, Rose needed five of his men upstairs to be on alert to "repeat" for their comrades toiling in the cellar. Fortunately, Lieutenant Moran boasted that Rose's trick worked, "making Ross's book balance."[20]

There were, however, unforeseen problems even with this tactic: The men enjoyed the repeating a bit too much. Soon, other prisoners joined in the tunnelers' "prank," racing back and forth from room to room to undermine Ross's count "just for the fun of the thing."[21] In words of Captain Caldwell, it was "Yankee fun . . . to deceive these confederates, by means of this small door."[22] However, so many prisoners joined in the frenzy that the clerk's tallies greatly exceeded the number of prisoners that should have been housed in Libby. Ross would sternly rebuke the "grinning" prisoners: "Now, gentlemen, look yere," he once roared in his high-pitched drawl. "I can count a hundred as good as any 'blank' man in this yere town, but I'll be 'blank blanked' if I can count a hundred of you 'blanked' Yankees."[23]

Ross's castigation had the opposite effect: "Now, gentlemen," he complained, "there's one thing sho: there's eight or ten of you-uns yere that ain't yere!" The men broke into a raucous laughter that "brought down the house." Lieutenant Moran remembered the hilarity being so "contagious" that it "shook the rafters of Libby."[24] One prisoner, however, did not find it amusing; Rose worried that his crews in the cellar would soon be caught now that Ross was wise to the repeating ploy. Of course, he and the other prisoners did not know that the "diminutive" clerk was actually one of Van Lew's spies and was helping them. But with such regular and wide discrepancies in the roll call, Ross was having trouble covering up the issue. Soon Inspector Turner and Lieutenant LaTouche started overseeing the counts.[25]

Early one morning as Rose and Hamilton returned to their barracks from another shift of digging, the doors to the "Lower Chickamauga Room" burst open. Several armed guards entered, followed by the clerk and Lieutenant LaTouche: Under their eye, Ross would not be able to forge the count. Two of Rose's digging crew, Captain Isaac N. Johnston and Major Bedan B. McDonald, were still in the tunnel. Rose and Hamilton prepared to cover for their fellow diggers by repeating during the head count. However, when they tried to duck back into formation, their fellow prisoners, perhaps alarmed by the show of force, did not cooperate. The count came up two prisoners shy. To Rose's horror, Ross was sent back downstairs by LaTouche to get the roster of all the prisoners. He returned and ordered the prisoners to line up outside one of the doorways and then walk one at a time through a gauntlet of guards by the door while he called out the names. When the tally was finished, Ross read the names of the two missing prisoners. Commandant Turner was summoned and ordered an investigation. After weeks of digging, several failed attempts, and many long and brutal nights in the cellar, it appeared the tunnelers had finally been caught.[26]

In all the fuss, Rose and Hamilton had been unable to sneak downstairs to warn Johnston and McDonald. And neither could the two diggers simply return to the Chickamauga Room as if nothing had happened. Prisoners were being killed for less. Late that night after Turner placed the prison on lockdown, Rose and Hamilton managed to evade the guards and make it back to the cellar. They informed their two colleagues that their "absence was detected," as Rose described the situation in his characteristic matter-of-fact manner. The men wanted to reenter the prison population, but Rose asked them what explanation they would give for not being at the roll call. Their appearance back upstairs would likely compromise the tunnel, and the two men would, at best, be locked in solitary in the cellar. They were so weak that Rose doubted they would survive the ordeal. At worst, they would be shot or hanged.[27]

The colonel put the decision before the two men. McDonald believed he might be able to lie his way out of it but seemed also to be dreading the prospect of living in the putrid cellar for the next few days. Or longer. Johnston decided to remain in hiding in the cellar. This, of course, meant he would have to sleep in Rat Hell and, he recalled, endure "the sickening air, the deathly chill, and the horrible interminable darkness." His fellow diggers would also have to bring him water and food each day.[28] Living "among the squealing rats" in the dank, cramped cellar would be difficult for anyone, but Johnston had grown up on a farm. Being in prison and unable to enjoy open spaces had been difficult for the Kentuckian. However, Rose had faith in the tough veteran who had made it through the bloody battles at Shiloh, Chickamauga, and Stones River.[29]

So, in the predawn hours, McDonald snuck back upstairs to the Chickamauga Room and appeared at the morning roll call. McDonald was promptly discovered and ordered to report to Ross. The major concocted a lie, claiming he had been sick and gone to the hospital the day before to see if any physicians were still there. There had been no doctors there, but before returning to the barracks, he claimed, he had gone to the third floor to visit friends and ended up sleeping upstairs. It was a dangerous gamble and a suspect story. The prisoners would have known that the hospital had been closed and the privilege of visiting other rooms had been revoked a few days earlier by the commandant. Fortunately, Ross covered up the incident by accepting the lie. However, Commandant Turner, who had already ordered a manhunt for the two prisoners, did not believe Ross's report and demanded answers. The major from Ohio responded to the questioning by claiming he had hidden because he was afraid of being caught in the wrong room. To his amazement, Turner accepted the account and even commended the major for his honesty, saying, "An open confession is good for the soul." The commandant, McDonald guessed, was as dumb as he had always suspected. Rose wondered if perhaps he wasn't simply hesitant to report yet another escape from his prison. The tunnel might not have been compromised after all.[30]

Captain Johnston was not as lucky. He was still trapped in "purgatory." It was hellish, Johnston later recalled, to take "up his abode in this cellar" amid the swarms of "squealing rats." Rose informed him that the commandant had announced to the prisoners that the captain had escaped but would be recaptured. The members of Rose's crew had even been questioned by the commandant but had a lie ready; they claimed they had heard that Johnston had stolen a Confederate uniform and walked out of the prison, aided by disloyal guards who also happened to be relatives of the officer from Kentucky. They went so far as to suggest that they had heard that Johnston had fashioned a wooden sword that he'd hooked on his belt to complete the ruse. It worked; the commandant even started questioning his guards' loyalty.[31]

Rose decided that further digging during the day was simply too dangerous. There were liable to be additional roll calls. Sure enough, multiple tallies continued through early February. Rose's crews had thus far been lucky but could not risk another incident during the roll calls. However, this meant Johnston would have to wait until nightfall for water and food. The crewmembers did help Johnston to occasionally sneak upstairs so he could sleep in the barracks and free himself from the horrors of the dungeon for at least a few hours. This was done with the utmost care, Johnston remembered, in order that "his presence was never known" to the other prisoners.[32] Before dawn, he would then sneak back down to the cellar with Rose, giving the colonel time to replace the bricks by the fireplace and make it back upstairs for the roll call.

The unfortunate turn of events had an unintended benefit: Johnston occupied his time digging. Like Rose, he worked tirelessly, claiming there was nothing else to do, and idle time alone in the foul dungeon was too awful. Besides, the captain told his accomplices good-naturedly, "I had plenty of company—little of it, however, agreeable." After all, "it consisted of rebels, rats, and other vermin!"[33] The rodents, it turned out, did come in handy. Whenever a guard patrolled nearby or came to inspect the cellar, the rats grew loud and agitated. Fortunately, Johnston later recalled, the rats seemed to have grown accustomed to his presence but warned him when the guards were near. At the same time, they gave him an idea, albeit a repulsive one: He dug a "pit" under the straw pile. Despite being surrounded by rats, it was a safe hiding place in which to sleep.

On the morning of February 6, when the captain was trying to relax after hours of digging, the door to the cellar burst open, and several guards entered. There was only a moment's notice from the other occupants of the cellar, allowing Johnston insufficient time to make it to the tunnel. He dove into the pile of straw, thinking quickly enough to bring the loose digging tools with him. Johnston watched in horror as the guards walked toward the tunnel but stopped just shy of the entrance. However, as he hid, the straw began to tickle his nose. He felt a sneeze coming on. The guards relaxed and simply stood in the center of the cellar talking. Johnston could hold his sneeze no longer. He let loose what seemed to him to be a "loud explosion," but the guards seemed not to notice and soon exited the cellar.[34]

That night, the captain shared the details of his near capture with Rose, who expressed concern that the guards were again inspecting the cellar. It was not normal; Rose concluded that the commandant or guards must have been expecting an escape. Lieutenant Moran later remembered that even the "stout-hearted" Hamilton "was for once excited" and worried. Moran noted that Rose's "unflinching fortitude had thus far inspired his little band," but now their "spirits were dashed." The risk of capture was weighing on the men, and the ordeal of sneaking extra rations of water and food to the cellar each night was precarious. At the same time, Johnston's physical and mental health were deteriorating from being stuck in the wretched dungeon days on end. "It soon became apparent that a man could not long exist in such a pestilential atmosphere," Moran felt. As a result, Rose announced that they had no option but to complete the digging within a night or two. It was time to escape.[35]

RAID ON RICHMOND

The tunnelers were nervous with anticipation. But they were not the only ones; as rumors of an impending Union raid on Richmond again swirled through the city and prison, the tension grew palpable among both prisoners and guards. Confederate authorities responded accordingly. Defenses in and around the city were reinforced, and security inside the bastille was tightened. These developments threatened to undermine the pending escape in a number of ways. On one extreme was the thought among some of the crew that they should simply wait to be liberated; on the other hand, hearsay suggested Turner would kill everyone inside Libby as soon as the raid commenced.

In early February 4, a teenage boy had arrived at Fortress Monroe on the Virginia coast with an urgent dispatch for Union general Benjamin Butler. It was another encrypted note from Elizabeth Van Lew, writing under her alias as his "niece . . . Eliza A. Jones." One of Van Lew's informants had been studying Confederate troop positions around the capital city and estimated, "Richmond could be taken easier now than at any other time since the war began." The defenses were spread too thin because of pressing needs elsewhere and the reinforcements ordered to defend Richmond had not yet arrived.[36] The message contained more pressing news. Van Lew warned, "It is intended to remove to Georgia very soon all the federal prisoners." Libby and other Richmond prisons were so grotesquely overcrowded that General Winder was planning to move as many as thirteen thousand Union prisoners from Richmond to Georgia. The idea had originated with none other than General Robert E. Lee, who had grown concerned with the security threat posed by so many starving and desperate prisoners in the capital city. Van Lew warned that most of the prisoners were so weak that they would not survive the journey. Moreover, their destination would be Andersonville, the dismal holding pen that would become the most notorious prison in American history.[37]

The heavyset, droopy-eyed Butler dispatched an urgent telegram to Edwin Stanton, the secretary of war, with the recommendation that they strike Richmond immediately. "You will see that the prisoners are to be sent away to Georgia," wrote Butler. "Now, or never, is the time to strike." He further reminded the war secretary, "If we fail, it will be at least an attempt to do our duty and rescue our friends." However, there was insufficient time to plan the raid, and Butler's Eighteenth Army could only muster about six thousand soldiers for the emergency mission.[38]

Nevertheless, the gruff Stanton, who had long complained of the South's treatment of Union prisoners, supported the effort. Furthermore, Northern politicians and family members whose loved ones continued to suffer in Richmond's prisons urged action. Three months earlier, the influential *New York Herald* had written of the prisoners: "They must not be permitted to perish!" The paper pushed for an assault on the Confederate capital, writing, "Those prisoners at Richmond must be rescued by force of arms; and this can be done."[39] Likewise, the US Senate had released a report chronicling the abuses in Richmond's prisons. The graphic details and extent of inmate injustices shocked the public. The Senate even debated raising one million volunteers for a three-month tour whose sole purpose would be the sacking of Richmond. The new army's mission might be to "carry food and freedom to every captive held in rebel prisons, and to plant the flag of the United States upon every prison they occupy." The crimes in Libby must be stopped and the prisoners saved, the report argued.[40]

Frustratingly, the Union had not seriously put Richmond in the crosshairs since General George McClellan's failed incursion back in 1862. Butler had been itching to strike Richmond, so it was with urgency that he gave orders to General Isaac J. Wistar to prepare to attack the Confederate capital. The objective: "To relieve our prisoners who must otherwise, it seems to me, of necessity be starved." The hastily made plan called for Wistar to conduct a hit-and-run raid that would destroy as much of Richmond as possible in a short amount of time, with priority targets such as the Tredegar Iron Works and the railways that advanced the Southern war effort. If the opportunity presented itself, Wistar was to try and capture Jefferson Davis and other Confederate leaders. The mission to the Confederate capital would, predicted Butler, deliver a "blow . . . from which it will never recover." They would also try to liberate Libby.[41]

As Rose's crew was digging in the cellar on the night of February 6, General Wistar, with far too few troops—mostly light cavalry—set out from Williamsburg to strike Richmond. It was intended to be a lightning strike, and the force was moving quickly, with each soldier carrying only seventy rounds of ammunition and rations for just six days. They passed the Pamunkey and Chickahominy Rivers, then entered the fields surrounding Richmond. Just before dawn on the seventh, the small company approached the city from the south, which they believed would be largely undefended. The plan was to cross Bottoms Bridge and race into the city before its residents and defenders awoke. However, they found the bridge destroyed and Confederate forces dug in on the opposite bank of the river with artillery. The Confederates had learned the raid was coming. Worse yet, as the fighting broke out, a train full of reinforcements arrived to join their brothers in gray.

General Wistar probed enemy lines for an opportunity to pass but saw none. His mounted units were no match for the artillery and strong Confederate defenses. Wistar had to abandon the effort and withdraw back to Williamsburg. In the city, the predawn artillery barrage had shaken both residents and prisoners from their slumber. Civilians, militia units, and even sickly children took to the streets in panic, guns in hand, expecting an invasion. Inside Libby, Colonel Bartleson remembered his fellow prisoners gathering excitedly for the moment of liberation. In the bleak cellar, Rose's crew continued to dig but prepared to rush upstairs for whatever happened next. Back at Fortress Monroe, General Butler was outraged. He would later read a newspaper account in the *Richmond Examiner* that a "Yankee deserter" named William Boyle had tipped the Confederates off regarding the pending attack. The reaction inside Libby was hopelessness and defeat . . .[42]

BREAKING GROUND!

. . . That is, except for Rose. He remained focused on tunneling to the storage shed just outside the perimeter fencing of the prison. The shed was used by another warehouse known as Kerr's and not by the Libby Prison, so Rose assumed no guards would be in or around the shed. The shed would provide cover for the crew as they emerged from the tunnel. From there, the prisoners could make it to the small alley sitting between the prison and the canal, known as Dock Street or Canal Street, which ran parallel to the James River. Rose had been interrogating every new prisoner who had arrived at the bastille. From them, he knew the exact position of the nearest Union lines. The target would be Williamsburg, roughly fifty miles east of Richmond. The important city had been taken during the Peninsula campaign in the spring of 1862 after Confederate forces had abandoned it and retreated toward Richmond.

The digging continued at a frantic pace, but Rose added a new order for his three crews: In preparation for the escape, they had to start saving as much nonperishable food as possible. This would not be easy; the rations were barely sufficient for a man to stay alive, and some days there was no food at all, meaning the men were already dying a slow death from starvation. Over the next few days, each man managed to save a few bites, hiding morsels of smoked tongue, dried beef, and hard bread in their pockets. The provisions would have to sustain them during their race to freedom, which would most likely require several nights of travel.

Around midnight on February 6, Major McDonald, Captain Terrance Clark, and Captain W. S. B. Randall of the Second Ohio were on the rotating digging shift. Based on Rose's calculations, their tunnel had extended to just over fifty feet, which should have placed its exit directly below the shed. It was time to begin digging the few feet upward to freedom. Randall was in the tunnel and used the chisel to dig directly overhead. An avalanche of dirt and rocks poured down on him, but the major persisted and "soon broke through to the surface." To his horror, when he rubbed the debris out of his eyes, Randall saw a guard "standing nearby!" The sentry appeared to have heard a noise, turned, and walked directly over the small hole made by Randall. The captain's heart was racing. He recalled, "The events of my life seemed to flit before me." Beside the sentry was the fence. The sentry walked over to it and leaned on the fence for what to Randall seemed an eternity. The guard casually looked around for the source of the sound. Satisfied it had been nothing, he casually turned and continued his patrol.[43]

Captain Randall took one last, quick glance. What he saw was nearly as disturbing as the sentry: The tunnel emerged on the wrong side of the fence. The opening came up next to the fence, but on the prison side of the perimeter. They had been short by a few feet. The captain quickly crawled back to the entrance of the tunnel. McDonald and Clark reached in and yanked Randall out and onto his feet. In a panicked tone, he informed the others of his "nearly fatal blunder." They agreed to get Colonel Rose, who had already finished his shift and returned to the Lower Chickamauga Room to sleep; so one man climbed the rope ladder to the kitchen and snuck upstairs to awaken the colonel. Rose immediately headed to the cellar. There, Randall described the encounter, insisting, "All is lost!"[44]

Rose ordered McDonald, Clark, Randall, and the two other men on that night's rotation to do nothing—to wait for him. The burly colonel grabbed the chisel and dove into the tunnel. He wanted to examine the damage. Rose reached the exit point and peered quietly up into the cold, dark sky. He saw the yard around the prison and then spied the sentry standing guard. Fortunately, the opening in the ground above was very small. It would be hard to detect, especially at night and if the sentries were not looking for it. Rose also saw that the tunnel had come up a bit short. The digging must not have been perfectly straight, which then threw off their count for the length of the excavation. Suddenly, Rose heard the voice of another guard: "What is it?" Two sentries were now directly overhead. One looked down at the hole, seeming to stare directly at Rose, but in the black night could not see into the tunnel. However, the guard thrust the tip of his bayonet into the hole. With no room to move, Rose held his breath as the steel tip of the bayonet came toward his face but only "grazed" his cheek. A tense moment later, one of the guards grumbled, "a thundering big rat!" Both sentries agreed and casually walked away. Rose had been lucky.[45]

The good news was that the guards' demeanor indicated that they had not detected the escape. Rose pushed an old shoe through the small opening and then quickly and quietly patched up the exit with a shirt and dirt. The colonel returned to the cellar and notified the men that he had misjudged the distance and they were, indeed, on the prison side of the fence; however, the guards had not detected them, and a slight corrective expansion of the tunnel would place them by the shed on the other side of the fence. Rose said it would only take one more night of digging. The important thing was to not panic. He would alert the others of the next step in the plan after peering out the windows by the dockside of the prison in order to confirm the location of the old shoe and use it as the vantage point for extending the tunnel a few additional feet. The men calmed down, hid the evidence of their night's work, and went back upstairs before the morning roll call.

The next day, Rose and the crewmembers saw the old shoe. It was close to the fence and shed on the other side. The tunnel was only a little over five feet shy of their target. February 7 was a Sunday, and Rose decided to risk a daytime operation, hoping to finish the tunnel's extension that night and believing the guards would not inspect the cellar or conduct surprise roll calls on a Sunday. Rose, Hamilton, McDonald, and Clark began their work with a renewed sense of "urgency," knowing that they were so close. Indeed, as Rose remembered, "the diggers rejoiced at the prospect of the speedy completion." Throughout the day and night, the other members of the crews stole glances out the window in the direction of the shed and canal, looking to spot any Confederate soldiers who might be in the area, and hoping to see Rose break ground at any moment. Unfortunately, the digging progressed slower than expected, and the tunnel was not yet complete by that night. However, Rose and his crews were back at it the following night, working throughout the evening of February 8.[46]

According to Lieutenant Moran, "from this time forward . . . [Rose] never once turned over the chisel to a relief." The tunnelers remembered that, "all day long he worked with the tireless patience of a beaver." Rose finally took a short break around midnight but was back in the tunnel a few moments later, "possessed." He reached the base of a fence post, indicating that they were close. Only then did Rose turn the chisel over to McDonald and Clark for the final push. An "upward shoot was made" at an angle, just large enough, in the words of Hamilton, to "squirm through." After a few more hours of "tireless" digging, McDonald and Clark broke ground in the predawn hours. They peered aboveground and saw the shed.[47]

The cold, fresh air that greeted the men was a relief. The diggers returned to the cellar to announce the good news to Rose. The colonel instructed them to wait and immediately raced through the tunnel, then crawled out of the hole to inspect the small shed and high fence. He stood quietly under "the pale gleam of a star" and looked around. Rose saw the street and the glimmer of the old gas lamp and knew they were at the "desired point." As hoped, the shed would provide cover from the guards and any prying eyes in the prison. Careful to hide in the shadows, Rose snuck to the large gate below the archway that opened to the street. An iron bar rested across the latch, but to his amazement, it was unlocked. The guards' incompetence continued to prove fortuitous. Rose opened the gate and crept quietly out to Canal Street and the docks behind the prison. A lesser person might have been overcome by the urge to run, but after his brief reconnaissance, Rose closed the gate and climbed back into the tunnel. He quickly widened the exit, then concealed the tunnel with a pair of old pants filled with straw "to replace some of the earth at the surface" and "bolstered" it with a wood plank. Satisfied, the colonel crawled back into the cellar to inform his crewmembers of the good news.[48]

McDonald, Clark, and Johnston "almost wept with delight" as Rose, his muscles trembling from overwork and dehydration, announced to the men, "The underground railroad to God's country was open!"[49] He was so exhausted that he needed to be lifted out of the tunnel. The men covered the entrance of the tunnel by pushing a hogshead[50] into it. As soon as their handiwork was concealed, the tunnelers heard a nearby sentry holler, "Half-past one, and all's well!" Indeed, all was well. As the tunnelers helped Rose up the rope ladder and upstairs to the Chickamauga Room, he thought to himself, "Godspeed."[51]

Later that same day, Abraham Lincoln would sit for a photograph that would become perhaps the most famous image of the president. It would later grace the five-dollar bill.

15

Exodus

He went again to make escape.
Just as affairs were in this fix,
The guard on nine came down to six
And seeing Joe stand near the door,
He gave a yell, half cry, half roar
"Whose there?" and then (fe-fi-fo-fum!)
He came to a charge and cocked his gun.
"Don't shoot! Don't Shoot!" cried Joe, "Damn the luck"
"Lower the rope! Draw me up! Draw me up!"
The guard on six was just in time
In sezing the gun of number nine
And crying, "Don't shoot! Oh, don't shoot, Dan,
Jesus Christ, don't kill the man!"

—Robert Cornwell, Libby Prison, 1864[1]

It had been fully fifty-three days since Colonel Rose and Major Hamilton had re-moved the first brick from the fireplace in the Libby kitchen, including thirty-eight total days of digging, thirteen of them on the last tunnel. The crews had averaged five feet per night during the final few days of digging. If one accounted for the upward chute to the exit and the twists and turns to avoid rocks and the building's foundation, the "underground road to liberty" now extended nearly sixty feet from the cellar out to the shed on the perimeter of the prison grounds. They had done it.[2]

As Hamilton recounted later, "believing a fresh and early start would be to our ad-vantage we closed up the hole and came upstairs for orders from Colonel Rose." The men quietly woke the other members of the crews and informed them that they had "broke through the wall" and that the tunnel was complete. On Rose's instructions, they were all to meet in the kitchen at three o'clock in the morning for instructions.[3]

Down in the kitchen, Rose announced, "Boys, the tunnel is finished." Lieutenant Moran remembered that, with their day of liberation at hand, the men lined up in front of Rose and "wrung his hand again and again, and danced about with childish joy." As Rose detailed the next steps of the escape, "perspiration dripped from every pore of his exhausted body."[4] There was not enough time remaining for them to attempt their escape before daylight and the morning roll call, he cautioned. In addition, they would all need their rest for the arduous road ahead. Rose also invited each member of the secret party to select one trusted friend to join them on the escape. Once the fifteen diggers and their fifteen friends were out of the tunnel, it was decided that one trusted prisoner would seal the tunnel's entrance and exit and then replace the bricks around the kitchen fireplace. That prisoner was then to wait one hour in order to give the escapees ample head start and then either escape himself or notify the other prisoners. Rose selected Colonel Harrison C. Hobart of the Twenty-First Wisconsin Infantry for the important task. Like many of the crew, Hobart had been captured at Chickamauga; he was also trusted by all.[5]

As the fifteen tunnelers discreetly invited partners to join them on their escape, a few of their fellow prisoners declined, believing it to be too risky given their advanced age or deteriorated health. Colonel James Sanderson, for instance, decided not to go, believing he was about to be exchanged; the commissary was always cutting deals both inside and outside of the prison. Another offer was extended to General Neal Dow, the famed abolitionist and advocate for temperance. It devastated Dow to reject the offer, but he believed himself to be too old and far too sick for the journey. He did not want to slow the men down because "My naturally strong constitution had been broken down."[6] Colonel Bartleson wrote to his wife that day about the pending escape, admitting, "The difficulties after getting out are very formidable." He bemoaned, "The country is swarming with scouts and patrols," all of whom are "on the lookout for deserters" and escaped prisoners. Bartleson worried about his friends' chances and even asked his wife for her opinions on the escape plan. He also lamented the fact that he would not soon be reunited with her, stating that it would be "impossible" with just one arm for him to "crawl or make the descent, which was through a fireplace." He hoped his friends could beat the odds but doubted their chances.[7]

The city was crawling with Union-hating residents, soldiers, and militiamen, while Confederate pickets ringed the city. The escapees would have to forge creeks, rivers, and bogs and cover many miles traveling only in the middle of the night. The men were weak, hungry, and ill, and had but little food and no means for carrying water. Eventually, the alarm would be sounded, and Commandant Turner would organize an aggressive and massive manhunt. The prisoners would be on foot and unarmed; the Confederates would have horses and bloodhounds and be armed. On top of that, the weather was bitterly cold, and there was a chance of snow and freezing rain. A lot could go wrong.

Rose composed a map of Richmond and the Virginia peninsula, which he shared with his compatriots. Based on intelligence received from Van Lew's spies, Rose showed the men the possible locations of the Confederate defensive positions ringing the city. Likewise, Colonel W. P. Kendrick of the Third Cavalry from the Washington Territory had mapped out routes toward Norfolk, Fortress Monroe, Williamsburg, and other destinations. Armed with this knowledge, the escapees planned to move by night, hide by day, and avoid the Confederate pickets that surrounded the city. It would be a long and precarious journey to the nearest Union positions east of Richmond. With enough luck, they just might make it. Before the crewmembers crept back upstairs, Rose reminded them to say nothing about the plan, to discreetly gather food and supplies, and to meet back that night after dark for the escape.

That final day, Rose crept to one of the high windows and surveyed the area by the tunnel's exit, marked by the old shoe he had placed aboveground only a few hours earlier. He took note of the fence, gate, and path from the shed away from the prison. The exit, he observed, was "within sight" of one of the nearby sentries and just "a few yards" from the nightly route another sentry patrolled. They would need to be cautious and time their run eastward to the canal at the very moment the guards turned to begin their "westward course." Rose figured he would have to remain in the "shadows" and hug the "adjoining house as to make the color of his uniform indiscernible to the guard."[8] It was risky, but the plan had a chance of succeeding.

The men spent that final day gathering as much warm clothing, hard bread, dried meat, matches, and other supplies as possible without drawing attention to their efforts. They had been hoarding their meager rations for days in anticipation of this moment. Captain David Caldwell, a military chaplain, had managed to retain an old sack in which he had been collecting supplies for the big moment. His final day in the bastille also brought an unexpected event. Caldwell had always made himself available to all the prisoners for prayer, sermons, and just to lend a friendly ear. That final day, one of the prisoners died, and the men asked him to officiate at an informal funeral. Caldwell gave the service, but, despite the somber and serious matter, his mind was elsewhere. It also surely prompted him to think of his own mortality and the many hazards that faced him that night.[9]

At the prompting of Lieutenant James Wells and in anticipation of the long walk to freedom, the men had for days been working on their endurance. Wells organized walks each day, whereby the members of the crew would pace circles around the crowded rooms in order to keep their legs in condition. Wells gradually increased the distance each day until they were walking an estimated twenty-two miles a day around the room! Wells had also spent the final days trying to trade for boots. His were completely worn out. Nevertheless, none of the prisoners would take the deal. He decided he would escape even though he would be walking barefoot in the dead of winter.[10]

Major McDonald may have put the entire plan at risk when he asked Colonel Sanderson, a former hotelier, for money. Sanderson had been feuding with Colonel Streight, and most of the prisoners disliked and distrusted him. Ironically, McDonald had selected Colonel Streight as his "partner" for the escape. Even still, Sanderson offered his help; he procured a hatchet, a bottle of brandy, and a few other items and some currency for the prisoners. He also advised McDonald to take Streight to the Van Lew mansion and even provided directions to Church Hill. They would be safe there, the former commissary advised. Van Lew had likely been the source for Sanderson's last-minute supplies and was already preparing to receive the prisoners. Importantly, everyone kept the escape a secret that final day . . . except for one anonymous informant.[11]

The plot was also almost derailed just hours before the escape was to commence. One man whose emotions ran high that final day was Captain Johnston, who was still stuck in the east cellar. "Never was my anxiety as great as for the setting of that day's sun, and more than once during its long, dreary hours I feared that the cup of happiness, now so near our lips, would be rudely dashed away." Johnston recalled that their plan was nearly dashed that final day when an informant snitched on the crews! As the former farmer whittled away the final hours of his incarceration in the cellar, the guards unexpectedly burst through the bolted door. The captain again dove for cover under the straw pile. The guards looked around hurriedly but then departed just as quickly as they had come. However, they returned with a dog. Johnston's heart sank as he realized he was about to be captured just hours before escaping. The dog began sniffing around the cellar and then headed to the pile of straw. Fortunately, startled rats darted in and out of the straw, distracting the dog, who gave chase to one rodent after another. The guards called the dog off and again departed. Of the close encounter with the dog, Johnston exhaled and mused, "I was too large game for him!"[12]

Sleep eluded all of the men that final day. The long day inside Libby—their last—was made all the more emotional because, as Bartleson recalled, the newspapers were filled with "a great commotion in Richmond" regarding General Wistar's unsuccessful raid. The city remained in a state of "excited uneasiness." Adding to the tension, another rumor was circulating that General Meade was advancing from the Rapidan River. As anticipated, no mail or boxes arrived at the prison on February 8 or 9, and neither did the prisoners get but a morsel of "entirely spoiled" food. Bartleson suspected that their rations had again "undoubtedly been pilfered by the guards."[13]

To the tunnelers, Tuesday, February 9, 1864, "seemed to them all the longest day in their lives."[14]

THE GREAT ESCAPE

It was seven o'clock on a chilly, forty-two-degree Tuesday night, February 9. Nightfall came early, and the temperature dropped quickly. The new moon was only two days into its cycle, and the men thanked their luck that the night remained dark. It was time to go. Thirty men gathered in the kitchen, which "seemed alive with the stir of preparation, so many were making ready to leave." Rose and Hamilton had given each of the crewmembers a secret password to share with the companion invited to join in the escape. In hushed tones in the kitchen, the two leaders asked each of the fifteen invitees their password, and then Rose opened the fireplace wall. The men climbed down the narrow, Z-shaped chute for the final time—a few for the first time.[15]

Colonel Hobart had joined them in the kitchen. It was his job to pull up the rope ladder and seal the bricks by the fireplace after the men had escaped. It would then, Rose agreed, be up to Hobart whether and when he wanted to escape or invite other prisoners to do so. Rose then took his fellow colonel by the hand, said his goodbyes, and went down into the cellar. The former principal was the last man down the passageway. As he scaled down the narrow, winding chute, he heard Hobart sealing the brick entrance above him as planned. At the site of Rose descending into the cellar, the men had to suppress the desire for "whooping" and "dancing." The colonel calmed them by announcing final instructions.[16]

Rose advised the men to go their separate ways once out of the prison in order to assure that someone would escape. A large group would draw attention, but scattering thirty prisoners across different routes toward City Point or Williamsburg might serve to confuse the inevitable manhunt that would follow. Finally, Rose explained that they would escape in intervals every several minutes as a security measure. The men agreed that Rose and Hamilton should be the first pair to escape. Afterward, the men departed more or less by rank, in descending order, with a few exceptions made for men who had been with the expedition since the beginning. The colonel then gave everyone "parting caution" and "thanked his brave comrades for their faithful labors." They all shook hands with the big man, who offered "Godspeed and farewell"; then Rose and Hamilton turned and crawled into the tunnel they had excavated.[17]

Rose went first. He crawled on his stomach over fifty feet. At some places, the tunnel was tight and perilously narrow. Rose's shoulders scraped the sides for the entire duration of the crawl. Then he angled upward to the small shed that had formerly held tobacco. At the point of egress, he peered around the shed, fence, alley, and canal. In the cold, clear night sky, he saw one of the guards about "twenty steps" from him and halted until the sentry was far enough away. There was no sign of anyone else, so at roughly eight o'clock that evening, Rose climbed out of the tunnel and signaled behind him to Hamilton that "all was clear." The colonel and major snuck to the sidewalk, and, as soon as the lone sentry turned to bring his patrol some "forty or sixty paces" in the other direction, the two men quickly and quietly opened the gate and hustled down the dark, narrow alley called Dock Street, heading east. They were soon out of sight.[18]

After Rose and Hamilton, the second pair in the tunnel was Captain John Gallagher and Major George Fitzsimmons, followed by Captain Isaac Johnston and Lieutenant John Fislar. The others "followed at intervals of a few minutes and, running low past the shed and fence, headed out through the gate and to the street." One of the most difficult parts of the escape was at its very start: sentries were patrolling, the street lamps remained lit, and an occasional resident walked by. If they had waited until midnight, it would have been easier, as the street lamps were put out and the city quieted down. However, that would have limited the amount of time for them to get out of the city before dawn broke. Once the prisoners made it to the dock, "there they disappeared in various directions in groups" of two.[19]

One of the last teams was Major Bedan McDonald and his partner, Colonel Abel Streight. It was a good thing, as the famous colonel "was too large to easily pass one obstruction in the tunnel, and got wedged in so that quite an effort was necessary to get him out of his predicament." He was stuck in the tunnel at the narrow point where it began angling upward. Time was of the essence, and so McDonald tried to help the colonel. After considerable effort, Streight was forced to strip off his clothing. With much difficulty and harassed by agitated rats, he tied a few items to his feet and pushed the remainder of his possessions ahead of him in the tunnel. He eventually made it out.[20]

Behind McDonald and Streight were Captain Charles Earle and Captain Charles Rowan, two of the Ninety-Sixth Illinois Infantry. Earle had wandered into the cellar one evening, surprising the crew working on the tunnel. To their relief, he had not caught wind of the operation; rather, he had been restless and looking for his own way to escape. Rose agreed that Earle could join the digging crews, and he became a helpful addition to the expedition when it turned out he had a map of Tidewater Virginia and the Peninsula, which he shared with Rose. Earle invited Rowan to be his partner for the escape, and the two men had stowed away some pieces of corn, stale meat, an empty bottle in the event they found water on the journey, and a bible. Earle recalled that it took him fifteen minutes to crawl through the passageway by the fireplace and through the length of the tunnel. He described being in the tunnel as "terrifying" because there was "no light." While the opening was "airy," the tunnel was but "a narrow, dark, damp hole, just large enough for one to pull himself through." Unfortunately for Earle and Rowan, they brought up the end of the escape and so were momentarily stuck behind Colonel Streight, who was wedged in the tunnel "kicking and floundering."[21]

Streight's escaping partner, Major McDonald, had been given information about Elizabeth Van Lew. Streight had also received a secret message—most likely hidden in a compartment in one of "Crazy Bette's" custard bowls. It had encouraged him to make his way to her mansion, which would serve as a safe house where the escapees could hide, sleep, eat, and prepare for the next leg of their journey. The note said only that Van Lew was a "negro woman."[22] Streight, McDonald, and a few other men headed the six blocks up Church Hill to the home.

On the way, they were careful to keep to the shadows beside the homes. However, on the street leading to the Van Lew mansion they passed a pub where several Confederates were, according to Streight, "drinking and carousing." The establishment was lit up, and the men realized too late that they should have avoided it altogether and moved a block in either direction. However, they were in a hurry and, starving and exhausted, were not thinking clearly. They decided to simply walk past the open door in a calm manner. However, as Streight passed the wooden frame, a "heavy" hand grabbed him by the shoulder. A drunken Confederate standing just inside the door confronted him. "Make that fellow give back my hat," the soldier slurred. Streight froze but a moment later calmly stated that he could not make the "fellow" return the soldier's hat and politely excused himself. The big soldier in gray was either too drunk to make sense of Streight's blue uniform or too used to seeing them around the city. Either way, Streight walked hurriedly from the pub and joined a relieved McDonald. The men agreed that they had to be more careful.[23]

Soon afterward, a young "negress" met Streight and McDonald on the street and informed them that she would take them to the Van Lew mansion. They followed their own Harriet Tubman a short distance up Church Hill to a mansion encircled by extensive grounds and large trees. There Miss Van Lew welcomed them. Inside the house the men were given food and water and escorted to a secret chamber where they would hide. Other prisoners arrived later that night. Streight and McDonald remained in hiding at the safe house for seven days—as Van Lew explained, time enough to let the panic from the large prison break and subsequent manhunt pass. After a week in hiding, the two prisoners were sent out of the house at night by Van Lew, who had provided them with "food, arms, and full directions," and they made their way toward the nearest Union lines. The two prisoners traveled for thirteen more nights, one of which was interrupted by a near run-in with a hunting party of Confederate soldiers and militiamen. They eventually arrived at the Potomac. Van Lew's instructions had been to wait on a small islet in the middle of the river, known as Blackistone Island. They did as instructed and were joined by two other escapees from Libby—William W. Scearce of the Fifty-First Indiana Infantry and Lieutenant John Sterling of the Thirtieth Indiana Infantry, who was still nursing wounds he had suffered at the Battle of Chickamauga back in the autumn of 1863. On February 28, the Union ship *Ella* arrived and rescued the men.[24]

Streight's escape caused perhaps the most commotion in Richmond of any of the prisoners. The city's newspapers later reported on the escapees that "among them we regret to include . . . notorious Colonel Straight." The *Richmond Examiner* lamented that "disloyal" Unionists must have helped them.[25] Amusingly, on February 9, Captain Cornwell recorded in his diary that "the day has been barren of any unusual incidents." The escape started well and was going according to Rose's plan . . . at least for a little while.[26]

"THE WILD STAMPEDE TO LIBERTY"

Back in the bastille's kitchen, after Rose had vanished into the passageway, Colonel Hobart had sealed the entrance to the fireplace immediately. He then snuck upstairs to his assigned barracks and went to the window to try and watch the escape unfolding just beyond the fence on Canal Street. By the dark window, Hobart watched what he described as a "living drama" of "dark shadows disappearing in another part, and the same shadows appearing on the opposite walk" by the canal. However, the orderly flight would not last.[27]

Word of the escape spread like wildfire through the prison. By nine o'clock that evening, the rumors sparked "a convention of excited and whispering men." Anxious and desperate prisoners confronted Hobart. He tried to deny the escape but soon had to admit it had happened, trying instead to calm the growing throng of prisoners. It did not work. Soon a "frenzied crowd" clamored down the steps. Hobart followed them, pleading with them to be quiet. In the kitchen, they found the fireplace entrance and "fiercely struggled" with one another, clawing at the bricks. Pushing and shoving, a near riot ensued as prisoners tried to get down the Z-shaped passageway to the tunnel. Hobart gave up trying to restore order and took his place in line to escape. Men rushed into the passageway one after the other and began tumbling out into the cellar. After the mob had disappeared into the cellar, Hobart grabbed the rope ladder and crawled down into the dungeon.[28]

In the cellar, prisoners scrambled to find the tunnel. Once it was located, a wide-eyed race ensued, with prisoners cramming into the passageway with no plan, rations of food, or idea of where they were going. In total, an additional sixty-nine prisoners followed the original thirty members of Rose's tunnelers that evening, running in every direction. Another ten would later find their way to the cellar and out of the tunnel.

General Dow remained behind. Much to his chagrin, he was unable physically to escape. He knew about the details of "the great escape" but "believed" that the riot that followed the orderly break out was the result of "a spy in their midst who communicated much of what took place to the officers in charge of the prison."

Dow reasoned, "Only a select few knew that preparations for this were going on." Someone had talked. Dow also worried that so many escapees would quickly expose the plot. It did.[29]

The prisoners continued to clamor into the cellar until around three or four in the morning. Surprisingly, despite the commotion in the kitchen and sheer number of escapees, the guards remained unaware of what was happening under their noses. Colonel Bartleson attributed this to a bit of luck, the incompetence of the guards, and freezing weather. Not long before the escape, the commandant had punished prisoners by boarding up the windows around the kitchen, which ended up having the effect of helping to muffle the riot there. Likewise, the sentry on duty outside the kitchen had spent the night bundled from head to toe with Union overcoats and blankets, while stamping his feet in an attempt to keep warm. He was, reasoned the one-armed colonel, disinterested in anything but trying to stay warm. The sentries patrolling the perimeter of the grounds had indeed spotted figures moving around the shed, but they had assumed it was fellow guards again "taking advantage of the night to pilfer the Yanks' boxes sent from home." In the cold night, they all were desperate for blankets.[30]

One of the mob to escape that night was Lieutenant Frank Moran. He had gone to sleep early, weak from the lack of food and water. Next to him in the barracks were two friends—Sprague and Duenkel. The commotion awakened Duenkel, who then wrested Moran from his slumber and "whispered excitedly the fact that Colonel Rose had gone out at the head of a party through a tunnel." Moran sat up and observed several fellow prisoners hurriedly gathering their belongings and putting on any available clothing. Men were running down the stairs, so Moran ran to one of the windows and peered out. He saw figures in the dark night sneaking along the alleyway beyond the fence. The lieutenant felt "a current of electricity" rush through him. "Thrilled," he headed down the stairs to join them.[31]

So many men poured into the stairway that in their panic they were knocking one another off the steps. Without a banister, many were tumbling to the ground below. Moran was of slight built and was quickly elbowed off the steps. He landed hard, hitting his head and cutting one of his hands. As he tried to get up, several prisoners trampled over him. One landed forcefully on his shoulder, and Moran felt the searing pain from the heavy boot. He managed to stand and was almost carried into the kitchen by the mob as if caught in a wave.

When Moran entered the kitchen he looked around for Duenkel, but his friend was nowhere to be found. The lieutenant glanced excitedly around the dark kitchen, wondering how the prisoners had escaped. All around, men were overturning tables and rushing about trying to find the way out. At that moment, another acquaintance, Lieutenant Harry Wilcox of the First New York, rushed into the kitchen and announced that the prisoners had escaped from a hole by the fireplace. Unfortunately, a scrum of desperate prisoners shoved their way to the stoves and brick fireplace. "Blocking the way," Moran and Wilcox were knocked to the ground by the throng of prisoners and "nearly suffocated."[32]

As Moran disappeared down the passageway, he heard others yelling, "The guards! The guards!" The alarm only further excited the chaotic scene in the kitchen. Worried their opportunity to escape was ending, men in the kitchen "begged in vain" to get into the hole. The prisoners had been descending by the rope ladder left by Colonel Hobart, but so many of them were hanging onto it that it tore. Men were sent crashing down onto the floor, one of them being Moran. For a third time, he landed hard, this time on top of squealing rats—"several of which I must have been killed in my fall." The panicked rodents were running for cover and "swarming" over his body. He felt a "troop" race across his face and hands. Instinctively, Moran jumped to his feet in the "cold" dark cellar and felt a rat standing on top of his shoulder. He shuddered and flung it off. Nearby was a stick, which he picked up and swung wildly at the rats while groping about for the entrance to the tunnel.[33]

Only when he was in the cellar with no way to get back to the barracks did Moran realize his mistake: he was utterly unprepared. He had "not a crumb of food saved up," and his shoes were "thin and ragged." He doubted that, "nearly worn out," he would survive the long run to freedom. He was snapped out of his anxiety by the ghastly tunnel. As he knelt down and crawled in, Moran's first feeling was that it was "indescribably horrible" and less a passageway than a "grave." Even though Moran was thin, the tunnel was so narrow that he was forced to shed his overcoat in order to wriggle through. There was such a commotion behind him that it sounded as if there were "several hundred men struggling" to get into the cellar and tunnel. It inspired Moran to crawl faster. He shoved his coat ahead and crawled as fast as possible through the tunnel, which, amid the adrenaline and panic, seemed to be "a mile long."[34]

As the lieutenant pulled himself through the tunnel, he bumped into the heels of a boot ahead of him. He followed closely, and as he reached the end of the passageway, he felt two men lift him out of the opening. He was standing next to Lieutenant Charles H. Morgan and Lieutenant William L. Watson. Both men were with the Twenty-First Wisconsin and had fought at Chickamauga. Moran looked for Wilcox but could not find him in the "stampede" of prisoners pouring out of the hole. Moran learned from Morgan and Watson that Colonel Rose and his party "were several hours on their journey." As such, the prison guards would likely soon discover the plot and sound the alarm; at best, he and the other prisoners would have only until the morning roll call before their absence at the prison was detected. The three men knew that Confederate pickets surrounded Richmond, so they needed to hurry but also be careful. On their journey, Morgan and Watson quickly discussed some of the details of their travel to Richmond. Moran had served in McClellan's Peninsula campaign in 1862 and recalled the maps he had seen, which he shared with the other two men. The three lieutenants quickly formulated a plan for getting out of the city and to Union lines. They ran using the North Star shining in the clear, cold night for bearing.[35]

Another prisoner among the "wild stampede" was James Wells, second lieutenant in the Eighth Michigan Cavalry. He had raced down to the kitchen with a friend named Plympton White, a young lieutenant from Erie, Pennsylvania, who was with the Eighty-Third Pennsylvania Infantry. Lieutenant White had managed to secure a haversack with "a scant supply of rations saved for the occasion and a map of the country which we had drawn up with a pencil."[36] These two prisoners were likely the only ones in that unorganized second wave of escapees to have prepared for the possibility of escape. However, they were not prepared for the melee that met them in the kitchen, as prisoners pushed and shoved to get into the passageway.

As the two friends tried to force their way through the throng of panicked prisoners, an exasperated White told the Michigander that, if they became separated, "Wells, I will wait for you" outside the tunnel. Wells managed to finally make it down the passageway and proceeded to follow roughly one dozen prisoners who were crawling into the tunnel. But just as Wells was about to enter the tunnel, "a noise at the outside door caused a report to be circulated that those who had gone out had been captured, and that the guards were coming in to take us all under arrest." Prisoners overreacted, with some trying to get back up the passageway to return to their barracks, and others clamoring to get into the tunnel. Wells soon learned that it had been a false alarm.[37]

The air inside the narrow shaft was so "foul" that Wells felt himself growing nauseated. Like others, Wells was forced to take off his overcoat and drag it behind him through the tunnel. When he climbed out of the opening by the shed, he looked for Lieutenant White but could not find him. He later discovered that when the prisoners had sounded the false alarm, White had raced back up to the barracks. Later that night after realizing the guards had not discovered the escape plan, White returned to the cellar and fled. Unfortunately, Lieutenant White was caught five days later.

After waiting some time for his friend, Wells decided to flee on his own and ran to Canal Street. Without White's map, Wells tried to recall the travel plan they discussed. He remembered the Chickahominy River, which was "not more than six miles distant."[38] However, amid the excitement Wells admitted that he ended up "guided wholly by impulse, and by circumstances as they were presented." He ran "two squares" down Canal Street then tried to angle in the direction of the river and closest Union lines. Wells was less concerned about wearing his blue uniform because so many Confederate soldiers and the city's residents had stolen Union coats and uniforms that blue had become the color of Richmond. He was, however, worried about dogs. The prison commandants and search parties organized to hunt down escapees routinely included bloodhounds and a few large and aggressive dogs.[39]

16

Manhunt

The measureless torments of the . . . helpless young men, with all their humilia-
tions, hunger, cold, filth, despair, hope utterly given out.

—Walt Whitman, Union nurse, Washington, D.C., 1864[1]

The "wild stampede for liberty," Major Hamilton would later argue, was what "attracted the attention of the Confederate guards." While in actuality the guards had
not been aware of the stampede down in the kitchen and cellar, it may be true that
Hamilton and other members of the original group of escapees would have stood
a better chance of making it to the Union lines had it not been for a total of 109
prisoners breaking out of Libby. On the other hand, Hamilton believed the panic of
the second wave of escapees cost the inmates dearly: "had the prisoners kept cool and
collected, I believe that the prison would have been almost emptied before daylight
the next morning."[2]

At the morning roll call on February 10, it was obvious that something was
wrong. Not only were many prisoners missing, but also the ones who assembled
for the tally were buzzing with excitement and gossip. That morning Captain
Robert Cornwell recorded with delight in his diary, "The first news that greeted
my ears this morning when I awoke was the startling intelligence that on last night
Libby had sprung a very big leak."[3] Bartleson, who had been forced to stay behind
on account of his lost arm, remembered that the initial roll call was off, but only
by nine prisoners. The prison clerk then ordered a second count. This time the
prisoners were "packed like sardines" into one of the rooms upstairs and made
to walk one at a time through the door to be counted.[4] General Dow, ranking
officer among the inmates, was ordered to go first; he noted the look of concern

on the "faces" of the guards. A second count, he recalled, produced a much larger "discrepancy." He described a "great . . . panic" among the guards.[5] Bartleson remembered that part of the concern was because "many of the most prominent and some of the most obnoxious of the prisoners were missing."[6]

Ross organized a third tally. It was a quick and simple head count, but according to General Dow, the prisoners "tried to confuse him." It worked. They also disrupted a fourth tally. The general described the scene of how "they would dodge in and out, get counted twice, put hats and caps on sticks and try to get them counted for heads." The prison commandant and authorities were summoned, and yet another count was ordered. With his superiors breathing over his shoulder, Ross became so flustered that he lost his place during the "tally" and had to start over. Dow described the shock of the commandants and guards turning to "blank astonishment and despair" when they realized the extent of the escape. As for the prisoners, they found the whole affair "amusing." The whole morning was occupied with tallies, each of which produced different results, cheers by the prisoners, and exasperation among the officials! Of course, it is probable that Ross purposely miscounted in order to cover for the escapees and buy them time.[7]

Commandant Turner was "stumped" as to how so many prisoners had managed to escape. When pressed for answers, the guards were "unable to determine how it was done." Bartleson remembered "great consternation among the officials" and hot disagreements among them and accusations of disloyalty leveled at the guards, who were then ordered to find evidence of the escape. The search took much of the day, and yet no clue was found. Predictably, the guards bungled the effort; yet Hobart had done a respectable job concealing the means of escape, despite the second "wild stampede" out of the prison.[8]

Because of the high profile of Libby Prison and ongoing fears about a massive uprising among the Union inmates, word spread quickly. The day after the breakout was discovered, the *Richmond Examiner* reported the "Escape of one hundred and nine commissioner Yankee officers from the Libby prison." They claimed the breakout was discovered during morning roll call when "the count" failed to "correspond with the number booked." The newspaper admitted that "the calling of the roll consumed nearly four hours" but spun the story to emphasize that it had only taken so long because there were over a thousand inmates in Libby and because the guards had been so thorough.[9] Three days later the *Richmond Enquirer* expressed disbelief that so many prisoners could have escaped, writing, "This is almost incredible." Other papers labeled it "miraculous."[10]

After the count was finalized and the extent of the breakout known, General Winder was notified; he was "furious." He immediately inspected Libby and dressed down Major Turner. The two wardens joined the guards in searching the perimeter fencing, the building, windows, and other possible routes of escape but found nothing. "At first it was suspicioned that the night sentinels had been bribed, and connived at the escape," recalled one of the remaining prisoners. Likely trying to shift the blame, Winder and Turner agreed: "Such an escape had but one explanation—the guards had been bribed." The prisoners seized the opportunity and suggested the guards had been complicit. "This suspicion," the newspapers reported, "received some credence from the statements of the Yankee officers, who said the guards had passed them out by their posts." Again, the prisoners had outsmarted their captors. Winder and Turner ordered that sentries be arrested and "searched for greenbacks." Although "the fruits of their supposed bargain and sale" were not found, the guards were still accused of disloyalty and sent to Castle Thunder for incarceration. Turner announced his decision "in order that further developments might either establish their innocence or fix their guilt upon them."[11]

"After a long time," according to the papers, the tunnel was finally discovered. Prison authorities ordered a "terrified negro boy" into the tunnel to find the place of exit. The young slave hesitated but was forced into the hole "at the point of a bayonet." He was told to shout if he found anything. The *Charleston Mercury* newspaper described these events: "At the base of the east wall, and about twenty feet from the Cary Street front, was discovered a tunnel, the entrance to which was hidden by a large rock, which fitted the aperture exactly." The paper continued, noting that when the rock was "rolled away" it revealed the tunnel. The "small negro boy was sent into the tunnel on a tour of exploration, and by the time Major Turner and Lieutenant LaTouche gained the outside of the building, a shout from the negro announced his arrival at the terminus of the subterranean route." The paper echoed other Southern papers' complaints that the fifty-plus-foot tunnel "lay directly beneath the tread of three sentinels, who walked the breadth of the east end of the prison."[12]

It took "until a few days after" the discovery of the tunnel before the guards found the opening by the fireplace, and this only after the heavy-handed interrogation of one of the prisoners who had been recaptured. With "the testimony afforded by the revelation of the tunnel," the guards were finally released from custody in Castle Thunder.[13] General Dow took further pleasure when prison officials reluctantly admitted that the "Yanks" were actually rather "smart."[14] Still, Winder and Turner refused to acknowledge their own mistakes, the incompetence of the guards, or the ingenuity and ability of their foe. Bartleson watched the blame game with amusement and concluded that Inspector Turner seemed less upset that the prisoners had escaped and angrier that he had not received any bribes. Behind his "jealousy" was his concern that there were "reports set on foot previously of his complicity with attempts to escape through bribes." Turner was in trouble. Obviously, the prisoners observed these antics with deep satisfaction, feeling "compensated" that their tormentors were furious, embarrassed, stumped, and now facing arrest.[15] Moreover, Winder and Turner had wasted valuable time blaming the guards and having them arrested. Each passing hour had allowed Rose, Hamilton, and the escapees to put distance between themselves and the prison.

HEAD START

Rose, Hamilton, and their fellow tunnelers had a full night and half a day's head start on the search parties; the other seventy-nine prisoners who had flooded out after them had a lead of several hours on their pursuers. After hours of roll-call checks and bickering, Winder had finally sounded the alarm. The first to give chase was Inspector Turner, joined by a few armed guards. Meanwhile, Winder and Commandant Turner had ordered local Rebel soldiers, including the dragoons of Richmond, to hunt down the escapees.[16] The groups departed on horseback and on foot, taking bloodhounds to track the escaped prisoners. At the same time, volunteers were dispatched on horseback "in every direction" to alert the Confederate "pickets" around the city. Sentries were also "double posted on all the roads and bridges" in and out of the city.[17]

It would be a massive manhunt. Everyone, it seemed, was eager to join the chase. Locals took to the streets to look for runaway prisoners. They grabbed their guns and rounded up packs of dogs. The affair was beginning to evince a spirit of both revenge and sport. Reading about the response to the escape, Bartleson worried about his former inmates. They were, he groused sarcastically, being "hunted down by armed citizens and some bloodhounds, those instruments, under a beneficent Providence employed by the South in humanizing and Christianizing the African race."[18] Turner ordered the entrance and exit of the now-famous tunnel sealed, then grabbed his sword and pistol and took off on horseback with a "small escort" of guards and two policemen to find "his" prisoners. As to the path the prisoners had taken, he guessed correctly, riding toward the Chickahominy River and Peninsula.[19]

Both within the prison and throughout Richmond, news of the escape spread rapidly. The event "continued to be the liveliest topic of yesterday," reported the *Richmond Enquirer* two days after the breakout, "and diverse conjectures were rife as to the means of the escape." As per the usual propaganda, the *Enquirer* and other newspapers were quick to point out that, however, "this grand deliver does not exceed in glory or secrecy the escape of John Hunt Morgan."[20] Never mind that the famous Confederate raider's escape had involved only seven prisoners. Southern newspapers also claimed that the escape from Libby had only succeeded because the guards "were enriched with laurels." This would be only the beginning of a serious propaganda effort in the South to discredit and minimize the escape.[21]

The *Enquirer* went so far as to credit Morgan with the breakout from Libby, writing, "It is most probably, in fact, that [Morgan] is, more than anybody else, responsible for the success with which Streight and his chums made their exit from the Libby." The Union soldiers, it was alleged, would have been incapable of mounting such an ambitious mission had it not been for "the experience and example" of Morgan and his fellow Confederates. The escapees simply stole "an admirable lesson," the newspapers claimed. Even after details of the remarkable Libby escape emerged, the papers still dismissed the ingenuity it had entailed and later credited Captain J. N. Johnston of the Sixth Kentucky Cavalry with being the planner rather than Rose, a Pennsylvanian. Being from the South, it was claimed that Johnston was "different" than the other escapees; apparently it was important in the South that the escape be credited to a Southerner.[22]

Throughout the tense days of the manhunt, Southern newspapers such as the *Enquirer* continued to sing Morgan's praises, even complaining that he had not "received any credit" from "historians" for his feat and war record. The *Richmond Examiner* joined in the distraction campaign, focusing much of its attention on the recapture of prisoners. "Half the loaf," they opined, "is better than no loaf." So too did they evoke Morgan. After a few days, when the reviled Streight had still not been apprehended, the paper wrote, "The Confederacy got more than ten times his value when it received Morgan back, and can afford to let him run. Bon Voyage, whiskey Straight!"[23]

Inside the prison, news of the escape had been met by jubilation among the Union officers. The morning roll calls and whispering among the prisoners indicated that many prisoners had in fact escaped—not just those initially suspected, Streight and Rose. Bartleson reported that news of a large escape imbued the prisoners with much-needed purpose, although he later admitted that he did not want to discuss any details of the breakout in his journal "for fear that may not be so and that this journal might accidentally fall into their hands." He was right to worry about further inspections inside the prison. Of Commandant Turner's rage and participation in the manhunt, Bartleson suggested, "his zeal was to disprove the rumors" of his incompetence and complicity rather than to do his job and apprehend the escapees. However, it was also apparent that, if prisoners were caught, they would be dealt with very, very harshly.[24]

The one-armed colonel also "predicted" in his diary that the escape would be "the grandest thing that ever took place in Libby Prison." He mused, "As Mother Goose might say, 'If the night had been longer, my story would have been longer.'" Everyone might have escaped! As it was, fully 109 prisoners broke out of the prison that night, among them approximately sixteen colonels, eight majors, over thirty captains, and in excess of fifty lieutenants.[25]

48!

During the harrowing escape, two of the prisoners perished quickly. They apparently drowned while crossing the James River behind the prison, either succumbing to the shock of the icy river or perhaps underestimating how weak they really were. They were not the only escapees whose flight was cut short. By the end of the first day, Captain Junius Gates of the Thirty-Third Ohio was apprehended within the Richmond city limits near Bottoms Bridge. He was dragged back to Libby and thrown into a cell in the prison's dungeon. By the end of that first day, seven more prisoners were captured and returned to the bastille. By the end of the next evening—February 11—another fourteen escapees were back in Libby. The captured prisoners had been paraded through the streets of Richmond, "footsore" and showing signs of "fatigue" and defeat. Bartleson noted that many had been caught by locals who had turned them in to the search parties. Sick, starving, and freezing, the escapees had mistakenly approached homes and farms in the area, begging for food and warm clothing. Each successful apprehension was met with great disappointment inside the prison. The one-armed colonel wrote in his journal that thirty prisoners had been recaptured by the night of February 12 and thrown into the cells in the dungeon.[26]

"The Rebs are very anxious to catch Colonel Streight," recalled Captain Cornwell. This was an understatement. The famous raider's escape had angered the Southerners and became the focus of several newspaper reports, all demanding that he be apprehended. Throughout the manhunt, his status became part of most newspaper accounts, Winder's orders, and gossip inside Libby. Cornwell expressed the sentiments of other prisoners when he wrote, "I think however they will miss him." Hearsay of the Union raider's whereabouts abounded: "It has been rumored that Colonel Streight had been overtaken and ordered to halt, refusing to do which he was shot and wounded." Upon reading the report in the newspaper, Cornwell defiantly recorded, "I do not rely on the statement."[27]

One of the 109 prisoners to escape was Lieutenant James Wells of the Eighth Michigan Cavalry, whose story mirrors that of many of the escapees. He wisely kept clear of street lamps and raced down a road "as quietly and rapidly as possible" to get out of Richmond. He discovered that the outskirts of the city were ringed by Confederate defenses, which made his escape fraught with "great danger and difficulty." One evening, Wells spotted a light, but it turned out to be a Confederate camp. As Wells was preparing to turn around, a soldier in gray had walked by with a musket on his shoulder. The Michigan cavalryman hugged the ground, then crawled on his hands and knees around the camp to continue his run to freedom. Wells crossed fields, hiked through woods, and worried about being lost—especially at night.[28]

Another dark evening, he came across a body of water and was unsure whether it was a river or lake and so he threw a stick into it. The stick floated off, indicating it was a river, and Wells correctly guessed that it was the Chickahominy. This was one of a few instances when he had to "wade in water and mud waist deep." He kept going and made it to higher and drier ground. Wells hid and slept during the days, preferring to find "a dense thicket of laurel and other brush" for cover, then walked by night. Wells was awakened one evening by the sound of men talking. It was another

Confederate picket. Soon, a cavalry unit rode by him at, he estimated, a distance of only two hundred yards. The concern was whether they had dogs with them.[29]

On another occasion, Wells was walking on the side of a road when it came to a fork. As he was was deciding which branch to take, a man suddenly appeared before him, not giving the prisoner time to take cover. The Michigander remained calm and tried not to "show any signs of fear or hesitation." Rather, Wells casually remarked, "Good evening, sir." He completed the ruse by asking, "Can you tell me which of these roads will take me to the mill?" The unsuspecting man offered directions and believed Wells's story that he was a Confederate soldier on furlough coming to visit a relative in the area.[30]

Besides these near run-ins with Confederate soldiers and local civilians, Wells faced other obstacles. In two full nights of travel, he had only managed to cover about twelve miles. He needed to move more quickly but was slowed by hunger and fatigue, both of which were "closing in on me with a death-grip," he later remembered. This prompted him to take risks, such as when he came across a camp comprised of Confederate supply crews with mules and wagons. Rather than walk some distance around the camp, he adopted a Southern accent and strolled casually through it. Afterward, he realized how foolish he had been. But he'd made it. Soon thereafter, however, while resting, two men appeared at his hiding place. Wells froze, but the men turned out to be two of his fellow escapees—Lieutenant Nineoch McKean of the Twenty-First Illinois and Captain William Randall of the Second Ohio. The three men whispered excitedly and decided to travel together. McKean and Randall had saved some rations and shared them with Wells. It was the first food he tasted in three days.[31]

Later on their journey, the three men stumbled upon another Confederate outpost. Unfortunately, they had a dog. The animal barked "furiously" at the three prisoners, who turned and started to run. Immediately, Confederate soldiers were chasing them. Three or four shots were fired, causing the three prisoners to scatter in panic. Soon, Confederates on horseback were everywhere. McKean and Wells veered off into a bog and hid, crouching as low as possible. They could not find Randall and assumed he had been shot.[32] They spent the night in hiding and never saw Randall again.[33] Not long thereafter, McKean and Wells ran out of food and were driven more by hunger than caution. They encountered a man and took a big risk by approaching him to ask for food. The stranger knew all about the escape and told them he was a veteran who had served with the Confederacy. The two prisoners admitted that they were from the notorious bastille. To their amazement, he said simply, "But I never turned a hungry man away from my door yet, and do not propose to do so now." He took them to his home, where the two prisoners half expected to be shot or arrested. Instead, the stranger gave them a few dry biscuits. The generous veteran apologized that the biscuits constituted "his whole store of provisions." Their luck continued: The good Samaritan pointed out how to get to Williamsburg and York-town, where there were large camps of Union soldiers.[34]

The biscuits helped, but McKean and Wells were still very weak and in a state of starvation. They struggled on wearily. On their seventh day on the run, the skies opened up in a "terrible storm of sleet and rain." The two prisoners dug into the side of a massive, old log and covered themselves with leaves—not so much to stay dry but in a futile effort to stay warm. They were freezing. Wells believed he would "perish" and did not know if he could walk any further, even though they were not far from Williamsburg. That was when they spotted a small force of about twenty soldiers on horseback. The soldiers rode directly toward the spot where the two men stood. McKean dove for cover and urged Wells to do the same. In their condition, it would have been impossible to run; plus, the soldiers were on horseback. The captain from Michigan did not know what overcame him; he stood feebly and yelled, "What regiment is that?" The cavalrymen drew swords and pistols and demanded, "Surrender immediately or else!" McKean joined Wells at his side; both men raised their hands in surrender. To their delight, it turned out to be a patrol from the Eleventh Pennsylvania Cavalry! Their mission: To find prisoners from Libby who had escaped before Confederates in the area found them. The two escapees were rescued. They imagined their appearance—dirty, torn rags for clothing, emaciated, desperate—must have alarmed their rescuers. But they were free![35]

Over the next few days, more escapees were caught. Soon the cells in Libby's dungeon were "over full." Prisoners had been caught by the Chickahominy River, at the Pamunkey Indian Reservation, in the village of Hanover, just south of the Chickahominy, trying to cross Bottoms Bridge, and throughout the region. A few had headed toward Fredericksburg, in the direction of Washington, D.C. Some had been caught "only a few miles from the city," while others were retaken within sight of Union lines. Richmond's newspapers celebrated each capture, especially those stories—real or invented—lending themselves to the Southern cause. One escapee was alleged to have been caught by a slave who had been digging up potatoes in a field. When the prisoner in blue had approached the farm, the slave "held" his captive with a raised "hoe at the ready to strike." The plantation master then turned the prisoner over to Confederate soldiers. The newspaper story was replete with condescending references to "mammy" and offensive "slave talk"—such as quoting the enslaved man as saying, "You done broke out o' one o' dem prisons." Of course, like so many articles in the Southern press, it was likely just propaganda and lies.[36]

Other captures were also celebrated. It was said that everyone from local residents to some of the South's most famed fighters had captured prisoners. Reading the exaggerated accounts, it would seem that hundreds upon hundreds of prisoners had escaped—and even more had been apprehended. One story claimed a lieu-tenant had entered the ballroom in the city's Concert Hall but was immediately arrested by locals after they recognized his "Yankee jib." Another prisoner was said to have "stumbled" into a saloon on Main Street for a drink and had become "garrulous." He was apprehended by men of the celebrated "Mosby's Rangers." Again, what tipped them off was his strange "Yankee" accent. Even a young "newspaper boy" was in on the action, allegedly alerting the authorities after seeing a Union prisoner trade his uniform for a "negro's great coat." They had all given chase and caught the "Yankee."[37]

Meanwhile, the prisoners inside Libby struggled to keep up hope that their compatriots would make it across Union lines. The weather, after all, remained "damp and chilly" only to turn "still colder." One of the inmates anxious about the fate of the prisoners was Bartleson, who wrote sarcastically, "The absence of so many has made the rest of us quite lonesome." He added, more seriously that "many are filled with additional regret that they are still here when so large a number are toward the Land of Liberty."[38] At the same time, Libby's commandant imposed further restrictions and frequent roll calls inside, leading the one-armed colonel to gripe, "They intend to put little annoyances upon us." He and other prisoners hoped that "it is one of those things, however, of which they will soon tire." The men endured, drawing strength from the fact that the "famous or infamous Streight"—as Richmond's newspapers called him—was still unaccounted for and, they prayed, might even be "out of reach" and "now under the protection of the Stars and Stripes." Little did they know, but Streight was still in the heart of Richmond, hiding at the Van Lew mansion.[39]

In total, forty-eight of the prisoners were recaptured.

ROSE

Back on the night of the breakout, Rose and Hamilton, once clear of the vicinity of the prison, had crept along the shadows of buildings for two "squares" before changing direction. The two friends said what must have been a very difficult goodbye and each went their own way, hoping the separation would improve the chances that at least one of them would make it to freedom. Surely they must have agreed to meet again once they had made it across the Union lines. That night, Hamilton had gone off on his own and made it out of the city, traveling an estimated eight miles that first night and afterward walking by night and hiding by day, often in "half-frozen swamps." But he was a young man and in reasonable health, despite the months of imprisonment and exhausting task of working on the tunnel night after night. He also pushed himself hard, trying to suppress the pangs of hunger and anxieties about being caught.[40]

The path to Williamsburg and the Union lines required that Hamilton pass through several creeks, where he found himself "in ice and water to my knees the greater part of the time." He also forged a river and the tributaries of the James and Appomattox where he was "up to my waist" in bone-chilling water. The Kentuckian traveled quicker than most of the other escapees and was the third person to reach freedom. Ultimately, he traveled for seven days before arriving at the Union defenses around Williamsburg, where he was greeted by news that two men had arrived the day before him. Equally satisfying, he had the opportunity to welcome two more prisoners the following day. But there was no sign of Rose.[41]

After leaving Hamilton, Rose had turned the corner by a hospital. Just as he did, an armed guard was standing in front of him. There was not enough time to run or fight. The guard drew his weapon and ordered Rose to report to the head guard. The two men walked a short distance, whereupon the senior soldier stationed at the hospital questioned Rose. Thinking quickly, the colonel concocted a lie and talked his way out of the jam. Fortunately, so many prison guards, veterans, and residents of the city had stolen blue Union coats and pants that he blended in. Fresh off his close call with the guards at the hospital, Rose rushed back to the canal and followed the path he had earlier outlined on the map. Thirty minutes later, he spotted a few prisoners, and they traveled together, quietly and quickly, through Richmond and beyond the city limits. He resisted the urge to join his compatriots; instead, he stuck to the plan and traveled alone and by night, hiding and sleeping during the daylight hours.

Rose made it out of Richmond and traveled to the York River Railroad, which ran to the Chickahominy bridge. However, the bridge was guarded, so the colonel turned and headed further along the tracks, eventually crossing some distance away. Once again, he came upon another Confederate defensive position, this one an artillery battery. He passed stealthily around the camp, close enough to hear men talking and horses winnowing. As dawn threatened, Rose crawled inside a hollowed-out sycamore log. It was not an ideal place to hide and sleep, but it would do.

At sunset, Rose continued his journey. He had to cross the Chickahominy and thus walked along the banks, identifying what appeared to be one of the narrowest and—presumably—shallowest spots. Halfway through the river, however, he stepped into an unseen hole and went under. Head to toe, he was now soaking wet. He kept walking in order to try to keep warm. It did not work; in the bitter cold of night he found himself shivering uncontrollably. Cavalry units in gray rode by, appearing to be looking for prisoners. It was another incentive to press on. Despite being wet, cold, hungry, and exhausted, Rose somehow managed to once again walk all night. That morning, he hunkered down and hid, but sleep eluded him. He was so wet and cold that, in his head, he heard his teeth chattering violently. Worse yet, the pack of matches he had stolen was now wet and useless. There would be no fire to warm him.

When he awoke at sunset, he was in trouble. His muscles ached, and his body was stiff. His broken foot, which had only partially healed during his imprisonment, was now worse. He could hardly stand, much less walk. Rose somehow continued his journey, but soon came upon a Confederate outpost. The problem was that, in order to outflank it, he had to cross a swamp; he quietly waded through the "morass" and once again found himself wet and shivering. When he made it to high ground in a grove of cedars, Rose was completely fatigued. He had also repeatedly stubbed and bumped his broken foot in the wooded area, and it was now throbbing in pain. Rose could not stand, let alone walk; he had to sit and rest and promptly fell asleep. A noise awakened him. More Confederate soldiers were passing by. Rose decided he needed to keep to the woods in order to avoid potential captors.[42]

Rose again awoke in trouble. Not only was his foot swollen and too sore to support his weight, but his uniform was now covered in ice. The temperature had dropped while he'd slept. Mustering every bit of his strength, Rose willed himself forward and continued to Crump's Crossroads in the eastern part of the state, where he outflanked and avoided yet another Confederate camp. The colonel was now so desperately hungry, cold, and in pain that he walked both day and night, risking being seen in daylight. He came upon an open field. His instincts told him to walk well around the open terrain and follow the tree line. However, he doubted he had the energy for such a long detour; the open field was the fastest and most direct way toward the Union positions by Williamsburg. As Rose crossed the half-mile-wide field, a soldier on horseback approached and saluted. Rose returned the gesture. The man asked if he was "part of the New Kent Cavalry," to which the colonel responded, "Yes." Shockingly, the cavalryman turned and rode away. Rose thought him incredibly "stupid" and himself incredibly lucky.

As soon as the man was gone, Rose resumed his journey but headed for cover in a "laurel thicket" in the center of the field. However, several men on horseback approached. Rose darted into the thicket, but the riders simply surrounded it. Rose ran to the eastern side of the thicket, his foot exploding in pain with each step. But there, on the easternmost perimeter of the trees, was yet another Confederate picket. He was trapped. He could not leave the thicket, but neither could he stay, and he had to cross the open field if he wanted to proceed to Williamsburg. Rose contemplated hunkering down but worried that he would be stuck there, and he desperately needed food and water. Rose spotted a shallow gully. It was the answer: It ran through the field, toward the tree line. Very carefully but as quickly as possible, Rose crawled across the field and then dropped down in the ditch. It was a step closer to getting to the tree line and out of the open field.[43]

The problem was that the gully was lined with briers and thistles. Rose's hands now bled and ached, but he pulled his body forward through the shallow trench. But again he heard voices, and they were getting nearer. Rose froze and listened to the men talking and realized they had discovered him. It was a group of Confederate cavalrymen. With renewed determination, Rose dragged his body through the briers and gully as fast as possible. The horses headed to the thicket in the center of the field, which gave him a chance. Reaching the end of the gully, Rose raced into the pine forest bordering the field. He was "breathless" and "half-dead," but he'd managed to elude the cavalry detachment looking for him. Williamsburg was just ahead.[44]

The Williamsburg Road ran from the other end of the field to the city, now under Union control. It was too dangerous to cross the field, so Rose stayed in the cover of the pine forest and worked his way in an arcing semicircle to the edge of the road. As he emerged onto the roadside, he looked back and saw Confederate cavalrymen riding to and fro. They were, he reasoned, searching for him. There were more Confederate pickets by the road. In fact, the entire region from Richmond eastward was brimming with Confederate defenses. Rose again stayed to the woods and worked his way past the defenses and some distance parallel to the road. As he snuck through the woods, small units of cavalry raced by him down the road every so often. Each time they neared, Rose hugged the ground until they had passed. He was almost to Williamsburg and the Union lines. Peering out from the tree line, Rose did not see any Confederate camps or cavalry. He could not wait any longer to cross the short field to the road into Williamsburg.

The colonel crawled into the field and, to his "utterable joy," saw smoke from campfires and Union soldiers marching just a short distance down the road. It was, he recalled, a site for "sore eyes." Rose contemplated the safest path across the field to the road and, stooping low, stepped out into the field and began carefully creeping toward the campfires. No sooner had he started than he heard the sound of men behind him. Rose swung around to see three Confederate soldiers dressed in a mix of regulation uniforms and Union blue.[45]

The colonel immediately dove for cover. The three soldiers were on foot, and they continued walking past him. Somehow they had missed seeing him! Rose waited a short time and then hurried on toward the Union line. He made it roughly one hundred yards before the three soldiers turned and spotted him. The soldiers rushed forward, one of them yelling "Halt!" Rose contemplated running, but he could hardly walk, and the distance was too great across the open field and road. Once the three soldiers were close enough to him, they commanded him to come to them. Rose was a strong and big man but in no condition to fight. In addition, there were three of them, and they were armed. He surrendered to the officer, while one of the two enlisted men detained him. It was February 14, and the Union line was visible at the end of the field. The three Confederates escorted Rose at gunpoint back to the nearest Confederate picket.[46]

Part V

FREEDOM

17

"Kill Cavalry"

> But through the clouds the sun is slowly breaking;
> Hope from her long, deep sleep is re-awaking:
> Speed the time, Father! when the bow of peace,
> Spanning the gulf, shall bid the tempest cease,
> When foemen, clasping each other by the hand,
> Shall shout once more, in a united land,
> "All's well!"
>
> —Frederick A. Bartleson[1]

Rose walked beside his captors, struggling to keep up on his broken foot and despite his exhaustion. He purposely fell a bit behind. It worked. The soldier assigned to detain him approached; Rose observed that the man's guard was down. When the Confederate was next to Rose, the big colonel "suddenly sprang upon the man." Rose grabbed the musket and, in the struggle, it discharged but fired harmlessly into the air. The prisoner overpowered the guard and forcefully yanked the weapon out of his hand. Rose threw it to the ground, turned, and ran.[2]

The other soldier raised his musket, but, rather than fire, the three Confederates turned and ran away from Rose. The colonel guessed that they felt the nearby Union soldiers might hear the gunshot and ride out from the defensive lines; or perhaps Rose's strength dissuaded them from chasing him down, as surely they could have done. Rose continued to run and, stealing a quick look behind him, saw the three Confederates running away. As the colonel turned back around, he saw that it was too late: Many Confederate soldiers suddenly appeared, directly in front of him. They had been hiding in the tall grass of the field, apparently ready to ambush any

Union soldiers venturing out from Williamsburg or to spring upon any escapees trying to get to the city. That quickly, a few men were on top of Rose and beat him savagely with the butts of their guns.

It took several soldiers to pin Rose to the ground. After subduing the Union soldier, the Confederates yanked him to his feet and dragged him back toward the nearest pickets. Blood ran down Rose's face, and his eyes began to swell from the beating. He heard one of the Confederates yell, "Hurry up, boys; the Yankees are right here!" As he arrived back at the Confederate picket, he was greeted by the soldier he had just overpowered. The man growled and threated to "fill [him] full of Confederate lead."[3]

The Confederates seemed, Rose recalled, rather excited to have a Union prisoner in their custody. They took him to Barhamsville, then across the Pamunkey River, and back to Richmond, to the wretched bastille, where he was locked in a "narrow and loathsome cell" in the dark "dungeon" near where he had spent roughly eight weeks excavating the tunnel.[4] As punishment, Turner left Rose there in solitary confinement for several days and with only morsels to eat. Rose's capture had a disastrous effect on the prisoners, who by now knew the colonel had been the ringleader of the great escape. Bartleson recorded that the prisoners were also upset because Rose had obviously been badly beaten and locked in the cellar, which he called "that repentance place of all unfortunates."[5] Morale inside Libby plummeted.

Local newspapers reported that by February 15 nearly fifty of the escaped prisoners had been apprehended.[6] Of the successful manhunt, one newspaper wrote that the prisoners "were found, like sheep scattered from the fold, spread about in individual spots, all over the country below Richmond and above, their faces set towards the Yankee lines as truly as the needle to the pole."[7] Indeed, it was a brutal and difficult return for Rose. And for everyone else interned there. The entire prison was in the grips of fear over Turner's threats to kill everyone. Security was increased, patrols were doubled, the cellar was sealed, stronger iron bars were put in all the windows, inspections were held in the upstairs barracks, roll calls were convened at all hours, and bloodhounds accompanied the sentries everywhere they went. The prisoners who had been recaptured, General Dow recorded in his diary, "are confined in dark underground cells, and fed only on corn bread and water—the cells so densely crowded that there is not room on the floor to lie down." He added, "The cells are also foul."[8]

However, a group of prisoners went on the offensive, targeting Turner with psychological warfare. The commandant received an anonymous note claiming the prisoners were planning to cut his throat. Turner became especially paranoid. He ordered all one thousand men into the cramped kitchen—which had been built to accommodate only a fraction of that number. While the prisoners stood in formation there, the other rooms were searched for knives and any kind of weapon. The treatment was even worse for those who had escaped and been recaptured—especially Rose. Indeed,

Turner had been embarrassed by the mass escape; he was out for vengeance. At the same time, rations were again cut, leaving prisoners in a perpetual state of starvation, and guards were given orders to shoot first, ask questions second. The meals now consisted of nothing but water and some days "3 small turnips." "Everything done here, is calculated, and we believe, *intended* to annoy us and make us suffer," General Dow wrote; the food and treatment were simply "vile."[9] Yet Turner was noticeably less aggressive, spending his time hiding in his office; he was clearly unnerved. As one of the prisoners sneered, "Really, when our distracted little Commandant now comes into our rooms, he keeps his knees well together . . . some of us might slip out between his legs!"[10] He was also watching his back and expecting an attack.

A full investigation was underway, and Turner found himself under attack from the authorities. The prison was simply too important, and too much effort had been invested into using Libby for propaganda purposes. Moreover, one of the escapees who remained at large was Colonel Streight. The realization that the "biggest fish," as he was now called in the Southern press, might have made it to Union lines was simply too much for Richmond to digest. With Streight gone, Southern politicians and newspapers reframed the manhunt as a success, because "two big fish who slipped through the prison net" had been recaptured. They were speaking not of Streight but of Colonel Rose and Colonel Ely of Connecticut.[11]

The papers took to inventing new explanations for the mass escape, while also returning to the argument that it had been an inside job or orchestrated from the highest echelons of the Yankee government. "The intended exodus was known in Lincoln's Cabinet before it was revealed in Richmond by its accomplishment," wrote the *Richmond Examiner*. "The column of the enemy was thrown forward in order to be in readiness to succor any of the escaping prisoners who might break through the Confederate lines." The effort to frame the escape as a failure also continued: "It is also plain that the escape was delayed several nights beyond its actual accomplishment, and that it was intended to be far more successful than it was."[12]

The prison, like the city, remained in a state of alarm. Newspapers continued to cover every detail surrounding the escape. They also continued their not-so-subtle campaign of propaganda, celebrating the manhunt as "admirable" and "extraordinary" despite the fact that fully fifty-nine escaped prisoners had made it to Union lines, a number that constitutes perhaps the largest and most successful prison break in American history.[13]

"A GREAT EXCITEMENT IN RICHMOND"

Elizabeth Van Lew's role in the famous prison break included passing valuable information to the prisoners concerning the location of the nearest Union lines, bringing food into Libby, and sheltering escaped prisoners in her home. All the while, she had been in communication with General Butler and other Union commanders about both the escape and the deteriorating conditions in Richmond. In February, she had also urged Butler to strike at the Confederate capital in order to free the remaining prisoners languishing inside the wretched facility. After the mass escape, Van Lew warned Union commanders of the harsh reprisals being meted out by the embarrassed and outraged commandant in Libby. Van Lew worried that the prisoners in Libby, Belle Isle, and elsewhere would not long endure their poor treatment. In addition, the Confederacy was about to relocate thousands of Richmond's prisoners outside of the city.

Of the many secret dispatches Van Lew had sent to General Butler, only one batch remains. It contains letters written in the early months of 1864 for the purpose of providing details on the situation in Richmond and Confederate troop movements. In the dispatch, Van Lew encourages Butler to attack the capital city, writing, "It is intended to remove to Georgia all the Federal prisoners . . . Quaker (a Union man whom I know) knows this to be true." She adds intelligence and words of caution about newly added defenses, writing that the Confederates "are building batteries on the Danville road . . . Do not underrate their strength and desperation." However, she adds that Confederate units were being called up, which would provide an opportunity for a Union strike on Richmond. "Forces could probably be called into action in from five to ten days; 25,000, mostly artillery. Hoke's and Kemper's brigades gone to North Carolina; Pickett's in or about Petersburg. Three regiments of cavalry disbanded by General Lee for want of horses."[14]

Butler and other Union commanders agreed to conduct a cavalry assault on Richmond. One of the main objectives would be to liberate the prisoners suffering in Libby. The attack would be led by the flamboyant general H. Judson Kilpatrick and Colonel Ulric Dahlgren, the dashing twenty-one-year-old son of Admiral John Dahlgren. Young Dahlgren—of whom it would soon be said by Secretary of the Navy Gideon Welles "a more gallant and brave-hearted fellow was not to be found"[15]—had lost his right leg after the Battle of Gettysburg while in pursuit of General Lee's retreating army. Dahlgren looked the part—tall, handsome, and charismatic. After months of recuperation, he was eager to get back into the fight. He would, however, soon show that his talents did not extend to battlefield tactics.[16]

In the early days of February, General Kilpatrick conferred with President Lincoln and his cabinet. The plan would be to strike at Richmond in a lightning cavalry attack from the south while Dahlgren swooped in undetected from the southeast. Infantry and other mounted units would simultaneously hit Charlottesville and sites to the north in an effort to distract the Confederate defenders. The raid became known as "Kill Cavalry" in honor of its commander. The braggadocious Kilpatrick guaranteed success, even wagering his commanding officer, General Alfred Pleasonton, a whopping five thousand dollars that he would take Richmond. The day of the raid, Kilpatrick offered to double the bet.

With very little planning, Kilpatrick and Dahlgren departed the night of February 28 from their camp near Culpeper and Stevensburg in Virginia. Nearly 3,500 cavalrymen from the First Cavalry and other units set out with rations for only three days on what was described as "the most ambitious and daring" mission of the war.[17] It was believed that the Union force would encounter little opposition on the path they had selected to enter Richmond, which was roughly seventy miles to the southeast—that is, as long as the raiders struck quickly and without being detected. Neither happened.

One day later, on March 1, Kilpatrick stopped at Beaverdam to destroy railways and Confederate installations, which only delayed their attack on the capital city. They then crossed the lower Rapidan River but found their progress slowed by snow and sleet. Along the way, Confederate scouts observed the raiders and reported the movements back to Richmond. Kilpatrick's main force of almost three thousand then arrived on the outskirts of the capital around ten in the morning on March 2. He was only about a mile from the center of the city yet hesitated. Not receiving word as to whether or not Dahlgren had made it into the city, Kilpatrick pulled back; known for being bold, the Union general uncharacteristically missed an excellent opportunity to strike. Timidity now seemed to define his command. And this gave Confederate general Wade Hampton time to organize additional defenses and dispatch Confederate cavalry units to pursue both Union commanders. From that point on, everything in the Union assault went wrong.[18]

The day prior, on March 1, Colonel Bartleson had recorded in his diary that there was "a great excitement in Richmond." A day later, he noted there was "still great excitement." Word had arrived in the city that Kilpatrick was only six miles away from the Confederate capital. The sounds of artillery fire boomed outside the city. Panic ensued, as every able-bodied Confederate man and child was scrambled to defensive positions near Libby, while newspapers warned of "indiscriminate pillage, rape, and slaughter" at the hands of soldiers in blue and from the prisoners who, it was feared, were about to revolt. Crowds gathered in the streets and outside the bastille, shouting threats of death to the prisoners inside. The Libby guards, remembered Bartleson, were now "unusually vigilant" and violent. Something big was happening.[19]

Inside Libby, the prisoners buzzed with anticipation, feeding off rumors of the impending attack. Commandant Turner had announced on March 1 that guards were to fire at any prisoner exhibiting the least action that might be construed as threatening. Likewise, he warned "against going near the windows, under penalty of being shot." At nearby Castle Thunder, one of the prisoners threw hard, stale bread out a window at the guard below. The guard fired at his tormentor but missed. The head of the guards proceeded to race inside to find the perpetrator. Not finding any obvious suspects, the officer "thrust his head out of the window to notify the guard" below, who mistakenly shot and killed his commander. The same thing happened at Libby, when one of the guards leaned out the window to shout orders to his fellow sentry below and was summarily shot and killed.[20]

Winder and Turner approved a plan to booby-trap the bastille. Slaves and captured blacks were sent to Libby to begin digging a large ditch under the entire perimeter of the prison. The workers whispered to the prisoners that they had been told to place gunpowder under the buildings. Deputy commandant Inspector Turner confirmed the worst when he "stated to several that there were one thousand pounds of powder deposited there." The "idea," he threatened, was to "blow us up rather than allow us to be released by our forces."[21]

Rose remembered that Commandant Turner sent guards every half hour with a lighted candle to inspect the fuses connecting the large, buried kegs of gunpowder under the prison. With each inspection, more and more prisoners began to suspect the inevitability of their demise. Some began trying to bore holes through the roof of the bastille; others began to refer to Libby as a "volcano."[22]

"THE DAHLGREN AFFAIR"

The prisoners debated whether to try to escape or to wait for General Kilpatrick's Union forces. Either way, they worried they might not make it out alive. Many of the prisoners believed that the commandant and deputy commandant were entirely capable of destroying the prison and killing everyone in it. "It is," marveled Bartleson, "incredible that men could resort to such a desperate measure." The one-armed colonel, who, like others inside the bastille, was slowly starving to death, argued that the South's hatred of Northerners was such that anything was possible. "Notions die hard," he explained. Even Kilpatrick's "attack and capture of Richmond" might not save Libby's inmates. Mindsets were such that "the enemy will retain prisoners to the very end of the struggle." Moreover, even if the prisoners tried to fight their way out, "hundreds will be killed."[23]

Similarly, Captain Szabad cautioned his compatriots against believing liberation was at hand. He reminded them of other failed attempts to seize Richmond. Anger and frustration inside the prison were building. Prisoners began planning to rise up when Kilpatrick struck the city. On March 2, Bartleson again put quill to paper, writing, "I would at this time wish for power to crush my enemies, did I not know when I obtained the power I would lose the heart."[24]

General Kilpatrick's "lightning" strike was anything but. He had made it to Richmond in a day but had neglected to account for the weather and so many Confederate spies along the route. When they had first stopped by the rail depot to destroy it, they mistakenly failed to stop a train that sped past them on its way to Richmond. Those on board the train would also warn Richmond's officials of the impending raid. Even the city's newspapers were publishing details of the coming attack. Yet Kilpatrick pressed on when he should have postponed and reconfigured the assault. So too had Dahlgren's smaller force already headed off on its own path into the city.

On March 1, Dahlgren and roughly five hundred raiders finally reached Dover Mills by the James River. They foolishly burned installations in the area, which further warned the Confederates of looming attack. From there, the Union forces planned to cross the river into Richmond. However, the rain and snow had swollen the river, which had become impassable. The young colonel blamed the fiasco on his Black scout, whom he ordered hanged by the reins of his horse after an impromptu trial. Lacking the element of surprise, Dahlgren tried to approach Richmond farther to the east but was repelled by a superior Confederate force waiting on him. He was forced to retreat and, shockingly, took the time to sack farms in the area. Again moving too slowly on his way back to the Peninsula after the embarrassing defeat, Dahlgren's cavalrymen were ambushed near the Mattaponi River. Dahlgren, riding out in front of his men, was shot and killed. Not far away, Kilpatrick's larger force was also beaten and forced to retreat.[25]

Roughly 135 of Dahlgren's troops were captured, along with forty freed Blacks marching with them. All were promptly and savagely beaten and paraded through Richmond. Dahlgren's body was dragged through the city in a grisly display, and his fake leg kept as a souvenir. Then came the spark that ignited one of the most controversial episodes of the American Civil War: A thirteen-year-old boy allegedly found on Dahlgren's body a handwritten order to burn Richmond and assassinate Jefferson Davis. The story of "The Dahlgren Affair" spread throughout the country, with both Northerners and Southerners decrying the order. In Richmond, Confederate officials propagandized the incident, as newspapers expressed outrage. The *Richmond Examiner* went so far as to argue that "the depredations of the last Yankee raiders, and the wantonness of their devastation equal anything heretofore committed during the war." The prisoners rightly worried about further reprisals against them, such was the city's militant "indignation against the raiders."[26]

The authenticity of the orders have never been confirmed and continue to be debated. For instance, Union general George C. Meade, the victor at Gettysburg, felt the need to contact Confederate general Robert E. Lee to assure him that any such action was not sanctioned by Union commanders. Kilpatrick also denied the authenticity of the controversial order. It seems highly unlikely that the Union would have ordered the assassination of Davis and that those commanders would have then carried an enabling handwritten note into battle. Either way, the alleged note soon disappeared.[27]

Here Elizabeth Van Lew reentered the affair. Dahlgren's body had been hung up for public display, and angry crowds spit upon and desecrated the corpse, after which the body was hastily buried. A Black servant who had observed the burial notified Van Lew of the location of the interment. The Yankee spy sent members of the Unionist underground "to discover the hidden grave and remove his honored dust to friendly care."[28] Dahlgren's mutilated corpse was "exhumed and furtively transported in a wagon to a farm north of the city to have it properly reinterred."[29] When Dahlgren's father later requested that his son's body be returned to the family, the grave was then found to be empty; the *Richmond Examiner* suggested colorfully that "Dahlgren had risen, or been resurrected."[30] Van Lew later notified the Dahlgren family of her actions on behalf of the deceased colonel.

WAITING

During the days surrounding the failed raid on Richmond, there was no roll call in Libby Prison. However, neither were there mail deliveries or food rations. Rather, the spectacularly failed Union attack on Richmond prompted celebrations throughout the capital city. Confederate reinforcements also arrived in the city as insurance against another attempt. Inside the prison, the defeat generated despair and hopelessness. There now appeared to be no way out of the bastille until war's end, and even then the prisoners' fate was uncertain. Newspapers continued to buzz with speculation about further attempts to take Richmond. Bartleson described the reaction inside Libby, grumbling, "Richmond has been taken so often that we are incredulous."[31] Of the attack, the one-armed colonel described the two failed Union raiders as "blathering simpletons who talk about taking Richmond with cavalry, and who then think they enhance their reputations for sagacity and boldness." Bartleson knew that he and his fellow prisoners would now face vicious retaliation for the raid.[32]

Indeed, the conditions inside the bastille continued to deteriorate. At the same time, the threat to move the prisoners became a reality. No less than General Lee urged that Richmond's prison population be moved outside of the city and farther to the south. Just days after the mass escape, some prisoners had been sent from Richmond prisons to internment camps in North Carolina, others to Georgia, including several from Libby, who found themselves in Macon and Andersonville.

The Confederate States Congress formed a joint committee and, on March 3, agreed to retain the option of mining and exploding the prison. It was necessary, they maintained, because of the threat a mass prison break would pose to the city's civilians. "Had the prisoners escaped," the congressional committee warned, "the women and children of the city, as well as their homes, would have been at the mercy of 5,000 outlaws." Commandant Turner was given permission to blow up the prison. "Humanity," the order from the congress read, "required that the most summary measures should be used to deter them from any attempt at escape."[33]

18

The Fall of Richmond

I know that I am free, for I have seen Father Abraham.

—Unidentified Black woman, Richmond, April 4, 1865[1]

The Confederate capital fell on April 2, 1865, almost four years to the day that shots had been fired on Fort Sumter, starting the war. It had long been the goal of the Union to seize Richmond and thereby expedite the end of the war, but the objective had long eluded President Lincoln and his generals. Ironically, Richmond was only about one hundred miles from Washington, D.C. It was the assault on Petersburg that finally marked the end for Richmond.

The strategic city sat only twenty-four miles from Richmond at the junction of five railroads that supplied the larger James River region. The fall of Petersburg would mean that Richmond would be cut off from its supply and communication channels. Commanders of both Northern and Southern forces—Ulysses S. Grant and Robert E. Lee—knew this and raced reinforcements to the key city. Ultimately, a total of 104,000 troops were thrown into the long and bloody campaign. From June 15, 1864, until April 2, 1865, Grant laid siege to the heavily fortified Confederate positions. After months of fighting, and with Confederate troops starving and cut off from supplies, Grant ordered an attack on all fronts. On April 2, General Philip Sheridan was able to penetrate Confederate defenses, forcing the end to the fighting. It had been 292 days in the making, but an American flag once again flew over Petersburg.[2]

General Lee informed Confederate president Jefferson Davis that the end was at hand and recommended that Richmond be evacuated. A reporter covering the action wrote eloquently of the carnage: "With that Sunday's sun the hope of the Rebels set, never to rise again."[3] There was now nothing between the advancing blue wave and the Confederate capital. Lee's Army of Northern Virginia was on the run to Danville to try to link up with General Joseph Johnston's forces there. Likewise, Richmond's militia units were soon in full retreat. Civilians began evacuating the city, amid unfounded rumors that they would all be killed by invading Union troops. Such was the state of war and result of the fearful and hateful propaganda promulgated by the Confederacy for four long years. More practically, the complete and utter defeat of the Confederacy was at hand.

In the chaos of those final days, looters set fire to much of the city and pillaged public buildings. They were joined by Confederate officials who spent their final hours in power desperately trying to burn or pack their official records. Lee ordered General Richard S. Ewell, Richmond's highest-ranking commander, to burn the city's tobacco stores and anything else of value. Thus warehouses and supplies that would have been vital for the reconstruction of the city were put to the torch. In the inferno that followed, Libby was nearly engulfed. Inside, prisoners worried that they would be trapped in a burning building. Even though they were spared from the flames, it was uncertain whether the commandant would order them to be killed or transferred as the city fell. Prison officials and guards simply ran for their own lives. Ironically, the last remaining official was Major Thomas Turner, who stayed just long enough to burn many of the prison's records before he too finally fled.[4] The prison remained with no guards, food, or water, its doors locked and the prisoners uncertain as to what would happen next.

One eyewitness described the scene in Richmond: "All that Sabbath day the trains came and went, wagons, vehicles, and horsemen rumbled and dashed to and fro, and, in the evening, ominous groups of ruffians—more or less in liquor—began to make their appearance on the principal thoroughfares of the city. At night came on pillage and rioting took place." The remaining prisoners were simply left alone, locked in the bastille in a once-glorious city now in complete ruin. Most of the Confederate government and military were gone when General Godfrey Weitzel, a German-American officer who had overseen the occupation of New Orleans, arrived with Union forces. He accepted the surrender at 8:15 a.m. at City Hall.[5] Nearby, Major Atherton H. Stevens Jr., an officer with the Fourth Massachusetts Volunteer Cavalry, raised the American flag over the statehouse.[6] The long national nightmare was at an end.

"LET 'EM UP EASY"

With the victory at Petersburg and subsequent fall of Richmond, General Grant invited President Lincoln to visit his headquarters at City Point, near Petersburg. The news prompted curious crowds in Washington, D.C., to gather at the Seventh Street Wharf along the Potomac River to watch the president depart on the steamer *River*

Queen. Although emotionally exhausted, Lincoln was temporarily reinvigorated by the good news and opportunity to tour the battlefields and meet with generals Grant, Sherman, and Sheridan. He chatted warmly with the soldiers and even grabbed an ax to help chop wood for the army. According to Lincoln's bodyguard, Colonel William H. Crook, who chronicled the tour, Grant took Lincoln out to the battlefields. Both men were avid riders, so they traveled by horseback. "Mr. Lincoln was seen to be on a black pony belonging to General Grant. The name of the animal was Jeff Davis. Everybody laughed at the idea, and at the sight, too, for the President's feet nearly touched the ground." Quipped the good-natured president of the irony of the horse's name, "Well, he may be Jeff Davis and a little too small for me, but he is a good horse."[7]

The president and his son Tad then boarded a boat for Richmond. Sailing the James River proved to be precarious, as Confederates had placed obstacles all along the river to deter Union warships. The sailing was slow, and the scene all around them was one of destruction and despair. One passenger described "Dead horses, broken ordinance, wrecked boats" . . . everywhere. The flagship *Malvern* under the command of Admiral David Dixon Porter arrived at the Confederate capital at nine in the morning on April 4 and docked a mere hundred yards from Libby. Lincoln requested to immediately be taken into the city and was rowed ashore under armed escort. Worried about Lincoln's safety, Admiral Porter sent one dozen sailors and marines to form a protective circle around the president.[8] The admiral wanted to send more troops, but Lincoln would barely agree to the token force. "I should have preferred to see the President of the United States entering the subjugated stronghold of the rebels with an escort more befitting his high station," complained Porter, "yet that would have looked as if he came as a conqueror to exult over a brave but fallen enemy. He came instead as a peacemaker, his hand extended to all who desired to take it."[9]

Lincoln was, of course, eager to see the war end and to meet with Confederate leaders in Richmond. According to Colonel Crook, Lincoln's bodyguard, the president "had no wish to see the spectacle of the Confederacy's humiliation." He did not want the trip to be a celebration. Likewise, "Mr. Lincoln knew perfectly well how dangerous the trip was."[10] Yet grateful crowds of Black residents, servants, and former slaves soon surrounded Lincoln with affectionate greetings of "Father Abraham." The gesture was returned. Meanwhile, nervous marines found it impossible to secure the president, who was almost swallowed up by the crowds.[11] The admiral took note of the remarkable event unfolding before him. "No electric wire could have carried the news of the President's arrival sooner than it was circulated through Richmond," he wrote. Indeed, all present remembered it as an ethereal moment—the tall president comforting throngs of the suffering amid the smoldering ruins of the enemy capital. "As far as the eye could see the streets were alive with negroes and poor whites rushing in our direction, and the crowd increased so fast that I had to surround the President with the sailors with fixed bayonets to keep them off," remembered Porter. Yet "they all wanted to shake hands with Mr. Lincoln or his coat tail or even to kneel down and kiss his boots!"[12] Lincoln seemed taken aback by the outpouring of support but also by the scenes of destruction and want throughout the city. With his characteristic magnanimity and humility, he managed only a few words: "Kneel to God only, and thank him for the liberty you will hereafter enjoy."[13]

Lincoln and his son met with General Weitzel. The president had hoped to meet with the Confederacy's senior political leaders and commanding general, but they had all fled. Only a small delegation of soldiers and citizens including a judge and one general were on hand. After a brief meeting with them, Lincoln joined Weitzel for lunch and then set off in a carriage for an afternoon tour of Richmond. They passed cheering crowds of Black residents and a few of the city's White residents who came out to leer maliciously at the villainous Lincoln. The party, now supplemented by Weitzel's own guard, visited the State Capitol. The president held Tad's hand throughout most of the tour.

The day was documented by Thomas Thatcher Graves, aide to Weitzel, who remembered Lincoln "walking with his usual long, careless stride, and looking about with an interested air and taking in everything." Graves saluted his president, who asked casually, "Is it far to President Davis's house?" Weitzel had just commandeered the White House of the Confederacy as his interim headquarters, and Lincoln was eager to see it. Graves recorded the president as grinning in almost "boyish" excitement, "Come, let's look at the house!" The tall president looked around with great interest but was especially keen to sit in the office chair, remarking, "This must have been President Davis's chair."[14]

By the afternoon, the crowds were dangerously large and growing larger with every passing hour. The presidential party headed to Libby Prison so Lincoln could see for himself the infamous site of so much suffering.[15] He walked to the prison, where a crowd quickly assembled and began chanting for the building to be torn down. As the commander in chief surveyed the site, someone near him yelled, "We will pull it down." Lincoln, however, with an eye to history and thinking of those who had been lost, responded solemnly, "No, leave it as a monument."[16]

Lincoln's bodyguard recorded that the devastation of Richmond, the plight of the citizens, and ghosts of the wretched bastille "wore new furrows in his face." Crook added, "Mr. Lincoln never looked sadder."[17] When asked by Weitzel what should be done "in regard to the conquered people," Lincoln replied only "that he did not wish to give any orders on that subject" for the moment. He then added in a solemn tone, "If I were in your place I'd let 'em up easy, let 'em up easy."[18]

IRONY

With the fall of Richmond, the few remaining Union soldiers suffering in the bastille were freed and taken to City Point by ship. However, the notorious Libby complex would remain in use as a prison. In the ultimate twist of fate, the facility would now hold Confederate prisoners—and would do so until 1868. Approximately seven hundred Confederate soldiers and government workers were detained in the former warehouse. With Richmond still smoldering and chaos reigning throughout the city, the conditions inside the new Libby Jail remained deplorable. They were, however, much improved over what inmates had borne under Confederate management. Importantly, the inmates were no longer subjected to beatings, harsh interrogations, robbery, starvation, or summary execution. In the subsequent months and years, the federal government under Lincoln's policy of Reconstruction would send food, physicians, and supplies to rebuild the city.[19]

Poetically, a few of the former Confederate officials who had overseen Richmond's prisons and some of the guards who had not evacuated the city were incarcerated in Libby. One of the new inmates was Richard Turner himself, the former deputy commandant. The *Richmond Examiner* noted the irony of the situation when they reported that a special cell had been prepared for the "inspector."[20]

Sadly, as history has so abundantly recorded, the end of the war and policy of forgiveness under Reconstruction did little to soften hearts. In the years after the war, racial tensions heightened throughout Richmond as local newspapers stoked the fears of White residents. The arbitrary arrests, beatings, and lynchings of Black residents became so oppressive that some people of color fled to Libby Prison for the protection of the federal soldiers on guard there.

One of the city's residents whose safety was in real jeopardy after the fall of the Confederacy was Elizabeth Van Lew. The former Yankee spy suffered constant threats and harassment from the city's newspapers and ardent secessionists. As Northern newspapers reported, "So offensive had Miss Van Lew become to her rebel neighbors that two nights before the evacuation of Richmond a mob was organized to burn her house down." Disturbingly, the incident only repeated itself, with Van Lew bravely confronting the crowds and calling out the "ringleaders" by name.[21] In the chaotic final days of the war, General Butler had been so concerned for the life of his spy that he had sent Colonel David B. Parker of the Seventy-Second New York to Richmond to protect her. Soon thereafter, amid the chaos and vigilantism in Richmond, General Grant sent a small unit of men to Van Lew's home. When they arrived at her mansion, she was not at home. A servant directed them to the Richmond Library, where she was found combing through the remaining government documents to prepare her next intelligence report!

Van Lew invited newly arrived Union commanders to dine with her. Eager to begin the healing, she even invited "several prominent Confederate officials" and Erastus Ross, the clerk she had placed inside Libby, to the affairs.[22] However, Richmond newspapers covered her events with much mockery and derision, even reporting the names of guests as a not-so-thinly veiled threat because of their "disloyalty."[23] Indeed, many residents never forgave her, most especially because it was none other than "Crazy Bette" who'd had an eighteen-by-nine-foot American flag snuck into the city and flown over her home—the first stars and stripes to fly over Richmond since before the war had started.[24]

19

Liberation!

Let us have peace.

—General Ulysses S. Grant[1]

Of the 109 men to break out of Libby Prison on the night spanning February 9 and 10, 1864, forty-eight were recaptured in the days and weeks following their escape, and two died trying; but fifty-nine men made it across Union lines. All of them had stories to tell, from the drama of the escape to the horrors of the wretched prison. Yet so too were their lives after Libby just as compelling. For instance, two of the escapees, Major Ivan Walker and Captain Ithamer Phelps, had both served in the Seventy-Third Indiana Infantry and been friends since before the war. They had spent the five days after tunneling out of Libby hiding in swamps, freezing, and Walker grew too ill and weak to go any farther. He begged his friend to continue without him, but Phelps refused to leave. On the sixth day of their ordeal, they were recaptured and confined to Libby's dungeon cells. From there they were sent to prisons in Macon, Georgia, and in Charleston and Columbia, South Carolina. Somehow the friends survived the war.

Another among the recaptured was William Grosvenor Ely of the Eighteenth Connecticut Infantry, who, after being paroled near the end of the war, rejoined fighting and was twice wounded in combat. He would survive the war and live another forty-one years. Others were not so lucky. One of the veterans of the Battle of Chickamauga, Charles Morton of the Eighty-Fourth Illinois Infantry, was also recaptured after his escape from Libby. He became a police magistrate after the war but suffered mightily during his long convalescence and was never able to deal with painful bouts of depression—likely caused from the trauma of imprisonment. Of course, such afflictions were, at best, misunderstood in the mid-nineteenth century, and it is believed Morton committed suicide on July 26, 1880. Another veteran of Chickamauga, David Flansburg of the Fourth Indiana Artillery, was also recaptured. The Confederacy sent him to prisons in Macon and Columbia, where his health declined. Sadly, he died in prison in November of 1864.

Like Flansburg, others who were recaptured suffered while back in Libby and in other foul prisons. One of them was Edwin Hayes of the One Hundredth Ohio Infantry, who was sent to the dreaded Andersonville stockade and then later to a prison in Charleston. He managed to survive each ordeal, including a disquieting episode in which the Confederacy sent prisoners to the front lines to serve as fodder during attacks and bombardments. Hayes would go on to be promoted to the rank of general and was appointed governor of North Carolina during Reconstruction. He was also the oldest living former Union general when he died in New Jersey on January 1, 1917. Another prisoner placed on the front lines by Confederates to be sacrificed during the artillery barrage at Charleston was David Miles of the Seventy-Ninth Pennsylvania Infantry. In addition to somehow making it through the Battle of Chickamauga, Libby, and the bombardment of Charleston, he survived captivity in a prison in Macon. So too was John Spofford of the Ninety-Seventh New York Infantry recaptured and incarcerated in both Macon and Charleston, where he was also one of the prisoners placed by his captors at the front to be killed. Spofford somehow survived all these horrors as well as the earlier Battle of Gettysburg.

Another veteran of Gettysburg also escaped from Libby. Charles Tilden of the Sixteenth Maine Infantry immediately returned to combat after the escape but was again captured at the Weldon Railroad on August 19, 1864. Upon discovering he was to be taken back to the dreaded Libby, Weldon was prompted to escape during the transit to Richmond. Once again, he rejoined the fight and was badly wounded in the final weeks of the war during the attack on Petersburg; he survived his wounds and lived into his eighties. Junius Gates of the Thirty-Third Ohio Infantry, another veteran of Chickamauga, was recaptured after the great escape. He was reincarcerated in Macon but managed to escape again. So did William Rossman of the Third Ohio Infantry, who after recapture was detained in both Macon and Charleston but managed to escape in November of 1864, going on an agonizing month-long run through South Carolina and Georgia before finding a Union camp.

A similar adventure faced Lewis Sutherland of the 126th Ohio Infantry, who was also recaptured. After breaking out of the bastille, Sutherland was forging a muck-filled swamp when his boots were "sucked" off his feet. He walked barefoot for days in freezing temperatures and suffered frostbite on his toes. He was retaken by Confederate troops and interned in prisons in Macon, Charleston, and ultimately Columbia, remaining gravely ill. He escaped from the latter facility in November of 1864 but was quickly caught by guards with bloodhounds, severely punished, and returned to the prison. Though seriously ill, he managed to escape three weeks later, finally making it to Union lines.

Another officer with a record of escaping was George Starr of the 104th New York Infantry. The veteran of Gettysburg not only escaped from Libby but prisons in Macon, Columbia, and elsewhere. In October of 1864, he was aided by a widow with two sons in the Confederate army who told him that she hoped one day someone would help her boys. Likewise, Robert Bradford of the Second West Tennessee Cavalry managed to elude his would-be captors after the great escape from Libby. Remarkably, this was only one of the three times that he was captured and then managed successfully to escape. However, he could not overcome a bad bout of pneumonia and passed away in Paducah, Kentucky, near the end of the war in February of 1865.

A few of the men who escaped Libby died either in subsequent fighting or in service of the nation. Michael Gallagher of the Second New Jersey Cavalry escaped and, like his fellow prisoners, immediately returned to active duty. Tragically, he was killed in Mississippi in 1864. A naval engineer assigned to the warship *Satellite* named Isaac Johnson was recaptured after getting out of Libby and sent to prison in Macon, then later to Savannah and Charleston. He survived all four prisons and remembered that he'd never had a blanket at Libby and had gone days without food in the wretched facility. Sadly, when the war ended he was serving on the ship *Juno* that, in March of 1866, was lost at sea with all hands.

James Fales of the First Rhode Island Cavalry was also recaptured after the great escape. During transfer back to Libby, he jumped off the train and ran but was later recaptured and again locked up in the bastille. Fales had the unfortunate distinction of being one of the very last Union prisoners held at the infamous facility at war's end in 1865.

Of the thirteen prisoners who had joined Rose and Hamilton in their tunnel, some had managed to elude Commandant Turner's search parties; others did not. Of them, Major George Fitzsimmons of the Fortieth Indiana, Major Bedan McDonald of the 101st Ohio, Captain John Gallagher of the Second Ohio, and Lieutenant David Garbett of the Seventy-Seventh Pennsylvania all died soon after the war, having never recovered their health from the trials they had suffered inside Libby. Captain Isaac Johnston of the Sixth Kentucky survived the war and lived out his life in Pleasantville in his home state. Captain Terrence Clark of the Seventy-Ninth Illinois also survived the war, as did Lieutenant Eli Foster of the Thirtieth Indiana, Lieutenant Nineveh McKeen of the Seventy-Ninth Illinois, and Lieutenant John Fislar of the Seventh Indiana. All of them returned to their home states after the war, except Foster, who moved to Chicago.

Both Rose and Hamilton lost contact with Captain John Lucas of the Fifth Kentucky, Lieutenant John Mitchell of the Seventy-Ninth Illinois, and Lieutenant John Simpson of the Tenth Indiana, and the latter chapters of their lives are unknown.

However, the two leaders recorded that Captain William S. B. Randall of the Second Ohio Infantry survived the war. Incredibly, the veteran of the bloody fighting at Chickamauga had arrived at Libby with several wounds, including a fractured skull from a musket ball suffered from a shot taken at the Battle of Stones River on New Year's Eve of 1862. Randall moved home to Hillsboro, Ohio, after the war.

Colonel Harrison Hobart of the Twenty-First Wisconsin Infantry—the man Rose had entrusted to replace the bricks by the fireplace and remove other evidence of the mass escape once the tunnelers had fled that momentous February night—escaped. He managed to elude the ensuing manhunt and, after six nights of running and hiding, made it to a Union camp. He continued to serve, leading troops in the siege of Atlanta and Sherman's famous March to the Sea. After the war, the veteran of Chickamauga met with President Lincoln and later was elected to public office. He would go on to serve as president of the Libby Prison Tunnel Association, the organization formed by the former prisoners, until his passing on January 26, 1902, in Milwaukee.

LIBBY'S LEADERS

The mastermind of the escape, Thomas Rose, was recaptured while in sight of the Eleventh Pennsylvania Cavalry near Williamsburg and severely punished by a vengeful Commandant Turner. The stoic colonel survived two months of abuse back in Libby before being exchanged on April 30, 1864. Despite his deteriorated health, a broken foot that had never healed, and a bout with scurvy brought on by malnutrition suffered during his roughly seven and a half months in the bastille, Rose was eager to get back into uniform. After a brief leave of duty, he rejoined the Seventy-Seventh Pennsylvania in June. Again leading from the front, he was wounded at the end of the month in the fighting at Kennesaw Mountain in Georgia. But Rose was back in command on July 6 and participated in General Sherman's famed victory at Atlanta. That same summer he was promoted to the rank of brigadier general and served until the end of the war. Rose was mustered out of service on December 6, 1865.

After the war, Rose reenlisted as an officer with the Eleventh US Infantry and then in 1870 was transferred to the Sixteenth US Infantry, where he served with great distinction until his retirement at Fort Ringgold in Texas on March 12, 1894. Over the course of his military career Rose had won numerous awards for meritorious service. The former school principal gained a degree of fame once stories of the great escape were published after the war and was frequently asked about the prison and tunnel. Yet the humble officer rarely spoke of his service, never boasted, and dismissed talk of his heroism. His friend and co-leader of the great Libby Prison escape, Major

Andrew G. Hamilton, even cautioned people against listening to Rose's account of the escape, on account of Rose's tendency to downplay and understate the details; Rose, his friend noted, was a "particularly modest and unassuming gentleman." In fact, Rose never wanted to write his story and did so only after "hundreds of requests from all over the country" and pleas from Hamilton. The account was published in the *National Tribune* in 1884. Even after the accolades poured in, Hamilton remembered Rose saying to him, "I do not want to be distinguished, particularly so if distinction must come through so much pain and sorrow as the little I gained from the event in Libby."[2]

Lieutenant Moran went so far as to say of Rose that "No one meeting him now would hear from his reticent lips, or read in his placid face, the thrilling story that links his name in so remarkable a manner with the history of the famous Bastille of the Confederacy."[3] Rose died of a cerebral hemorrhage on November 6, 1907, in the nation's capital and was buried in Arlington National Cemetery.

It was said of Rose's co-conspirator, Andrew G. Hamilton, that he possessed "almost superhuman powers of energy." The tunneling crews credited him with "keeping up the flagging interest, mental spirits, and physical condition of the men." It was also Hamilton who helped find the "few poor tools" used to dig the tunnel and devised creative solutions to many of the obstacles the prisoners faced when trying to dig out of the prison.[4] Like his co-leader of the excavation, the cavalryman with the Twelfth Kentucky Volunteers never took credit for the remarkable escape; instead, he attributed everything to Rose, saying time and again, "He was the acknowledged leader of the tunnel party . . . and it was through his good sense, energy and management, aided by the devotion and labor of his fourteen comrades in the secret tunnel, that the escape was a success." The major even claimed he had been asked to write his account of the story of the prison break because Rose was too humble and unassuming to admit to the many incredible details of the ordeal.[5]

Hamilton was Rose's original partner in the plan and was the only other member of the expedition to serve from the start through the completion of the tunnel. Unlike Rose, however, Hamilton made it to the Union lines after the escape, where he immediately rejoined the war effort and served with distinction until the very end of the fighting. Like Rose, Hamilton served in General Sherman's army, where his cavalry unit cut the supply lines necessary for the Confederacy during the fighting around Macon and Atlanta. Hamilton resigned his commission on June 5, 1865, and moved to Reedyville in his native Kentucky.

Tragically, one warm spring night in Morgantown, Kentucky, in 1895, two miscreants, Sam Spencer, aged twenty-one, and Alfred Belcher, aged twenty-two, decided to get drunk. As Belcher later described, after an evening of hard drinking, "at about 12 o'clock . . . we . . . went to our boarding-house and went to bed. In an hour or so Spencer and I got up" and started drinking again. Both young men packed pistols and headed to a local "booze pen." After leaving for "the whiskey house just outside of town" around two in the morning, they were walking along Bowling Green Road when they passed two older men. One of them was Major Hamilton. The other man asked the two youngsters where they were going. According to Belcher, "We replied that it was none of his —— business." The older man stood and "started toward us," but Hamilton "raised up and called his companion to come back." Spencer pulled his .32 caliber pistol and fired, hitting the Civil War hero between the second and third ribs beside his heart. Hamilton fell to the ground, mortally wounded. The two young troublemakers attacked Hamilton, lying defenseless on the side of the road, and the other man. They then went back to their boardinghouse.[6]

Hamilton's body was discovered at dawn, and the two culprits were quickly apprehended. Spencer denied the charges, but Belcher confessed to everything. The man who had helped so many to escape from one of the most notorious prisons in history had been murdered on April 3, 1895, while enjoying a night's conversation with a friend.

LIBBY'S LUMINARIES

General Neal Dow of Maine had been unable to join the tunnel escape, lamenting his declining health and saying, "Only the vigorous could hope to succeed." The general was sixty at the time of the mass escape. He referred to the event, however, as "the most famous of all jail deliveries" in history.[7] Fortunately, the general's release was forthcoming. On March 14, 1864, just one month after the breakout, he was part of an exchange involving General Robert E. Lee's son. The famous general had a number of prominent backers seeking to secure his release, including Vice President Hannibal Hamlin and Lot Morrill, who would serve as both governor of and senator from Dow's home state.

The next day, Dow boarded the steamer *New York*, which was docked behind Libby, and sailed east on the James River for Fortress Monroe. Upon his arrival, he was met at the port by General Benjamin Butler and other Union commanders. Afterward, he was escorted to Annapolis until an invitation arrived to come to Washington, where he was debriefed and dined with political leaders, including the vice president. Though weak from eight and a half months of captivity, Dow took only thirty days' leave. He had not been home in two years and so the general returned to Maine on March 23, receiving a hero's welcome. Fully "five companies of infantry" met him, and they were "followed by a large concourse of citizens" that escorted him to City Hall in Portland. The grateful general was taken aback, observing that "the public buildings and hundreds of dwelling-houses and stores were gaily decorated."[8]

A grand celebration followed. The general took the stage and treated the audience to an eloquent oration: "When this war shall be ended, and liberty shall be proclaimed through the land to all the inhabitants thereof . . . the survivors of it will see that the value to the nation and to mankind will be far beyond its cost." As to the terrible sacrifices made, Dow added, "those who now mourn the death of father, brother, son, slain in battle, or starved in prison, will be comforted by the thought that their dear ones perished in the cause of civilization, humanity and Christianity, and that by their death Justice and Truth are established on an everlasting throne."[9]

Beginning on December 6, 1863, Dow had kept a hidden journal of his time in Libby, written in small print. Yet one of the highest-ranking prisoners of the entire war would wait fifteen years—until he was nearly seventy-five—before assembling his letters and recollections. Like Rose and Hamilton, "he had an almost morbid disinclination to talk of his personal efforts and experiences."[10] Rather, Dow dedicated his life to abolition and temperance. After the war he traveled widely and internationally to raise awareness of and support for the temperance movement. In 1880, he was even nominated as the Prohibition Party's choice for president of the United States. In fact, so identified was Dow with prohibition, abolition, and other social reforms that, after his funeral, his family received a letter from a rum merchant who had written somewhat insensitively but comically, "I am glad to have lived to know that my natural enemy, Neil Dow, is dead." The bibulous writer had been forced to wait a long time; Dow passed in 1897 at the ripe old age of ninety-three.[11]

After escaping from the bastille, Abel Streight had been aided by Elizabeth Van Lew, who had fed and hid the famous raider and a few of his fellow prisoners in her Richmond mansion. From there, she had provided the escapees with directions to get to Blackistone Island in the Potomac and notified Union commanders that the prisoners were on their way. Two and a half weeks after escaping, Streight and his compatriots were rescued by sailors aboard the USS *Ella*. Like other veterans of the wretched prison, he reupped and returned to service just three months after his liberation. The colonel of the Fifty-First Indiana Infantry served through the remainder of the war, achieving the rank of brigadier general on March 13, 1865, as the fighting was drawing to an end.

In 1883, Streight returned to Richmond and the prison where he had spent nearly nine grueling months. Like Rose, Hamilton, and Dow, he reluctantly shared his story of the great escape. Some of the versions of the prison break that appeared in newspapers and popular magazines after the war attributed the planning to Streight on account of his fame. However, like Hamilton, Streight credited Rose with the leadership and planning of the escape. Streight passed on May 26, 1892, and was mourned as a national hero.

LIBBY'S LITERARIES

Colonel Frederick Bartleson, the one-armed veteran of many battles and budding poet, had not been a part of the great escape, feeling that his disability would prevent him from digging, accessing the tunnel via the passageway, or climbing through it. After the mass breakout, he had felt "abandoned" and bemoaned his inability to join his brothers-in-arms. Bartleson chafed under the vengeful punishments, depleted food rations, and restrictions on sending and receiving letters imposed on the remaining prisoners in Libby, saying there was no good news in the prison "for a long time."[12]

Then, in March, word arrived that there might be a prisoner exchange. Bartleson was skeptical; the exchanges had always been hit-or-miss—and mostly the latter of late—and Richmond's newspapers, politicians, and commandants were claiming to have ended the practice. But on March 4, a ship arrived from City Point carrying eight hundred enlisted Confederate men and sixty-two Confederate officers, brought for a reciprocal exchange. Some of the prisoners in the bastille allowed themselves to be "carried away and nervous with excitement," but Bartleson remained "perfectly incredulous," even penning another poem for his compatriots titled "There's a Good Time Coming, Boys; Wait a Little Longer."[13]

The Confederate soldiers were marched past the prison, but authorities announced that they had enough troops and did not need another exchange. Two days later, however, prison officials organized the Union men for an exchange. Bartleson discovered the previous announcement had been yet another instance of Confederate leaders playing cruel games with the inmates suffering in Libby. Bartleson heard his name called, writing that he was one of the "lucky ones" who were lined up and searched before being marched to the ship. Aboard the federal steamer, the prisoners were "chattering . . . shouting . . . singing." Bartleson remembered, "we could not sleep." On March 8, they arrived at Fortress Monroe by City Point before being transferred to another ship, the *Schultz*, and on March 9 they headed up the Chesapeake for Annapolis. Bartleson celebrated in a letter, "No more prisons for me!"[14]

On March 11, Bartleson was given an audience with members of the House of Representatives and delegates from the War Department. Ever the soldier, he avoided small talk and instead informed the leaders about the war, maintaining, "We must make more exertions than we are doing . . . if we want to whip" the Rebels. He was invited to attend a reception hosted by the first lady but skipped it; instead, he went to Ford's Theater to see a production of *Hamlet*. After his short stay in Washington, Bartleson took a train to New York, arriving in Brooklyn on March 14. He then boarded another train to head home to Joliet, Illinois, where on March 20 he was "restored to the bosom of my family."[15] He had been in Libby for over eight months, and it showed.

The once-strong and proud colonel who now arrived in Illinois was "pale and emaciated." His was a hero's welcome, with a grand event hosted by the town in his honor, featuring remarks and appearances from public figures. Friends and family urged the colonel to retire, while leaders encouraged him to run for office; but he had made his decision already. "The question," Bartleson announced," is still unsettled whether we are to have another Congress, or country, and it can only be settled by the success of our armies." Few were surprised when their hometown hero told them that, "Until it is settled, I want no nomination, and no office but the one I now hold, and I shall return to my post, and give my life, if need be, to secure to us a free Government."[16]

The colonel reported for duty at Camp Chase in Columbus, Ohio, on April 21, wasting no time to get back into uniform, rushing his convalescence. His troops greeted him with gusto and paid respects to his "indomitable patriotism." They were deployed immediately as part of the campaign in Georgia. Bartleson's regiment was dispatched to Kennesaw Mountain, where Rose and Hamilton had earlier fought. However, there were mistakes made in planning the attack, and Bartleson's unit lacked accurate maps and reinforcements. Sadly, a letter written on June 25, 1864, by Doctor H. T. Woodruff, a Union surgeon with the One Hundredth Illinois, arrived back to Illinois with the news. It announced "the death of our gallant and noble Colonel." He had died while riding to the front of the line in the early afternoon of June 23 to "spur" the men on; the colonel had been shot in the right side of his body, the musket ball "passing through the body and coming out on the left side." Stretcher-bearers from the Fifty-Seventh Indiana had seen an officer fall and hoped it was not Bartleson. But it was. They had rushed him back to the field hospital, but Dr. Woodruff later noted, "His death was probably instantaneous." The surgeon added, "I have seen many officers and men killed on the field, but never saw one whose death seemed to strike such a blow to everyone as his did." When the three generals on the field of battle heard the news, they all came to pay their respects to the heroic colonel. Bartleson had been only thirty-one.[17]

Fortunately for history, Bartleson's daughter, Minnie Bartleson King, saw fit to save her father's poetry, letters, and diary from Libby. They were passed on to Margaret W. Peelle, his grandniece, who assembled them into a book.[18]

The Reverend Louis Napoleon Beaudry of the Fifth New York Cavalry by way of Canada and New England had been paroled on October 7, 1863, four months before the great escape, and just as the conditions inside Libby had begun their downward spiral, leading to the darkest days in the prison's history. It had happened suddenly: A guard had burst into the upstairs room and demanded, "Are there any chaplains in this room?" Beaudry had stepped forward. He was then ordered to leave immediately but risked reprimand or worse by quickly gathering letters from his fellow prisoners. In all, he "hastily" filled his pockets and boots with 123 letters.

Some of the men "sought to have me leave them" behind, fearing that the reverend would be searched and caught. "Their discovery by the authorities," he admitted, "would cost me prolonged imprisonment and, doubtless too, in a dingy cell" in the dungeon. Beaudry also "stuffed" the crosses and small "treasures of worked bone" he had carved into his pants. Surprisingly, the guards paid him no attention, and the reverend boarded the flag-of-truce steamer *New York*. Fortunately, some of the items he had taken with him upon his release were copies of the *Libby Chronicle*, the clever "newspaper" he had "published" inside the prison.[19]

Beaudry's wife had given birth to a son shortly after the reverend had enlisted with the cavalry, so Beaudry's was a joyful homecoming. His wife begged him to stay home, but Beaudry took just one month's leave before reenlisting and serving until the end of the war. Fortunately, the reverend had started keeping a diary when he was nineteen, which had become a passion and lifelong pursuit. He had kept a daily journal of his time at war—opening with the line "Away to war!" on February 16, 1863—and his imprisonment. By the time of his death in 1892, his writings totaled thirty volumes! Ultimately, Beaudry published a book about the Fifth New York Cavalry in 1865 and then organized the issues of the *Chronicle* as a book that was released in 1889. Beaudry was but one of the prisoners who had inspired the men suffering in the bastille with his comical poems, newspaper, sermons, and prayers.[20]

LIBBY'S LIBERATORS

Captain Emeric Szabad of Hungary had a front-row seat to the great escape, the subsequent manhunt, Kilpatrick's failed raid to free the prisoners, and the vengeful response by Libby's commandant. Szabad had also been in the thick of the fighting at Gettysburg in July of 1863, before his capture later that October. His detailed writings on all of these events as well as on the trials and tribulations in the prison during the most critical period in its history are invaluable. Szabad was exchanged on March 15, 1864, in the next wave of prisoners released after the one that freed Bartleson. Close to death, having suffered through numerous diseases and bouts of starvation, Szabad's convalescence upon gaining his freedom was long and precarious. It took nearly a full year before his health was recovered.

Nonetheless, like other prisoners, Szabad was back in uniform and was promoted to the rank of major. He was assigned in February of 1865 to the Fifth Army Corps under General Romeyn Beck Ayres but later recommended to the headquarters of General Gouverneur K. Warren at Petersburg. Szabad brought his formidable intellect and knowledge of military strategy to the planning of the final stage of the siege of Petersburg and was rewarded with a promotion to the rank of lieutenant colonel.

However, the Hungarian was severely wounded in the neck and right shoulder in March of 1865. He once again faced a difficult rehabilitation, never having fully recovered from his wounds or the illnesses contracted inside Libby.

Szabad finished the war with the rank of colonel and was honorably discharged on October 7, 1865. Szabad joined the Continental Masonic Lodge in New York City while convalescing there after his release from the bastille. Afterward, he moved to Texas, where he was appointed assistant customs collector at the Port of Galveston. The former professor continued to write prolifically, penning a book on General Grant in 1868 and another on economics and currency the following year. His remarkable diary written while in Libby Prison formed the basis for a series of articles published in magazines in America, newspapers such as the *New York Tribune*, and *Fraser's Magazine* in England. He also published his account of Libby Prison.[21]

After his stint at the Port of Galveston, Szabad moved to Laredo, where he bought land and remained an active Mason for the remainder of his days, passing in the year 1894 in Boerne, Texas. The official cause of death was listed as an "alarming malady" remaining from the war. Szabad's will provided funds to build a memorial to his long military service. It took a full century, but on August 14, 1997, the local chapters of the Masonic Lodge, Veterans of Foreign Wars, and a historical society eventually erected a monument to his service against tyranny in Hungary and Italy and his efforts to preserve the Union and end slavery in America.[22]

Szabad had visited with Bartleson while they were both in the bastille. Their meeting had been recorded by both men and occurred on February 28, 1864—only days after the great escape and days before the two would be exchanged. Both men were seriously ill and wondered whether they would survive their captivity. The one-armed colonel doubted he would make it and gave Szabad a poem titled "All Is Well" that he had written on New Year's Eve.[23] Like many of the prisoners, Szabad appreciated Bartleson's verses but commented that, amid so much starvation, despair, and death, the touching poem was "a strange infant for Libby!" Szabad made sure the poem was preserved.[24]

Szabad had also met Colonel Federico Fernández Cavada inside Libby. Like Szabad, Fernández Cavada was a multilingual intellectual and talented writer. He was also a liberator. The two men shared a deep passion for opposing tyranny and were willing to be a part of military campaigns to end persecution and subjugation. Much as Hamilton later reminded readers that Rose's account of life in Libby had been understated—in that the colonel was never one to claim credit for his accomplishments or complain about his struggles—so it was the case that Szabad considered Colonel Fernández Cavada's book *Life in Libby* to be "a very mild account without the usual atrocity stories."[25] Where Rose's stoic temperament and tight-lipped brevity were defining characteristics, so it was that Fernández Cavada's courteous and aristocratic inclinations limited his bravado and bluster. Nonetheless,

Fernández Cavada eloquently detailed the sufferings of the prisoners and cruelty of the commandants and guards.

The Cuban-American colonel was also exchanged in the spring of 1864. After his recovery, Fernández Cavada was appointed by the United States to serve as the American consul to Cuba. When the insurrection against Spanish rule began in the island nation, he resigned his post and, ever the liberator, joined the revolution. Given his service as an officer in the Civil War, Fernández Cavada was given the rank of general and made commander in chief of all Cuban forces. His younger brother, Adolphus, had also served in the Civil War as a captain. Both Cavada men were engineers, possessing a number of skills and talents, and both joined the fight for independence in Cuba. The eldest of the three brothers, Emilio, remained in Philadelphia but raised money, arms, and supplies for the war.

The Ten Years' War, also known as the Great War,[26] began in 1868 by Cuban-born planters and wealthy citizens. It grew to include much of the island's population. In the bitter conflict, Federico Fernández Cavada earned the moniker "General Fire" for burning Spanish property. He continued his literary pursuits, publishing articles in American magazines in the hopes of building support for Cuban independence. In 1871, Fernández Cavada led his forces to Camagüey in central Cuba, and from there he intended to go to the island's western coast to secretly board a boat to travel to the United States. His objective was to press for American support and raise arms and funds for the struggle. However, Spanish authorities were tipped off, and the general was captured by the gunboat *Neptuno* and taken prisoner to Puerto Principe.

Former Civil War commanders such as Generals S. Ulysses Grant, George Meade, and Daniel Sickles tried desperately to secure their former colleague's release. However, on July 1, 1871, Cavada was put to death by firing squad. His final words were "Adios, Cuba, para siempre" (Goodbye, Cuba, forever). On February 24, 1929, a monument was erected in the town of Nuevitas in the Province of Camagüey. It honored those who fought for Cuban independence. Likewise, in the city of Cienfuegos, a medical clinic was named for him, and back in the United States, he was posthumously awarded the military's Campaign Medal.[27]

FATE

The incompetent provost marshal of Richmond, General John Winder, grotesquely mismanaged the city's prisons, hired commandants and guards ill-equipped to handle their responsibilities, and had a hand in the tragedy that was Andersonville, the worst and most deadly prison in American history. The "short-tempered," "aloof," and controversial marshal died of a heart attack in February of 1865 while inspecting a prison in Florence, South Carolina. Had Winder lived, it is possible that he may have been tried for war crimes.

The same is true for Commandant Thomas Turner—if Union officials had been able to find him. As Richmond was falling in early April of 1865, Turner was preparing his escape. On the evening of April 3, he burned most of Libby's official records, thus denying history many of the details of the brutal prison. A few documents were recovered and made it into the hands of federal leaders, and they paint a gruesome picture. Though President Lincoln had urged reconciliation and reconstruction, Secretary of War Edwin Stanton, shocked by the accounts coming out of Libby, ordered that Dick be investigated for wartime atrocities.[28] It seems probable the Union would have been interested in Major Thomas Turner as well.

It did little good; Major was nowhere to be found. The violent commandant had fled "the day on which the Yankees entered" the Confederate capital. He described the fall and "evacuation" of Richmond as tragic, adding, "I found every thing chaos and confusion." As he traveled from the city, he noted, "The roads and avenues were filled with fugitives, hurrying on God knows where." Turner joined them, racing on horseback to General Robert E. Lee's headquarters, but he then discovered the Confederate general had surrendered. A diehard secessionist, Turner had grumbled that the capitulation was "very sudden and unexpected." Turner then headed off toward General Johnston's headquarters, but the Union Army was in the path, so he snuck to Augusta in Georgia, hoping to unite with Confederate units. After encountering two Southern generals—Franklin Gardner and Henry B. Carrington—the three unrepentant Confederates arrived just miles from where Jefferson Davis had been captured only days earlier. The situation looked hopeless: Southern leaders were either on the run or surrendering, and Union forces were everywhere. The two generals with whom he was traveling were ill, so Turner abandoned his comrades and headed on alone, back toward the Mississippi River, adopting a fake name and ditching his uniform for civilian clothing.[29]

In Yazoo City, Mississippi, Turner abandoned his horse, stole a dugout canoe, and crossed the Yazoo River on his trek toward the Mississippi. He canoed across the river hoping to find Confederate forces and put distance between himself and Union armies in the east. What he found were mosquitoes. After lashing his canoe in the thick brush on the shore of the river, he hid on the banks of the river for a few days, where he recorded that he was "almost bitten to death by mosquitoes, buffalo gnats, and every other pestiferous creature imaginable." Eager to get out of the country, he proceeded on foot to Arkansas. It seems he avoided heading south to New Orleans because it was occupied by Union forces and he'd had enough of the region's "suffocating bogs" and mud. In the "Natural State," the commandant met up with a few other Confederate soldiers on the run. Together they traveled to Waco, Texas, arriving in August of 1865.[30]

While preparing to cross the Rio Grande into Mexico, the expats met General Jubal Early, who, like the others, was using an "alias"[31] and shared their interest in traveling to Mexico in order to "free ourselves from Yankee thraldom." Not finding Mexico to their liking, however, that October the small band boarded a ship "bound for Liverpool" and, according to Turner, were thrilled to be leaving "the so-called US behind us, with its abolition crew." Turner remained on the lam, traveling to the Bahamas, England, Canada, and Cuba—anything to avoid the perceived horrors of living in the United States. Interestingly, Turner and his fellow Confederates believed they were not free in the United States; rather, they were "oppressed" because they could not own slaves. He described the journey abroad as an effort "to free ourselves from atrocious persecution, tyranny, and oppression." Reflecting Southern propaganda, the unrepentant Turner referred to his former fellow countrymen as the "barbarians of the North," "dogs" who only wanted to kill "women and children of the South."[32]

Turner remained on the run. The news that a few co-conspirators behind the assassination of Lincoln had been hanged and that Captain Henry Wirz, commandant of Andersonville Prison, had been sentenced to death on November 10, 1865, convinced Turner that he and all Confederates would "one of these days share the same fate." Never mind that Wirz was the only Confederate soldier charged with war crimes during the entire bloody conflict and nearly all Southern commanders and politicians had been allowed to go free. Disliking every country where he hid, ironically Turner ultimately returned to the United States, and it is possible he moved to Tennessee and there worked as a dentist. Not much is known about his final years, as he—understandably—kept a low profile. Accounts claim he died the day after Christmas in 1900 at the Odd Fellow Retirement Home in Clarksville, Tennessee, not far from Nashville, and was buried at the Odd Fellow Cemetery in the city; other accounts suggest we do not know what came to be of Turner.[33]

Some Confederate prison officials and guards were caught and arrested by the Union at the end of the war. Some of the former guards were held at Libby for a short time before simply being released. Inspector Dick Turner, the deputy commandant, had been captured and placed in the same cages in Libby's dungeon he used to punish his former charges. The inspector was released on June 18, 1866, after only one year in prison. Lieutenant Moran claimed he remained unrepentant, "disagreeable and revolting," throughout the ordeal perhaps because his view in the dark, foul cellar included the entrance to the tunnel dug by Rose and Hamilton. One of the former prison officials who avoided jail was Erastus Ross, the clerk who had secretly helped some of Libby's prisoners to escape. He died in a hotel fire in the city in 1870.[34]

Curiously, after the end of hostilities, the War Department returned some of the secret messages Elizabeth Van Lew had sent to Union commanders. Tragically, she seems to have destroyed most of them, likely in order to protect the identity of the couriers who had worked for her and to cover her own complicity in working against the Confederacy. She was, after all, still living in Richmond, and sectional animosities and bitterness remained strong during the postwar years. Unfortunately for the Yankee spy, the end of the war did not mean the end of difficulties. Richmond's newspapers frequently published critical stories about Van Lew long after the war's end, informing their readers that she had been "a Federal spy," a "traitor" who was "disloyal." The threats and ostracization weighed on her. "No one will walk with us on the street," she complained. "No one will go with us anywhere; and it grows worse and worse as the years roll on." Richmond's citizens even accused her of being a witch and claimed her Church Hill mansion was haunted, prompting Van Lew to groan that she was "shunned . . . like the plague."[35]

However, grateful generals, politicians, and former prisoners in the North all extended heartfelt thanks to Elizabeth Van Lew, inviting her to visit Washington, D.C., in November of 1867. Deeming her a hero, General Ulysses S. Grant even made a point of visiting her in Richmond. Van Lew suffered financially after the war, having spent the family fortune in the service of the prisoners. To ease her financial burden, on March 17, 1869, newly sworn-in President Grant appointed her postmaster of Richmond, a post she held until 1877, when Grant's second term ended. The president even wrote that she would be his "warm friend until his death." In 1883, President Chester A. Arthur reappointed her to the position. Although her assignment was bitterly opposed in the South, as one newspaper opined, the trailblazing appointments were "looked upon as a big thing for the women's rights people" across the country. The famous Yankee spy died on the twenty-fifth of September 1900.[36]

20

Museum and Memory

We are not fighting for slavery. We are fighting for independence, and that, or extermination, we will have.

—Jefferson Davis[1]

It seems that warfare is a foundational part of human nature. Clearly war, violence, and brutality are present in every chapter of the human story, and one of those appalling chapters was the Civil War. In many ways, the horrors and heroism of Libby was but a microcosm of the larger struggle from 1861 to 1865; focusing on what happened at Libby Prison provides us with important insights and lessons into both war and human nature. Indeed, as tensions increased during the war, so did the violence and punishments inside the prison. Prisoners were beaten, denied blankets during winter, robbed, arbitrarily punished, restricted in receiving mail, threatened with shootings, starved, and placed in solitary confinement in the dungeon for the slightest infraction or, at times, without cause. Others were executed. General John Winder, provost marshal of Richmond, boasted that in his prisons "I'm killing more Yankees than Lee at the front." Jefferson Davis seemed to be just fine with the executions and death toll in Libby and other Southern prisons, wearing the horrors as a perverse badge of honor.[2]

In April of 1864, two Confederate spies were caught recruiting soldiers in Kentucky and carrying secret war documents. The two men—Captain William F. Corbin and Captain T. G. McGraw—were arrested and found guilty by military tribunal. On May 15, 1864, Union general Ambrose Burnside ordered their execution. The event roiled the South, eventually leading to Libby's infamous "Lottery of Death."

As soon as Confederate authorities learned of the fate of their two spies, an order was given that "two captains now in our custody shall be selected for execution in retaliation for this gross barbarity." On July 6, authorities ordered seventy-four Union prisoners inside Libby with the rank of captain to fall into formation. They were forced to draw names as part of a cruel lottery, and those selected would be executed as a reprisal. One can only imagine the horror they must have felt upon hearing the order. Accordingly, Henry Sawyer, one of the Union captains, suggested the prison chaplains draw the names. Reverend Joseph Brown of Maryland agreed quite reluctantly to perform the gruesome task. The first name he selected was Sawyer's; the second was John M. Flinn of the Fifty-First Indiana. According to the *Richmond Dispatch*, "When the names were read out, Sawyer heard it with no apparent emotion, remarking that someone had to be drawn, and he could stand it as well as anyone else." However, the paper gloated, "Flinn was very white and much depressed."[3]

Sawyer had enlisted in the war on April 15, 1861—the very day that President Lincoln had called for volunteers—and gone on to serve with the Allentown Rifles, a Pennsylvania unit, before joining the First New Jersey Cavalry. At Brandy Station in Virginia on June 9, 1863, the cavalrymen conducted a brave charge into the Confederate ranks of General J. E. B. Stuart, and Sawyer was shot in the neck and thigh. Severely wounded, he was left for dead on the battlefield. However, Sawyer had survived; he was caught by the Rebels and imprisoned in Libby.

The story of the South's plan to enact reprisal executions gained attention throughout the North and South. The Confederacy had been systematically brutalizing and even murdering prisoners, threatening to end exchanges, robbing inmates, and so much more. President Lincoln had repeatedly been advocating dialogue and conciliation, but it was not working. Upping the ante, the Union announced "that for each officer so executed one of your officers in our hands will immediately be put to death and this number be not sufficient it will be increased." When the South remained defiant, they were reminded that the North held the sons of Robert E. Lee and General Winder in custody. The situation threatened to devolve further into a macabre series of high-stakes retaliations and executions. Cooler heads finally prevailed. After outcries from the public and pleas from politicians, both sides stepped back from the brink. Sawyer and Flinn were spared, and high-level exchanges were negotiated.[4]

But it would be a mistake to think the mistreatment in Libby could not have gotten worse; and in fact, it was about to.

THE LIBBY ZOO

General Dow noted in his diary, "We had frequent visitors who came from curiosity, and to many of these I was pointed out as a special object of interest." The famous

New Englander dismissed all the fuss to see him, writing, "To all this I paid no attention."[5] Captain Szabad also found the stream of visitors—which included the city's residents, "tourists" from across the South, and celebrities—to be unusual, noting that those who came to see the prisoners did not do so because they were "sympathetic." Rather, the Hungarian freedom fighter described the reason as a mix of morbid curiosity and prideful gloating. In January of 1864, during the worst days in the prison's history, and just as Rose, Hamilton, and their crews were tunneling to freedom, Szabad remembered that "more than the usual number of visitors" came to see "Yankees." They were treated to the sight of men starving, dying, and unable to stand up. That was the purpose.[6]

Appallingly, the bastille functioned as something of a sick carnival show for prominent Southerners amused by the prisoners "in the same manner as the animals do" in zoos.[7] A reporter from the *New York Tribune* described the scene: "The Rebels would walk about the rooms very much as if they were in a zoological garden . . . and this General, that Colonel, or that Major, was pointed out as would be a Bengal tiger, an African giraffe, or a Polar bear."[8] One of the prisoners echoed the point, remembering the prison officials "pointing out some of the better-known prisoners as if they were zoological specimens."[9] Guards were always nearby, of course.

The tours commenced outside the prison at "welcome" tents. Always, the Union officers were referred to as "abolition prisoners" and the Union Army as the "Abolition army," conveniently forgetful, of course, that Confederate authorities claimed the war was not about slavery. The "tour" included Libby's kitchen and offices, where the guests enjoyed walls adorned with US flags captured during the fighting, including one from Vicksburg, "splattered with blood." But the highlight would be to peer into the doors of the upstairs barracks. There they might see such celebrities as General Dow or the despised Colonel Streight. Many came to see David Campbell Van Buskirk of the Twenty-Seventh Indiana Infantry, billed as the "largest Yankee prisoner." Van Buskirk was said to stand at six feet, eleven inches, and weigh in at nearly four hundred pounds. He added a carnival-show atmosphere to the tours. President Jefferson Davis even came to see him. Often these "sightseeing tours" included politicians, such as Congressman Henry S. Foote of Mississippi, Confederate generals, such as John C. Breckinridge[10] and John Hunt Morgan, and other leading citizens; and one time Richmond's mayor, Joseph Mayo, took the tour. Famed Southern raider John Singleton Mosby visited in order to see some of the soldiers his unit had captured.[11]

CONDUCT OF THE WAR

In April of 1864, just two months after the great escape from Libby, Secretary of War Edwin Stanton was so enraged with reports of grotesque mistreatment of Union prisoners in Richmond that he formed the Joint Committee on the Conduct of the War. Among their charges was to visit Union soldiers who had returned from Southern prisons. Committee members went to the hospitals in Annapolis, Baltimore, and other communities where the prisoners were recovering. What they discovered shocked them. The prisoners told of frostbite, neglect, starvation, beatings, and executions. The men, though some had been freed weeks earlier, were still "emaciated, filthy, listless." In short, reported the committee, they "resembled skeletons."[12]

In May, the committee reported, "The evidence proves, beyond all manner of doubt, a determination on the part of the rebel authorities, deliberately and persistently practiced for a long time past, to subject those of our soldiers who had been so unfortunate as to fall in their hands to a system of treatment which has resulted in reducing many of those who have survived and been permitted to return to us to a condition, both physically and mentally, which no language can adequately describe." The final report, issued a year later, chronicled the gamut of abuses included starvation, theft, and arbitrary killings.[13] In 1869, the House of Representatives authorized another report on Southern prisons—*Treatment of Prisoners of War by the Rebel Authorities.*[14] Over three thousand witnesses were interviewed and numerous documents examined. The findings echoed those of the earlier study undertaken by the War Department, and both reopened old wounds, educating the public about the horrors of these prisons. At the same time, however, the attention paid to the prisons was generally resented in Dixie. Sadly, the reports did little to heal the deep divides between North and South. However, the House report along with lobbying efforts by the National Ex-Prisoner of War Association helped build support for pension benefits for the former prisoners. Finally, in 1880, Congress passed a bill that provided eight dollars a month to any veteran who had spent at least six months in a Southern prison.[15]

Bartleson pondered why the prisoners had been forced to suffer such monstrous mistreatment. He correctly noted that prisoners everywhere and in all wars were generally treated wretchedly. He also admitted that neither side was innocent of abuses. Indeed, both had held political prisoners, suspended *habeas corpus*, and held inmates in unacceptable conditions. However, the one-armed colonel stated, the South had treated its prisoners far worse. He postulated a few reasons for this: "They haven't got the means to treat them well," he pointed out, recognizing the shortages of food and clothing the entire Southern population had suffered during the war. But, Bartleson added, "They haven't got the disposition" either. "They are fighting from different motives from us. We are fighting for the Union, a sentiment, a high and noble experiment, but after all a sentiment," whereas, he felt, the South is "fighting for independence and are animated by passion and hatred against invaders." In his candid letter to his wife in late February of 1864, Bartleson reasoned, "When men fight for independence, it makes no difference whether the cause is just or not." He concluded his thoughts with a stark and harsh assessment, maintaining that Southerners were "filled with hate." As a result, he felt, "public sentiment there will justify almost any treatment of Yankees." He would know.[16]

General Dow agreed, suggesting in genteel terms that the "hearts and minds" of Confederate leaders and prison authorities lacked the "kindly phases of human nature." Rather, he felt, their "disposition," so consumed with hate and anger, had deteriorated to the point of a "tendency to use the great power in their hands for evil." Dow concluded, "Civilization blushes as the horrors of Andersonville, Belle Isle, Libby, and other prison pens are recalled."[17]

MEMORY

The federal government finally shut down Libby Prison in 1868. Desperate locals broke into the abandoned warehouse and looted what little remained. Invaluable connections to the past were, invariably and most likely irrevocably, lost. In time, as is sometimes the case for such harrowing events during war, the prison "faded into memory." Today it has been largely forgotten. Rarely has the history of this important prison even been mentioned in textbooks, taught in schools, appeared in our newspapers and magazines today, or graced the silver screen.[18] Of course, families remembered the loved ones they had lost to the prison, but few of them ever received a fitting memorial or even a proper burial. Countless thousands of prisoners of war had been buried quickly, with no service, and in mass graves throughout Richmond, including many dead coming from the infamous bastille. Even today unmarked gravesites pock the city, rendering the exact location of the remains of so many Union soldiers a mystery. Some who perished at Libby were buried at Oakwood Cemetery, but the spotty recordkeeping for most means they are lost. One exception was Major Robert Morris of the Pennsylvania Sixth Cavalry who died at the prison in 1863 at the age of twenty-six. Morris was grandson of Robert Morris, the revolutionary Founding Father.[19]

The old Libby warehouse and prison sat idle and in disrepair for several years after its closing. Then, in 1880, the west building was sold to the Southern Fertilizer Company for use in processing fish and animal carcasses into fertilizer for farmers. In the late 1880s, William H. Gray of the Knights Templar Assurance Association in Chicago visited the former prison and began inspecting the buildings.[20] It was so foul from the smell of fertilizer that Gray was said to have commented, "Beside it, the Chicago stockyards are a bed of roses." Likewise, the telltale signs of suffering and prison life were still quite visible throughout the facility. The floors still had checker and chessboards carved into them, and the blood-soaked "heavy timbers" were still carved with names and initials of the prisoners as well as marks to indicate the rooms, such as "Third Floor E" and "Second Floor M."[21]

It was rumored that the old prison would be bought. Some veterans and news-papers in the North complained about both the dilapidated condition of the warehouses and its sale to an investor. They wanted the site of so much suffering to be memorialized. There was, sadly, "no local sentiment" or interest in either the building or its upkeep in the South. However, Gray and a group of Chicago investors had an idea.[22]

In 1888, the three buildings that comprised the prison were bought for $23,000 by Gray and a group of investors that included Josiah Cratty, John A. Crawford, and Charles Miller. The architectural firm of Burnham & Root assisted with the detailing of the buildings, and the law firm Rawlings & Rose managed the deal.[23] The plan was to move the entire complex to Chicago, where it would form the basis for a new museum dedicated to the Civil War. Famed Philadelphia archi-tect Louis M. Hallowell traveled to Richmond to supervise the sensitive process of disassembling the building, brick by brick. That labor-intensive and arduous enterprise took place in December of 1888 and is estimated to have cost roughly $200,000. Each piece of wood, for example, was numbered so as to be identified and reassembled in Chicago.

It was "a project never before equaled in the history of building moving." Fully 132 railway cars were required to transport tons of bricks, doors, barred windows, and even the roof of the bastille by way of the Chesapeake and Ohio Railway, which operated near the prison in Richmond. Libby seemed to remain cursed: On the way to Chicago, the train derailed near Ashtabula, Ohio, spilling bricks and artifacts everywhere. It took weeks and a major salvage operation to recover much—but not all—of the prison. Some bricks were simply left on the ground.[24]

The old prison would rise again like the phoenix: The building was reassembled by the Libby Prison Museum Association, which had been founded in Chicago on February 4, 1888. Quarried artesian stone from throughout Illinois was used to build a high stone walled entrance that resembled a medieval fortress, which sat on Wabash Avenue between Fourteenth and Sixteenth streets.[25] After over a full year of construction, the Libby Prison War Museum held its grand opening on Sep-tember 20, 1889. Unlike other museums of the time, it was open daily, including Sundays, from nine in the morning until ten at night. The cost of admission was a lofty fifty cents, but children under fifteen got in for half that price. Advertised as the "great" Libby Prison War Museum, it featured the doors and keys to the prison, iron bars from the windows, and the chisel "said to have been used by escaping prisoners" of the "great Yankee tunnel." There were curiosities such as the pillow, clothing, and bedding alleged to have been from Lincoln's assassination, complete with old bloodstains.[26]

Of course, the main attraction was the "tunnel entrance" from which 109 Union officers had escaped. It had been, of course, "moved from its original location." Civil

War veterans made pilgrimages to the museum, and vets ran featured tours for other vets. General Dow even visited the museum and was taken to see a plate that marked the spot in the prison where he had been held.[27]

The museum enjoyed large crowds and a few years of success. However, the operators missed a lucrative opportunity to include it as part of the Chicago World's Fair in 1893.[28] By 1897, the museum was no longer making money, and attendance had slowed, so it was closed to make space for another project. Many of the items, including the bricks and timbers, were auctioned. Some artifacts were sold as souvenirs or handed out to the final patrons as keepsakes,[29] a sad demise for the relics marking a tragically important chapter of the Civil War.[30]

LEGACY

A farmer named Frank Davis from LaPorte County in Indiana purchased some of the bricks and wooden beams sold at the museum auction. Davis bought a significant quantity to use in building a large barn near the small village of Hamlet in the northwestern part of the state, not far from Chicago.[31] One account described the "beams and rafters of a peaceful Indiana barn" still containing initials and carvings of the Union soldiers incarcerated in the infamous prison. The protests etched on the old walls—"United We Stand, Divided We Fall" and "The Union Must and Shall be Preserved"—still beckoned so many years later. The barn stood from about 1900 to 1962. On October 20, 1962, the Richmond Civil War Centennial Committee, in cooperation with the LaPorte County Historical Society and the Indiana Centennial Commission, erected a historic marker along a nearby road. It prompted curious tourists driving on the lonely highway to stop, and, angered by the attention, the family that owned the barn sold it, and over time the old sign was never replaced. However, Davis's daughter, Ella J. Davis, used some of the wood to have a gavel fashioned, which she presented to the city of Richmond.[32]

A few remaining artifacts from Libby are found today in museums around the country in locations as far from Richmond as Illinois, Massachusetts, Ohio, and Vermont. Oddly, in 1907, nails and iron from the prison were melted down and used to cast the Pokahuntas Bell,[33] which was used in the Jamestown Exposition commemorating the founding of the colony. Several items remain in Richmond in such locations as the American Civil War Museum–Historic Tredegar, and the Virginia Museum of History and Culture. Some of the records from Libby Prison are in the National Archives.

Over time, the site of the prison at Twentieth and Cary Streets became a cluttered assortment of debris and miscellany from a salvage company. Today a small marker stands at the site, affixed to the side of the Richmond Floodwall, which runs straight through the former prison grounds and by the James River. Next to it is a small interpretive sign near a passageway through the floodwall that is popular with joggers and folks taking their dogs for a walk; it contains information on the history and suffering of the infamous prison and on one of history's most daring and successful prison escapes. Perhaps fittingly, the lot immediately adjacent to the site now houses the Virginia Holocaust Museum.

Reverend Beaudry reflected on his incarceration there, noting, "Libby prison became almost as notorious as its enlisted men's counterpart, Andersonville, because of its overcrowded, cold and damp conditions with theft by their captors and a constant hunger."[34] Robert Cornwell, who had suffered in the bastille, observed, "Libby, probably more than any other Southern prison, was well known in the North during the war." He supposed "there were two reasons for this: the prisoners were officers and the prison was located in the enemy's capitol city. This made it a perfect subject for Northern newspapers and magazines, and Libby coverage was frequent."[35] The *New York Times*, for instance, ran stories under such headlines as "Horrors of Richmond Prisons."[36] It and other papers provided gripping details from firsthand accounts by prisoners who had been exchanged or paroled.

Of course, Libby's legacy also contains the remarkable prison break and the incredible stories of suffering and survival of the incarcerated. One of the 109 escapees who later wrote of his adventure was Lieutenant Frank Moran of the Seventy-Third New York Infantry, only twenty-one while imprisoned in the bastille. He noted, "Among all the thrilling incidents in the history of Libby Prison, none exceeds in interest the celebrated tunnel escape."[37] According to Major Andrew Hamilton, coleader of the famous breakout, "in the history of all of them there is not one that compares."[38]

Appendix: Colonel Bartleson's Poem

In Libby Prison, New Year's Eve, 1863–64

'T is twelve o'clock! Within my prison dreary,
My bed upon my hand, sitting so weary,
Scanning the future, musing upon the past,
Pondering the fate that here my lot has cast,
The hoarse cry of the sentry on his beat
Wakens the echoes of the silent street,—
    "All 's well!"

Ah! is it so? My fellow-captive sleeping
Where the barred window strictest watch is keeping,
Dreaming of home and wife and prattling child,
Of the sequestered vale, the mountain wild,—
Tell me, when cruel morn shall break again,
Wilt thou repeat the sentinel's refrain,
    "All 's well!"

And thou, my county! Wounded, pale, and bleeding,
Thy children deaf to a fond mother's pleading,
Stabbing with cruel hate and nurturing breast
To which their infancy in love was prest,—
Recount thy wrongs, thy many sorrows name,
Then to the nations, if thou canst, proclaim,
    "All 's well!"

But through the clouds the sun is slowly breaking;
Hope from her long, deep sleep is re-awaking:
Speed the time, Father! when the bow of peace,
Spanning the gulf, shall bid the tempest cease,
When foemen, clasping each other by the hand,
Shall shout once more, in a united land,
          "All 's well!"

> —Frederick A. Bartleson, Colonel,
> One Hundredth Illinois Volunteers

Notes

PREFACE

1. Andrew G. Hamilton, *The Story of the Famous Tunnel Escape from Libby Prison, as Told by Maj. A. G. Hamilton, One of the Projectors* (Chicago: N.p., 1893) (Reprint, [N.p.]: Digital Text Publishing, 2017), facsimile online, https://babel.hathitrust.org/cgi/pt?id=loc.ark:/13960/t5z60zp4d&view=1up&seq=1.

PROLOGUE: THE TUNNEL

1. Robert T. Cornwell, *Libby Prison and Beyond*, edited by Thomas Boaz, 1999, p. 201.
2. Andrew G. Hamilton, *The Story of the Famous Tunnel Escape*, n.p.
3. Hamilton, *The Story of the Famous Tunnel Escape*, n.p.
4. Hamilton, *The Story of the Famous Tunnel Escape*, n.p.
5. Angela M. Zombek, "Libby Prison," Encyclopedia Virginia, encyclopediavirginia.org/entries/libby-prison/.
6. Thomas E. Rose, *Col. Rose's Story of the Famous Tunnel Escape from Libby Prison*, 1884, n.p.
7. Hon. H. L. Morey, Member of Congress, "Libby Prison: The Experience of One of the Successful Tunnelers," *National Tribune*, March 27, 1890.
8. Rose, *Col. Rose's Story of the Famous Tunnel Escape*, n.p.
9. Rose, *Col. Rose's Story of the Famous Tunnel Escape*, n.p.

CHAPTER 1. "THE GREAT UNPLEASANTNESS"

1. Abraham Lincoln, "The Perpetuation of Our Political Institutions," known as "The Lyceum Address," made to the Young Men's Lyceum of Springfield, Illinois, January 27, 1838,

in Roy P. Basler, Marion Dolores Pratt, and Lloyd A. Dunlap, eds., *Collected Works of Abraham Lincoln*, vol. 1, 108–15 (New Brunswick, NJ: Rutgers University Press, 1953), text online, http://www.abrahamlincolnonline.org/lincoln/speeches/lyceum.htm.

2. Her book *Uncle Tom's Cabin* was released in 1852. Harriet Beecher Stowe, *Uncle Tom's Cabin; or, Life among the Lowly* (Boston: John P. Jewett and Company, 1852).

3. Library of Congress, "Elijah Parish Lovejoy Was Killed by a Pro-slavery Mob, November 7, 1837," Jump Back in Time: Western Expansion and Reform (1829–1859), *America's Story from America's Library* (website), http://www.americaslibrary.gov/jb/reform/jb_reform_lovejoy_1.html, http://www.americaslibrary.gov/jb/reform/jb_reform_lovejoy_2.html, http://www.americaslibrary.gov/jb/reform/jb_reform_lovejoy_3.html, and http://www.americaslibrary.gov/jb/reform/jb_reform_lovejoy_4.html.

4. Lincoln, "Lyceum Address."

5. "Missouri Compromise," History Net, accessed February 11, 2021, https://www.historynet.com/missouri-compromise; "Missouri Compromise (1820)," *Our Documents*, US National Archives and Records Administration, accessed February 11, 2021, https://www.ourdocuments.gov/doc.php?flash=false&doc=22.

6. "Pottawatomie Massacre," *Kansaspedia*, Kansas Historical Society, accessed February 11, 2021, https://www.kshs.org/kansapedia/pottawatomie-massacre/16699.

7. National Park Service, "Charles Sumner," US Department of the Interior, last updated November 9, 2020, https://www.nps.gov/people/charles-sumner.htm; United States Senate, "The Caning of Senator Charles Sumner," Art and History, Senate Historical Office, accessed February 22, 2021, https://www.senate.gov/artandhistory/history/minute/The_Caning_of_Senator_Charles_Sumner.htm.

8. Abraham Lincoln, letter to Joshua Speed, August 24, 1855, reproduced at *Abraham Lincoln Online*, accessed February 11, 2021, http://www.abrahamlincolnonline.org/lincoln/speeches/speed.htm, emphasis original.

9. Goodrich, "From Slaves of Sin to Slaves of God," 510–11; Rae, "How Christian Slaveholders Used the Bible to Justify Slavery."

10. The Civil War—or "War Between the States"—was referred to by numerous names, perhaps the most genteel of which was "The Late Unpleasantness" or "The Great Unpleasantness," terms used in the South. Additional names such as "The War of Northern Aggression" or "The Great Rebellion" also originated in Dixie.

11. Michael E. Woods, "What Twenty-First-Century Historians Have Said about the Causes of Disunion: A Civil War Sesquicentennial Review of the Recent Literature," *The Journal of American History* 99, no. 2 (September 2012): 415–39, https://academic.oup.com/jah/article/99/2/415/860501.

12. John Hope Franklin, *From Slavery to Freedom: A History of African Americans* (New York: McGraw-Hill, 1947) (reprint, New York: Knopf, 2000), 123.

13. South Carolina General Assembly, "Resolution to Call the Election of Abraham Lincoln as U.S. President a Hostile Act and to Communicate to Other Southern States South Carolina's Desire to Secede from the Union," November 9, 1860, *Resolutions of the General Assembly, 1779–1879*, S165018, South Carolina Department of Archives and History, Columbia, South Carolina.

14. "The Civil War's Last Great Peace Effort," *Shotgun's Home of the American Civil War*, last updated February 16, 2002, https://civilwarhome.com/peaceconference.html.

15. The inaugural date was moved from March 4 to January 20 in 1937, as per the Twentieth Amendment.

16. Texas Secession Convention, "A Declaration of the Causes which Impel the State of Texas to Secede from the Federal Union," February 2, 1861, text online, https://avalon.law.yale.edu/19th_century/csa_texsec.asp.

17. Lincoln, First Inaugural.

18. American Battlefield Trust, "Fort Sumter," *Battlefields.org*, Learn: Civil War: Battles, accessed February 11, 2021, https://www.battlefields.org/learn/civil-war/battles/fort-sumter.

19. Lonnie R. Speer, *Portals to Hell: Military Prisons of the Civil War* (Mechanicsburg, PA: Stackpole Books, 1997), 12.

20. Source: *The New York Times*, October 3, 1862, p. 2; for information on Lincoln's legal rationale for declaring the South in "open insurrection," see Nicolay and Hay, *Abraham Lincoln*, vol. 3, p. 143.

21. Walter Coffey, "Lincoln's Militia Proclamation (April 15, 1861)," *The Civil War Months*, April 15, 2016, archived online, https://web.archive.org/web/20200616132629/https://civilwarmonths.com/2016/04/15/lincolns-militia-proclamation/.

22. History.com editors, "Confederate States of America," *History.com*, A&E Television Networks, updated August 21, 2018, https://www.history.com/topics/american-civil-war/confederate-states-of-america.

23. American Battlefield Trust, "Civil War Casualties," Learn: Civil War: History, *Battlefields.org*, accessed February 11, 2021, https://www.battlefields.org/learn/articles/civil-war-casualties.

24. Robert P. Watson, *America's First Crisis: The War of 1812* (Albany: State University of New York Press, 2014), 353.

25. American Battlefield Trust, "Fort Sumter."

CHAPTER 2. LIBBY & SON

1. Emeric Szabad quoted in Stephen Beszedits, ed., *The Libby Prison Diary of Colonel Emeric Szabad*, 1999 (reprint).

2. Of Pocahontas fame.

3. For a helpful discussion, see University of Richmond, "Explore the City: History," Visit, *Richmond.edu*, accessed February 11, 2021, https://www.richmond.edu/visit/city.html; and also see Jack Trammell and Guy Terrell, *A Short History of Richmond* (Mount Pleasant, SC: The History Press, 2017).

4. Patrick Henry, "Give Me Liberty or Give Me Death," address made to the Second Virginia Convention, St. John's Church, Richmond, Virginia, March 23, 1775, text reproduced online, http://www.gutenberg.org/files/6/6-h/6-h.htm.

5. Joseph Wheelan, *Libby Prison Breakout: The Daring Escape from the Notorious Civil War Prison* (New York: PublicAffairs, 2010), 2.

6. Author visit to and interviews with staff of the American Civil War Museum–Historic Tredegar, in Richmond, Virginia.

7. Author visit to and interviews with staff of the American Civil War Museum–Historic Tredegar and the Virginia Museum of History and Culture, in Richmond.

8. James Munroe Wells, "Tunneling Out of Libby Prison: A Michigan Lieutenant's Account of His Own Imprisonment and Daring Escape," *McClure's Magazine* 22 (November 1903–April 1904): 319.

9. Richmond Deed Book, 69B, June 1, 1854, 635–50.

10. Source: "Libby Prison," Encyclopedia Virginia.

11. In *Frederick A. Bartleson: Letters from Libby Prison*, ed. Margaret W. Peelle (New York: Greenwich Book Publishers, 1956), 41.

12. Wheelan, *Libby Prison Breakout*, 3; T. C. De Leon, *Four Years in Rebel Capitals: An Inside View of Life in the Southern Confederacy from Birth to Death; From Original Notes, Collated in the Years 1861 to 1865* (Mobile: The Gossip Printing Company, 1892), 86, text online, https://archive.org/details/fouryearsinrebel00deleiala/page/86/; History.com editors, "Confederate States of America," https://www.history.com/topics/american-civil-war/confederate-states-of-america.

13. Sally Putnam's diary, as quoted in Wheelan, *Libby Prison Breakout*, 3–4.

14. Roger Pickenpaugh, *Captives in Blue: The Civil War Prisons of the Confederacy* (Tuscaloosa: University of Alabama Press, 2013), 1.

15. It was also known as simply Henry Hill.

16. Source: "Stonewall Jackson at First Manassas," Encyclopedia Virginia.

CHAPTER 3. "WHAT IS TO BE DONE WITH THE PRISONERS?"

1. Letter to H. L. Pierce and others, April 6, 1859, reproduced at *Abraham Lincoln Online*, accessed February 16, 2021, http://www.abrahamlincolnonline.org/lincoln/speeches/pierce.htm.

2. Speer, *Portals to Hell*, 12.

3. Speer, *Portals to Hell*, 9.

4. Stephen Beszedits, ed., *The Libby Prison Diary of Colonel Emeric Szabad* (Toronto: B & L Information Services, 1999), 29.

5. Speer, *Portals to Hell*, 11.

6. Speer, *Portals to Hell*, 12.

7. Congressional Report on Confederate Prisons, Congressional Record: Proceedings and Debates, Vol. 21, part 9.

8. Congressional Report on Confederate Prisons, Congressional Record: Proceedings and Debates, Vol. 21, Part 9.

9. Beszedits, *Libby Prison Diary*, 33–34.

10. *Richmond Dispatch*, July 2, 1861, text online, https://chroniclingamerica.loc.gov/lccn/sn84024738/1861-07-02/ed-1/; Robert Thompson Cornwell, *Libby Prison and Beyond: A*

Union Staff Officer in the East, 1862–1865, ed. Thomas M. Boaz (Shippensburg, PA: Burd Street Press, 1999), 48.

11. Pickenpaugh, *Captives in Blue*, 2; Cornwell, *Libby Prison and Beyond*, 48.

12. Cornwell, *Libby Prison and Beyond*, 48.

13. *Richmond Examiner*, October 24, 1861, text online, https://chroniclingamerica.loc .gov/lccn/sn84024738/1861-10-24/ed-1/; Cornwell, *Libby Prison and Beyond*, 52.

14. As quoted in Pickenpaugh, *Captives in Blue*, 1.

15. *Richmond Whig*, August 5, 1861, as quoted in Pickenpaugh, *Captives in Blue*, 3.

16. *Richmond Enquirer*, September 20, 1861, text online, https://chroniclingamerica.loc .gov/lccn/sn84024738/1861-09-20/ed-1/.

17. *Richmond Examiner*, numerous issues printed throughout August and September 1861.

18. Ibid., 4–5; and see *Charleston Mercury*, 1861, in Pickenpaugh, *Captives in Blue*, 4.

19. *Richmond Whig*, August 5 and 10, 1861.

20. Speer, *Portals to Hell*, 15.

21. Woods, "What Twenty-First Century Historians Have Said."

22. Courtesy of the *New York Times*' American Civil War (1861–1865) archives, searchable at https://www.nytimes.com/topic/subject/american-civil-war-18611865.

23. Goldberg, "George Wythe Randolph," Encyclopedia Virginia; see also Beszedits, "Frederick Knefler," Jewish-American History Foundation.

24. Foote quoted in Ken Burns, *The Civil War: A Film by Ken Burns*, Kenneth Lauren Burns Production (Burbank, CA: PBS Home Video, 1990).

25. Cornwell, *Libby Prison and Beyond*, 48.

26. William Best Hesseltine, *Civil War Prisons: A Study of War Psychology* (Columbus: The Ohio State University Press, 1930) (reprint, Kent, OH: Kent State University, 1962), 5.

27. Beszedits, *Libby Prison Diary*, 35–36; see also Saunders, "A Flower at Elmire," *Florida Historical Quarterly*, 445.

28. See National Park Service, "The Raiders," Learn: History and Culture: People, Andersonville, National Historic Site, Georgia, US Department of the Interior, last updated April 14, 2015, https://www.nps.gov/ande/learn/historyculture/the_raiders.htm; United States War Department, ed., *War of the Rebellion: A Compilation of the Official Records of the Union and Confederate Armies War of Rebellion; A Compilation of the Official Records of the Union and Confederate Armies*, 128 volumes (Washington, DC: Government Printing Office, 1880–1901). And also see Cornwell, *Libby Prison and Beyond*, 46.

29. Speer, *Portals to Hell*, 14.

30. Beszedits, *Libby Prison Diary*, 46 and 51.

31. Mary DeCredico, "Richmond during the Civil War," Encyclopedia Virginia; see also Beszedits, *Libby Prison Diary*, 51–52.

32. Richmond's newspapers such as the *Dispatch*, *Examiner*, and *Whig* repeatedly referred to Northern prisoners with such terms.

33. Ibid.

34. Adjutant General F. C. Ainsworth offered an estimate based on his counting of 193,743 Union and 214,865 Confederate troops captured and imprisoned during the war.

See also Alan Marsh, "POWs in American History: A Synopsis," Learn: History and Culture, National Park Service, US Department of the Interior, last updated January 13, 2021, https://www.nps.gov/ande/learn/historyculture/pow_synopsis.htm. Also see the eight volumes of United States War Department, *War of the Rebellion*, particularly the second series, which focuses on the prisons (Series 2: *Prisoners of War, Etc.*, 8 vols., prep. Robert N. Scott [Washington, DC: Government Printing Office, 1894–1899], facsimiles of vols. 1–5 and 8 online, https://catalog.hathitrust.org/Record/004388999).

35. Hamilton, *Story of the Famous Tunnel Escape*, n.p.

CHAPTER 4. TO WAR

1. "Important from Montgomery.; Speech of Hon. Jefferson Davis. Declaration of the Policy of the Southern Confederacy. Montgomery, Saturday, Feb. 16. Arrival of Hon. Jefferson Davis. Important Army News," *New York Times*, February 18, 1861, https://www.nytimes.com/1861/02/18/archives/important-from-montgomery-speech-of-hon-jefferson-davis-declaration.html.

2. The city was sometimes spelled with an "h" and sometimes without an "h" at the time.

3. John Obreiter, *The Seventy-Seventh Pennsylvania at Shiloh: History of the Regiment* (Harrisburg: Harrisburg Publishing Co., 1908), vol. 2, 985–92.

4. Also known as the Battle of Pittsburg Landing.

5. Obreiter, *Seventy-Seventh Pennsylvania*; see also *PA-Roots*, "77th Regiment: Pennsylvania Volunteers," Pennsylvania in the Civil War, accessed February 17, 2021, https://www.pa-roots.com/pacw/infantry/77th/77thorg.html.

6. *PA-Roots*, "77th Regiment," citing Samuel P. Bates, *History of Pennsylvania Volunteers, 1861–5*, 5 vols. (Harrisburg, PA: B. Singerly, 1869–1871), .

7. National Park Service, "The Civil War: Battle Unit Details: Union Kentucky Volunteers: 12th Regiment, Kentucky Cavalry," US Department of the Interior, accessed February 11, 2021, https://www.nps.gov/civilwar/search-battle-units-detail.htm?battleUnitCode=UKY0012RC.

8. *Richmond Examiner*, February 15, 1864, as quoted in https://www.civilwarrichmond.com/written-accounts/newspapers/richmond-examiner/2783-1864-02-15-richmond-examiner-recapturing-libby-escapee-anecdotes.

9. Garfield was elected in 1880 but assassinated in 1881, little more than seven months into his term.

10. Hebert, "Streight's Raids," Encyclopedia of Alabama, www.encyclopediaofalabama.org/article/h-1380.

11. Frederick N. Dow, *The Reminiscences of Neal Dow: Recollections of Eighty Years* (Portland, ME: The Evening Express Publishing Co., 1898), (reprint, London: Forgotten Books, 2017), 23 and 28.

12. Maine became a state in 1820.

13. Dow, *Reminiscences*, 58.

14. Dow, *Reminiscences*, 20.

15. Dow, *Reminiscences*, 618 and 621.

16. Dow, *Reminiscences*, 60, 620–21.

17. Dow, *Reminiscences*, 629, 632, 635. Dow makes reference to a *Boston Evening Traveler* article of February 19, 1863, and also to a letter he received from Simon Cameron, secretary of war, dated October 12, 1861.

18. Dow, *Reminiscences*, 618; Hesseltine, *Civil War Prisons*, 60–61.

19. Bartleson, *Letters from Libby Prison*, 11.

20. Bartleson, *Letters from Libby Prison*, 11.

21. Some sources list the ancestral family name as "Boudrye," and the War Department used both spellings.

22. Louis N. Beaudry, *War Journal of Louis N. Beaudry, Fifth New York Cavalry: The Diary of a Union Chaplain, Commencing February 16, 1863*, ed. Richard E. Beaudry (Jefferson, NC: McFarland & Co., 1960), 2 (1st ed. published 1896).

23. Beaudry, *War Journal*, 45.

24. He sometimes spelled it "Freyreich."

25. Beszedits, *Libby Prison Diary*, v and 56.

26. Beszedits, *Libby Prison Diary*, 57.

27. Beszedits, *Libby Prison Diary*, 8.

28. Beszedits, *Libby Prison Diary*, 11.

29. "The Thirteen Martyrs of Arad" was the name given to the thirteen Hungarian generals who were executed on October 6, 1849, by the Austrian Empire, in the city of Arad. See "164th Anniversary: The 13 Martyrs of Arad of October 6, 1849," *Daily News Hungary*, October 6, 2013, https://dailynewshungary.com/164th-anniversary-the-13-martyrs-of-arad-on-october-6-1849/.

30. Ella Lonn, *Foreigners in the Union Army and Navy* (Baton Rouge: Louisiana State University, 1951).

31. Beszedits, *Libby Prison Diary*, 64.

32. The French Zouaves were established in 1830 and were inspired by the Berbers of North Africa.

33. William J. Wray, *Birney's Zouaves Civil War: Life of the 23rd Pennsylvania Volunteers*, 5th ed. (New York: Bloch Publishing Co., 2000). See also Steve A. Hawkes, "23rd Pennsylvania Voluntary Infantry Regiment," *The Civil War in the East* (website), accessed February 17, 2021, https://civilwarintheeast.com/us-regiments-batteries/pennsylvania/23rd-pennsylvania-infantry/.

34. Wray, *Birney's Zouaves Civil War*; see also Hawkes, "23rd Pennsylvania Volunteers"; and Fernández Cavada, *Libby Life*.

CHAPTER 5. "THE CASTLE OF DESPAIR"

1. Beszedits, *Libby Prison Diary*.

2. Records indicate payments of seven to thirty dollars made to Libby during this period.

3. Bartleson, *Letters from Libby*, 84. An unsigned letter from another prisoner discusses Independence Day of 1863; from the Bartleson family collection.

4. With the Southern economy collapsing, it appears that only the one payment was ever made.

5. Michael D. Gorman, "Summary of Libby & Son," file M346, submitted January 2001, National Archives and Records Administration, Washington, DC, text online, https://www .civilwarrichmond.com/images/pdf/Summary_of_Libby.pdf.

6. Cornwell, *Libby Prison and Beyond*, 52; see also Howard Bartholf, "Significant Dates in the History of Libby Prison," *Civil War Richmond*, accessed February 10, 2021, https:// www.civilwarrichmond.com/images/pdf/SIGNIFICANT_DATES_IN_THE_HISTORY_ OF_LIBBY_PRISON.pdf.

7. Frank E. Moran, "Colonel Rose's Tunnel," in *Famous Adventures and Prison Escapes of the Civil War*, edited by G. W. Cable (New York: The Century Co., 1885), 185, text online, http://www.loyalbooks.com/download/text/Famous-Adventures-and-Prison-Escapes-of-the -Civil.txt.

8. Beszedits, *Libby Prison Diary*, 45; Beaudry, *War Journal*, 56.

9. R. W. Wiatt, *Libby Civil War Prison*, Official Publication #12 (Richmond: Richmond Civil War Centennial Committee, 1961–1965).

10. Wiatt, *Libby Civil War Prison*.

11. *Richmond Dispatch*, January 10, 1863.

12. Federico Fernández Cavada, *Libby Life: Experiences of a Prisoner of War in Richmond, VA, 1863–1864* (Philadelphia: King, Roger & Baird, 1864), (reprint, New York: University Press of America, 1985), 24–25.

13. Wells, "Tunneling Out of Libby Prison," 319; Moran, "Colonel Rose's Tunnel," 185.

14. Fernández Cavada, *Libby Life*, 24–25; see also United States War Department, *War of Rebellion*, series 2, vol. 6, 544–45.

15. Moran, "Colonel Rose's Tunnel," 189.

16. Wells, "Tunneling Out of Libby Prison," 320.

17. Moran, "Colonel Rose's Tunnel," 187; see also Wells, "Tunneling Out of Libby Prison," 321.

18. Moran, "Colonel Rose's Tunnel," 187.

19. Moran, "Colonel Rose's Tunnel," 188.

20. J. L. Burrows, "Recollection of Libby Prison," *Southern Historical Society Papers* 11, nos. 2 and 3 (February–March, 1883): 83–92, text online, https://civilwarrichmond.com/ prisons/prison-depot/4421-1883-southern-historical-society-papers-11-1883-pp-83-92-bur rows-j-l-recollections-of-libby-prison.

21. Beszedits, *Libby Prison Diary*, 79.

22. Beszedits, *Libby Prison Diary*, 46. See also Willard W. Glazier, *The Capture, the Prison Pen, and the Escape: Giving a Complete History of Prison Life in the South* (Hartford, CT: H. E. Goodwin, 1867), 60.

CHAPTER 6. CAPTURED

1. Hamilton, *Story of the Famous Tunnel Escape*, 2.

2. Moran, "Colonel Rose's Tunnel," 185.

3. Moran, "Colonel Rose's Tunnel," *Famous Adventures and Prison Escapes of the Civil War* (New York: Century Co., 1885), 185; Bruce Catton, *Civil War* (Boston: Houghton Mifflin Co., 1978), 179–81; Obreiter, *Seventy-Seventh Pennsylvania*, 230; Wheelan, *Libby Prison Breakout*, 105.

4. Moran, "Colonel Rose's Tunnel," 185.

5. Benjamin F. Booth, *Dark Days of Rebellion: Life in Southern Military Prisons* (Garrison, IA: Meyer Publishing, 1996), 55–56; Wheelan, *Libby Prison Breakout*, 105.

6. Wheelan, *Libby Prison Breakout*, 105.

7. Hamilton, *Story of the Famous Tunnel Escape*, 4–5.

8. Hamilton, *Story of the Famous Tunnel Escape*, 4–5.

9. Hamilton, *Story of the Famous Tunnel Escape*, 4–5.

10. Dow, *Reminiscences*, 689–90.

11. Dow, *Reminiscences*, 693–94.

12. Dow, *Reminiscences*, .

13. Dow, *Reminiscences*, 700–701.

14. Dow, *Reminiscences*, 704.

15. Dow, *Reminiscences*, 706.

16. Dow, *Reminiscences*, 708.

17. Dow, *Reminiscences*, 706–8.

18. With roughly 3,500 killed and over sixteen thousand wounded, at the time it was fought Shiloh had the highest casualty rates of the war.

19. Bartleson, *Letters from Libby*, 50.

20. Bartleson, *Letters from Libby*, 12–13.

21. Bartleson, *Letters from Libby*, 14–15.

22. Bartleson, *Letters from Libby*, 55–73.

23. Bartleson, *Letters from Libby*, 50.

24. Bartleson, *Letters from Libby*, 50.

25. Letter from Fred Bartleson to Kate Bartleson, February 26, 1864, in Bartleson, *Letters from Libby*, 66–67.

26. Bartleson, *Letters from Libby*, 67.

27. Beaudry, *War Journal*, 45 and 49.

28. Beaudry, *War Journal*, 49.

29. Beaudry, *War Journal*, 49.

30. Beaudry, *War Journal*, 51.

31. Beaudry, *War Journal*, 51.

32. Beaudry, *War Journal*, 55.

33. Beszedits, *Libby Prison Diary*, 27.

34. Beszedits, *Libby Prison Diary*, 24–27.

35. Beszedits, *Libby Prison Diary*, .

36. Banks would later lead the assault on Port Hudson in New Orleans with General Neal Dow.

37. Emeric Szaba, *Modern War: Its Theory and Practice* (New York: Harper & Bros., 1863).

38. Szabad, *Modern War*; Beszedits, *Libby Prison Diary*, 68.

39. See "To Bind Up the Nation's Wounds," National Museum of Health and Medicine, www.medicalmuseum.mil.

40. Beszedits, *Libby Prison Diary*, 74.

41. The caps had been named for the Union general George McClellan.

42. Beszedits, *Libby Prison Diary*, 75.

43. Beszedits, *Libby Prison Diary*, 75.

44. Beszedits, *Libby Prison Diary*, 76.

45. American Battlefield Trust, "Civil War Ballooning," Learn: Civil War: Quick Facts, *Battlefields.org*, accessed February 11, 2021, https://www.battlefields.org/learn/articles/civil-war-ballooning.

46. Steve A. Hawkes, "23rd Pennsylvania Volunteer Infantry Regiment," Pennsylvania Monuments at Gettysburg: Pennsylvania Infantry, *The Battle of Gettysburg* (website), accessed February 11, 2021, https://gettysburg.stonesentinels.com/union-monuments/pennsylvania/pennsylvania-infantry/23rd-pennsylvania/.

CHAPTER 7. "ALL HOPE ABANDON, YE WHO ENTER HERE"

1. Fernández Cavada, *Libby Life*.

2. Wells, "Tunneling Out of Libby Prison," 317.

3. Wells, "Tunneling Out of Libby Prison," 319.

4. For a helpful discussion, see Charles Carleton Coffin, *The Boys of '61; or, Four Years of Fighting* (Boston: Estes & Lauriat, 1884).

5. Moran, "Colonel Rose's Tunnel," 189–91.

6. Beszedits, *Libby Prison Diary*, 80.

7. Hesseltine, *Civil War Prisons*, 56–58.

8. Bezsedits, *Libby Prison Diary*, 48.

9. Bezsedits, *Libby Prison Diary*, 48.

10. Wells, "Tunneling Out of Libby Prison," 319.

11. Bezsedits, *Libby Prison Diary*, 78.

12. Meaning "shit."

13. Bezsedits, *Libby Prison Diary*, 79.

14. Bezsedits, *Libby Prison Diary*, 80–81 and 95.

15. James Gindlesperger, *Escape from Libby Prison* (Shippensburg, PA: White Mane Publishing, 1996), 5; Wells, "Tunneling Out of Libby Prison," 319.

16. Beaudry, *War Journal*, 55.

17. Beaudry, *War Journal*, 56–57.

18. Beaudry, *War Journal*, 55 and 65.

19. Beaudry, *War Journal*, 49 and 55.

20. Bezsedits, *Libby Prison Diary*, 80.

21. Beaudry, *War Journal*, 65.

22. Letter dated July 21, 1863, in Beaudry, *War Journal*, 57.

23. Fernández Cavada, *Libby Life*, 26.

24. Fernández Cavada, *Libby Life*, 33–34.

25. Fernández Cavada, *Libby Life*, 32–34.

26. Beszedits, *Libby Prison Diary*, 81.

27. Ibid., 48; Bartleson, *Letters from Libby*, 72.

28. Hesseltine, *Civil War Prisons*; diary entry for July 22, 1863, in Beaudry, *War Journal*, 57; Bartleson, *Letters from Libby*, 51; and "The Richmond Prisoners," *New York Herald*, November 28, 1863.

29. Bartleson, *Letters from Libby*, 15.

30. Bartleson, *Letters from Libby*, 15.

31. Beszedits, *Libby Prison Diary*, 31 and 57.

32. Bartleson, *Letters from Libby*, 57.

33. Emeric Szabad, "Diary in Libby Prison," *Fraser's Magazine for Town and Country* 77, no. 459 (March 1868): 385–406 (facsimile online, https://babel.hathitrust.org/cgi/pt?id=uc1.a0007087596&view=1up&seq=393); Beszedits, *Libby Prison Diary*, 82.

34. Beszedits, *Libby Prison Diary*, 82.

35. Bartleson, *Letters from Libby*, 70.

36. Letter from Robert T. Cornwell to Lydia Cornwell, December 9, 1863, in Cornwell, *Libby Prison and Beyond*, 61; Moran, "Colonel Rose's Tunnel," 185–86.

37. Cornwell, *Libby Prison and Beyond*, 56.

38. Bartleson, *Letters from Libby*, 70; Fernández Cavada, *Libby Life*, 41–47; letter from Robert T. Cornwell to Lydia Cornwell, December 9, 1863, in Cornwell, *Libby Prison and Beyond*, 61; Hesseltine, *Civil War Prisons*, 433.

39. Beszedits, *Libby Prison Diary*, 82.

40. Bartleson, *Letters from Libby*, 68.

41. Beszedits, *Libby Prison Diary*, 81.

42. Beszedits, *Libby Prison Diary*, 81–82.

43. Literally, "bad subjects" in French.

44. Beszedits, *Libby Prison Diary*, 87.

45. Beszedits, *Libby Prison Diary*, 85.

46. Beszedits, *Libby Prison Diary*, 85; Fernández Cavada, *Libby Life*, 29; Beszedits, *Libby Prison Diary*, 79.

47. Wells, "Tunneling Out of Libby Prison," 317; Bartleson, *Letters from Libby*, 17 and 68.

48. Bartleson, *Letters from Libby*, 17; Beszedits, *Libby Prison Diary*, 80.

49. Beaudry, *War Journal*, 57.

50. Beszedits, *Libby Prison Diary*, 79.

51. Bartleson, *Letters from Libby*, 68.

52. Fernández Cavada, *Libby Life*, 29.

53. Beszedits, *Libby Prison Diary*, 80 and 84.

54. Bartleson, *Letters from Libby*, 26.

55. Letter from Robert Ould to the War Department of the Confederate States of America, March 21, 1863, in John William Jones, ed., *Southern Historical Society Papers*, vol. 1, no. 3 (March) (Richmond, VA: Southern Historical Society Papers, 1876), 21, text online, https://en.m.wikisource.org/wiki/Southern_Historical_Society_Papers/Volume_01/March/Judge_Ould%27s_reply_to_charges_against_him.

56. Beszedits, *Libby Prison Diary*, 80.

57. Beszedits, *Libby Prison Diary*, 84.

58. Beszedits, *Libby Prison Diary*, 79.

59. Cornwell, *Libby Prison and Beyond*, 57; Beaudry, *War Journal*, 57.

60. Beaudry, *War Journal*, 57, letter of July 22, 1863.

61. Beszedits, *Libby Prison Diary*, 48.

62. Beaudry, *War Journal*, 57, letter of July 22, 1863.

63. Beszedits, *Libby Prison Diary*, 36; letter from Robert T. Cornwell to Lydia Cornwell, December 9, 1863, in Cornwell, *Libby Prison and Beyond*, 61.

64. Bartleson, *Letters from Libby*, 68.

65. "The Prisons at Richmond," *Harper's Weekly*, October 17, 1863, 667–69, facsimile online, http://www.sonofthesouth.net/leefoundation/civil-war/1863/october/libby-prison.htm.

66. See diary entries of June 4 and 5, 1863, in Cornwell, *Libby Prison and Beyond*, 42–45.

67. "The Richmond Prisoners," *New York Herald*, November 28, 1863; *Richmond Dispatch*, February 21, 1863; Beaudry, *War Journal*, 58, letter of July 24, 1863.

68. Malaria or another illness involving fever and shivering.

69. See letters from Robert T. Cornwell to Lydia Cornwell, October 26, 1863, and December 9, 1863, in Cornwell, *Libby Prison and Beyond*, 59 and 61.

70. Beszedits, *Libby Prison Diary*, 36.

71. *Richmond Dispatch*, January 24, 1863.

72. *Richmond Examiner*, July 23, 1862.

73. See National Archives and Records Administration, "Statistical Reports of Hospitals in Virginia, 1862–1864," record group 109, vol. 151, p. 59, Washington, DC, linked online, https://civilwarrichmond.com/hospitals/3971-statistics-of-hospitals-in-richmond-va-during-the-civil-war.

74. National Archives and Records Administration, "Statistical Reports of Hospitals," 59.

75. Bartleson, *Letters from Libby*, 70.

CHAPTER 8. THE LIBBY LYCEUM

1. From Bartleson's poem "Libby Prison, New Year's Eve, 1863–64," found in Bartleson, *Letters from Libby Prison*.

2. Bartleson, *Letters from Libby Prison*, 51.

3. Fernández Cavada, *Libby Life*, 185–87.

4. Bartleson, *Letters from Libby Prison*, 52–53.

5. Beszedits, *Libby Prison Diary*, 80–81.

6. The game of faro originated in France in the seventeenth century.

7. Beszedits, *Libby Prison Diary*, 80–81.

8. Beszedits, *Libby Prison Diary*, 82.

9. Beszedits, *Libby Prison Diary*, 82.

10. Fernández Cavada, *Libby Life*, 41–47.

11. Bartleson, *Letters from Libby Prison*, 31.

12. Dow, *Reminiscences*, 719.

13. "Grape" was short for grapevine.

14. Bartleson, *Letters from Libby Prison*, 19.

15. Bartleson, *Letters from Libby Prison*, 20.

16. See the diary entry for February 6, 1864, in Cornwell, *Libby Prison and Beyond*, 102.

17. Bartleson, *Letters from Libby Prison*, 58 and 71.

18. Bartleson, *Letters from Libby Prison*, 40 and 72.

19. Bartleson, *Letters from Libby Prison*, 57–58.

20. Dow, *Reminiscences*, 721.

21. "A Prisoner's Letter," *The Christian Recorder*, February 11, 1865.

22. Dow, *Reminiscences*, 722.

23. Dow, *Reminiscences*, 704, 718–19.

24. Bartleson, *Letters from Libby Prison*, 55.

25. Thomas Ellwood Rose, *Col. Rose's Story of the Famous Tunnel Escape from Libby Prison: A Thrilling Account of the Daring Escape of 109 Union Officers from Libby Prison Through a Famous Yankee Tunnel* (1884), (reprint, London: Forgotten Books, 2017), .

26. See diary entry for February 12, 1864, in Cornwell, *Libby Prison and Beyond*, 104; Rose, *Col. Rose's Story*, .

27. Bartleson, *Letters from Libby Prison*, 70–71.

28. Wells, "Tunneling Out of Libby Prison," .

29. Dow, *Reminiscences*, 718.

30. See the diary entry for January 11, 1864, in Bartleson, *Letters from Libby Prison*, 15–16.

31. Bartleson, *Letters from Libby Prison*, 15–16.

32. Beaudry, *War Journal*, 62.

33. Bartleson, *Letters from Libby Prison*, 52 and 69.

34. Beaudry, *War Journal*, 64; see the diary entry for January 3, 1864, in Cornwell, *Libby Prison and Beyond*, 101.

35. Beszedits, *Libby Prison Diary*, 84.

36. Beaudry, *War Journal*, 1, 58–60, diary entries for August 22 and 24, 1863, 62.

37. Fernández Cavada, *Libby Life*, 186–87.

38. Bartleson, *Letters from Libby Prison*, 52–53.

39. Letter from Robert T. Cornwell to Lydia Cornwell, December 9, 1863, in Cornwell, *Libby Prison and Beyond*, 61.

40. Dow, *Reminiscences*, 719.

41. Wells, "Tunneling Out of Libby Prison," 319.

42. Dow, *Reminiscences*, 729.

43. Beszedits, *Libby Prison Diary*, 84.

44. Bartleson, *Letters from Libby Prison*, 69.

45. Beszedits, *Libby Prison Diary*, 84–85.

46. Cornwell, *Libby Prison and Beyond*, 57.

47. Bartleson, *Letters from Libby Prison*, 69.

48. Bartleson, *Letters from Libby Prison*, 85.

49. Bartleson, *Letters from Libby Prison*, 85–86; Hebert, "Streight's Raid," n.p.

50. Bartleson, *Letters from Libby Prison*, 86.

51. Bartleson, *Letters from Libby Prison*, 86.

52. Bartleson, *Letters from Libby Prison*, 86.

53. Beszedits, *Libby Prison Diary*, 90–91.

54. Beszedits, *Libby Prison Diary*, 91.

55. Beaudry, *War Journal*, 62–63. And see Louis N. Beaudry, ed., *The Libby Chronicle: Devoted to Facts and Fun; A True Copy of the Libby Chronicle as Written by the Prisoners of Libby in 1863* (Albany: Louis N. Beaudry, 1889), text online, https://play.google.com/books/read er?id=WQNPAhEtLxMC&hl=en&pg=GBS.PP1; all *Libby Chronicle* citations drawn from this volume.

56. Beaudry, *War Journal*, 62.

57. Beaudry, *War Journal*, 62–63.

58. Private, "Castle Thunder, Part II," *Libby Chronicle* 1, no. 2 (August 28, 1863): 7.

59. Beaudry, "Notes and Notices," *Libby Chronicle* 1, no. 3 (September 4, 1863): 1.

60. Bartleson, *Letters from Libby Prison*, 69.

61. Lieut.-Col. N., "Who Is Responsible for Non-exchange of Prisoners," *Libby Chronicle* 1, no. 2 (August 28, 1863): 8.

CHAPTER 9. "THE UNDERGROUND ROAD TO LIBERTY"

1. Rose, *Col. Rose's Story*, n.p.

2. Beszedits, *Libby Prison Diary*, 50.

3. *Richmond Examiner*, October 30, 1863, November 20, 1863, and November 23, 1863.

4. James M. Sanderson, *My Record in Rebeldom . . .* (New York: W. E. Sibell, 1865), 23–28, facsimile online, https://babel.hathitrust.org/cgi/pt?id=loc.ark:/13960/ t6tx3rd4r&view=1up&seq=14; Frank L. Byrne, "Libby Prison: A Study in Emotions," *Journal of Southern History* 24, no. 4 (November 1958): 436.

5. Dow, *Reminiscences*.

6. Beszedits, *Libby Prison Diary*, 50; Dow, *Reminiscences*.

7. Dow, *Reminiscences*.

8. Beszedits, *Libby Prison Diary*, 51.

9. Dow, *Reminiscences*.

10. Beszedits, *Libby Prison Diary*, 85; United States War Department, *War of the Rebellion*, series 1: 701 and 706.

11. Beszedits, *Libby Prison Diary*, 88–89.

12. Beszedits, *Libby Prison Diary*, 88–89.

13. Beszedits, *Libby Prison Diary*, 85–87; United States War Department, *War of the Rebellion*, series 1: 973–74.

14. Hesseltine, *Civil War Prisons*, 63.

15. Wells, "Tunneling Out of Libby Prison," 320.

16. Wells, "Tunneling Out of Libby Prison," 320.

17. Wells, "Tunneling Out of Libby Prison," 320; Dow, *Reminiscences*, 720 and 726.

18. Rose, *Col. Rose's Story*, i.

19. Moran, "Colonel Rose's Tunnel," i.

20. Moran, "Colonel Rose's Tunnel," I, 184, and 190.

21. Rose, *Col. Rose's Story*, n.p.

22. Bartleson, *Letters from Libby*, 55.

23. Fernández Cavada, *Libby Life*, 138.

24. Moran, "Colonel Rose's Tunnel," 193–95.

25. Moran, "Colonel Rose's Tunnel," 189–90.

26. Hamilton, *Story of the Famous Tunnel*, 4–5.

27. Rose, *Col. Rose's Story*, ii.

28. Wheelan, *Libby Prison Breakout*, 108.

29. Hamilton, *Story of the Famous Tunnel*, 5.

30. Hamilton, *Story of the Famous Tunnel*, 7; Rose, *Col. Rose's Story*, 2.

31. Wheelan, *Libby Prison Breakout*, 109.

32. Rose, *Col. Rose's Story*, n.p.

CHAPTER 10. "RAT HELL"

1. Cornwell, *Libby Prison and Beyond*.

2. Rose, *Col. Rose's Story*, n.p.

3. Hamilton, *Story of the Famous Tunnel*, 5.

4. Hamilton, *Story of the Famous Tunnel*, 5.

5. Rose, *Col. Rose's Story*, n.p.

6. Hamilton, *Story of the Famous Tunnel*, 5.

7. Hamilton, *Story of the Famous Tunnel*, 5; Moran, "Colonel Rose's Tunnel," 201–2; Wells, "Tunneling Out of Libby Prison," 98–99.

8. Hamilton, *Story of the Famous Tunnel*, 5–6.

9. Hamilton, *Story of the Famous Tunnel*, 5–6.

10. Wheelan, *Libby Prison Breakout*, 109.

11. Rose, *Col. Rose's Story*, n.p.

12. Hamilton, *Story of the Famous Tunnel*, 5.

13. Hamilton, *Story of the Famous Tunnel*, 5.

14. Moran, "Colonel Rose's Tunnel," 203; Wheelan, *Libby Prison Breakout*, 109.

15. Moran, "Colonel Rose's Tunnel," 203; Hamilton, *Story of the Famous Tunnel*, 6.

16. Hamilton, *Story of the Famous Tunnel*, 6.

17. "The Recent Escape from the Libby Prison—Recapture of Twenty-Two Officers," *Richmond Enquirer*, February 12, 1864. Read the entire story at https://civilwarrichmond .com/written-accounts/newspapers/richmond-enquirer/2644-1864-02-12-richmond-en quirer-description-of-the-libby-prison-breakout-and-list-of-escapees-re-captured.

18. Hamilton, *Story of the Famous Tunnel*, 6.

19. Rose, *Col. Rose's Story*, n.p.

20. Moran, "Colonel Rose's Tunnel," 204; Rose, *Col. Rose's Story*.

21. Hamilton, *Story of the Famous Tunnel*, 6; Rose, *Col. Rose's Story*, n.p.

22. Hamilton, *Story of the Famous Tunnel*, 6; Rose, *Col. Rose's Story*, n.p.

23. Hamilton, *Story of the Famous Tunnel*, 6; Rose, *Col. Rose's Story*, n.p.

24. Rose, *Col. Rose's Story*, n.p.; Hamilton, *Story of the Famous Tunnel*, 6.

25. Hamilton, *Story of the Famous Tunnel*, 6.

26. "The Recent Escape from the Libby Prison—Recapture of Twenty-Two Officers," *Richmond Enquirer*, February 12, 1864.

27. Moran, "Colonel Rose's Tunnel," 204–5; Virgil Carrington Jones, "Libby Prison Break," *Civil War History* 4, no. 2 (June 1958): 96–97.

28. Hamilton, *Story of the Famous Tunnel*, 6.

29. *Richmond Enquirer*, "The Recent Escape from the Libby Prison—Recapture of Twenty-Two Officers," February 12, 1864.

30. A cuspidor is a vase-shaped spittoon with a wide opening. Hamilton, *Story of the Famous Tunnel*, 6–7.

31. *Richmond Enquirer*, "The Recent Escape from the Libby Prison—Recapture of Twenty-Two Officers," February 12, 1864.

32. Hamilton, *Story of the Famous Tunnel*, 5; Rose, *Col. Rose's Story*, n.p.

33. Moran, "Colonel Rose's Tunnel," 204–6; Hamilton, *Story of the Famous Tunnel*, 6.

34. Moran, "Colonel Rose's Tunnel," 203–4; Hamilton, *Story of the Famous Tunnel*, 4–5; Frank E. Moran, "The Bright Side of Libby Prison," in *Living History: The Civil War*, ed. Henry Steele Commager, rev. and exp. Erik Brunn (New York: Tess Press, 1950), 31; Jones, "Libby Prison Break," 97.

CHAPTER 11. CLOSE CALLS

1. Cornwell, *Libby Prison and Beyond*.

2. Frank E. Moran, "Libby Prison's Tunnel," *Toledo Blade*, November 9, 1892, facsimile online, https://news.google.com/newspapers?nid=1350&dat=18821109&id=TzsxAAAAIBAJ &sjid=a_4DAAAAIBAJ&pg=5431,1130354.

3. Hamilton, *Story of the Famous Tunnel*, 5.

4. Rose, *Col. Rose's Story*, n.p.

5. Hamilton, *Story of the Famous Tunnel*, 7.

6. Moran, "Colonel Rose's Tunnel," 205–6.

7. Moran, "Colonel Rose's Tunnel," 205–6; Hamilton, *Story of the Famous Tunnel*, 7; Rose, *Col. Rose's Story*, 2; Wheelan, *Libby Prison Breakout*, 117.

8. Hamilton, *Story of the Famous Tunnel*, 5–6.

9. Hamilton, *Story of the Famous Tunnel*, 5–6.

10. Major Brendon B. McDonald, 101st Ohio; Captain Terrance Clark, Seventy-Ninth Illinois; Captain John Lucas, Fifth Kentucky; Captain W. S. B. Randall, Second Ohio; Lieutenant John C. Fislar, Seventh Indiana; Lieutenant Eli Foster, Thirtieth Indiana; Lieutenant David Garbett, Seventy-Seventh Pennsylvania; Lieutenant Nineveh S. McKean, Twenty-First Illinois; Lieutenant John Mitchell, Seventy-Ninth Illinois; and Lieutenant John D. Simpson, Tenth Indiana.

11. Hamilton, *Story of the Famous Tunnel*, 6.

12. Moran, "Colonel Rose's Tunnel," 210.

13. Bartleson, *Letters from Libby*, 37.

14. Moran, "Colonel Rose's Tunnel," 210–12; Hamilton, *Story of the Famous Tunnel*, 5.

15. Wheelan, *Libby Prison Breakout*, 116.

16. Rose, *Col. Rose's Story*, 2.

17. Moran, "Colonel Rose's Tunnel," 205–6; Hamilton, *Story of the Famous Tunnel*, 6–7.

18. Moran, "Colonel Rose's Tunnel," 206.

19. Rose, *Col. Rose's Story*, 2.

20. Moran, "Colonel Rose's Tunnel," 205–8.

21. Hamilton, *Story of the Famous Tunnel*, 6.

22. Moran, "Colonel Rose's Tunnel," 199–200; Rose, *Col. Rose's Story*, n.p.

23. Moran, "Colonel Rose's Tunnel," 199–200.

24. Moran, "Colonel Rose's Tunnel," 199–200; Fernández Cavada, *Libby Life*, 138.

25. Cornwell, *Libby Prison and Beyond*, .

26. Cornwell diary entry dated January 1, 1864, in Cornwell, *Libby Prison and Beyond*, 61–62.

27. Hesseltine, *Civil War Prisons*, 64.

28. Cornwell diary entry dated January 2, 1864, in Cornwell, *Libby Prison and Beyond*, 62.

29. Hamilton, *Story of the Famous Tunnel*, 5.

30. Hamilton, *Story of the Famous Tunnel*, 5.

31. Hamilton, *Story of the Famous Tunnel*, 5.

32. David Stidmond Caldwell, *Incidents of War and Southern Prison Life* (Dayton, OH: United Brethren Printing, 1864) (reprint, [Ohio]: The Wyandot Tracers, Chapter of the Ohio Genealogical Society, 2002), 31.

33. Moran, "Colonel Rose's Tunnel," 204, 207–8.

34. Moran, "Colonel Rose's Tunnel," 204–8.

35. Hamilton, *Story of the Famous Tunnel*, 5.

36. Moran, "Colonel Rose's Tunnel," 207–8.

37. Moran, "Colonel Rose's Tunnel," 207–8.

38. Moran, "Colonel Rose's Tunnel," 208.

39. Jones, "Libby Prison Break," 97–98; Moran, "Colonel Rose's Tunnel," 207–8.

40. Moran, "Colonel Rose's Tunnel," 206.

41. Isaac N. Johnston, *Four Months in Libby, and the Campaign against Atlanta* (Cincinnati: Methodist Book Concern, 1864), 63, facsimile online, https://babel.hathitrust.org/cgi/pt?id=hvd.32044020270237&view=1up&seq=9; Hamilton, *Story of the Famous Tunnel*, 5.

CHAPTER 12. THE EVIL TURNERS

1. Beszedits, *Libby Prison Diary*.

2. Watson, *America's First Crisis*, 275.

3. Arch Fredric Blakey, *General John Winder, CSA* (Gainesville: University Press of Florida, 1990); Matt Atkinson, "John H. Winder (1800–1865)," in *Encyclopedia Virginia*,

Virginia Humanities, April 7, 2016, http://encyclopediavirginia.org/winder_john_h_1800 -1865#start_entry.

4. Blakey, *General John Winder*, 4.

5. "The Rebel Guardians of National Prisoners in Richmond," *New York Times*, November 15, 1863, https://www.nytimes.com/1863/11/15/archives/the-rebel-guardians-of -national-prisoners-in-richmond.html; Beszedits, *Libby Prison Diary*, 45.

6. Winder's portfolio was gradually expanded during the war from Richmond's provost marshal, to overseer of the city's defenses, to being responsible for nearly all prisons in the South, including Andersonville.

7. At its peak, Andersonville held a staggering thirty-three thousand prisoners of war within its grounds, thousands of whom would die during their internment, making it the worst and most infamous prison in American history.

8. Byrne, "Libby Prison," 431; Blakey, *General John Winder*, 6.

9. Letter from George C. Gibbs to John H. Winder, September 7, 1861, in United States War Department, *War of Rebellion*, series 2, vol. 3.

10. *Richmond Enquirer*, September 4, 6, 14, and 18, 1863.

11. Pickenpaugh, *Captives in Blue*, 6.

12. Pickenpaugh, *Captives in Blue*, 6.

13. Beszedits, *Libby Prison Diary*, 34.

14. Sarah Johnson, "'A Very Brutal Man': Lewis Horton, David Todd, and Prisoner Torture," *The Gettysburg Compiler* (website), September 30, 2013, Civil War Institute at Gettysburg College, http://gettysburgcompiler.org/2013/09/30/a-very-brutal-man-lewis-horton -david-todd-and-prisoner-torture/.

15. Pickenpaugh, *Captives in Blue*, 7 and 10.

16. *Harper's Weekly*, "Mrs. Lincoln, Wife of the President," November 8, 1862, 709, facsimile online, http://www.sonofthesouth.net/leefoundation/civil-war/1862/november/mary -todd-lincoln.htm.

17. Angela Zombek, "Libby Prison," *Encyclopedia Virginia*, December 7, 2020, https:// encyclopediavirginia.org/entries/libby-prison/.

18. National Archives and Records Administration, "T. P. Turner," *Compiled Service Records of Confederate Generals and Staff Officers, and Non-regimental Enlisted Men*, file M331 and M346, Washington, DC.

19. National Archives and Records Administration, "T. P. Turner"; Byrne, "Libby Prison," 431.

20. Byrne, "Libby Prison," 431.

21. Byrne, "Libby Prison," 431.

22. United States War Department, *War of the Rebellion*, Series 2, vol., 4, 928; Peter Carlson, "The Pirate-Warden of Richmond," Disunion, *New York Times*, June 3, 2013, http:// opinionator.blogs.nytimes.com/2013/06/03/the-pirate-warden-of-richmond/.

23. United States War Department, *War of the Rebellion*, Series 2, vol., 4, 928; Peter Carlson, "The Pirate-Warden of Richmond," Disunion, *New York Times*, June 3, 2013, http:// opinionator.blogs.nytimes.com/2013/06/03/the-pirate-warden-of-richmond/. At the end of

the war, Alexander was tried and acquitted by a military court. Yet, facing additional war crimes, he fled to Canada.

24. Beszedits, *Libby Prison Diary*, 47; Byrne, "Libby Prison," 431; Caldwell, *Incidents of War*, 7.

25. Beszedits, *Libby Prison Diary*, 47.

26. Carlson, "Pirate-Warden of Richmond"; Caldwell, *Incidents of War*, 7; diary entry dated January 5, 1864, in Cornwell, *Libby Prison and Beyond*, 63.

27. Letter, from T. P. Turner to G. W. Alexander, November 19, 1862, record group 109, chapter 9, vol. 199, 33, National Archives.

28. Beszedits, *Libby Prison Diary*, 47.

29. Cornwell, *Libby Prison and Beyond*, 52.

30. Cornwell, *Libby Prison and Beyond*, 52.

31. Byrne, "Libby Prison," 431.

32. Beszedits, *Libby Prison Diary*, 47–48.

33. Beszedits, *Libby Prison Diary*, 48.

34. National Archives and Records Administration, "T. P. Turner."

35. The quartermaster was responsible for provisioning the prison.

36. Beaudry, *War Journal*, 58; Cornwell, *Libby Prison and Beyond*, 52.

37. Bernard Domschcke, *Twenty Months in Captivity: Memoirs of a Union Officer in Confederate Prisons*, ed. and trans. Frederic Trautmann (Rutherford, NJ: Farleigh Dickinson University Press, 1987), 39–40; Cornwell, *Libby Prison and Beyond*, 52.

38. Cornwell, *Libby Prison and Beyond*, 52–53.

39. Elizabeth L. Ryan Van Lew, *A Yankee Spy in Richmond: The Civil War Diary of "Crazy Bet" Van Lew*, ed. David D. Ryan (Mechanicsburg, PA: Stackpole Books, 1996), 108–9 (first published January 24, 1864).

40. Bartleson, *Letters from Libby*, 52.

41. Pickenpaugh, *Captives in Blue*, 6.

42. Bryne, "Libby Prison," 430.

43. Bryne, "Libby Prison," 430; Bartleson, *Letters from Libby*, 52.

44. Bartleson, *Letters from Libby*, 52–53.

45. Bartleson, *Letters from Libby*, 32.

CHAPTER 13. DESPERATION

1. Rose, *Col. Rose's Tunnel*, n.p.

2. From Dow's diary, in Hesseltine, *Civil War Prisons*, 64 and 69.

3. Diary entry dated January 22, 1864, in Cornwell, *Libby Prison and Beyond*, 70.

4. Beszedits, *Libby Prison Diary*, 94.

5. Beszedits, *Libby Prison Diary*, 94.

6. Beszedits, *Libby Prison Diary*, 94–95.

7. From Dow's diary, in Hesseltine, *Civil War Prisons*, 67.

8. Fernández Cavada, *Libby Life*, 137.

9. Beszedits, *Libby Prison Diary*, 94.

10. Diary entry dated January 22, 1864, in Cornwell, *Libby Prison and Beyond*, 7.

11. Diary dated February 5, 1864, in Cornwell, *Libby Prison and Beyond*, 102; Bartleson, *Letters from Libby*, 20.

12. Fernández Cavada, *Libby Life*, 133–39, 166–67; Dow, *Reminiscences*, 722.

13. Benjamin F. Butler, *Private and Official Correspondence of General Benjamin F. Butler during the Period of the Civil War* (Norwood, MA: Plimpton Press, 1917), 3:435–36; Cornwell, *Libby Prison and Beyond*, 97.

14. Bartleson, *Letters from Libby*, 20.

15. Beszedits, *Libby Prison Diary*, 94.

16. Diary entry dated January 19, 1864, in Cornwell, *Libby Prison and Beyond*, 68–69.

17. Bartleson, *Letters from Libby*, 16.

18. Diary entry dated November 31, 1864, in Cornwell, *Libby Prison and Beyond*, 73.

19. Bartleson, *Letters from Libby*, 16–17.

20. Bartleson, *Letters from Libby*, 16–17.

21. Bartleson, *Letters from Libby*, 18.

22. Bartleson, *Letters from Libby*, 18.

23. Bartleson, *Letters from Libby*, 18; Moran, "Colonel Rose's Tunnel," 213; Caldwell, *Incidents of War*.

24. Bartleson, *Letters from Libby*, 16–20.

25. Hesseltine, *Civil War Prisons*, 69.

26. Bartleson, *Letters from Libby*, 38.

27. Diary entry dated January 8, 1864, in Cornwell, *Libby Prison and Beyond*, 62–63.

28. Wheelan, *Libby Prison Breakout*, 126.

29. Diary entry dated January 11, 1864, in Cornwell, *Libby Prison and Beyond*, 64–65.

30. Sitting at the confluence of the James and Appomattox Rivers, City Point was then held by the Union and served as the site for prisoner exchanges. It would function as General Grant's field headquarters at the end of the war.

31. Beszedits, *Libby Prison Diary*, 86.

32. Wheelan, *Libby Prison Breakout*, 123.

33. Alva C. Roach, *The Prisoner of War, and How Treated: Containing a History of Colonel Streight's Expedition . . .* (Indianapolis: Robert Douglass, 1887), 318 (facsimile of earlier edition online, https://babel.hathitrust.org/cgi/pt?id=yale.39002004517323&view=1up&seq=12); Wells, "Tunneling Out of Libby Prison," 97.

34. Wells, "Tunneling Out of Libby Prison," 97–98.

35. Beszedits, *Libby Prison Diary*, 88.

36. Cate Lineberry, "Elizabeth Van Lew: An Unlikely Union Spy," Special Report: The Civil War, *Smithsonian Magazine*, May 4, 2011, https://www.smithsonianmag.com/history/elizabeth-van-lew-an-unlikely-union-spy-158755584/.

37. Elizabeth R. Varon, *Southern Lady, Yankee Spy: The True Story of Elizabeth Van Lew, A Union Agent in the Heart of the Confederacy* (New York: Oxford University Press, 2003), 24–29; Van Lew, *Yankee Spy*, 5–7.

38. Wheelan, *Libby Prison Breakout*, 99.

39. "Richmond's Prominent Unionists," *Richmond Times-Dispatch*, April 13, 2014, https:// richmond.com/news/local/richmond-s-prominent-unionists/article_895662b9-6286-51ed -9cee-edef8f7c90fe.html (paywall).

40. Van Lew Papers, 1818–1900, call number MssCol 3135, New York Public Library Archives & Manuscripts Division, 3; David D. Ryan, *Cornbread and Maggots Cloak and Dagger: Union Prisoners and Spies in Civil War Richmond* (Richmond: Dietz Press, 1994), 17–19; Wheelan, *Libby Prison Breakout*, 87.

41. Varon, *Southern Lady*, 86.

42. *Burlington Weekly Free Press*, July 20, 1883, 3, text online, https://chroniclingamerica .loc.gov/lccn/sn86072143/1883-07-20/ed-1/seq-3/.

43. "Elizabeth Van Lew, 1818–1900(?)," *Shotgun's Home of the American Civil War* (website), accessed February 22, 2021, https://civilwarhome.com/vanlewbio.html; Rebecca Beatrice Brooks, "Elizabeth Van Lew: Spymaster," Civil War Saga, www.civilwarsaga.com/ elizabeth-van-lew-spymaster/.

44. Van Lew, *Yankee Spy*, 49; Van Lew Papers; Brooks, "Elizabeth Van Lew."

45. *Richmond Enquirer* (Richmond, Va.), 1815–1867, Library of Congress, www.loc.gov/ item/sn84024735/.

46. *Richmond Dispatch* (Richmond, Va.), 1850–1884, Library of Congress, www.loc.gov/ item/sn84024738/.

47. Varon, *Southern Lady*, 64–68.

48. "Nomination of Miss Van Lew as Postmistress of Richmond," *Richmond Dispatch*, March 18, 1869, 3, text online, https://chroniclingamerica.loc.gov/data/batches/vi_kors_ ver02/data/sn84024738/00271741960/1869031801/0275.pdf.

49. Varon, *Southern Lady*, 113; Butler, *Correspondence*, vol. 5, sect. 3, 319.

50. *Richmond Dispatch*, July 18, 1864, 2; Wheelan, *Libby Prison Breakout*, 87.

51. Beszedits, *Libby Prison Diary*, 92–93.

52. Beszedits, *Libby Prison Diary*, 86, 94.

53. Fernández Cavada, *Libby Life*, 132–33, 137.

54. From Dow's diary, in Hesseltine, *Civil War Prisons*, 67–68.

55. John B. Jones, *John B. Jones: A Rebel Clerk's Diary*, ed. Earl Schenck Miers (New York: Sagamore Press, Inc., 1958), 154–56.

56. Van Lew, *Yankee Spy*, 54.

57. *Southern Punch*, October 10, 1863, p. 5, quoted in Jones, *Rebel Clerk's Diary*, 137.

58. *Richmond Examiner*, January 5, 1864.

59. James I. Robertson Jr., "Houses of Horror: Danville's Civil War Prisons," *The Virginia Magazine of History and Biography* 69, no. 3 (July 1961): 329–45; Hesseltine, *Civil War Prisons*, 66.

60. Diary entries dated January 9 and January 19, 1864, in Cornwell, *Libby Prison and Beyond*, 64, 68–69.

61. From Dow's diary, in Hesseltine, *Civil War Prisons*, 68.

62. Wheelan, *Libby Prison Breakout*, 137.

63. Wheelan, *Libby Prison Breakout*, 128.

64. Wheelan, *Libby Prison Breakout*, 129.

65. Moran, "Colonel Rose's Tunnel," 209–10.

66. Johnston, *Four Months in Libby*, 82.

67. Rose, *Col. Rose's Story*, 2; Hamilton, *Story of the Famous Tunnel*, 3, 6; Moran, "Colonel Rose's Tunnel," 207.

68. Moran, "Colonel Rose's Tunnel," 221–22.

69. Hamilton, *Story of the Famous Tunnel*, 6.

70. Johnston, *Four Months in Libby*, 83.

71. Moran, "Colonel Rose's Tunnel," 211–12.

72. Moran, "Colonel Rose's Tunnel," 207.

CHAPTER 14. "GODSPEED!"

1. Fernández Cavada, *Libby Life*.

2. Fernández Cavada, *Libby Life*, 156–57.

3. Albert Heffley and Cyrus P. Heffley, *Civil War Diaries of Capt. Albert Heffley and Lt. Cyrus P. Heffley: Company F, 142nd Regt. Penna. Vol., Army of the Potomac* (Apollo, PA: Closson Press, 2000), 66–67.

4. Cornwell, *Libby Prison and Beyond*, 97.

5. Heffley and Heffley, *Civil War Diaries*, 101.

6. Wheelan, *Libby Prison Breakout*, 101.

7. Robert Knox Sneden, *Robert Knox Sneden Diary, 1861–1865*, vol. 5: *1863 November 9–1864 August 10*, December 1863–February 1864, part 2, p. 237, in the Robert Knox Sneden Papers, Virginia Historical Society, Richmond, guide to vol. 5 of Sneden papers online, https://www.virginiahistory.org/collections-and-resources/how-we-can-help-your-research/researcher-resources/finding-aids/sneden-0-3.

8. Fernández Cavada, *Libby Life*, 141; diary entry dated February 7, 1864, in Cornwell, *Libby Prison and Beyond*, 102; Beszedits, *Libby Prison Diary*, 90; United States Sanitary Commission, *Narrative of Privations and Sufferings of United States Officers and Soldiers while Prisoners of War in the Hands of the Rebel Authorities* (Philadelphia: King & Baird, 1864), 152, facsimile of alternate edition online, https://babel.hathitrust.org/cgi/pt?id=loc.ark:/13960/t2v415d5q&view=1up&seq=1.

9. Van Lew, *Yankee Spy*, 59–60; Varon, *Southern Lady*, 130–32; Wheelan, *Libby Prison Breakout*, 101–2.

10. Hamilton, *Story of the Famous Tunnel*, 5.

11. Rose, *Col. Rose's Story*, 3; see also *National Tribune*, March 13, 1890, text online, https://chroniclingamerica.loc.gov/lccn/sn82016187/1890-03-13/ed-1/.

12. Johnston, *Four Months in Libby*, 77–78.

13. Wheelan, *Libby Prison Breakout*, 146.

14. Moran, "Colonel Rose's Tunnel," 211–12.

15. Diary entries dated February 1 and 2, 1864, in Cornwell, *Libby Prison and Beyond*, 100–101.

16. Diary entry dated January 3, 1864, in Cornwell, *Libby Prison and Beyond*, 101.

17. Frank E. Moran, "Colonel Rose's Tunnel at Libby Prison," *Century Illustrated Monthly Magazine* (March 1888): 780, text online, https://civilwarrichmond.com/prisons/libby-prison/4437-1888-03-century-magazine-march-1888-pp-770-790-moran-frank-e-colonel-rose-s-tunnel-at-libby-prison-excellent-account-of-the-tunneling-effort-and-subsequent-escape-of-109-libby-prisoners.

18. Fernández Cavada, *Libby Life*, 141; diary entry dated February 7, 1864, in Cornwell, *Libby Prison and Beyond*, 102; Beszedits, *Libby Prison Diary*, 90; US Sanitary Commission, *Narrative of Privations and Sufferings*, 152.

19. Varon, *Southern Lady*, 121–22; see also *New York Herald*, February 15, 1864, accessed via *Civil War: A Newspaper Perspective*, database, Accessible Archives.

20. Rose, *Col. Rose's Tunnel*, n.p.; Moran, "Colonel Rose's Tunnel," 213.

21. Moran, "Colonel Rose's Tunnel," 213.

22. Wheelan, *Libby Prison Breakout*, 126.

23. Moran, "Colonel Rose's Tunnel," 213.

24. Moran, "Colonel Rose's Tunnel," 213.

25. *New York Herald*, February 15, 1864, accessed via *Civil War: A Newspaper Perspective*, database, Accessible Archives; Varon, *Southern Lady*, 121–22.

26. Moran, "Colonel Rose's Tunnel," 215–16; Caldwell, *Incidents of War*, 25.

27. Wheelan, *Libby Prison Breakout*, 147.

28. Wheelan, *Libby Prison Breakout*, 147; Johnston, *Four Months in Libby*, 77–79, 217.

29. Wheelan, *Libby Prison Breakout*, 147.

30. Caldwell, *Incidents of War*, 25–26; Moran, "Colonel Rose's Tunnel," 216–17.

31. Bartleson, *Letters from Libby*, 37–38; Wheelan, *Libby Prison Breakout*, 148.

32. Johnston, *Four Months in Libby*, 78–79.

33. Johnston, *Four Months in Libby*, 78–79.

34. Johnston, *Four Months in Libby*, 79–80.

35. Johnston, *Four Months in Libby*, 79–82; Moran, "Colonel Rose's Tunnel," 219–20.

36. Wheelan, *Libby Prison Breakout*, 130, 132; Butler, *Private and Official Correspondence*, 3:331–33.

37. Butler, *Private and Official Correspondence*, 3:331–33.

38. Ibid.; Butler, *Private and Official Correspondence*, 3:331–34.

39. "They Must Not Be Permitted to Perish," *New York Herald*, October 31, 1863, text online, https://www.loc.gov/resource/sn83030313/1863-10-31/ed-1/?st=gallery.

40. Francis Preston Blair and Franklin Rives, eds., *The Congressional Globe: Debates and Proceedings*, 1st ed., 38th Congress (Washington, DC: Congressional Globe Office, 1864), 118–19.

41. Butler, *Private and Official Correspondence*, 3:351.

42. Butler, *Private and Official Correspondence*, 3:396–402, 421–25; Bartleson, *Letters from Libby*, 31–32.

43. *National Tribune*, March 27, 1890, text available https://chroniclingamerica.loc.gov/lccn/sn82016187/1890-03-27/ed-1/; Wheelan, *Libby Prison Breakout*, 151.

44. Wheelan, *Libby Prison Breakout*, 151–52.

45. Moran, "Colonel Rose's Tunnel," 218–19; Johnston, *Four Months in Libby*, 86–87.

46. Moran, "Colonel Rose's Tunnel," 221–22.

47. Moran, "Colonel Rose's Tunnel," 221–22; Hamilton, *Story of the Famous Tunnel*, 6–7.

48. Rose, *Col. Rose's Tunnel*, n.p.

49. Moran, "Colonel Rose's Tunnel," 222.

50. A large barrel.

51. Moran, "Colonel Rose's Tunnel," 222–23.

CHAPTER 15. EXODUS

1. Cornwell, *Libby Prison and Beyond*.

2. *National Tribune*, March 27, 1890, text online, https://chroniclingamerica.loc.gov/lccn/sn82016187/1890-03-27/ed-1/; Johnston, *Four Months in Libby*, 83–84.

3. Hamilton, *Story of the Famous Tunnel*, 7.

4. Moran, "Colonel Rose's Tunnel," 224.

5. Hamilton, *Story of the Famous Tunnel*, 7.

6. From Dow's diary in Hesseltine, *Civil War Prisons*, 71.

7. Bartleson, *Letters from Libby*, 57.

8. Rose, *Col. Rose's Tunnel*, n.p.

9. Caldwell, *Incidents of War*, 34–35.

10. Wells, "Tunneling Out of Libby Prison," 100.

11. Sanderson, *My Record in Rebeldom*, 48–49.

12. Johnston, *Four Months in Libby*, 90–91.

13. Bartleson, *Letters from Libby*, 33.

14. Moran, "Colonel Rose's Tunnel," 222–23.

15. Dow, *Reminiscences*, 727; Wheelan, *Libby Prison Breakout*, 158.

16. Caldwell, *Incidents of War*, 37.

17. Wheelan, *Libby Prison Breakout*, 160; Moran, "Colonel Rose's Tunnel," 225.

18. Wells, "Tunneling Out of Libby Prison," 323.

19. Hebert, "Streight's Raid."

20. Hamilton, *Story of the Famous Tunnel*, 7; Dow, *Reminiscences*, 726–27.

21. Charles Warrington Earle, "In and Out of Libby Prison (Read November 11, 1886)," in *Military Essays and Recollections: Papers Read before the Commandery of the State of Illinois, Military Order of the Loyal Legion of the United States*, vol. 1, ed. Military Order of the Loyal Legion of the United States, Commandery of the State of Illinois (Chicago: Commandery of the State of Illinois, 1891), 279–83, text online, https://ia800307.us.archive.org/35/items/militaryessaysa02illigoog/militaryessaysa02illigoog.pdf; see also *National Tribune*, August 30, 1906, text online, https://chroniclingamerica.loc.gov/lccn/sn82016187/1906-08-30/ed-1/.

22. Meaning she was an abolitionist.

23. Wheelan, *Libby Prison Breakout*, 170.

24. Dow, *Reminiscences*, 725–27.

25. Dow, *Reminiscences*, 727; "Escape of One Hundred and Nine Commissioned Yankee Officers from the Libby Prison," *Richmond Examiner*, February 11, 1864, text online, https://

www.civilwarrichmond.com/events/libby-prison-breakout/2781-1864-02-11-richmond-ex
aminer-good-description-of-the-great-escape-from-libby-prison-castle-thunder-mentioned.

26. Diary entry dated February 9, 1864, in Cornwell, *Libby Prison and Beyond*, 103.

27. Wheelan, *Libby Prison Breakout*, 162.

28. Wheelan, *Libby Prison Breakout*, 162–63.

29. Dow, *Reminiscences*, 726; Bartleson, *Letters from Libby*, 78.

30. Bartleson, *Letters from Libby*, 39.

31. Moran, "Colonel Rose's Tunnel," 223–28.

32. Moran, "Colonel Rose's Tunnel," 223–28.

33. Moran, "Colonel Rose's Tunnel," 223–28.

34. Moran, "Colonel Rose's Tunnel," 223–28.

35. Moran, "Colonel Rose's Tunnel," 223–28.

36. Wells, "Tunneling Out of Libby Prison," 322–23.

37. Wells, "Tunneling Out of Libby Prison," 323.

38. Wells, "Tunneling Out of Libby Prison," 323. His estimates were short by several miles.

39. Wells, "Tunneling Out of Libby Prison," 323.

CHAPTER 16. MANHUNT

1. Walt Whitman, letter to the editor, "The Prisoners," *New York Times*, December 27, 1864, https://www.nytimes.com/1864/12/27/archives/the-prisoners.html.

2. Hamilton, *Story of the Famous Tunnel*, 7.

3. Diary entry dated February 10, 1864, in Cornwell, *Libby Prison and Beyond*, 103–4.

4. Bartleson, *Letters from Libby*, 40.

5. Dow, *Reminiscences*, 727.

6. Bartleson, *Letters from Libby*, 40.

7. Dow, *Reminiscences*, 728.

8. Bartleson, *Letters from Libby*, 34.

9. *Richmond Examiner*, February 11, 1864, text online, https://www.civilwarrichmond
.com/events/libby-prison-breakout/2781-1864-02-11-richmond-examiner-good-description
-of-the-great-escape-from-libby-prison-castle-thunder-mentioned.

10. "Recapturing Libby Escapees, and List of Re-captured Prisoners," *Richmond Enquirer*, February 13, 1864, text online, https://www.civilwarrichmond.com/events/libby-prison
-breakout/2645-1864-02-13-richmond-enquirer-recapturing-libby-escapees-and-list-of-re
-captured-prisoners.

11. "Recapturing Libby Escapees, and List of Re-captured Prisoners," *Richmond Enquirer*, February 13, 1864, text online, https://www.civilwarrichmond.com/events/libby
-prison-breakout/2645-1864-02-13-richmond-enquirer-recapturing-libby-escapees-and-list
-of-re-captured-prisoners; *Richmond Examiner*, February 11, 1864, text online, https://www
.civilwarrichmond.com/events/libby-prison-breakout/2781-1864-02-11-richmond-examiner
-good-description-of-the-great-escape-from-libby-prison-castle-thunder-mentioned.

12. "Particulars of the Escape of the Yankee Officers from the Libby Prison," *Charleston Mercury*, February 16, 1864.

13. *Richmond Examiner*, February 11, 1864, text online, https://www.civilwarrichmond .com/events/libby-prison-breakout/2781-1864-02-11-richmond-examiner-good-description -of-the-great-escape-from-libby-prison-castle-thunder-mentioned.

14. Dow, *Reminiscences*, 728.

15. Bartleson, *Letters from Libby*, 40.

16. The term *dragoon* comes from British cavalry units.

17. Bartleson, *Letters from Libby*, 40–41.

18. Bartleson, *Letters from Libby*, 41.

19. "Escape of One Hundred and Nine," *Richmond Examiner*, February 11, 1864; "The Recent Escape from the Libby Prison—Recapture of Twenty-Two Officers," *Richmond Enquirer*, February 12, 1864.

20. "The Recent Escape from the Libby Prison—Recapture of Twenty-Two Officers," *Richmond Enquirer*, February 12, 1864. The dashing "guerrilla" fighter had escaped on November 27, 1863, from the Ohio Penitentiary also by digging a tunnel.

21. "The Recent Escape from the Libby Prison—Recapture of Twenty-Two Officers," *Richmond Enquirer*, February 12, 1864.

22. "The Recent Escapes from Libby Prison—Recapture of Twenty-Two Officers," *Richmond Enquirer*, February 12, 1864.

23. "No More Escapees from Libby have been Captured," *Richmond Examiner*, February 16, 1864; "The Recent Escape from the Libby Prison—Recapture of Twenty-Two Officers," *Richmond Enquirer*, February 12, 1864.

24. Bartleson, *Letters from Libby*, 34–35.

25. Bartleson, *Letters from Libby*, 35, 40.

26. "Escape of One Hundred Yankee Officers from the Libby Prison—A Scientific Tunnel—Their Underground Route to Liberty," *Richmond Examiner*, February 11, 1864; "The Recent Escape from the Libby Prison—Recapture of Twenty-Two Officers," *Richmond Enquirer*, February 12, 1864.

27. Cornwell, *Libby Prison and Beyond*, 104.

28. Wells, "Tunneling Out of Libby Prison," 323.

29. Wells, "Tunneling Out of Libby Prison," 323–24.

30. Wells, "Tunneling Out of Libby Prison," 325.

31. Wells, "Tunneling Out of Libby Prison," 325.

32. Captain Randall's name does not appear on the lists of recaptured prisoners published in the Richmond newspapers, so it is probable that he was never caught.

33. Wells, "Tunneling Out of Libby Prison," 325.

34. Wells, "Tunneling Out of Libby Prison," 325–26.

35. Wells, "Tunneling Out of Libby Prison," 326.

36. "Recapture of More Yankee Officers," *Richmond Enquirer*, February 13, 1864; diary entry dated February 13, 1864, in Cornwell, *Libby Prison and Beyond*, 104–5.

37. "Two More Libby Escapees Re-captured," *Richmond Enquirer*, February 16, 1864.

38. Bartleson, *Letters from Libby*, 35.

39. Bartleson, *Letters from Libby*, 19; diary entry dated February 14, 1864, in Cornwell, *Libby Prison and Beyond*, 105.

40. Hamilton, *Story of the Famous Tunnel*, 7.

41. Hamilton, *Story of the Famous Tunnel*, 7.

42. Rose, *Col. Rose's Tunnel*, n.p.

43. Rose, *Col. Rose's Tunnel*, n.p.

44. Rose, *Col. Rose's Tunnel*, n.p.

45. Rose, *Col. Rose's Tunnel*, n.p.

46. Rose, *Col. Rose's Tunnel*, n.p.

CHAPTER 17. "KILL CAVALRY"

1. Excerpt from his poem "In Libby Prison, New Year's Eve, 1863–64," found in Bartleson, *Letters from Libby*.

2. Moran, "Colonel Rose's Tunnel at Libby Prison," 788.

3. Moran, "Colonel Rose's Tunnel at Libby Prison," 788.

4. Moran, "Colonel Rose's Tunnel at Libby Prison," 788.

5. Bartleson, *Letters from Libby*, 21.

6. The exact number of men recaptured after the mass breakout was forty-eight.

7. "The Re-captured Yankee Officers," *Richmond Examiner*, February 15, 1864, text online, https://civilwarrichmond.com/prisons/libby-prison/2783-1864-02-15-richmond-ex aminer-recapturing-libby-escapee-anecdotes.

8. See Dow's diary entry dated February 14, 1864, in Hesseltine, *Civil War Prisons*, 70.

9. From Dow's diary entries dated February 12, 27, and then 5, 1864, in Hesseltine, *Civil War Prisons*, 69, 72 (italics original), and 69 again.

10. Fernández Cavada, *Libby Life*, 192.

11. "The Re-captured Yankee Officers," *Richmond Examiner*, February 15, 1864, text online, https://civilwarrichmond.com/prisons/libby-prison/2783-1864-02-15-richmond-exam iner-recapturing-libby-escapee-anecdotes. And see "Re-capture of Twenty-Two of the Escaped Yankee Officers," *Richmond Examiner*, February 12, 1864, text reproduced online, http://www.migenweb.org/montcalm/military/civilwar/civilwarhindshh.html.

12. "The Re-captured Yankee Officers," *Richmond Examiner*, February 15, 1864, text online, https://civilwarrichmond.com/prisons/libby-prison/2783-1864-02-15-richmond-ex aminer-recapturing-libby-escapee-anecdotes.

13. Fernández Cavada, *Libby Life*, 189–92; Szabad, *Diary in Libby Prison*, 432; Hesseltine, *Civil War Prisons*, 69.

14. Letters from Elizabeth Van Lew to General Benjamin Butler, date unknown, likely written from January 30 to February 5, 1864, in United States War Department, *War of the Rebellion*, series 1, vol. 33, 519–21.

15. Diary entry dated March 8, 1864, in Gideon Welles, *Diary of Gideon Welles, Secretary of the Navy under Lincoln and Johnson*, intro. John T. Morse Jr., vol. 1 of 3: *1861–March 30, 1864* (Boston and New York: Houghton Mifflin Company, 1911), 538.

16. Beszedits, *Libby Prison Diary*, 53.

17. "Elizabeth L. Van Lew," Dictionary of Virginia Biography, Library of Virginia, www .lva.virginia.edu/public/dvb/bio.php?b=van_lew_elizabeth.

18. Wiatt, *Libby Civil War Prison*.

19. Bartleson, *Letters from Libby*, 75.

20. Hesseltine, *Civil War Prisons*, 132.

21. Bartleson, *Letters from Libby*, 75–76.

22. Rose, *Col. Rose's Story*, .

23. Bartleson, *Letters from Libby*, 27.

24. Bartleson, *Letters from Libby*, 76.

25. For a helpful discussion of the affair, see Stephen W. Sears, *Controversies and Commanders: Dispatches from the Army of the Potomac* (Boston: Houghton Mifflin, 2001).

26. *Richmond Examiner*, March 5, 1864.

27. Sears, *Controversies and Commanders*.

28. Lineberry, "Elizabeth Van Lew."

29. Lineberry, "Elizabeth Van Lew."

30. Peter Luebke, "Kilpatrick-Dahlgren Raid," in *Encyclopedia Virginia*, Virginia Humanities, last modified April 5, 2011, https://www.encyclopediavirginia.org/kilpatrick-dahlgren_raid.

31. Bartleson, *Letters from Libby*, 77.

32. Bartleson, *Letters from Libby*, 77.

33. Report by a joint committee of the Confederate States Congress, March 3, 1864, as quoted in "Colonel Ulrich Dahlgren," *Encyclopedia Virginia*, visited February 26, 2021, https://encyclopediavirginia.org/274hpr-b3b6015c14752b5/.

CHAPTER 18. THE FALL OF RICHMOND

1. As reported from a liberated slave jail, by T. Morris Chester for the *Philadelphia Press*, found in James M. McPherson, *The Negro's Civil War: How American Blacks Felt and Acted during the War for the Union* (New York: Vintage Books, 2003), 68.

2. See the American Battlefield Trust's online history of the siege of Petersburg at "Petersburg: Assault on Petersburg," https://www.battlefields.org/learn/civil-war/battles/petersburg; "Petersburg," https://www.battlefields.org/learn/articles/petersburg; and "Petersburg Breakthrough," https://www.battlefields.org/learn/articles/petersburg-breakthrough; *Battlefields.org*, all accessed February 26, 2021.

3. Reported variously, and in Walter Coffey, "The Fall of Petersburg," *The Civil War Months* (website), April 2, 2020, https://civilwarmonths.com/2020/04/02/the-fall-of-petersburg/.

4. Beszedits, *Libby Prison Diary*, 54.

5. Godfrey Weitzel, *Richmond Occupied: Entry of the United States Forces into Richmond, Va. April 3, 1865 . . .* ed. and intro. Louis H. Manarin (Richmond: Richmond Civil War Centennial Committee, 1965), 12, text online, https://www.civilwarrichmond.com/images/pdf/occupied.pdf.

6. As reported by Loomis L. Langdon, in "Memoranda on the Life of Lincoln," *The Century Illustrated Monthly Magazine* 40 (May–October 1890): 309. And see "President Lincoln Enters Richmond, 1865," *EyeWitness to History*, 2000, http://www.eyewitnesstohistory.com/richmond.htm.

7. From chapter 3, "The Entrance into Richmond," in William Henry Crook, *Through Five Administrations: Reminiscences of Colonel William H. Crook, Body-Guard to President Lincoln*, comp. and ed. Margarita Spalding Gerry (New York: Harper & Brothers, 1910), 42.

8. Crook, *Through Five Administrations*, 52.

9. National Park Service, "Lincoln's Visit to Richmond," Richmond: National Battlefield Park, Virginia, US Department of the Interior, last updated February 1, 2018, https://www.nps.gov/rich/learn/historyculture/lincvisit.htm.

10. Crook, *Through Five Administrations*, 50.

11. National Park Service, "Lincoln's Visit to Richmond." For a helpful discussion of Lincoln's visit to Richmond, see also James M. McPherson, *The Battle Cry of Freedom: The Civil War Era*, Oxford History of the United States, vol. 6 (New York: Oxford University Press, 1988).

12. National Park Service, "Lincoln's Visit to Richmond."

13. As reported with slightly different wording in David Dixon Porter, *Incidents and Anecdotes of the Civil War* (New York: D. Appleton and Co., 1885), 295, facsimile online, https://babel.hathitrust.org/cgi/pt?id=loc.ark:/13960/t3zs35c3t&view=1up&seq=301.

14. "President Lincoln Enters Richmond, 1865," *EyeWitness to History*.

15. On the 138th anniversary of Lincoln's visit to Richmond, the National Park Service unveiled a life-size sculpture of Lincoln and his son sitting on a bench in the city. It is located near the Tredegar Iron Works, James River, and Libby and is inscribed with the words, "To bind up the Nation's wounds." (Taken from Lincoln's second inaugural address.) National Park Service, "Lincoln's Visit to Richmond."

16. David Dixon Porter, *Incidents and Anecdotes of the Civil War* (New York: D. Appleton & Co., 1885) (reprint, Charleston: Nabu Press, 2010), 298–99.

17. Crook, *Through Five Administrations*, 59.

18. "President Lincoln Enters Richmond, 1865," *EyeWitness to History*.

19. Wiatt, *Libby Civil War Prison*; Beszedits, *Libby Prison Diary*, 54.

20. *Richmond Examiner*, February 10 and February 28, 1866.

21. "Personal," *Burlington Weekly Free Press*, July 20, 1883, p. 3, col. 6, text online, https://chroniclingamerica.loc.gov/lccn/sn86072143/1883-07-20/ed-1/seq-3/.

22. "Elizabeth L. Van Lew," Dictionary of Virginia Biography.

23. "The 'Loyal' 'Union' Hop at the Spotswood Last Night," *Richmond Examiner*, February 5, 1866, p. 3, c. 3, text online, https://www.civilwarrichmond.com/people/richmond-unionists/van-lew-house-elizabeth-van-lew/6104-1866-02-05-richmond-examiner-republication-and-expansion-of-very-lengthy-and-descriptive-account-of-a-loyal-union-hop-at-the-spotswood-hotel-names-of-many-attendees-including-john-van-lew-erastus-ross-and-many-others-greatly-expanded-since-earlier-publication.

24. David. B. Parker, *A Chautauqua Boy in '61 and Afterward: Reminisces* . . . ed. Torrance Parker, intro. Albert Bushnell Hart (Boston: Small, Maynard and Company, 1912), 54–64,

text online, https://books.google.com/books?id=0OoSAAAAYAAJ&printsec. See also "Elizabeth Van Lew," *Shotgun's Home of the American Civil War.*

CHAPTER 19. LIBERATION!

1. Ulysses S. Grant, in his letter formally accepting his nomination as the Republican Party's candidate for president of the United States, 1868.

2. Hamilton, *Story of the Famous Tunnel*, 3.

3. Frank E. Moran, "The Tunnel at Libby Prison: A Civil War Escape," in *Great American Adventure Stories*, ed. Tom McCarthy (Guilford, CT: Lyons Press Classics, 2017), 45.

4. Rose, *Col. Rose's Story*, n.p.

5. Hamilton, *Story of the Famous Tunnel*, 3.

6. "A Veteran Murdered in Cold Blood by Drunken Youths," *Louisville Courier-Journal*, April 4, 1895, p. 1, text online, https://bigfamilytree.weebly.com/uploads/2/4/8/2/2482186/hamiltonagshooting2.pdf.

7. Dow, *Reminiscences*, 726.

8. Dow, *Reminiscences*, 734.

9. Dow, *Reminiscences*, 735.

10. Dow, *Reminiscences*, v.

11. Dow, *Reminiscences*, vii and 99.

12. Bartleson, *Letters from Libby*, 77–78.

13. Bartleson, *Letters from Libby*, 78.

14. Bartleson, *Letters from Libby*, 79–80.

15. Bartleson, *Letters from Libby*, 81.

16. Bartleson, *Letters from Libby*, 12, 83, and 89.

17. Bartleson, *Letters from Libby*, 11, 90–91.

18. Bartleson, *Letters from Libby*, 11 and 95.

19. Beaudry, *War Journal*, 65.

20. Beaudry, *War Journal*, 3.

21. Beszedits, *Libby Prison Diary*, 72.

22. Beszedits, *Libby Prison Diary*, 73.

23. The poem is included in this book's appendix.

24. Beszedits, *Libby Prison Diary*, 102.

25. Beszedits, *Libby Prison Diary*, 102; note that Cavada published his account of his time in prison in 1864. It was titled *Libby Life: Experiences of a Prisoner of War in Richmond, VA, 1863–1864.*

26. In Cuba, it was known as *la Guerra Grande* and also nicknamed the War of '68.

27. Fernández Cavada published articles, including one in *Harper's New Monthly Magazine* in November of 1870, on the importance of the Bellamar Caves on Cuba's northern coast.

28. Allen O. Abbott, *Prison Life in the South: At Richmond, Macon, Savannah, Charleston, Columbia, Charlotte, Raleigh, Goldsborough, and Andersonville; During the Years 1864 and*

1865 (New York: Harper & Brothers, 1865), 23–34, alternate edition available at https://babel.hathitrust.org/cgi/pt?id=coo1.ark:/13960/t3pv72x6x&view=1up&seq=1.

29. "Major Turner's Escape; How the Ex-Commandant of Famous Libby Prison Fled to Cuba. His Experiences as Told by Himself; An Interesting Letter Written by Him from Havana Just after the War to a Friend in Virginia," *New York Times*, July 7, 1895, https://timesmachine.nytimes.com/timesmachine/1895/07/07/105981304.pdf; see also "Thomas Turner," Civil War Richmond, www.civilwarrichmond.com.

30. "Major Turner's Escape," *New York Times*.

31. General Early was using the alias "Anderson" when he met Turner.

32. "Major Turner's Escape," *New York Times*.

33. "Major Turner's Escape," *New York Times*. See also National Park Service, "Captain Henry Wirz," Andersonville, National Historic Site, Georgia, US Department of the Interior, last updated July 21, 2020, https://www.nps.gov/ande/learn/historyculture/captain_henry_wirz.htm.

34. Moran, "Colonel Rose's Tunnel," .

35. Quoted in "Elizabeth Van Lew," Shotgun's Home of the American Civil War, www.civilwarhome.com/vanlewbio.html.

36. See "Rewarding a Spy," *Nashville Union and American*, March 25, 1869, p. 3, c. 1, text online, https://chroniclingamerica.loc.gov/lccn/sn85033699/1869-03-25/ed-1/seq-3/; "The Richmond Postoffice," *Nashville Union and American*, May 28, 1870, p. 1, c. 1, text online, https://chroniclingamerica.loc.gov/lccn/sn85033699/1870-05-28/ed-1/seq-1/; *Charleston Daily News*, November 24, 1870, p. 2, text online, https://chroniclingamerica.loc.gov/lccn/sn84026994/1870-11-24/ed-1/seq-2/; *New York Tribune*, April 18, 1877, p. 1, text online, https://www.loc.gov/resource/sn83030214/1877-04-18/ed-1/?sp=1.

CHAPTER 20. MUSEUM AND MEMORY

1. Quoted in Horace Greeley, "Some Words on Peace and War," *The New York Times*, July 29, 1864.

2. Beszedits, *Libby Prison Diary*, 37.

3. James M. Powels, "Civil War Stories: Libby Prison's 'Lottery of Death,'" *Warfare History Network* (website), December 7, 2014, http://warfarehistorynetwork.com/2014/12/07/civil-war-stories-libby-prisons-lottery-of-death/.

4. Powels, "Civil War Stories."

5. Dow, *Reminiscences*, 720.

6. Beszedits, *Libby Prison Diary*, 92.

7. Beszedits, *Libby Prison Diary*, 49.

8. Junius H. Browne, *Four Years in Secessia: Adventures within and beyond the Union Lines* (Hartford, CT: O. D. Case and Company, 1865), 269.

9. Wheelan, *Libby Prison Breakout*, 189. And see *Richmond Dispatch*, January 30, 1863.

10. Breckinridge had run for president in 1860.

11. Wheelan, *Libby Prison Breakout*, 135. See also *Richmond Dispatch*, April 4, 1864.

12. Beszedits, *Libby Prison Diary*, 37–38; see also Joint Committee of the Conduct of the War. Report of the Joint Committee on the Conduct of the War, at the Second Session, Thirty-Eighty Congress. US Senate, report no. 142. Washington, DC. Government Printing Office, 1865.

13. Joint Committee on the Conduct of the War, US Senate, May 22, 1865, https://www.senate.gov/artandhistory/history/common/investigations/jointcommittee_conductofwar.htm. For a helpful discussion of the committee, see also Bruce Tap, *Over Lincoln's Shoulder: The Committee on the Conduct of the War* (Lawrence: University Press of Kansas, 1998).

14. United States House of Representatives, *Report on the Treatment of Prisoners of War by the Rebel Authorities . . .* (Washington, DC: Government Printing Office, 1869), text online, https://memory.loc.gov/cgi-bin/ampage?collId=llss&fileName=1300/1391/llss1391.db&recNum=8.

15. House Report No. 85, 40th Congress, 3rd Session, 1869; note that the first general law for pensions for Union Civil War veterans was in 1862, Congress then studied the issue in the 1869 report, and increased pensions in 1880.

16. Bartleson, *Letters from Libby*, 71.

17. Dow, *Reminiscences*, 725–26.

18. The 1985 television series *North and South* featured a character named General George Hazard (played by James Read) who was captured and taken to Libby, where he suffered at the hands of the sadistic Commandant Turner (played by Wayne Newton), until rescued by Orry Main (played by Patrick Swayze). The series is based on John Jakes's novel of the same title and also features the prison.

19. Speer, *Portals to Hell*, 170; *Richmond Sentinel*, August 15, 1863, p. 2.

20. Charles W. Sanders, *While in the Hands of the Enemy: Military Prisons of the Civil War* (Baton Rouge: Louisiana State University Press, 2005).

21. Beaudry, *War Journal*, 236.

22. Beaudry, *War Journal*, 236.

23. One of the officers who would later join their team was Albert G. Spalding, founder of Spalding sporting goods.

24. Neil Gale, "The History of Charles 'Carl' Frederick Günther, Known as 'The Candy Man' and 'The P. T. Barnum of Chicago,'" *Digital Research Library of Illinois History Journal*, October 20, 2017, https://drloihjournal.blogspot.com/2017/10/history-of-charles-carl-frederick-gunther.html; John J. Flinn, ed. "Libby Prison Museum," in *Chicago: The Marvelous City of the West; A History, Encyclopedia, and Guide*, 2nd ed. (Chicago: National Book and Picture Co., 1893), 126, text online, https://archive.org/details/chicagomarvelous00flin/page/126/mode/2up?q=libby+prison+museum.

25. For years there was an inaccurate rumor that the stone was from Libby.

26. Speer, *Portals to Hell*, 172.

27. Beaudry, *War Journal*, 237.

28. Known as the "World's Columbian Exposition."

29. Fortunately, some items were sold to the Chicago Historical Society.

30. Gale, "History of Charles 'Carl' Frederick Günther"; Flinn, "Libby Prison Museum."

31. A recent census put the population of Hamlet at just eight hundred residents.

32. "Prison Timers in Barn," *National Tribune*, June 13, 1940; Wiatt, "Libby Civil War Prison"; Beszedits, *Libby Prison Diary*, 44–45.

33. Named for Pocahontas, the bell was to be placed in the Virginia gallery but was not hung there. It was subsequently to be donated to the University of Virginia, but the present location of the bell remains uncertain.

34. Beaudry, *War Journal*, 236.

35. Cornwell, *Libby Prison and Beyond*, 46.

36. "Horrors of the Richmond Prisons; An Average of Fifty Victims Every Day. Disease, Starvation and Death. The Sick Denied Hospital Treatment. Shocking Pictures of Destitution and Abject Wretchedness. Official Statement of the Released Surgeons," *New York Times*, November 28, 1863, https://www.nytimes.com/1863/11/28/archives/horrors-of-the-richmond-prisons-an-average-of-fifty-victims-every.html. And see Zombek, "Libby Prison."

37. Moran, "Colonel Rose's Tunnel," 184.

38. Hamilton, *Story of the Famous Tunnel*, 3.

Bibliography

HISTORICAL SOURCES

Abbott, Allen O. *Prison Life in the South: At Richmond, Macon, Savannah, Charleston, Columbia, Charlotte, Raleigh, Goldsborough, and Andersonville; During the Years 1864 and 1865.* New York: Harper & Brothers, 1865. Alternate edition available at https://babel.hathitrust .org/cgi/pt?id=cool.ark:/13960/t3pv72x6x&view=1up&seq=1.

Bartleson, Frederick A. *Frederick A. Bartleson: Letters from Libby Prison.* Edited by Margaret W. Peelle. New York: Greenwich Book Publishers, 1956.

Bates, Samuel P. *History of Pennsylvania Volunteers, 1861–5.* 5 vols. Harrisburg, PA: B. Singerly, 1869–1871.

Beaudry, Louis N., ed. *The Libby Chronicle: Devoted to Facts and Fun; A True Copy of the Libby Chronicle as Written by the Prisoners of Libby in 1863.* Albany: Louis N. Beaudry, 1889. Text online, https://play.google.com/books/reader?id=WQNPAhEtLxMC&hl=en& pg=GBS.PP1.

———. *War Journal of Louis N. Beaudry, Fifth New York Cavalry: The Diary of a Union Chaplain, Commencing February 16, 1863.* Edited by Richard E. Beaudry. Jefferson, NC: McFarland & Co., 1960. First edition published 1896.

Benjamin F. Butler Papers. Manuscript/mixed-material collection: 1831–1896. Manuscript Division, Library of Congress, Washington, DC. See https://www.loc.gov/item/ mm82014514/.

Beszedits, Stephen, ed. *The Libby Prison Diary of Colonel Emeric Szabad.* Toronto: B & L Information Services, 1999.

Brock, Sallie A. *Richmond during the War: Four Years of Personal Observation.* Introduction by Virginia Scharf. Lincoln: University of Nebraska Press, 1996. First published 1867. Facsimile of first edition online, https://www.google.com/books/edition/Richmond_Dur ing_the_War/q8FIAQAAMAAJ.

Blair, Francis Preston, and Franklin Rives, eds. *The Congressional Globe: Debates and Proceedings*, 1st ed., 38th Congress. Washington, DC: Congressional Globe Office, 1864.

Browne, Junius H. *Four Years in Secessia: Adventures within and beyond the Union Lines*. Hartford, CT: O. D. Case and Company, 1865.

Burrows, J. L. "Recollection of Libby Prison." *Southern Historical Society Papers* 11, nos. 2 and 3 (February–March, 1883): 83–92. Text online, https://civilwarrichmond.com/prisons/prison-depot/4421-1883-southern-historical-society-papers-11-1883-pp-83-92-burrows-j-l-recollections-of-libby-prison.

Butler, Benjamin F. *Private and Official Correspondence of General Benjamin F. Butler during the Period of the Civil War*. 5 vols. Norwood, MA: Plimpton Press, 1917.

Byers, S. H. M. "Letters from Libby." *National Tribune*, December 29, 1891. Text online, https://civilwarrichmond.com/written-accounts/other-newspapers/3695-1891-12-29-national-tribune-excellent-set-of-letters-from-libby-prison-recounting-treatment-and-life-in-prison-mentions-purchasing-one-of-the-rees-images-from-the-prison-guards-and-sending-it-north.

Caldwell, David Stidmond. *Incidents of War and Southern Prison Life*. Dayton, OH: United Brethren Printing, 1864. Reprint, [Ohio]: The Wyandot Tracers, Chapter of the Ohio Genealogical Society, 2002.

The Century Illustrated Monthly Magazine. "Memoranda on the Life of Lincoln." 40 (May–October 1890): 305–11.

Chamberlain, J. W. "Scenes in Libby Prison." In *Sketches of War History, 1861–1865: Papers Read before the Ohio Commandery of the Military Order of the Loyal Legion of the United States*, edited by the Commandery, 342–70. Volume 2, *1886–1888*. Cincinnati: Robert Clarke & Co., 1888.

Charleston Mercury. "Particulars of the Escape of the Yankee Officers from the Libby Prison." February 16, 1864. Text online, https://civilwarrichmond.com/prisons/libby-prison/4382-1864-02-16-charleston-mercury-description-of-the-libby-prison-escape-includes-a-very-good-description-of-the-physicality-of-the-escape.

Christian Recorder. "A Prisoner's Letter." (Philadelphia) February 11, 1865. Archived online, https://archive.org/stream/christianrecorder_1865_v5_no1_to_13/christianrecorder_1865_v5_no1_to_13_djvu.txt.

Coffey, Walter. "Lincoln's Militia Proclamation (April 15, 1861)." *The Civil War Months*, April 15, 2016. Archived online, https://web.archive.org/web/20200616132629/https://civilwarmonths.com/2016/04/15/lincolns-militia-proclamation/.

Coffin, Charles Carleton. *The Boys of '61; or, Four Years of Fighting*. Boston: Estes & Lauriat, 1884.

Congressional Report on Confederate Prisons, Congressional Record: The Proceedings and Debates, 51st Congress, 1st Session, Vol. 21, Part 9.

Convention of the People of Alabama. "An Ordinance to Dissolve the Union between the State of Alabama and the Other States United Under the Compact Styled 'The Constitution of the United States of America.'" Resolution submitted to the State of Alabama's Committee on Ordnance of Secession, Montgomery, Alabama, January 11, 1861. Text online, https://ehistory.osu.edu/exhibitions/Regimental/alabama/confederate/secession.

Cornwell, Robert Thompson. *Libby Prison and Beyond: A Union Staff Officer in the East, 1862–1865*. Edited by Thomas M. Boaz. Shippensburg, PA: Burd Street Press, 1999.

Crook, William Henry. *Through Five Administrations: Reminiscences of Colonel William H. Crook, Body-Guard to President Lincoln*. Compiled and edited by Margarita Spalding Gerry. New York: Harper & Brothers, 1910.

Davis, Jefferson. "Address to Congress, July 20, 1861." In *The Papers of Jefferson Davis*, vol. 7, *1861*, edited by Lynda Lasswell Crist and Mary Seaton Dix. Baton Rouge: Louisiana State University Press, 1992, 48–51. Text online, https://en.wikisource.org/wiki/Jefferson_Davis %27_Message_to_the_Third_Session_of_the_Provisional_Confederate_Congress.

———. *The Rise and Fall of the Confederate Government*. New York: D. Appleton and Co., 1881.

De Leon, T. C. *Four Years in Rebel Capitals: An Inside View of Life in the Southern Confederacy from Birth to Death; From Original Notes, Collated in the Years 1861 to 1865*. Mobile: The Gossip Printing Company, 1892. Text online, https://archive.org/details/fouryearsinre bel00deleiala/mode/2up.

di Cesnola, Louis [Luigi] Palma. *Ten Months in Libby Prison*. [Philadelphia]: N.p., 1865. Duke University Special Collections Library.

Domschcke, Bernard. *Twenty Months in Captivity: Memoirs of a Union Officer in Confederate Prisons*. Edited and translated by Frederic Trautmann. Rutherford, NJ: Farleigh Dickinson University Press, 1987.

Dow, Frederick N. *The Reminiscences of Neal Dow: Recollections of Eighty Years*. Portland, ME: The Evening Express Publishing Co., 1898. Reprint, [London]: Forgotten Books, 2017.

Earle, Charles Warrington. "In and Out of Libby Prison (Read November 11, 1886)." In *Military Essays and Recollections: Papers Read before the Commandery of the State of Illinois, Military Order of the Loyal Legion of the United States*, vol. 1, edited by the Military Order of the Loyal Legion of the United States, Commandery of the State of Illinois, 247–92. Chicago: Commandery of the State of Illinois, 1891. Text online, https://ia800307.us.archive. org/35/items/militaryessaysa02illigoog/militaryessaysa02illigoog.pdf.

Ely, Alfred. *Journal of Alfred Ely, a Prisoner of War in Richmond*. Edited by Charles Lanman. New York: D. Appleton and Co., 1862.

Fernández Cavada, Federico. *Libby Life: Experiences of a Prisoner of War in Richmond, VA, 1863–1864*. Philadelphia: King, Roger & Baird, 1864. Reprint, New York: University Press of America, 1985.

Flinn, John J., ed. "Libby Prison Museum." In *Chicago: The Marvelous City of the West; A History, Encyclopedia, and Guide*, 2nd ed., 126. Chicago: National Book and Picture Co., 1893. Text online, https://archive.org/details/chicagomarvelous00flin/page/126/ mode/2up?q=libby+prison+museum.

Glazier, Willard W. *The Capture, the Prison Pen, and the Escape: Giving a Complete History of Prison Life in the South*. Hartford, CT: H. E. Goodwin, 1867.

Gorman, Michael D. "Summary of Libby & Son." File M346. Submitted January 2001. National Archives and Records Administration, Washington, DC. Text online, https://www .civilwarrichmond.com/images/pdf/Summary_of_Libby.pdf.

Hamilton, Andrew G. *The Story of the Famous Tunnel Escape from Libby Prison, as Told by Maj. A. G. Hamilton, One of the Projectors*. Chicago: N.p., 1893. Reprint, [N.p.]: Digital Text

Publishing, 2017. Facsimile online, https://babel.hathitrust.org/cgi/pt?id=loc.ark:/13960/t5z60zp4d&view=1up&seq=1.

Harper's Weekly. "Mrs. Lincoln, Wife of the President." November 8, 1862, 709. Facsimile online, http://www.sonofthesouth.net/leefoundation/civil-war/1862/november/mary-todd-lincoln.htm.

———. "The Prisons at Richmond." October 17, 1863, 667–69. Facsimile online, http://www.sonofthesouth.net/leefoundation/civil-war/1863/october/libby-prison.htm.

Heffley, Albert, and Cyrus P. Heffley. *Civil War Diaries of Capt. Albert Heffley and Lt. Cyrus P. Heffley: Company F, 142nd Regt. Penna. Vol., Army of the Potomac.* Apollo, PA: Closson Press, 2000.

Henry, Patrick. "Give Me Liberty or Give Me Death." Address made to the Second Virginia Convention, St. John's Church, Richmond, Virginia, March 23, 1775. Text reproduced online, http://www.gutenberg.org/files/6/6-h/6-h.htm.

Jeffrey, William H. *Richmond Prisons, 1861–1862: Compiled from the Original Records Kept by the Confederate Government; Journals Kept by Union Prisoners of War, Together with the Name, Rank, Company, Regiment and State of the Four Thousand Who Were Confined There.* St. Johnsbury, VT: The Republican Press, 1895. Facsimile online, https://babel.hathitrust.org/cgi/pt?id=uc2.ark:/13960/t1ng4gr3d&view=1up&seq=7.

Jones, John B. *John B. Jones: A Rebel Clerk's Diary.* Edited by Earl Schenck Miers. New York: Sagamore Press, Inc., 1958.

Jones, John William, ed. *Southern Historical Society Papers.* Vol. 1, no. 3 (March). Richmond, VA: Southern Historical Society Papers, 1876. Text online, https://en.m.wikisource.org/wiki/Southern_Historical_Society_Papers/Volume_01/March/Judge_Ould%27s_reply_to_charges_against_him.

Johnston, Isaac N. *Four Months in Libby, and the Campaign against Atlanta.* Cincinnati: Methodist Book Concern, 1864. Facsimile online, https://babel.hathitrust.org/cgi/pt?id=hvd.32044020270237&view=1up&seq=9.

Joint Committee on the Conduct of the War. US Senate (May 22, 1865). www.senate.gov/artandhistory/history/common/investigations/jointcommittee_conductofwar.htm.

Libby Prison War Museum Association. *Libby Prison War Museum Catalogue and Program.* Chicago: Libby Prison War Museum Association, [189–?]. Reprint, London: Forgotten Books, 2017. Facsimile online, https://babel.hathitrust.org/cgi/pt?id=loc.ark:/13960/t5x63xs5n&view=1up&seq=3.

Lincoln, Abraham. First Inaugural Address. Washington, DC, March 4, 1861. Transcript online, https://www.bartleby.com/124/pres31.html.

———. Letter to Henry L. Pierce and others. April 6, 1859. Reproduced at *Abraham Lincoln Online.* Accessed February 16, 2021. http://www.abrahamlincolnonline.org/lincoln/speeches/pierce.htm.

———. Letter to Joshua Speed. August 24, 1855. Reproduced at *Abraham Lincoln Online.* Accessed February 11, 2021. http://www.abrahamlincolnonline.org/lincoln/speeches/speed.htm.

———. "The Perpetuation of Our Political Institutions." Known as "The Lyceum Address," made to the Young Men's Lyceum of Springfield, Illinois, January 27, 1838. In Roy P.

Basler, Marion Dolores Pratt, and Lloyd A. Dunlap, eds., *Collected Works of Abraham Lincoln*, vol. 1, 108–15. New Brunswick, NJ: Rutgers University Press, 1953. Text online, http://www.abrahamlincolnonline.org/lincoln/speeches/lyceum.htm.

Moran, Frank E. "The Bright Side of Libby Prison." In *Living History: The Civil War*, edited by Henry Steele Commager, revised and expanded by Erik Brunn, 494–96. New York: Tess Press, 1950.

———. "Colonel Rose's Tunnel." In *Famous Adventures and Prison Escapes of the Civil War*, edited by G. W. Cable. 184–242. New York: The Century Co., 1885. Text online, http://www.loyalbooks.com/download/text/Famous-Adventures-and-Prison-Escapes-of-the-Civil.txt.

———. "Colonel Rose's Tunnel at Libby Prison." *Century Illustrated Monthly Magazine* (March 1888): 770–90. Text online, https://civilwarrichmond.com/prisons/libby-prison/4437-1888-03-century-magazine-march-1888-pp-770-790-moran-frank-e-colonel-rose-s-tunnel-at-libby-prison-excellent-account-of-the-tunneling-effort-and-subsequent-escape-of-109-libby-prisoners.

———. "Libby Prison's Tunnel." *Toledo Blade*, November 9, 1892. Facsimile online, https://news.google.com/newspapers?nid=1350&dat=18821109&id=TzsxAAAAIBAJ&sjid=a_4DAAAAIBAJ&pg=5431,1130354.

———. "The Tunnel at Libby Prison: A Civil War Escape." In *Great American Adventure Stories*, edited by Tom McCarthy. Guilford, CT: Lyons Press Classics, 2017.

Hon. H. L. Morey, Member of Congress, "Libby Prison: The Experience of One of the Successful Tunnelers," *National Tribune*, March 27, 1890.

National Archives and Records Administration. "Records of the Commissary General of Prisoners." Guide to Federal Records. Record group 249: 1961–1965. Washington, DC. Archival contents detailed online, https://www.archives.gov/research/guide-fed-records/groups/249.html.

———. Records relating to Individual Federal Prisoners of War: Registers, day books, daily lists of arrivals, and other records relating to federal prisoners confined in Libby Prison, Castle Thunder, and other prisons at Richmond, VA, 1861–65. September 1862–March 1865. Record group 249.3.2. Washington, DC. Collection description online, https://www.archives.gov/research/guide-fed-records/groups/249.html.

———. "Statistical Reports of Hospitals in Virginia, 1862–1864." Record group 109, vol. 151. Washington, DC. Linked online, https://civilwarrichmond.com/hospitals/3971-statistics-of-hospitals-in-richmond-va-during-the-civil-war.

———. "T. P. Turner." *Compiled Service Records of Confederate Generals and Staff Officers, and Non-regimental Enlisted Men*. File M331. Washington, DC.

New York Herald. "The Richmond Prisoners." November 28, 1863. Text online, https://civilwarrichmond.com/written-accounts/other-newspapers/4377-1863-11-28-new-york-herald-testimony-from-released-federal-surgeons-regarding-poor-conditions.

New York Times. "Important from Montgomery.; Speech of Hon. Jefferson Davis. Declaration of the Policy of the Southern Confederacy. Montgomery, Saturday, Feb. 16. Arrival of Hon. Jefferson Davis. Important Army News." February 18, 1861. https://www.nytimes.com/1861/02/18/archives/important-from-montgomery-speech-of-hon-jefferson-davis-declaration.html.

————. "Major Turner's Escape; How the Ex-Commandant of Famous Libby Prison Fled to Cuba. His Experiences as Told by Himself; An Interesting Letter Written by Him from Havana Just after the War to a Friend in Virginia." *New York Times*, July 7, 1895. https://timesmachine.nytimes.com/timesmachine/1895/07/07/105981304.pdf.

————. "The Rebel Guardians of National Prisoners in Richmond." November 15, 1863. https://www.nytimes.com/1863/11/15/archives/the-rebel-guardians-of-national-prisoners-in-richmond.html.

Nicolay, John George, and John Hay. *Abraham Lincoln: A History*, 3 volumes. New York: New Century, 1917.

Parker, David. B. *A Chautauqua Boy in '61 and Afterward: Reminisces by David B. Parker, Second Lieutenant and Seventy-Second New York, Detailed Superintendent of the Mails of the Army of the Potomac, United States Marshal, District of Virginia Chief Post Office Inspector.* Edited by Torrance Parker, introduction by Albert Bushnell Hart. Boston: Small, Maynard and Company, 1912. Text online, https://books.google.com/books?id=0OoSAAAAYAAJ&printsec.

Porter, David Dixon. *Incidents and Anecdotes of the Civil War*. New York: D. Appleton and Co., 1885. Facsimile online, https://babel.hathitrust.org/cgi/pt?id=loc.ark:/13960/t3zs35c3t&view=1up&seq=13.

Prisoners of Libby Prison, 1861–1865. *Walls that Talk: A Transcript of the Names, Initials and Sentiments Written and Graven on the Walls, Doors and Windows at the Libby Prison at Richmond.* Richmond: J. W. Randolph & English, 1889. Reprint, London: Franklin Classics, 2018. Facsimile online, https://babel.hathitrust.org/cgi/pt?id=uiug.30112054728925&view=1up&seq=1.

Richmond Enquirer. "City Intelligence: The Libby Prison and Its Contents." February 2, 1864. Text online, https://chroniclingamerica.loc.gov/lccn/sn84024735/1864-02-02/ed-1/.

Roach, Alva C. *The Prisoner of War, and How Treated: Containing a History of Colonel Streight's Expedition to the Rear of Bragg's Army, in the Spring of 1863, and a Correct Account of the Treatment and Condition of the Union Prisoners of War in the Rebel Prisons of the South in 1863–4, Being the Actual Experience of a Union Officer during 22 Month's Imprisonment in Rebeldom, with Personal Adventure, Biographical Sketches and History of Andersonville Prison Pen.* Indianapolis: Robert Douglass, 1887. Facsimile of earlier edition online, https://babel.hathitrust.org/cgi/pt?id=yale.39002004517323&view=1up&seq=12.

Rose, Thomas Ellwood. *Col. Rose's Story of the Famous Tunnel Escape from Libby Prison: A Thrilling Account of the Daring Escape of 109 Union Officers from Libby Prison Through a Famous Yankee Tunnel.* 1884. Reprint, London: Forgotten Books, 2017.

Sanderson, James M. *My Record in Rebeldom, as Written by Friend and Foe, Comprising the Official Charges and Evidence before the Military Commission in Washington, Brig. Gen'l J. C. Caldwell, Pres't, Together with the Report and Finding of the Court.* New York: W. E. Sibell, 1865. Facsimile online, https://babel.hathitrust.org/cgi/pt?id=loc.ark:/13960/t6tx3rd4r&view=1up&seq=14.

Sneden, Robert Knox. *Robert Knox Sneden Diary, 1861–1865.* Vol. 5: *1863 November 9–1864 August 10.* December 1863–February 1864, part 2. Robert Knox Sneden Papers, Virginia Historical Society, Richmond. Guide to vol. 5 of Sneden papers online, https://www

.virginiahistory.org/collections-and-resources/how-we-can-help-your-research/researcher-resources/finding-aids/sneden-0-3.

South Carolina General Assembly. "Resolution to Call the Election of Abraham Lincoln as U.S. President a Hostile Act and to Communicate to Other Southern States South Carolina's Desire to Secede from the Union." November 9, 1860. *Resolutions of the General Assembly, 1779–1879*, S165018. South Carolina Department of Archives and History. Columbia, South Carolina.

Stephens, Alexander Hamilton. "Speech Delivered on the 21st March 1861, in Savannah, Known as the 'Corner Stone Speech,' Reported in the *Savannah Republican*." In *Alexander H. Stephens, in Public and Private: With Letters and Speeches, Before, During, and Since the War*, edited by Henry Cleveland, 717–29. Philadelphia, Richmond, Atlanta, Cincinnati, St. Louis, Chicago, and New Orleans: National Publishing Company, 1866. Text online, https://archive.org/details/alexanderhstephe6114clev/page/n7/mode/2up.

Stowe, Harriet Beecher. *Uncle Tom's Cabin; or, Life among the Lowly*. Boston: John P. Jewett and Company, 1852.

Szabad, Emeric. "Diary in Libby Prison." *Fraser's Magazine for Town and Country* 77, no. 459 (March 1868): 385–406. Facsimile online, https://babel.hathitrust.org/cgi/pt?id=uc1.a0007087596&view=1up&seq=393.

———. *Modern War: Its Theory and Practice*. New York: Harper & Bros., 1863.

Texas Secession Convention. "A Declaration of the Causes which Impel the State of Texas to Secede from the Federal Union." February 2, 1861. Text online, https://avalon.law.yale.edu/19th_century/csa_texsec.asp.

Tower, Morton. *Army Experience of Major Morton Tower from 1861 to 1864*. Virginia Historical Society, 1870. Text online, https://civilwarrichmond.com/written-accounts/archival-sources/other-archives/4483-no-date-virginia-historical-society-morton-tower-memoir-excellent-account-of-conditions-in-libby-prison-in-1863-and-escape-through-the-famous-tunnel.

United States House of Representatives. *Report on the Treatment of Prisoners of War by the Rebel Authorities, during the War of the Rebellion: To Which Are Appended the Testimony Taken by the Committee, and Official Documents and Statistics, Etc.* Washington, DC: Government Printing Office, 1869. Text online, https://memory.loc.gov/cgi-bin/ampage?collId=llss&fileName=1300/1391/llss1391.db&recNum=8.

United States Sanitary Commission. *Narrative of Privations and Sufferings of United States Officers and Soldiers while Prisoners of War in the Hands of the Rebel Authorities*. Philadelphia: King & Baird, 1864. Facsimile of alternate edition online, https://babel.hathitrust.org/cgi/pt?id=loc.ark:/13960/t2v415d5q&view=1up&seq=1.

United States War Department, ed. *War of the Rebellion: A Compilation of the Official Records of the Union and Confederate Armies*. Series 2: *Prisoners of War, Etc.*, 8 vols. Prepared by Robert N. Scott. Washington, DC: Government Printing Office, 1894–1899. Facsimiles of vols. 1–5 and 8 online, https://catalog.hathitrust.org/Record/004388999.

———, ed. *War of the Rebellion: A Compilation of the Official Records of the Union and Confederate Armies War of Rebellion; A Compilation of the Official Records of the Union and Confederate Armies*. 128 volumes. Washington, DC: Government Printing Office, 1880–1901.

Van Lew, Elizabeth L. *A Yankee Spy in Richmond: The Civil War Diary of "Crazy Bet" Van Lew.* Edited by David D. Ryan. Mechanicsburg, PA: Stackpole Books, 1996. First published January 24, 1864.

Van Lew Papers, 1818–1900, call number MssCol 3135, Archives & Manuscripts Division, New York Public Library.

Wells, James Munroe. "The Tunnel Escape of Union Prisoners from the Confederate Libby Prison." In *The Most Incredible Prison Escape of the Civil War*, edited by W. Fred Conway, 91–113. New Albany, IN: FBH Publishers, 1991.

———. "Tunneling Out of Libby Prison: A Michigan Lieutenant's Account of His Own Imprisonment and Daring Escape." *McClure's Magazine* 22 (November 1903–April 1904): 317–26.

Wiatt, R. W. *Libby Civil War Prison.* Official Publication #12. Richmond: Richmond Civil War Centennial Committee, 1961–1965.

Wilkins, William D. "Forgotten in the Black Hole: A Diary from Libby Prison." *Civil War Times Illustrated* 15 (June 1976): 36–44.

BOOKS

Blakey, Arch Fredric. *General John Winder, CSA.* Gainesville: University Press of Florida, 1990.

Bonekemper, Edward H. III. *The Myth of the Lost Cause: Why the South Fought the Civil War and Why the North Won.* Washington, DC: Regnery History, 2015.

Bonner, Robert E. *Mastering America: Southern Slaveholders and the Crisis of American Nationhood.* New York: Cambridge University Press, 2009.

Booth, Benjamin F. *Dark Days of the Rebellion: Life in Southern Military Prisons.* Garrison, IA: Meyer Publishing, 1996.

Bristol, Frank Milton. *The Life of Chaplain McCabe: Bishop of the Methodist Episcopal Church.* New York: Eaton & Mains, 1908. Reprint, New York: Fleming H. Revell Co., 1908.

Burns, Ken. *The Civil War: A Film by Ken Burns.* Kenneth Lauren Burns Production. Burbank, CA: PBS Home Video, 1990.

Davis, William C. *Jefferson Davis: The Man and His Hour.* New York: HarperCollins, 1991.

Duke, Basil Wilson, and Thomas Henry Hines, eds. *Famous Adventures and Prison Escapes of the Civil War.* New York: The Century Co., 1913.

Eggleston, Larry G. *Women in the Civil War: Extraordinary Stories of Soldiers, Spies, Nurses, Doctors, Crusaders, and Others.* Jefferson, NC: McFarland & Co., 2009.

Franklin, John Hope. *From Slavery to Freedom: A History of African Americans.* New York: McGraw-Hill, 1947. Reprint, New York: Knopf, 2000. Citations refer to the Knopf edition.

Gindlesperger, James. *Escape from Libby Prison.* Shippensburg, PA: White Mane Publishing, 1996.

Hemmerlein, Richard F. *Prisons and Prisoners of the Civil War.* Boston: Christopher Publishing House, 1934.

Harper, Judith E., ed. *Women during the Civil War: An Encyclopedia.* Foreword by Elizabeth D. Leonard. New York: Routledge, Taylor & Francis Group, 2004.

Heidler, David Stephen, and Jeanne T. Heidler, eds. *Encyclopedia of the American Civil War: A Political, Social, and Military History*. Foreword by James M. McPherson. New York: W. W. Norton, 2002.

Hesseltine, William Best. *Civil War Prisons: A Study of War Psychology*. Columbus: The Ohio State University Press, 1930. Reprint, Kent, OH: Kent State University, 1962.

Hines, Emilee. *More than Petticoats: Remarkable Virginia Women*. Lanham, MD: TwoDot Press, 2003.

Hutchison, Coleman. *Apples and Ashes: Literature, Nationalism, and the Confederate States of America*. Athens: University of Georgia Press, 2012.

Krannawitter, Thomas L. *Vindicating Lincoln: Defending the Politics of Our Greatest President*. Lanham, MD: Rowman & Littlefield Publishers, 2010.

Lewis, Lloyd. *Sherman: Fighting Prophet*. Lincoln: University of Nebraska Press, 1993.

Longacre, Edward G. *Mounted Raids of the Civil War*. South Brunswick, NJ: A. S. Barnes, 1975.

Lonn, Ella. *Foreigners in the Union Army and Navy*. Baton Rouge: Louisiana State University, 1951.

McPherson, James M. *The Battle Cry of Freedom: The Civil War Era*. Oxford History of the United States, vol. 6. New York: Oxford University Press, 1988.

———. *The Negro's Civil War: How American Blacks Felt and Acted during the War for the Union*. New York: Vintage Books, 2003.

Nash, Howard P. *Stormy Petrel: The Life and Times of General Benjamin F. Butler, 1818–1893*. Rutherford, NJ: Farleigh Dickinson University Press, 1969.

Neely, Mark E., Jr. *Southern Rights: Political Prisoners and the Myth of Confederate Constitutionalism*. Charlottesville: University of Virginia Press, 1999.

Obreiter, John. *The Seventy-Seventh Pennsylvania at Shiloh: History of the Regiment*. Harrisburg: Harrisburg Publishing Co., 1908.

Pickenpaugh, Roger. *Captives in Blue: The Civil War Prisons of the Confederacy*. Tuscaloosa: University of Alabama Press, 2013.

Porter, David Dixon. *Incidents and Anecdotes of the Civil War*. New York: D. Appleton & Co., 1885. Reprint, Charleston: Nabu Press, 2010.

Rhodes, James Ford. *History of the Civil War, 1861–1865*. New York: Macmillan Co., 1917.

Ryan, David D. *Cornbread and Maggots Cloak and Dagger: Union Prisoners and Spies in Civil War Richmond*. Richmond: Dietz Press, 1994.

Sanders, Charles W. *While in the Hands of the Enemy: Military Prisons of the Civil War*. Baton Rouge: Louisiana State University Press, 2005.

Schultz, Duane P. *The Dahlgren Affair: Terror and Conspiracy in the Civil War*. New York: W. W. Norton, 1998.

Sears, Stephen W. *Controversies and Commanders: Dispatches from the Army of the Potomac*. Boston: Houghton Mifflin, 2001.

Speer, Lonnie R. *Portals to Hell: Military Prisons of the Civil War*. Mechanicsburg, PA: Stackpole Books, 1997.

Tap, Bruce. *Over Lincoln's Shoulder: The Committee on the Conduct of the War*. Lawrence: University Press of Kansas, 1998.

Trammell, Jack, and Guy Terrell. *A Short History of Richmond*. Mount Pleasant, SC: The History Press, 2017.

Vance, Jonathan F., ed. *Encyclopedia of Prisoners of War and Internment*. 2nd ed. Millerton, NY: Grey House Publishing, 2006.

Varon, Elizabeth R. *Southern Lady, Yankee Spy: The True Story of Elizabeth Van Lew, A Union Agent in the Heart of the Confederacy*. New York: Oxford University Press, 2003.

Watson, Robert P. *America's First Crisis: The War of 1812*. Albany: State University of New York Press, 2014.

Wheelan, Joseph. *Libby Prison Breakout: The Daring Escape from the Notorious Civil War Prison*. New York: PublicAffairs, 2010.

Wish, Harvey. *George Fitzhugh: Propagandist of the Old South*. Baton Rouge: Louisiana State University, 1943.

Wray, William J. *Birney's Zouaves Civil War: Life of the 23rd Pennsylvania Volunteers*, 5th ed. New York: Bloch Publishing Co., 2000.

ARTICLES, CHAPTERS, AND ONLINE SOURCES

American Battlefield Trust. "Civil War Ballooning." Learn: Civil War: Quick Facts. *Battlefields.org*. Accessed February 11, 2021. https://www.battlefields.org/learn/articles/civil-war-ballooning.

———. "Civil War Casualties." Learn: Civil War: History. *Battlefields.org*. Accessed February 11, 2021. https://www.battlefields.org/learn/articles/civil-war-casualties.

———. "Fort Sumter." *Battlefields.org*. Learn: Civil War: Battles. Accessed February 11, 2021. https://www.battlefields.org/learn/civil-war/battles/fort-sumter.

———. "Nathan Bedford Forrest." Learn: Civil War: Biographies. *Battlefields.org*. Accessed February 11, 2021. https://www.battlefields.org/learn/biographies/nathan-bedford-forrest.

———. "Petersburg." Learn: Articles. *Battlefields.org*. Accessed February 26, 2021. https://www.battlefields.org/learn/articles/petersburg.

———. "Petersburg: Assault on Petersburg." Learn: Civil War: Battles. *Battlefields.org*. Accessed February 26, 2021. https://www.battlefields.org/learn/civil-war/battles/petersburg.

———. "Petersburg Breakthrough." Learn: Articles. *Battlefields.org*. Accessed February 26, 2021. https://www.battlefields.org/learn/articles/petersburg-breakthrough.

———. "Purged Away with Blood: John Brown's War." Learn: Articles. *Battlefields.org*. Accessed February 11, 2021. https://www.battlefields.org/learn/articles/purged-away-blood.

Atkinson, Matt. "John H. Winder (1800–1865)." In *Encyclopedia Virginia*, Virginia Humanities, April 7, 2016. http://encyclopediavirginia.org/winder_john_h_1800-1865#start_entry.

Bartholf, Howard. "Significant Dates in the History of Libby Prison." *Civil War Richmond*. Accessed February 10, 2021. https://www.civilwarrichmond.com/images/pdf/SIGNIFICANT_DATES_IN_THE_HISTORY_OF_LIBBY_PRISON.pdf.

Beszedits, Stephen. "Frederick Knefler: Hungarian Patriot and American General." Jewish-American History Foundation. www.jewish-history.com/civilwar/knefler.html.

Blight, David W. "'He Knew How to Die': John Brown on the Gallows, December 2, 1859." *History News Network*. Accessed February 11, 2021. http://hnn.us/articles/120730.html.

Bonner, Robert E. "Proslavery Extremism Goes to War: The Counterrevolutionary Confederacy and Reactionary Militarism." *Modern Intellectual History* 6, no. 2 (August 2009): 261–85.

Bray, John. "My Escape from Richmond." *Harper's New Monthly Magazine* 28, no. 167 (April): 662–65. Text reproduced online, A. J., "My Escape from Richmond: John Bray's Account of His Escape from Libby Prison," *Civil War Sources* (blog), January 5, 2008, http://civilwarsources.blogspot.com/2008/01/john-brays-account-of-is-escape-from.html.

Bridge, Jennifer R. "A Shrine of Patriotic Memories." *Chicago History* 32, no. 1 (Summer 2003): 4–23. https://issuu.com/chicagohistorymuseum/docs/redacted-2003sum-chm-chicagohistory.

Brooks, Rebecca Beatrice. "Elizabeth Van Lew: Spymaster." Civil War Saga. www.civilwarsaga.com/Elizabeth-van-lew-spymaster/.

Buenger, Walter L. "Secession Crisis." In *Handbook of Civil War: Texas.* Texas State Historical Association. https://www.tshaonline.org/handbook/entries/secession.

Byrne, Frank L. "A General Behind Bars: Neal Dow in Libby Prison." *Civil War History* 8, no. 2 (1962): 164–83.

———. "A General Behind Bars: Neal Dow in Libby Prison." In *Civil War Prisons*, edited by William B. Hesseltine, 60–79. Kent, OH: Kent State University Press, 1962.

———. "Libby Prison: A Study in Emotions." *Journal of Southern History* 24, no. 4 (November 1958): 430–44.

Carlson, Peter. "The Pirate-Warden of Richmond." Disunion. *New York Times*, June 3, 2013. http://opinionator.blogs.nytimes.com/2013/06/03/the-pirate-warden-of-richmond/.

Chesson, Michael B. "Prison Camps and Prisoners of War." In *The American Civil War: A Handbook of Literature and Research*, edited by Steven E. Woodworth, 466–78. Hartford, CT: Greenwood Press, 1966.

Civil War Richmond. "Liggon's Prison." *Civil War Richmond* (website). Accessed February 11, 2021. https://www.civilwarrichmond.com/prisons/liggon-s-prison.

Coffey, Walter. "The Confederate Conscription Act." *The Civil War Months* (website), April 16, 2017. https://civilwarmonths.com/2017/04/16/the-confederate-conscription-act/.

———. "The Fall of Petersburg." *The Civil War Months* (website), April 2, 2020. https://civilwarmonths.com/2020/04/02/the-fall-of-petersburg/.

Daily News Hungary. "164th Anniversary: The 13 Martyrs of Arad of October 6, 1849." October 6, 2013. https://dailynewshungary.com/164th-anniversary-the-13-martyrs-of-arad-on-october-6-1849/.

DeCredico, Mary. "Richmond during the Civil War." Encyclopedia Virginia. www.encyclopediavirginia.org/entries/richmond-during-the-civil-war/.

DeMarco, Michael. "Elizabeth Van Lew (1818–1920)." In *Encyclopedia Virginia*, Virginia Humanities, last modified March 6, 2018. https://www.encyclopediavirginia.org/van_lew_elizabeth_l_1818-1900.

Dictionary of Virginia Biography. "Elizabeth L. Van Lew." Library of Virginia, www.lva.virginia.gov/public/dvb/bio.php?b=van_lew_elizabeth.

Encyclopedia Virginia. "Colonel Ulrich Dahlgren." Visited February 26, 2021. https://encyclopediavirginia.org/274hpr-b3b6015c14752b5/.

Eye Witness to History. "President Lincoln Enters Richmond, 1865." 2000. http://www.eyewitnesstohistory.com/richmond.htm.

Gale, Neil. "The History of Charles 'Carl' Frederick Günther, Known as 'The Candy Man' and 'The P. T. Barnum of Chicago.'" *Digital Research Library of Illinois History Journal*, October 20, 2017. https://drloihjournal.blogspot.com/2017/10/history-of-charles-carl -frederick-gunther.html.

———. "The History of Libby Prison War Museum, Chicago, Illinois (1889–1897)." *Digital Research Library of Illinois History Journal*. November 14, 2016. https://drloihjournal .blogspot.com/2016/11/libby-prison-war-museum-chicago.html.

Greeley, Horace. "Some Words on Peace and War." *The New York Times*, July 29, 1864, www.nytimes.com/1864/07/29/archives/some-words-on-peace-and-war-a-statement-by -mr-horace-greeley.html.

Goldberg, David E. "George Wythe Randolph." Encyclopedia Virginia. www.encyclopedia virginia.org/entries/randolph-george-wythe-1818-1867/.

Goodrich, John K. "From Slaves of Sin to Slaves of God: Reconsidering the Origin of Paul's Slavery Metaphor in Romans 6." *Bulletin for Biblical Research* 23, no. 4 (2013): 509–30.

Hawkes, Steve A. "The Civil War in the East." CWE home page. *The Civil War in the East* (website). Accessed February 11, 2021. https://civilwarintheeast.com/.

———. "23rd Pennsylvania Voluntary Infantry Regiment." *The Civil War in the East* (website). Accessed February 17, 2021. https://civilwarintheeast.com/us-regiments-batteries/ pennsylvania/23rd-pennsylvania-infantry/.

———. "23rd Pennsylvania Volunteer Infantry Regiment." Pennsylvania Monuments at Gettysburg: Pennsylvania Infantry. *The Battle of Gettysburg* (website). Accessed February 11, 2021. https://gettysburg.stonesentinels.com/union-monuments/pennsylvania/pennsylva nia-infantry/23rd-pennsylvania/.

Hebert, Keith S. "Streight's Raid." Encyclopedia of Alabama, www.encyclopediaofalabama .org/article/h-1380.

History.com editors. "Confederate States of America," *History.com*. A&E Television Networks. Updated August 21, 2018. https://www.history.com/topics/american-civil-war/ confederate-states-of-america.

History Net. "Missouri Compromise." *HistoryNet.com*. Accessed February 11, 2021. https:// www.historynet.com/missouri-compromise.

Hubbell, John T. "Abraham Lincoln and the Recruitment of Black Soldiers." *Journal of the Abraham Lincoln Association* 2, no. 1 (1980): 6–21. http://hdl.handle.net/2027/spo .2629860.0002.103.

Johnson, Sarah. "'A Very Brutal Man': Lewis Horton, David Todd, and Prisoner Torture." *The Gettysburg Compiler* (website), September 30, 2013. Civil War Institute at Gettysburg College. http://gettysburgcompiler.org/2013/09/30/a-very-brutal-man-lewis-horton-david -todd-and-prisoner-torture/.

Jones, Virgil Carrington. "Libby Prison Break." *Civil War History* 4, no. 2 (June 1958): 93–104.

Kansaspedia. "Pottawatomie Massacre." Kansas Historical Society. Accessed February 11, 2021. https://www.kshs.org/kansapedia/pottawatomie-massacre/16699.

Library of Congress. "Elijah Parish Lovejoy Was Killed by a Pro-slavery Mob, November 7, 1837." Jump Back in Time: Western Expansion and Reform (1829–1859). *America's Story from America's Library* (website). http://www.americaslibrary.gov/jb/reform/jb_re form_lovejoy_1.html, http://www.americaslibrary.gov/jb/reform/jb_reform_lovejoy_2.

html, http://www.americaslibrary.gov/jb/reform/jb_reform_lovejoy_3.html, and http://www.americaslibrary.gov/jb/reform/jb_reform_lovejoy_4.html.

Lineberry, Cate. "Elizabeth Van Lew: An Unlikely Union Spy." Special Report: The Civil War. *Smithsonian Magazine*, May 4, 2011. https://www.smithsonianmag.com/history/elizabeth-van-lew-an-unlikely-union-spy-158755584/.

LivingInVermont. "A Brave Drummer Boy." *A Day in the Life of the Civil War*, May 19, 2012. https://lifeofthecivilwar.blogspot.com/2012/05/brave-drummer-boy.html.

Luebke, Peter. "Kilpatrick-Dahlgren Raid." In *Encyclopedia Virginia*, Virginia Humanities, last modified April 5, 2011. https://www.encyclopediavirginia.org/kilpatrick-dahlgren_raid.

Marsh, Alan. "POWs in American History: A Synopsis." Learn: History and Culture. National Park Service. US Department of the Interior. Last updated January 13, 2021. https://www.nps.gov/ande/learn/historyculture/pow_synopsis.htm.

National Park Service. "Charles Sumner." US Department of the Interior. Last updated November 9, 2020. https://www.nps.gov/people/charles-sumner.htm.

———. "Captain Henry Wirz." Andersonville: National Historic Site, Georgia. US Department of the Interior. Last updated July 21, 2020. https://www.nps.gov/ande/learn/historyculture/captain_henry_wirz.htm.

———. "Charleston—Revolutionary City and Cradle of Secession." Fort Sumter and Fort Moultrie. US Department of the Interior. Last updated February 10, 2021. https://www.nps.gov/fosu/index.htm.

———. "The Civil War: Battle Unit Details: Union Kentucky Volunteers: 12th Regiment, Kentucky Cavalry." US Department of the Interior. Accessed February 11, 2021. https://www.nps.gov/civilwar/search-battle-units-detail.htm?battleUnitCode=UKY0012RC.

———. "Lincoln's Visit to Richmond." Richmond: National Battlefield Park, Virginia. US Department of the Interior. Last updated February 1, 2018. https://www.nps.gov/rich/learn/historyculture/lincvisit.htm.

———. "The Raiders." Learn: History and Culture: People. Andersonville, National Historic Site, Georgia. US Department of the Interior. Last updated April 14, 2015. https://www.nps.gov/ande/learn/historyculture/the_raiders.htm.

———. "Who Are These Men?" Learn: History and Culture. Andersonville: National Historic Site, Georgia. US Department of the Interior. Last updated April 14, 2015. https://www.nps.gov/ande/learn/historyculture/prisonerphotos.htm.

National Security Agency. "Women in American Cryptology: Elizabeth Van Lew." Cryptologic Heritage: Historical Figures and Publications: Women. *NSA.gov.* https://www.nsa.gov/about/cryptologic-heritage/historical-figures-publications/women/Article/1620966/elizabeth-van-lew/.

Our Documents. "Missouri Compromise (1820)." US National Archives and Records Administration. Accessed February 11, 2021. https://www.ourdocuments.gov/doc.php?flash=false&doc=22.

PA-Roots. "77th Regiment: Pennsylvania Volunteers." Pennsylvania in the Civil War. Accessed February 17, 2021. https://www.pa-roots.com/pacw/infantry/77th/77thorg.html.

Powels, James M. "Civil War Stories: Libby Prison's 'Lottery of Death.'" *Warfare History Network* (website). December 7, 2014. http://warfarehistorynetwork.com/2014/12/07/civil-war-stories-libby-prisons-lottery-of-death/.

Rae, Noel. "How Christian Slaveholders Used the Bible to Justify Slavery." *Time* (February 23, 2018). www.time.com/5171819/christianity-slavery-book-excerpt/.

Robertson, James I., Jr. "Houses of Horror: Danville's Civil War Prisons." *The Virginia Magazine of History and Biography* 69, no. 3 (July 1961): 329–45.

Saunders Jr., Robert. "A Flower at Elmire: The Prisoner of War Diary of Wilbur Wightman Gramling." *The Florida Historical Quarterly* 94, no. 3 (2016): 444–75.

Shotgun's Home of the American Civil War. "The Civil War's Last Great Peace Effort." Last updated February 16, 2002. https://civilwarhome.com/peaceconference.html.

———. "Elizabeth Van Lew, 1818–1900(?)." Accessed February 22, 2021. https://civilwar home.com/vanlewbio.html.

Smith, Steven Trent. "The Great Libby Prison Breakout." *Civil War Times* 49, no. 4 (August 2010): 46–53. https://www.historynet.com/great-libby-prison-breakout.htm.

"Stonewall Jackson at First Manassas." Encyclopedia Virginia. www.encyclopediavirginia .org/1139hpr-e3ea44372ec2cf5/.

Swanson, Diane. "Escape from Libby Prison." In *Tunnels! True Stories from the Edge*, 71–82. Toronto: Annick Press, 2003.

United States Senate. "The Caning of Senator Charles Sumner." Art and History, Senate Historical Office. Accessed February 22, 2021. https://www.senate.gov/artandhistory/history/ minute/The_Caning_of_Senator_Charles_Sumner.htm.

University of Richmond. "Explore the City: History." Visit. *Richmond.edu.* Accessed February 11, 2021. https://www.richmond.edu/visit/city.html.

Varon, Elizabeth R. "Women at War." Disunion. *New York Times*, February 1, 2011. https:// opinionator.blogs.nytimes.com/2011/02/01/women-at-war/.

Vega, Carolyn. "Ralph Waldo Emerson Praises Abolitionist John Brown." The Morgan Library & Museum (website), February 17, 2011. https://www.themorgan.org/blog/ralph -waldo-emerson-praises-abolitionist-john-brown.

Vollaro, Daniel R. "Lincoln, Stowe, and the 'Little Woman/Great War' Story: The Making, and Breaking, of a Great American Anecdote." *Journal of the Abraham Lincoln Association* 30, no. 1 (Winter 2009): 18–34. http://hdl.handle.net/2027/spo.2629860.0030.104.

Weitzel, Godfrey. *Richmond Occupied: Entry of the United States Forces into Richmond, Va. April 3, 1865; Calling together of the Virginia Legislature and Revocation of the Same.* Edited and introduction by Louis H. Manarin. Richmond: Richmond Civil War Centennial Committee, 1965. Text online, https://www.civilwarrichmond.com/images/pdf/occupied.pdf.

Welles, Gideon. *Diary of Gideon Welles, Secretary of the Navy under Lincoln and Johnson.* Introduction by John T. Morse Jr. Vol. 1 of 3: *1861–March 30, 1864.* Boston and New York: Houghton Mifflin Company, 1911.

Woods, Michael E. "What Twenty-First-Century Historians Have Said about the Causes of Disunion: A Civil War Sesquicentennial Review of the Recent Literature." *The Journal of American History* 99, no. 2 (September 2012): 415–39. https://academic.oup.com/jah/ article/99/2/415/860501.

Zombek, Angela. "Libby Prison." *Encyclopedia Virginia.* December 7, 2020. https://encyclo pediavirginia.org/entries/libby-prison/.

Index

About the Author

Robert P. Watson, PhD, is an author, historian, and media commentator who has published more than forty books, several of which have won book awards and been featured on C-SPAN's *Book TV* and at prominent literary festivals. His recent works include *America's First Crisis: The War of 1812* (2014), *The Nazi Titanic: The Incredible Untold Story of a Doomed Ship in World War II* (2016), *The Ghost Ship of Brooklyn: An Untold Story of the Revolutionary War* (2017), and *George Washington's Final Battle: The Epic Struggle to Build a Capital City* (2021). He lives in Boca Raton, Florida, where he is Distinguished Professor of American History, Avron Fogelman Research Professor, and director of Project Civitas at Lynn University.

www.ingramcontent.com/pod-product-compliance
Lightning Source LLC
Chambersburg PA
CBHW070402100426
42812CB00005B/1603